DIGITAL CONTENT & DISTANCE SALES

DIGITAL CONTENT & DISTANCE SALES

New Developments at EU Level

Edited by

Ignace Claeys
Evelyne Terryn

intersentia
Cambridge – Antwerp – Portland

Intersentia Ltd
Sheraton House | Castle Park
Cambridge | CB3 0AX | United Kingdom
Tel.: +44 1223 370 170 | Fax: +44 1223 370 169
Email: mail@intersentia.co.uk
www.intersentia.com | www.intersentia.co.uk

Distribution for the UK and Ireland:
NBN International
Airport Business Centre, 10 Thornbury Road
Plymouth, PL6 7 PP
United Kingdom
Tel.: +44 1752 202 301 | Fax: +44 1752 202 331
Email: orders@nbninternational.com

Distribution for Europe and all other countries:
Intersentia Publishing nv
Groenstraat 31
2640 Mortsel
Belgium
Tel.: +32 3 680 15 50 | Fax: +32 3 658 71 21
Email: mail@intersentia.be

Distribution for the USA and Canada:
International Specialized Book Services
920 NE 58th Ave. Suite 300
Portland, OR 97213
USA
Tel.: +1 800 944 6190 (toll free) | Fax: +1 503 280 8832
Email: info@isbs.com

Digital Content & Distance Sales. New Developments at EU Level

ISBN 978-1-78068-415-4
D/2017/7849/37
NUR 822

British Library Cataloguing in Publication Data. A catalogue record for this book is available from the British Library.

PREFACE

The Digital Single Market has recently been one of the priorities of the European Commission. As part of the implementation of its Digital Single Market Strategy,[1] the Commission adopted three proposals in December 2015: a proposal for a directive for the supply of digital content (DCD);[2] a proposal for a directive for the online and other distance sales of goods (ODSD);[3] and a proposal for a regulation on cross-border portability of online content services in the internal market.[4]

As these proposals may have a substantial impact not only for e-commerce and digital contracts, but also for the general rules on sales and services contracts, the UGhent and the KU Leuven organised a seminar with national and international specialists in the field to analyse the exact consequences of this proposed legislation. This book comprises the papers presented and discussed at this seminar. It combines contributions that set out the broader legislative and political context and give the reader a general overview of the impact of the proposals (chapters by *Marco Loos* and by *Gert Straetmans* and *Shana Meys*), with chapters with an in-depth analysis of specific aspects of the proposed legislation, its pros and cons and possible improvements. This approach inevitably involves some overlap but this was the deliberate choice of the editors, as it avoids excessive cross-references and allows for reading of the chapters separately, according to the needs of the reader for a helicopter view or a more detailed analysis.

The introductory and general chapter by *Marco Loos* sets out the lengthy road that led to the proposal for an online sales directive and of the proposal for a digital content directive, from the early legislative measures in European (consumer) contract law, to the academic initiatives, the DCFR, the Consumer Rights Directive and the (proposal for a) Common European Sales Law. In addition, he provides a global overview of the contents of both proposals. He

---

1 Communication from the Commission to the European Parliament, the Council, the European economic and Social Committee and the Committee of the regions: strategy for a digital single market for Europe, 6 May 2015, COM(2015) 192 final.

2 Proposal for a Directive of the European Parliament and of the Council on certain aspects concerning contracts for the supply of digital content, COM(2015) 634 final.

3 Proposal for a Directive of the European Parliament and of the Council on certain aspects concerning contracts for the online and other distance sales of goods, COM(2015) 635 final.

4 Proposal for a Regulation of the European Parliament and of the Council on ensuring the cross-border portability of online content services in the internal market, COM(2015) 627 final.

points out that certain matters remain unresolved, mainly where digital content and the consumer's digital environment are interdependent but without formal interconnection. He questions very critically the need for yet another separate sales regimes specifically for distance contracts and this sets the tone for what will be a recurring criticism throughout this book.

The subsequent chapters provide further detail and analysis of specific aspects of the proposals. *Sophie Stijns* and *Sanne Jansen* address the online sales proposal in more detail, more specifically its scope of application and the rules of conformity. They set out the differences and similarities with the Consumer Sales Directive, the CESL and national contract law. Although the authors see a number of improvements in the proposal in comparison with the Consumer Sales Directive, especially with regard to the rules on conformity, they also criticise the further fragmentation of consumer sales law which the adoption of this proposal would lead to. The application of a different legal system in face-to-face consumer sale transactions compared to online consumer transactions is not transparent to consumers or practicable for traders. They therefore plead for a comprehensive revised and uniform Consumer Sales Directive that would remain applicable to online and distance sales. The parallel chapter of *Reinhard Steennot* and *Simon Geiregat* addresses the scope of application and the conformity requirements in the proposal for a digital content directive. They applaud the broad approach towards digital content, whereby it is irrelevant whether the content is supplied on a tangible medium, whether it is tailor-made and also how the contract is classified. They also welcome the equation of actively provided data to money. The authors, however, propose a number of clarifications or adaptations to enhance legal certainty. They are more sceptical concerning the conformity provisions, as they consider that the provisions provide only limited protection: conformity is in principle only guaranteed by subjective criteria; objective criteria only apply if contractual provisions are absent or non-transparent.

Ignace Claeys and *Jan Vancoillie* address the remedies available to consumers under both proposed directives, as well as the specific provisions of the digital content directive concerning modification of digital content and termination of long-term contracts. The authors are not convinced that the proposals can effectively attain the goals pursued: a high level of consumer protection and increased legal certainty. There are firstly important aspects where the level of protection would be reduced under Belgian law, including the protection against hidden defects that now still applies after the expiry of the two-year period. The authors furthermore favour an integration of the DCD and the ODSD into one instrument, given the blurring borders between tangible goods and digital content. Legal certainty is further not necessarily enhanced by these proposals, which not only contain various ambiguous rules, but also increase the complexity of contract law in general and sales law in particular.

A more positive note on the ODSD proposal can be derived from the chapter by *Evelyne Terryn* and *Sanne Vandemaele* on commercial guarantees. The authors discuss the current legal framework, which they consider insufficient as it does not guarantee that commercial guarantees are transparent and provide added value to consumers. The additional information requirements imposed by the ODSD are therefore an improvement, but the authors once more see no justification for a limitation of the proposed changes to online and other distance sales of goods. *Bert Keirsbilck* discusses the provisions of the DCD and ODSD proposals that provide the seller/supplier with a right of redress in case of an act or omission by previous parties in the chain of transactions which triggered the seller/supplier's liability for the legal guarantee towards the consumer. These provisions are clearly inspired by the Consumer Sales Directive and as in the Consumer Sales Directive, the option of direct producer's liability is also disregarded in these proposals.

Eva Lievens has a closer look at the proposal for regulation on ensuring the cross-border portability of online content services, a complex matter that requires a careful balancing of the interests of rights-holders, online content service providers and consumers. The regulation has at least the potential to benefit all parties involved: through uninterrupted access to content for consumers when travelling to other Member States; through a (potential) decreased use of technical means to bypass current territorial restrictions for rights-holders, due to a (potential) increased legitimate access to content and for online content service providers; and through (possibly) new subscribers who value cross-border portability, without significant additional costs. However, Lievens also points out that amendments to the proposal are necessary for these benefits to materialise.

In a final horizontal chapter, *Gert Straetmans* and *Shana Meys* analyse in depth the impact of both proposed directives on the existing level of consumer protection, both from a Belgian and a European perspective. From a Belgian perspective, the answer is nuanced. They note changes that will benefit consumers, including the abolition of the obligation to notify the lack of conformity and the prohibition of the seller to stipulate such an obligation in the contract; the extension of the period during which the burden of proof is reversed and the possibility for the consumer to terminate the contract unilaterally in the case of a distance sales contract, even if the lack of conformity is minor. They also note some novelties that will benefit consumers; including the right to withhold performance and the right to damages for economic loss in the case of supply of digital content. However, *Straetmans* and *Meys* also regard the abolishment of the complementary regime concerning latent defects because of the full harmonisation as a major drawback of the proposals. The effect on the level of consumer protection receives an equally nuanced answer from a European perspective. Adoption of the proposals would entail problems of further fragmentation, delineation and a lower standard of consumer protection for specific aspects. In addition, the authors point out that the rather limited scope of application of the proposals – dealing only with certain aspects of the specific types of consumer contracts – will lead to different levels of protection between Member States which will thus undermine the uniformity aimed at by the proposals. A solution according to the authors, may therefore be the adoption, over time, of an overall horizontal measure in the form of a Regulation or a Directive that consolidates the consumer sales acquis by eliminating existing contradictions.

The chapters in this book are based on the text of the December 2015 proposals and further developments up to May 2016. At the time of writing this editorial (January 2017), discussions are still ongoing in the Council. An opinion of the European Economic and Social Committee (EESC) was published in July 2016.[5] Like the contributors to this book, the EESC also criticises the unacceptable difference in the treatment of online and offline sales of goods that the ODSD proposal creates. It considers it more appropriate to regulate online sales of tangible goods during the review of the Consumer Sales Directive as part of the REFIT exercise (Regulatory Fitness and Performance Programme). The results of the external studies supporting the Fitness Check are expected by February 2017[6] and will hopefully indeed support a revision of the Consumer Sales Directive that can at least incorporate the changes to sales law of the ODSD proposal and possibly also of the DCD. As to the DCD proposal that has been the subject of intense debate in the Council over the last months, political guidelines have been adopted,[7] as well as a revised text by the Dutch–Slovak presidency. The debate continues concerning a number of technical and policy questions (such as the approach on 'embedded digital content'; on consumer provision of data other than personal data as possible counter-performance; and on the balance between subjective and objective conformity criteria)[8] that are also raised by the contributors to this book. We therefore want to thank all the authors for their contribution to the ongoing debate and for their suggestions for improvement that will hopefully lead to better legislation for the Digital Single Market.

Ignace Claeys and Evelyne Terryn
Ghent and Kortrijk, 1 January 2017

---

5 Opinion of the European Economic and Social Committee on the 'Proposal for a directive of the European Parliament and of the Council on certain aspects concerning contracts for the supply of digital content' (COM(2015) 634 final – 2015/0287 (COD)) and the 'Proposal for a directive of the European Parliament and of the Council on certain aspects concerning contracts for the online and other distance sales of goods' (COM(2015) 635 final – 2015/0288 (COD)), OJ C 264, 20.7.2016.

6 http://ec.europa.eu/consumers/consumer_rights/review/index_en.htm.

7 Note on the Council Debate 2 June 2016, Interinstitutional file, 2015/0287 (COD), with Annex: 'basic principles and political guidelines for future work'.

8 Note on the Council Debate 1 December 2016, Interinstitutional file, 2015/0287 (COD).

CONTENTS

LIST OF AUTHORS

Ignace Claeys
Professor of Law, Centre for the Law of Obligations, Ghent University, Belgium; attorney at the Brussels bar, Belgium

Simon Geiregat
Doctoral researcher and fellow of the Special Research Fund (BOF), Consumer Law Institute, Ghent University, Belgium

Sanne Jansen
Postdoctoral BAEF fellow at the Yale / Columbia Law School, US; collaborator of the Institute for the Law of Obligations, KU Leuven, Belgium

Bert Keirsbilck
Professor of Commercial, Company and Economic Law, Consumer Competition Market, KU Leuven, Belgium; attorney at the Brussels bar, Belgium (of counsel Eubelius)

Eva Lievens
Professor of Law and Technology and member of the Human Rights Centre, Ghent University, Belgium

Marco B.M. Loos
Professor of Private Law, Centre for the Study of European Contract Law, University of Amsterdam, the Netherlands

Shana Meys
Doctoral researcher, Law Enforcement Unit, University of Antwerp, Belgium

Reinhard Steennot
Professor of Law, Financial Law Institute and Consumer Law Institute, Ghent University, Belgium

Sophie Stijns
Professor of Private Law, Institute for the Law of Obligations, KU Leuven, Belgium

Gert Straetmans
Professor of European Economic and Commercial Law, Consumer Law Institute, University of Antwerp, Belgium; substitute Judge of the Antwerp Court of Appeal, Belgium

Evelyne Terryn
Professor of Commercial and Consumer Law, Consumer Competition Market, KU Leuven, Belgium; attorney at the Kortrijk bar, Belgium

Jonas Vancoillie
Attorney at the Brussels bar, Belgium

Sanne Vandemaele
Doctoral researcher, Consumer Competition Market, KU Leuven Kulak, Belgium

PART I
INTRODUCTION

NOT GOOD BUT CERTAINLY CONTENT

The Proposals for European Harmonisation of Online and Distance Selling of Goods and the Supply of Digital Content

Marco B.M. Loos*

* This chapter is based in part on presentations during the *Workshop Digital Single Market: Stakeholders' Perspectives on Proposed new Contract Rules*, organised by the Centre for the Study of European Contract Law of the University of Amsterdam and the Dutch ministries of Economic Affairs and of Security and Justice in the context of the Dutch Presidency of the European Union on 4 February 2016, and the *Conference New EU Rules for Digital Contracts*, organised by the ERA and held in Brussels on 18 February 2016. The chapter was finalised on 31 May 2016.

1. INTRODUCTION

On 9 December 2015, the European Commission submitted the first three proposals for the implementation of the *Digital Single Market Strategy*.[1] These proposals identify obstacles to the conclusion of cross-border contracts and aim at taking away these barriers to the internal market by harmonising the contract law rules for such contracts.[2] A first proposal concerns a proposal for a regulation on cross-border portability of online content services in the internal market.[3] This proposal should result in the possibility for users that have concluded a contract for the supply of digital content services with a supplier (such as Netflix) in the EU Member State where they live, but that temporarily move to another Member State, to continue having access and being able to make use of the digital content during their stay in the other Member State. This proposal is primarily interesting from the perspective of copyright law. It will not be discussed any further here.[4] The second proposal concerns a directive for the supply of digital content,[5] the third proposal a directive for online and other distance contracts for the delivery of goods.[6] Both directives introduce harmonised rules on the basis of full harmonisation[7] and are intended to complement one another. These proposals are referred to hereinafter as the Digital Content Directive and the Online Sales and Distance Sales Directive (without indicating that these directives are currently only proposals).

In this chapter I will describe the contents of both proposals for directives globally. I will first address the Online Sales and Distance Sales Directive

---

1 Communication from the Commission to the European Parliament, the Council, the European Economic and Social Committee and the Committee of the Regions: Strategy for a Digital Single Market for Europe, 6 May 2015, COM(2015) 192 final.

2 See as to whether this goal may be achieved with the proposals discussed in this chapter in more detail V. Mak, 'Op weg naar een Europese "Digital Single Market"', *Nederlands Juristenblad* 2016/8, pp. 519 and 524.

3 Proposal for a Regulation of the European Parliament and of the Council on ensuring the cross-border portability of online content services in the internal market, COM(2015) 627 final.

4 See on this proposal D.J.G. Visser, P.J. Kreijger, 'Online diensten over de grens', *NtER* 2016/2, pp. 61–67.

5 Proposal for a Directive of the European Parliament and of the Council on certain aspects concerning contracts for the supply of digital content, COM(2015) 634 final.

6 Proposal for a Directive of the European Parliament and of the Council on certain aspects concerning contracts for the online and other distance sales of goods, COM(2015) 635 final.

7 See Art. 3 Online Sales and Distance Sales Directive and Art. 4 Digital Content Directive.

(Section 4) and then the Digital Content Directive (Section 5). I will conclude with some final comments on unresolved matters (Section 6) and conclusions (Section 7). However, before dealing with the two proposals, I will first sketch the road that has led to these proposals (Section 2). I will then deal with a preliminary question: is the introduction of a separate regime for distance sales contracts in addition of the existing raft of sale schemes a good idea (Section 3)?

2. THE ROAD LEADING TO THE CURRENT PROPOSALS[8]

2.1. THE EARLY LEGISLATIVE MEASURES

Where the laws of the Member States are the same, both businesses and consumers may profit from the internal market by selling and shopping cross-border. In an era of euro scepticism, European (consumer) contract and tort law offers the possibility for the European institutions to show that European integration is not only advantageous for businesses but also for consumers, i.e. for the citizens of the European Union. This is one of the reasons why the European Commission has been pushing for the harmonisation of consumer law. The Commission has done so consistently since the first Consumer Policy Programme, which was accepted in 1975.[9] Already at that time European consumer law was justified as being a measure to improve the quality of life of the peoples of the Member States of (then) the European Economic Community.

Yet, the road towards the 2015 proposals has been long. At first, rather isolated areas of private law were targeted, such as doorstep selling (1985), package travel (1990) and timeshare property (1994). The European legislation in these areas did not much influence the core of private law, and for that reason received relatively little attention from private law academics. This was different for the 1985 Product Liability Directive, but since that directive only provided remedies for very specific types of damage in addition to national contract and tort law remedies, and national law often was more generous to victims of product liability accidents, the Directive did not have as much of an impact as one might have expected from a full harmonisation directive. The 1993 Unfair

8 This section is an abbreviated and adapted version of M.B.M. Loos, A.L.M. Keirse, 'The Optional Instrument and the Consumer Rights Directive: alternative ways to a new ius commune in contract law – Introduction' in A.L.M. Keirse, M.B.M. Loos (eds.), *Alternative ways to Ius commune. The Europeanisation of private law*, Cambridge/Antwerp/Portland: Intersentia, 2012, pp. 1–20. Section 2.5 is largely taken from M.B.M. Loos, 'Consumer Sales in The Netherlands' in G. De Cristofaro, A. De Franceschi (eds.), *Consumer Sales in Europe*, Cambridge/Mortsel: Intersentia, 2016, pp. 109–130.

9 Council Resolution of 14 April 1975 on a preliminary programme of the European Economic Community for a consumer protection and information policy, *OJ* 1975, C 92/2.

Contract Terms Directive[10] and the 1999 Consumer Sales Directive[11] marked a different era, with consumer law legislation affecting the core of private law. This development has been continued into the twenty-first century, in particular with the 2005 Unfair Commercial Practices Directive[12] and the 2011 Consumer Rights Directive.[13]

2.2. THE POLITICAL DEBATE ON EUROPEAN CONTRACT LAW

The use of the Directive as the tool for harmonisation has not been unproblematic in the Member States. The implementation of, in particular, the Unfair Contract Terms Directive, the Consumer Sales Directive and recently the Consumer Rights Directive has had a profound influence on the national contract law systems. In each of these cases, for each Member State the question was how to implement the relevant directive without disturbing the inner coherence of the national legal system too much. Even though legislators have become increasingly more aware of the problem, this could not prevent the emergence of coherence problems within national law. By the year 2000, the question arose whether European patrimonial law or, slightly more limited, European contract law should not (ultimately) be fully harmonised in the form of a European Civil Code or at least a European Contract Law Code. The political debate on the issue really took flight with the 2001 Communication on European contract law,[14] followed by the 2003 Action Plan[15] and the 2004 Communication on European contract law and the revision of the acquis: The way forward.[16] In the Action Plan, the European Commission concluded from the responses to the 2001 Communication that at least for the moment, a majority of respondents was against a comprehensive body of legislation, but much support existed for the revision of the *acquis communautaire* and for the development of soft-law instruments. Consequently, the Commission proposed to undertake measures implementing these options. The Commission indicated that its priority was the improvement of the *acquis communautaire*, in order to increase the coherence

10 Council Directive 93/13/EEC, *OJ* 1993, L 95/29.

11 Directive 1999/44/EC, *OJ* 1999, L 171/12.

12 Directive 2005/29/EC, *OJ* 2005, L 149/22.

13 Directive 2011/83/EU, *OJ* 2011, L 304/64.

14 Communication of the Commission to the Council and the European Parliament on European contract law of 11 July 2001, COM(2001) 398 final, *OJ* 2001, C 255.

15 A more coherent European contract law: An Action Plan, Communication from the Commission to the Council and European Parliament of 12 February 2003, COM(2003) 68 final, hereinafter referred to as: Action Plan.

16 European contract law and the revision of the acquis: The way forward, Communication from the Commission to the Council and European Parliament of 11 October 2004, COM(2004) 651 final, hereinafter referred to as: 'The way forward'.

thereof.[17] An important step towards better coherence, the Commission indicated, would be the development of a 'Common Frame of Reference'. That Common Frame of Reference, or CFR, would establish common principles and terminology in the area of European contract law.[18] The purpose of the CFR was described as being threefold. The Commission indicated that the CFR could be used when preparing new legislation. To that extent, the CFR should provide for 'best solutions in terms of common terminology and rules', including definitions for terms such as 'contract' and 'damage', and rules pertaining to non-performance of contracts.[19] Secondly, the CFR should become an instrument in achieving a higher degree of convergence between the contract laws of the Member States.[20] Thirdly, the Commission indicated that the CFR would be the basis for the Commission's reflection on 'whether non-sector-specific measures such as an optional instrument' is needed.[21] The Commission further indicated that it would finance extensive research in this area within the Sixth Framework Programme.[22]

2.3. ACADEMIC GROUPS AND THE DEVELOPMENT OF THE DRAFT COMMON FRAME OF REFERENCE

At the same time, academics had organised themselves into small networks discussing the possibility to develop common principles of contract law. The two most influential groups, the Commission on European Contract Law (the Lando Commission) and Unidroit, consisted of scholars and sometimes also some practitioners. They prepared 'principles of contract law', based on comparative research. These 'principles' were drafted as general rules of contract law, and were accompanied by explanatory comments and comparative notes, explaining whether the rule existed in the reported legal systems. The first results from the academic groups were published in 1994 (the Unidroit Principles of International Commercial Contracts, second draft published in 2004) and 1995 (the Principles of European Contract Law, with much extended versions published in 1999 and 2003).

Later, the Study Group on a European Civil Code prepared Principles of European Law in different areas of private law, ranging from sales and service contracts to unjustified enrichment, tort law, and to transfer of ownership and

17 Action Plan, paras. 54–58.
18 Action Plan, para. 59.
19 Action Plan, para. 62.
20 Action Plan, para. 62.
21 Action Plan, para. 62.
22 Action Plan, paras. 63, 68.

security rights in movable goods.[23] At the same time, the Research Group on the Existing EC Private Law (Acquis Group) attempted to provide a restatement of existing Community private law in the Acquis Principles. A third group was the Project Group 'Restatement of European Insurance Contract Law', which published its own principles in 2009, and the *Association Henri Capitant des Amis de la Culture Juridique Française* and the *Société de Législation Comparée* developed guiding principles and model rules of European contract law.[24] These groups ultimately made a joint bid for funding under the Sixth Framework Programme establishing a Network of Excellence working together in the development of an academic Draft Common Frame of Reference (DCFR). The DCFR was prepared in an intensive co-operation between the Study Group and the Acquis Group, who established a joint Compilation and Redaction Team (CRT), which was to coordinate the work of these two groups. The CRT undertook to integrate both the Principles of European Contract Law and the draft texts of the various subgroups of the Study Group and the Acquis Group into the Draft Common Frame of Reference and to revise them for the purposes of the DCFR.[25] The final text of the DCFR was published in 2009 in no fewer than six volumes and consisted of model rules, comments and national notes on the law of contract and obligations in general (Books I–III), various specific contracts (Book IV),[26] benevolent intervention in another's affairs, tort law and unjustified enrichment (Books V–VII), acquisition and loss of ownership of goods, proprietary security in movable assets, and trusts (Books VIII–X). The scope of the DCFR was therefore a very wide one, but certainly not equal to that of a Civil Code: important areas that are traditionally regulated in Civil Codes are missing, notably family law, succession law, the law of legal persons and the law regarding the transfer of ownership pertaining to immovable property. Similarly, important specific contracts such as the labour contract, the package travel contract, and the lease of immovable property are not included in the scope of the DCFR.

2.4. THE CONSUMER RIGHTS DIRECTIVE

Parallel to the development of the DCFR a separate discussion on the review of the consumer acquis took place. This review was first announced in the

---

23 I have been involved with the Study Group since 1999, first as the team manager for service contracts and the Dutch reporter for sales contracts, and later as the team leader and the Dutch reporter for mandate contracts.

24 Other groups consisted of the European Group on Tort Law and the Académie des privatistes européen.

25 *Cf.* Ch. von Bar, E. Clive (eds.), *Principles, definitions and model rules of European private law. Draft Common Frame of Reference (DCFR). Full edition, Volume I*, Munich: Sellier, 2009, p. 31.

26 Sales, lease of movable goods, services, mandate, commercial agency, franchise and distributorship, loans, personal security, and donation.

Consumer policy strategy 2002–2006.[27] In its Communication 'The way forward',[28] the Commission indicated that in order to prepare a more coherent European contract law, a review of the consumer acquis was necessary. To this extent, it would prioritise the evaluation of whether eight existing directives in the area of consumer law[29] sufficiently contributed to the enhancement of consumer and business confidence in the internal market by way of a common high level of consumer protection and by eliminating barriers to the internal market and simplifying legislation.[30] In particular, the Commission would investigate the effects of minimum harmonisation clauses and whether the way in which Member States have implemented and applied directives meets these goals.[31]

By way of the *Green Paper on the Review of the consumer acquis*[32] the Commission delivered on its promise. Prior to the Green Paper consumer organisations and businesses had indicated various problems that consumers and businesses encounter. The European Commission concluded that these problems are the consequence of the use by Member States of the minimum harmonisation clauses that are included in most of the consumer directives: where Member States offer more protection than is required by a directive, by definition harmonisation can only be successful in part. Businesses and consumers would then in cross-border contracts again be confronted with differing rules.[33] Not surprisingly, the Commission took this as a sign that full harmonisation would be a better fit for the improvement of the functioning of the internal market.

---

27 Consumer policy strategy 2002–2006, Communication from the Commission to the European Parliament, the Council, the Economic and Social Committee and the Committee of the Regions, COM(2002) 208 final, *OJ* 2002, C 137/2.

28 'The way forward', pp. 4–5.

29 The directives that are subject to revision are Directives 85/577/EEC (doorstep selling), 90/314/EEC (package travel), 93/13/EEC (unfair contract terms), 94/47/EC (timeshare), 97/7/EC (distance selling), 98/6/EC (price indication), 98/27/EC (injunctions for the protection of consumers' interests), and 99/44/EC (consumer sales and guarantees). Given the fact that the Commission is also contemplating the possibility of introducing a direct action against producers in the case of non-conformity and the existing regulation on producers' guarantees (see Sections 4.8 and 4.9 below) it is remarkable that the revision of the Product Liability Directive (Directive 85/374/EEC) is not included in this list of directives.

30 *Cf.* also the then acting Commissioner for Consumer Policy M. Kuneva, 'The European Contract Law and Review of the Consumer Acquis', *Zeitschrift für Europäisches Privatrecht* 2007/4, p. 956.

31 The way forward, p. 4.

32 *Green Paper on the Review of the consumer acquis* of 8 February 2007, COM(2006) 744 final. The Green Paper's goal was to achieve a true internal market for consumers. In doing so, a balance must be struck between a high level of consumer protection and the competitiveness of companies, while the principle of subsidiarity must be respected, see Green Paper, p. 3.

33 Green Paper, p. 11.

In October 2008, the next step was made: the European Commission published its proposal for a Consumer Rights Directive,[34] indeed based on the idea of full harmonisation.[35] Whereas the Green Paper announced the review of eight existing directives, the proposal for a Consumer Rights Directive concerned only four of them: the Doorstep Selling Directive, the Unfair Terms Directive, the Distance Selling Directive, and the Consumer Sales Directive. The Commission's choice to opt for full harmonisation provoked very critical reactions in the academic literature: as a consequence of the full harmonisation clause, further-reaching national consumer protection measures would have to be abrogated. This might have been acceptable if this had been compensated for by a rise in the level of consumer protection in other areas, but this was not the case: almost throughout the proposal the *minimum* rules of the existing directives were taken over one-for-one, implying that the European minimum level of protection would become also the European maximum. In sum, this would mean that the level of consumer protection would decrease in all legal systems.[36] The critique concentrated in particular on the provisions on consumer sales and unfair terms, where most Member States had introduced or maintained higher levels of consumer protection in one way or another, ranging from longer conformity periods in the Netherlands, to the right to reject in the United Kingdom, or the use of much more extensive black-lists of clauses that are deemed to be unfair in consumer contracts in, for instance, Germany. Ultimately, the Council and the European Parliament – which were both very critical as well – agreed that these subjects would be left out of the new directive almost entirely. The final text of the Consumer Rights Directive, adopted on 25 October 2011,[37] therefore contained extensive rules on information obligations and the right of withdrawal for off-premises contracts and distance selling contracts, and only a very limited number of rules in other areas, in particular on subjects that were considered to be missing from the Consumer Sales Directive and the Unfair Contract Terms Directive.

2.5. THE PROPOSAL FOR A COMMON EUROPEAN SALES LAW

The timing of the proposal for a Consumer Rights Directive was not particularly fortunate: an interim version of the DCFR had been published at almost the

---

34 Proposal for a Directive of the European Parliament and of the Council on consumer rights of 8 October 2008, COM(2008) 614/4. This original proposal is available online at: http://eur-lex.europa.eu/LexUriServ/LexUriServ.do?uri=COM:2008:0614:FIN:EN:PDF (last visited on 15 March 2017).

35 See art. 4 of the CRD proposal.

36 See for instance the papers published in G. Howells, R. Schulze (eds.), *Modernising and Harmonising Consumer Contract Law*, Munich: Sellier, 2009.

37 Directive 2011/83/EU of the European Parliament and of the Council of 25 October 2011 on consumer rights, amending Council Directive 93/13/EEC and Directive 1999/44/EC of the

same time as the proposal was published, and the final version of the DCFR was only published in 2009. This meant that the Commission could not make use of the results of the work of the Network of Excellence, which it had established and financed for the very purpose of providing a toolbox for the enactment of new legislation and the improvement of the coherence and quality of the existing acquis. The partial failure of the full harmonisation approach in the Consumer Rights Directive, in particular with regard to consumer sales and unfair contract terms, opened the way for an alternative approach, in which the European Commission could take the results of the DCFR into account: after the preparatory work of an Expert Group, which published a Feasibility Study in May 2011,[38] the European Commission published a proposal for a Regulation on a Common European Sales Law, just two weeks before the formal adoption of the Consumer Rights Directive.[39]

If CESL had been adopted, this would have introduced an additional regime that might be applicable to a sales contract. It is uncertain how this would have affected national sales law, but it stands to reason that it would have contributed to the growing complexity of sales law. This might to some extent have been tempered by the fact that parties had to opt-in to CESL, whereas CISG applies automatically in a cross-border commercial sales contract that is governed by the law of a country that has ratified CISG. The complexity would also have been slightly diminished if the scope of CESL had been restricted to cross-border distance sales contracts, as the European Parliament had proposed.[40] The Parliament had not proposed to restrict the scope of CESL to consumer contracts. Instead, it had suggested extending the scope to all business-to-business (B2B) contracts, whether or not any of the parties is a small or medium-sized enterprise.[41] The consequence remains, however, that B2B contracts could have been governed by three instruments (national law, CISG and CESL), and consumer contracts by two (national law and CESL). Moreover, in those areas where CESL (or CISG) was silent, the otherwise applicable national law had to be applied. This meant that where the parties would have opted into CESL,

European Parliament and of the Council and repealing Council Directive 85/577/EEC and Directive 97/7/EC of the European Parliament and of the Council, *OJ* 2011, L 304/64.

38 Available online at: http://ec.europa.eu/justice/contract/files/feasibility_study_final.pdf (last visited on 15 March 2017).

39 Proposal for a Regulation on a Common European Sales Law (COM(2011) 635 final, http://eur-lex.europa.eu/LexUriServ/LexUriServ.do?uri=COM:2011:0635:FIN:en:PDF (last visited on 15 March 2017).

40 See Amendment 60 amending Article 4(1) CESL. The text adopted by the European Parliament in its first reading is produced in: European Parliament, Texts adopted Part III at the sitting of Wednesday 26 February 2014, P7_TA(2014)0159, http://www.europarl.europa.eu/sides/getDoc.do?pubRef=-//EP//TEXT+TA+P7-TA-2014-0159+0+DOC+XML+V0//EN&language=EN (last visited on 15 March 2017).

41 See Amendment 70 amending Article 7 CESL, deleting the second sentence of paragraph 1 and deleting paragraph 2 altogether.

problems of private international law would have continued to exist, but in fewer cases than presently is the case, since CESL would have covered more subjects than CISG does,[42] and CESL could have been applied to consumer contracts, whereas CISG is available only for B2B contracts.

Moreover, whereas the DCFR more or less covered the whole of the law on movable goods, and was thus capable of governing sales contracts to a larger degree even then CISG, CESL did not cover the whole of sales law. In fact, there were important caveats that would have prevented CESL from being considered an effective instrument for sales contracts.[43] First, matters of invalidity of the contract for reasons of public policy and good morals, and matters of representation had been left out of CESL and would therefore have had to be determined on the basis of the applicable national law. The same is true for matters of invalidity arising from incapacity of the buyer. The absence of Europeanised rules for the capacity of minors is problematic, in particular for businesses that conclude contracts online.[44] In this respect it is relevant to note that a relatively large number of distance sales contracts concluded online are concluded by minors, in particular in so far as the supply of digital content (including music and gaming) is concerned, and that Member States have very differing laws on incapacity of minors.[45] Thirdly, and probably most problematic, would have been the absence of any rules pertaining to the transfer of ownership from seller to buyer. This implies that the dispute between consensual systems, such as French and Italian law, and those that make the transfer of ownership

42 See M.B.M. Loos, H.N. Schelhaas, 'Commercial sales: the Common European Sales Law compared to the Vienna Sales Convention', *ERPL* 2013/1, 109–18.

43 These and other matters not regulated in CESL are listed in recital 27 of the Preamble to CESL (as proposed by the European Commission) and Amendment 76 of the European Parliament introducing the new Article 11a(2) CESL.

44 See M.B.M. Loos, N. Helberger, L. Guibault, C. Mak, L. Pessers, K.J. Cseres, B. van der Sloot, R. Tigner, *Analysis of the applicable legal frameworks and suggestions for the contours of a model system of consumer protection in relation to digital content contracts, Final Report: Comparative analysis, Law & Economics analysis, assessment and development of recommendations for possible future rules on digital content contracts*, 2011, p. 239. This report was prepared for the European Commission and is available at: http://csecl.uva.nl/research/projects/consumer-protection-in-relation-to-digital-content-contracts.html (last visited on 15 March 2017).

45 See M.B.M. Loos, N. Helberger, L. Guibault, C. Mak, L. Pessers, K.J. Cseres, B. van der Sloot, R. Tigner, *Analysis of the applicable legal frameworks and suggestions for the contours of a model system of consumer protection in relation to digital content contracts, Final Report: Comparative analysis, Law & Economics analysis, assessment and development of recommendations for possible future rules on digital content contracts*, 2011, pp. 138–41, referring to the laws of Finland, France, Germany, Hungary, Italy, the Netherlands, Poland, Spain, the United Kingdom, and that of non-Members Norway and the United States. See also the first report to the European Commission, which contains the national reports on these matters and which is also available at: http://csecl.uva.nl/research/projects/consumer-protection-in-relation-to-digital-content-contracts.html (last visited on 15 March 2017).

conditional upon delivery, such as Dutch and German law, would have remained unsettled: CESL would have required the seller to transfer ownership,[46] but the time at which ownership is transferred had expressly been left unregulated.[47] This implies that the national law applicable would have had to determine whether or not a buyer had already obtained the ownership of the goods – which is particularly relevant in the case of insolvency of any of the contracting parties. This does not seem to provide sufficient trust for the parties to be able to have relied on CESL: even for this fundamental issue a return to national law and to private international law would still have been needed. As a result, it seems unlikely that CESL would have been opted into by parties very often.

In sum, CESL was considered to lead to a too complex system of (sales) contract law at national level without providing an overarching legal system. And two of its advantages – it would apply only if the parties to a contract opted into the regime, and as a result it would not compromise the coherence of national law in the same way as a directive or regulation would – could also be considered as drawbacks: CESL would hardly lead to harmonisation, as parties were unlikely to opt-in and Member States need not take much account of the content of CESL as it was unlikely to apply to a contract anyway. These drawbacks were added to an extensive and critical discussion on the merits of introducing CESL as a second national system of contract law, thus evading the rules of the Rome I Regulation.[48] In addition, Member States were very critical as to the need for an optional instrument. In that sense, it did not come as a surprise that the Juncker Commission ultimately withdrew the proposal for a Common European Sales Law[49] and replaced it with two proposals within the framework of the Digital Single Market Strategy: the current proposals for an Online Sales and Distance Sales Directive and for a Digital Content Directive.

3. YET ANOTHER REGIME FOR SALES CONTRACTS?

The Online Sales and Distance Sales Directive contains rules for sales contracts concluded online or otherwise at a distance, i.e. contracts not concluded in the

46 *Cf.* Article 91(b) CESL.

47 The same is true for CISG, see Article 4(b) CISG.

48 See, for instance, G. Dannemann, 'Choice of CESL and conflicts of law' in G. Dannemann, S. Vogenauer (eds.), *The Common European Sales Law in context: interaction with English and German law*, Oxford: Oxford University Press, 2013, pp. 21–81; M. Heidemann, 'The parties choice of the Common European Sales Law – which governing law?', 2014, available at: http://ssrn.com/abstract=2725445 (last visited on 15 March 2017); S. Whittaker, 'The proposed "Common European Sales Law": legal framework and the agreement of the parties', *Modern Law Review* 2012, pp. 578–605.

49 *Commission Work Programme 2015, A New Start*, Strasbourg, 16 December 2014, COM(2014) 910 final, Annex 2, para. 60.

physical presence of both the seller and the buyer. For such consumer sales contracts the provisions of the Online Sales and Distance Sales Directive replace the current regime of the 1999 Consumer Sales Directive;[50] however, this old Directive continues to apply to consumer sales contracts that have not been concluded at a distance.[51]

If the Online Sales and Distance Sales Directive were adopted in its current form, the national legislators would be faced with an additional regime for sales contracts, similar to what would have been the case if the Common European Sales Law had been adopted. In many legal systems, this would lead to the co-existence of at least five regimes that might be applicable to sales contracts. The first and most general regime consists of the rules applicable to the sale of goods between two private parties in a purely domestic setting. In addition, all Member States have specific rules applying to the sale of immovable property. Many Member States also provide specific rules for domestic sales contracts between traders (domestic B2B sales contracts). The Vienna Sales Convention applies in most Member States to international sales contracts between professional sellers, unless the parties to the contract have excluded the applicability of that Convention, in which case national law for domestic B2B sales contracts or, in the absence thereof, that for private parties, applies. For contracts where the buyer is a consumer and the seller a professional party, the rules applicable to consumer sales contracts apply, with the newly introduced distinction between distance contracts and contracts concluded on- or off-premises. And on top of that a separate B2C regime for the supply of digital content is introduced as well. This seems unworkable. It seems therefore likely that the European Parliament and the Council will only agree to adopt the proposal for an Online Sales Directive if its scope is enlarged to include also on- and off-premises contracts.[52] If such an extension is not agreed upon, then each Member State would be faced with the question whether it should accept the addition of this additional regime, or whether to amend its existing consumer sales law by extending the scope of the provisions for distance sales contracts to on- and off-premises sales contracts and in that way prevent unnecessary differences between distance sales contracts and other sales contracts, which would severely complicate consumer sales law at the national level. The Online Sales and Distance Sales Directive would then

50 Directive 1999/44/EC of the European Parliament and of the Council of 25 May 1999 on certain aspects of the sale of consumer goods and associated guarantees, *OJ* 1999, L 171/12.

51 See art. 19(1) Online Sales and Distance Sales Directive.

52 Amendment 233 in the Draft Report of the Committee on the Internal Market and Consumer Protection of 18 November 2016 and 25 January 2017 indeed proposes to extend the scope of the directive in this sense (other amendments aim at accompanying provisions and recitals). The draft report is available at: http://www.europarl.europa.eu/oeil/popups/ficheprocedure.do?lang=en&reference=2015/0288(COD) (last visited on 15 March 2017) and will hereinafter be referred to as: Draft Report IMCO on the Online Sales and Distance Sales Directive.

on a national level lead to spontaneous harmonisation of consumer sales law – in other words: the provisions of the Online Sales and Distance Sales Directive would spill over to the regulation for other sales contracts, in effect leading to more or less the same result as an enlargement of the scope of the Directive itself would have. Obviously, the civil servants negotiating the content of the Directive within the Council of Ministers will be aware of the fact that the outcome of the negotiations will have consequences reaching far beyond the harmonised area.

It will not come as a surprise to the reader that the possible addition of another regime for consumer sales contracts has engaged the immediate attention of legal practitioners and academics. Without exception it has been argued that the rules for distance sales contracts should be as similar as possible to the rules for consumer sales contracts concluded on-premises and off-premises.[53] Staudenmayer, Head of Unit at the European Commission, defended the proposal both in a workshop in Amsterdam and a symposium in Brussels[54] by arguing that the earlier proposal for a Common European Sales Law, that provided for a uniform regulation for sales contracts met with a lot of criticism because its scope was regarded as too broad by many Member States. For that reason, the Juncker Commission ultimately withdrew the proposal and announced that it would come with much more limited proposals in the context of the *Digital Single Market Strategy*.[55] The European Commission could demonstrate for online and other distance contracts that there was a need for harmonisation, but it could not demonstrate such need for on- and off-premises contracts. Staudenmayer noted, however, that the forthcoming *fitness check* of the existing Consumer Sales Directive could show such a need after all, and if that is the case the Commission would propose to extend the scope of the Online Sales and Distance Sales Directive to cover also on- and off-premises contracts. When asked by several participants why the European Commission could not simply have waited with its proposal for an Online Sales and Distance

---

53 In this sense also Mak 2016a, p. 524; J.M. Smits, *The new proposal for harmonised rules for the online sales or tangible goods: conformity, lack of conformity and remedies. In-depth analysis*, Briefing note for the Legal Affairs Committee of the European Parliament, PE 536,492, 2016, pp. 7–8 and 9, presented during a workshop on 17 February 2016. This paper is available at: http://www.europarl.europa.eu/committees/nl/events-workshops.html?id = 20160217CHE00181 (last visited on 15 March 2017). See also R. Mańko, *Contracts for online and other distance sales of goods*, Briefing note of the European Parliamentary Research Service for the European Parliament, 2016, pp. 8–9, in which the at this point mostly critical views of consumer organisations, industry associations, organisations of legal practitioners and scientists are displayed. This briefing note can be downloaded from: http://www.europarl.europa.eu/thinktank/en/document.html?reference=EPRS_BRI(2016)577962 (last visited on 15 March 2017).

54 For details on the workshop in Amsterdam on 4 February 2016 and the symposium in Brussels on 18 February, see n. * above.

55 Commission Work Programme 2015, A New Start, Strasbourg, 16 December 2014, COM(2014) 910 final, Annex 2, para. 60.

Sales Directive until the *fitness check* would be completed, he could, however, not give a convincing answer. The real answer seems to be that here a political choice is made: in her speech in Brussels, EU Commissioner Jourová hinted that she wanted a 'result' during her term as Commissioner, and that she could therefore not wait for the implementation of the *fitness check*. So much for the ambition of 'better regulation', participants in the Brussels symposium sneered.

4. ONLINE SALES AND DISTANCE SALES DIRECTIVE

4.1. SCOPE OF THE ONLINE SALES AND DISTANCE SALES DIRECTIVE

The scope of the current proposal is expressly limited to *consumer* sales contracts,[56] in the same manner as the current Consumer Sales Directive is limited. Contracts between traders, even if one of them is an SME, are therefore not covered by the scope of the directive.[57] Although the heading of the Online Sales and Distance Sales Directive suggests otherwise, the Directive as such does not provide specific rules for consumer sales contracts concluded 'online' – the notion is only mentioned on a number of occasions in the preamble and in Article 19 of the Directive, where the full name of the Directive is listed as a Directive to which the Regulation on consumer protection cooperation[58] and the Injunctions Directive[59] apply.[60] In reality, therefore, the directive is aimed at consumer sales contracts concluded *at a distance*.[61]

The Directive contains, in particular, rules on (non-) conformity (Articles 4–8) and the consequences of non-conformity (Articles 9–14) of the delivered goods.

---

56 See Arts. 1(1) and 2(a) Online Sales and Distance Sales Directive.

57 See critically H. Beale, *Scope of application and general approach of the new rules for contracts in the digital environment, In-depth analysis*, Briefing note for the Legal Affairs Committee of the European Parliament, PE 536.493, 2016, p. 11, presented during a workshop on 17 February 2016; this paper is available at: http://www.europarl.europa.eu/committees/nl/events-workshops.html?id=20160217CHE00181 (last visited on 15 March 2017).

58 Regulation (EC) No 2006/2004 of the European Parliament and of the Council of 27 October 2004 on cooperation between national authorities responsible for the enforcement of consumer protection laws, *OJ* 2004, L 364/1.

59 Directive 2009/22/EC of the European Parliament and of the Council of 23 April 2009 on injunctions for the protection of consumers' interests, *OJ* 2009, L 110/30.

60 During the symposium held in Brussels on 18 February 2016, U. Pachl (BEUC) rightly asked why Article 19 of the Online Sales and Distance Sales Directive does not also amend the scope of the ADR Directive (Directive 2013/11, *OJ* 2013, L 165/63) and the ODR Regulation (Council Regulation (EU) 523/2013, *OJ* 2013, L 165/1). Staudenmayer could not answer this question.

61 This suggests that the word 'online' is used primarily to justify why this proposal is submitted within the context of the Digital Single Market Strategy.

The Directive does not, however, apply to the sale of tangible items on which digital content is stored, such as DVDs and CDs: such contracts fall within the scope of the Digital Content Directive.[62]

Article 1(2) Online Sales and Distance Sales Directive provides that with regard to mixed contracts under which both goods and services are supplied the Directive applies only to the supply of the goods.[63] Recital 12 of the preamble to the Directive suggests that this restriction would be in line with the Consumer Rights Directive. However, recital 50 of the preamble to the latter Directive merely provides that in so far as a consumer withdraws from a contract for the supply of both goods and services, the provisions on the return of the goods apply as to the goods delivered on the basis of the contract and the provisions on the compensation for services apply as to the services rendered on the basis of the contract.[64] The Consumer Rights Directive itself does not explicitly say this. Instead, it defines mixed contracts exclusively as *sales* contracts.[65] It is therefore uncertain whether the Court of Justice will follow the European Commission's interpretation of the Consumer Rights Directive on this point. The restrictive approach to mixed contracts also seems remarkable given the approach to similar situations: the Online Sales and Distance Sales Directive provides, in line with the provisions of the Consumer Sales Directive, that a contract under which goods are to be produced and then delivered is classified (only) as a sales contract[66] and that for contracts under which movable goods are installed by or under the responsibility of the seller, a defect in the installation of the goods equates to a lack of conformity of the goods themselves.[67] Moreover, delivery is only completed when the consumer or a third party designated by the consumer has obtained physical control over the goods. This is the case when the goods have been collected by or on behalf of the consumer or when the goods have been delivered to the consumer or a carrier nominated by the consumer. Until that moment the seller bears the risk of deterioration or destruction of the goods,[68] which implies that defects originating before this moment are to be considered as a lack of conformity of the goods for which the seller is liable.[69] This suggests

62 See Art. 1(3) Online Sales and Distance Sales Directive and Art. 3(3) Digital Content Directive.
63 Art. 1(2) Online Sales and Distance Sales Directive.
64 See recital 50, last sentence, of the preamble to the Consumer Rights Directive. In the Dutch implementation Act the Dutch legislator incorporated this in the law itself, see Art. 6:230g(2) Dutch Civil Code.
65 See the definition of 'sales contract' in Art. 2(5) Consumer Rights Directive.
66 See the definition of a sales contract in Art. 2(a) Online Sales and Distance Sales Directive; this definition is in line with the definition in Art. 1(4) Consumer Sales Directive.
67 See Art. 6 Online Sales and Distance Sales Directive; see also Art. 2(5) Consumer Sales Directive.
68 *Cf.* Art. 20 Consumer Rights Directive.
69 See Art. 8(1) Online Sales and Distance Sales Directive.

that Article 1(2) Online Sales and Distance Sales Directive concerns only services which are not directly related to the production, use or delivery of the goods, e.g. to services such as storage or maintenance of the goods. Since such services are not regulated at the level of the European Union, the regulation of this part of the mixed contract is thus left to national law.

The scope of the proposed directive is further limited to 'certain aspects' of sales law, as the heading of the Online Sales and Distance Sales Directive indicates. The Directive does not affect provisions of general contract law, such as the rules on the conclusion, validity and effects of contracts, in so far as these provisions do not concern matters that are regulated within the Directive.[70] Such provisions are not uncommon in European directives,[71] but are problematic with regard to this particular Directive. I will give two examples that demonstrate why this is the case.

The first example pertains to the remedies for lack of conformity. The Directive expressly provides that in the case of such non-conformity, the consumer is entitled to repair or replacement (Article 11) or to price reduction or termination (Articles 12–13). The Explanatory Memorandum to the Directive suggests that under Article 1(4) of the Online Sales and Distance Sales Directive the consumer may also claim damages in accordance with national law, since the Directive does not regulate this remedy.[72] It is, however, questionable whether the wording of the Directive supports this, as Article 9 Online Sales and Distance Sales Directive appears to contain an exhaustive list of remedies for lack of conformity. Moreover, Article 1(1) of the Online Sales and Distance Sales Directive clearly indicates that the Directive in particular relates to conformity, remedies for non-conformity and the modalities for the exercise of these remedies, whereas Article 1(4) expressly leaves the consequences of *termination* of the consumer sales contract to national law. Moreover, not even the preamble to the Directive refers to national law as regards the right to damages. It is noteworthy that the proposal for the Digital Content Directive *does* contain an explicit provision on damages. This again suggests that in the area of distance contracts such a remedy would not exist. Clearly, the Directive needs to provide a clear reference to national law here if damages may indeed be obtained under national law.[73]

Another ambiguity concerns the right of the consumer to invoke a defect of consent. In particular with regard to whether or not the consumer has a right to claim avoidance of the contract on the basis of mistake, it seems necessary to

---

70 Art. 1(4) Online Sales and Distance Sales Directive.

71 See for instance Art. 3(5) Consumer Rights Directive and Art. 3(3) Unfair Commercial Practices Directive (Directive 2005/29/EC, *OJ* 2005, L 149/22). See also Art. 3(9) Digital Content Directive, which will be discussed below in Section 6 of this chapter.

72 *Cf.* the Explanatory Memorandum to the Online Sales and Distance Sales Directive, p. 3.

73 Amendment 359 Draft Report IMCO on the Online Sales and Distance Sales Directive aims at introducing such clear reference.

include an explicit provision. At first glance one would think that this matter is simply left to national law, as Article 1(4) Online Sales and Distance Sales Directive indicates that the Directive 'shall not affect national general contract laws such as rules on formation, [or] the validity or effects of contracts, including the consequences of the termination of a contract'. However, that provision also indicates that the reference to national contract law only applies in so far as the matter is not regulated in the Directive. It is, however, uncertain whether or not the doctrine of mistake should be regarded as regulated by the Directive. In this respect it should be noted that in many cases the facts that justify a claim on the basis of a lack of conformity would also justify a remedy on the basis of mistake. Under the Vienna Sales Convention it is assumed that the absence of an explicit regulation for mistake does not mean that the matter is left to national law. Instead it is argued that where the facts could justify a claim on the basis of non-conformity, a claim under national law on the basis of mistake is excluded, as otherwise the uniform application of the rules for non-conformity could be undermined, which would jeopardise the uniformity that the Convention intends to provide.[74] A similar reasoning could also be developed under the Online Sales and Distance Sales Directive, as the Directive provides that the consumer may only invoke a remedy for non-conformity for a defect that has manifested itself within two years after delivery.[75] This limitation could be circumvented by invoking a remedy for mistake, as national rules on prescription may allow for a longer period to invoke the remedy, and it could be argued that such circumvention should not be allowed in order to ensure the intended harmonisation, particularly since the Directive aims at full harmonisation of the targeted matters.[76] In my view, the Directive should be explicit on this contested matter – and should allow such recourse to national rules on mistake. If the Directive does not address the question, then it is a matter of time before the Court of Justice will be asked to render its judgment on the matter.

4.2. CONFORMITY OF GOODS PURCHASED AT A DISTANCE

The rules in the Directive offer a detailed regulation of the rules on conformity (Articles 4–8). This may be seen as a consequence of the aim of fully harmonising the rules on conformity and leaving as little room as possible for diverging interpretations of these rules at the national level. Full harmonisation implies that with regard to harmonised matters Member States are not free to offer

74 See M. Djordjevic, 'Comment 21 to Art. 4 CISG' in S. Kröll, L. Mistelis, P. Perales Viscasillas, *UN Convention for the International Sale of Goods (CISG)*, Munich: C.H. Beck, 2011, p. 71.

75 *Cf.* Art. 14 Online Sales and Distance Sales Directive.

76 See Art. 3 Online Sales and Distance Sales Directive.

consumers more protection than follows from the Directive. Obviously this is a sensitive matter for the Member States in those areas where the introduction of the Directive would lead to a decrease in consumer protection. Almost by definition this will be the case for some Member States on some issues, as it seems unlikely that the European level of consumer protection could be set at the highest level of protection awarded in any of the Member States – bearing in mind that consumer protection always comes at a cost as it implies that the costs of traders are raised, which in turn means that traders will be forced to either raise prices or to accept lower profits.

One of the areas where a possible decrease in consumer protection is foreseeable pertains to the period during which consumers may invoke a remedy for lack of conformity. Article 14 Online Sales and Distance Sales Directive basically provides that this period is two years after the consumer has obtained physical possession of the goods or the goods have been installed.[77] This provision is in line with Article 5(1) of the Consumer Sales Directive, which, however, merely offers a minimum period for liability of the seller. According to the Explanatory Memorandum,[78] the two-year period has been adopted in 23 Member States: only Finland, Great Britain, Ireland, Sweden and the Netherlands allow for a longer period. This is, however, a misrepresentation of the facts. First, it is overlooked that in Belgium after the end of the period of two years the consumer can make use of the scheme for hidden defects.[79] The same is – since 2016 – true in France, where the scheme for hidden defects is applicable *alongside* the rules on conformity, and where the buyer may invoke a remedy for hidden defects within two years after discovery of the defect.[80] Moreover, in Belgium, the Czech Republic, Hungary, Malta, Slovakia and Spain, the two-year period is suspended during the period when the goods are being repaired and the consumer as a result cannot make use of the goods, or when negotiations take place between the parties regarding a remedy for performance.[81] For all these countries, this means that the period of two years can under certain circumstances be extended. Since the Online Sales and Distance Sales Directive does not provide for such a longer or extended period, effectively consumer protection is decreased in 12 Member States.[82]

---

77 See in more detail below in Section 4.3.

78 See the Explanatory Memorandum, p. 6.

79 H. Schulte-Nölke, Ch. Twigg-Flesner, M. Ebers (eds.), *EU Consumer Law Compendium, Comparative analysis*, 2008, p. 701.

80 See Articles 1643 and 1648 Code Civil and Article L217-13 Code de la Consommation; Article L217-13 Code de la Consommation was introduced by *Ordonnance n° 2016-301 du 14 mars 2016 relative à la partie législative du code de la consommation.*

81 See Schulte-Nölke/Twigg-Flesner/Ebers 2008, pp. 682–83.

82 Amendments 360–365 Draft Report IMCO on the Online Sales and Distance Sales Directive aim at remedying this by introducing either a conformity period of six years, the full economic lifespan of the goods, by leaving the matter to national law, or by providing that the two-year period is a minimum harmonisation rule only.

Moreover, there are also substantive reasons why the limitation of remedies for non-conformity to two years after delivery should not be adopted. First of all, it is difficult to explain why the seller should not be liable if durable goods – such as refrigerators, washing machines and (new) cars, which are bought by the consumer for use during a longer period and which the consumer may reasonably expect to last for a longer period than two years – break down at a moment when the consumer need not expect this, and the consumer has proven that this is due to a defect that already existed at the moment of delivery and therefore is not the result of normal tear and wear.[83] Secondly, the provision provides an incentive to producers of durable consumer goods to produce only goods that do not last significantly longer than two years.[84] By doing so, the producer would ensure that consumers are either forced to purchase, at the time of conclusion of the original sales contract, an extended warranty,[85] or to purchase replacement goods if such an extended warranty was not obtained and the goods indeed break down shortly after the two-year period has elapsed.[86] Clearly, from the point of view of sustainability, the two-year period does not provide an incentive for companies to show their interest in corporate social responsibility – and effective competition may even force willing companies to step away from such an approach. Moreover, if the consumer resold the later defective goods herself to another consumer (e.g. via an auction platform such as eBay), she might be held liable towards her buyer without having recourse to the original seller. Finally, the absence of a 'suspension period' such as in Belgium and the Czech Republic effectively renders the conformity period even shorter if a defect had already occurred during the two-year period and the consumer at that time had given the seller an opportunity to cure the lack of conformity through repair or replacement and as a result she has not been able to make use of the goods during the full two-year period. All of these objections show that introducing the two-year period on the basis of full harmonisation is not the right way forward.

The European Commission is persistent on this point: the original proposal for the Consumer Rights Directive contained a similar provision.[87] In that proposal also a full harmonisation approach was adopted, but throughout

83 See M.B.M. Loos, 'Consumer sales law in the proposal for a Consumer rights directive', *ERPL* 2010/1, p. 28; Ch. Twigg-Flesner, 'Fit for Purpose? The Proposals on Sales' in G. Howells, R. Schulze (eds.), *Modernising and Harmonising Consumer Contract Law*, Munich: Sellier, 2009, p. 172.

84 *Cf.* J. Hijma, 'De Koopregeling in het Richtlijnvoorstel Consumentenrechten' in M.W. Hesselink, M.B.M. Loos (eds.), *Het Voorstel voor een Europese Richtlijn Consumentenrechten. Een Nederlands Perspectief*, The Hague: Boom Juridische uitgevers, 2009, p. 177.

85 *Cf.* Hijma 2009, p. 178.

86 On this already Loos 2010, pp. 27–28.

87 See Art. 28(1) of the proposal for a Consumer Rights Directive, COM(2008) 614/4, on which critically Loos 2010, p. 28; Twigg-Flesner 2009, p. 172.

the proposal the European Commission had not raised the level of consumer protection above the minimum level that already resulted from the Consumer Sales Directive. Had this proposal been adopted in its original form then that would have meant that national legislators would have had to abolish national measures of consumer protection going beyond the European minimum without an increase in consumer protection on other points. That proved to be politically too problematic, and ultimately the Consumer Rights Directive was adopted without provisions replacing those of the Consumer Sales Directive (and those of the Unfair Contract Terms Directive).[88]

That is different in the proposal for the Online Sales and Distance Sales Directive, which on several points does go above the minimum level of consumer protection offered by the Consumer Sales Directive. The first example is the absence of a duty to notify. Under Article 5(2) of the Consumer Sales Directive Member States were given the possibility to introduce or maintain a provision that, in order to benefit from his rights, the consumer must inform the trader of the lack of conformity within a period of two months from the date on which she detected such lack of conformity. According to the Explanatory Memorandum, 17 Member States have made use of this option.[89] The duty to notify may have the effect that consumers lose well-substantiated claims for remedies. This is considered to be problematic especially in a cross-border transaction where the law of another Member State applies and the consumer may not be aware of this notification obligation resulting from the law of another Member State.[90] This is not a very convincing argument not to introduce a duty in this particular Directive, as the problem of the consumer being surprised by a duty to notify under a foreign national law would not exist – as the law would be fully harmonised anyway, and the duty to notify therefore would exist or not also in the consumer's national legal system. Nevertheless, it seems that the exclusion of the duty to notify is justified also from a substantive point of view. First, under the current regulation of the duty to notify the consumer is only required to notify as of the moment that she has actually discovered the defect. It seems likely that at that moment the consumer will in most cases indeed notify the defect to the seller whether or not she has a duty to that effect as she will not be satisfied and will want to invoke a remedy. Moreover, if the consumer were late in doing so, this could easily be concealed from the seller, as the consumer need only state that she found out 'just now' and it would be almost impossible for the seller to substantiate that the consumer in fact had noticed the defect earlier and had failed to notify at that time. And finally, it is doubtful whether a consumer should be under any *duty* to notify the seller for the *seller's* breach

88 See above, Section 2.4.
89 *Cf.* the Explanatory Memorandum, p. 6.
90 *Cf.* recital 25 of the preamble to the Online Sales and Distance Sales Directive.

of his contractual obligations to the extent that the seller could subsequently invoke the consumer's breach of this notification duty to escape liability for the breach of her own obligation as to conformity.

A second improvement of the position of the consumer is the limitation of the seller's defence against a claim for non-conformity by arguing that the consumer already was or should have been aware of the defect before the contract was concluded. Under Article 2(3) Consumer Sales Directive, this defence leads to the conclusion that the consumer had accepted that particular defect and therefore that there was no lack of conformity. Article 4(3) Online Sales and Distance Sales Directive, however, provides that the consumer only loses the right to invoke a remedy for lack of conformity if she not only *knew* of the defect at the time when the contract was concluded, but also had *accepted* that defect *explicitly*.[91] That will in any case prevent the discussion whether the consumer could reasonably have expected that the defect would have been repaired before delivery or that she had tacitly accepted the defect by not expressly demanding repair before that moment.

The third example pertains to termination in case of minor defects. Whereas Article 3(6) of the Consumer Sales Directive excludes termination in such cases, a similar exclusion deliberately has not been adopted in the Online Sales and Distance Sales Directive.[92] This implies that for consumers in legal systems where the exclusion had been adopted in national law, the new Directive enlarges the possibility for consumers to terminate the contract and therefore extends the extent of consumer protection on this point. This means that the contract for the sale of a car could be terminated for a small defect such as a scratch on the lacquer of the car, which may appear to be a disproportionate sanction. On the other hand, given the hierarchy of remedies (which will be discussed below, Section 5.1), termination is available only where neither repair nor replacement is available to the consumer, where the seller refuses to repair or replace the car, where the seller causes significant inconvenience to the consumer when repairing or replacing the car, or where the seller is required but neglects to repair or replace the car within a reasonable period. In most of these cases, the seller could have prevented the termination by complying with his obligation to repair or replace the goods. Where neither of these remedies is available to the consumer – implying that the seller is not capable of remedying the scratch herself or having it remedied on her behalf by a garage – the defect typically is not as minor as one would think. The choice made by the European Commission in any case prevents an otherwise complicated debate on the seriousness of the defect and thus facilitates a speedy resolution of the consumer's claim.

---

91 *Cf.* Beale 2016, p. 16.

92 *Cf.* recital 29 of the preamble to the Online Sales and Distance Sales Directive and the Explanatory Memorandum, pp. 3, 13 and 15; *cf.* also Smits 2016, p. 13.

Fourthly, whereas the consequences of termination have largely been left to national law,[93] Article 13(3)(d) of the Directive does provide that in the case where the goods are to be returned to the seller after termination, the consumer is only liable to compensate the trader for the loss of value due to the use of the goods in so far as the decrease in value is larger than would result from the normal use of the goods. The provision intends to reconcile on the one hand the effectiveness of the right to terminate and on the other hand the desire to avoid that the consumer unjustly is enriched as a result of the termination of the contract.[94] In this respect the Directive derogates to the benefit of consumers from the Consumer Sales Directive, where recital 15 of the preamble to that Directive explicitly left Member States the possibility to oblige the consumer to pay for the use of the goods prior to termination. The provision is, however, more restrictive than the corresponding provision for a decrease in value in the case of replacement, since for that situation Article 10(3) Online Sales and Distance Sales Directive excludes any right for the seller to claim compensation for the loss in value.

The last and arguably most important improvement of the consumer's position[95] pertains to the extension of the reversal of the burden of proof from six months[96] to two years.[97] This last improvement measure implies that throughout the full period during which the consumer can exercise rights due to non-conformity, the seller bears the burden of proof that the non-conformity did not already exist at the time of delivery. The *Faber* decision of the Court of Justice,[98] rendered under the current Consumer Sales Directive, brings about that this requires a full shift of the burden of proof, implying that the seller must prove that the defect was caused only after delivery; however, and in accordance with Article 5(3) Consumer Sales Directive, the burden of proof is not shifted if the nature of the goods or the nature of the defect is irreconcilable with the presumption that the defect already existed at delivery. If that is the case, the consumer not only must prove the lack of conformity itself but also that it existed already when the goods were delivered. If the seller indeed will be required to bear the burden of proof for the full period of two years after delivery, this will improve consumer protection considerably, as in many cases it is precisely she who bears the burden of proof who loses the procedure. Whether the extension

---

93 See Art. 1(4) Online Sales and Distance Sales Directive.

94 See recital 31 of the preamble to the Online Sales and Distance Sales Directive.

95 See in this respect expressly the Explanatory Memorandum, pp. 3 and 11.

96 See Art. 5(3) Consumer Sales Directive.

97 *Cf.* Art. 8(3) Online Sales and Distance Sales Directive.

98 CJEU 4 June 2015, Case C-497/13, ECLI:EU:C:2015:357 (*Faber v Autobedrijf Hazet Ochten BV*); see in contrast Smits 2016, p. 10, who is of the opinion that the seller need only shed doubt as to the correctness of the presumption that the defect already existed at the moment when the goods were delivered.

will be included in the final version of the Directive is, however, uncertain, as this is politically controversial.[99]

4.3. REMEDIES FOR NON-CONFORMITY OF GOODS PURCHASED AT A DISTANCE

From Article 9(3) Online Sales and Distance Sales Directive it becomes clear that the European Commission has adopted the Consumer Sales Directive's hierarchy of remedies for non-conformity – the primary remedies being repair or replacement, and the remedies of termination and price reduction fulfilling only a subsidiary role. Whereas, according to the Explanatory Memorandum, 20 Member States have adopted this hierarchy, eight have not[100] – which implies that the Online Sales and Distance Sales Directive, which is based on full harmonisation, would lead to a decrease of consumer protection on this point in eight Member States.

With regard to the right to repair and replacement, the Online Sales and Distance Sales Directive expressly provides that it is the *consumer* who may choose between the two remedies. Only if the chosen remedy is disproportionate for the seller, is the consumer required to accept the alternative remedy for bringing the goods into conformity.[101] In addition, the *Weber v Wittmer* and *Putz v Medianess* joined cases[102] are codified to the extent that when the consumer had installed the goods in accordance with their nature or purpose before discovering the non-conformity, the seller is obliged not only to provide replacement goods, but also to either remove the defective goods and reinstall the repaired or replacement goods, or to compensate the consumer for the costs thereof.[103] The provision that the consumer is not required to pay any compensation for the use of the goods prior to replacement[104] may be seen as codification of the *Quelle* judgment.[105] The Directive is, however, not clear whether in the case of a

---

99 See Amendments 277–284 Draft Report IMCO on the Online Sales and Distance Sales Directive, where diverging solutions are proposed ranging from a return to the current six-month period to a shift of the burden of proof during the full economic lifespan of the goods.

100 Explanatory Memorandum, p. 6.

101 Art. 11 Online Sales and Distance Sales Directive.

102 CJEU 16 June 2011, Joined Cases C-65/09 (*Gebruder Weber GmbH v Wittmer*) and C-87/09 (*Putz v Medianess Electronics GmbH*), ECLI:EU:C:2011:396. On these cases, see J.A. Luzak, 'Who should bear the risk of the removal of the non-conforming goods? Joined cases C-65/09 and C-87/09 (Weber and Putz)', *Zeitschrift für europäisches Unternehmens- und Verbraucherrecht/Journal of European Consumer and Market Law* 2012/1, pp. 35–40; J.A. Luzak, 'A storm in a teacup? On consumers' remedies for non-conforming goods after *Weber and Putz*', *ERPL* 2015/4, pp. 689–704.

103 *Cf.* Art 10(2) Online Sales and Distance Sales Directive.

104 *Cf.* Art 10(3) Online Sales and Distance Sales Directive.

105 CJEU 17 April 2008, Case C-404/06, ECLI:EU:C:2008:231 (*Quelle AG v Bundesverbraucherzentralen und Verbraucherverbände*).

non-conformity of, for instance, a television that has manifested itself after one and a half years, the consumer is entitled to a *new* television or to a replacement television that has already been used for one and a half years. If the latter is the case, replacement may be less burdensome for the seller, since the returned television could be repaired by the seller and then be used as a replacement television for another consumer claiming replacement for lack of conformity. A related question is whether after having received the replacement goods the consumer again is entitled to invoke a remedy for non-conformity during a further two years or merely during the remainder of the original period of the two years, possibly supplemented by the period between the notification of the non-conformity and the receipt of the replacement goods, such as is currently accepted in Belgium, the Czech Republic, Hungary, Malta, Slovakia and Spain.[106] Clarification on these matters, whether in the text of the Directive itself or in a recital in the preamble would be very welcome for practice.

For termination, a notice is required. Article 13 Online Sales and Distance Sales Directive makes clear that any means of communication suffices, thus indicating that no form requirement applies as to the termination of the contract. The Directive does not provide, however, when termination will take effect. Instead, this will have to be determined on the basis of the applicable national law.

After termination, the seller must return the price within 14 days of receipt of the termination notice, whereas the consumer is required to return the goods within 14 days following the dispatch of the termination notice.[107] This implies that the consumer's obligation to return the goods becomes due before the seller's obligation to return the price – in particular in cross-border cases where the consumer does not terminate by email but by a letter in writing. This implies that in such cases the seller may withhold repayment of the price until the consumer has returned the goods, burdening the consumer with the risk of the seller's insolvency or non-performance. Such an order of procedure is very well defensible in the case of the consumer's withdrawal during the cooling-off period,[108] as in such case the ending of the contract is caused by the consumer without this being in any way attributable to the seller. In the case of termination for non-conformity, however, this is different. First, termination is the result of the fact that the *seller* has not performed her original obligations under the sales contract. Moreover, due to the hierarchy of remedies, the seller was first put in the position to cure the defect through repair or replacement, and apparently has not cured the defect. Under these conditions it is difficult to see why the consumer should be required to – again – trust the seller to properly perform

---

106 *Cf.* Schulte-Nölke/Twigg-Flesner/Ebers 2008, pp. 682–83.

107 Art. 13(3)(a) and (b) Online Sales and Distance Sales Directive.

108 Arts. 13 and 14 Consumer Rights Directive.

her obligation where she has already has proven not to be trustworthy on several occasions.[109]

Article 13(3)(c) Online Sales and Distance Sales Directive provides that when the goods cannot be returned because they have been destroyed or lost, the consumer must reimburse the monetary value of the goods that these would have had at the time when the obligation to return them became due and which they would have had if the consumer at that time had returned them. A similar result, but in much simpler wording, is achieved by Article 7:10(3) of the Dutch Civil Code (Burgerlijk Wetboek (BW)), according to which the risk of loss or destruction of the goods is for the account of the seller if the buyer has invoked the right to termination or replacement on good grounds. In such cases, the consumer would be under a duty of care towards the goods as of the moment when she would reasonably have had to take the possibility of the future termination or replacement of goods into account, Article 7:10(4) BW provides. Moreover, under Dutch law the seller who wishes to claim the original value of the now destroyed or damaged goods will have to prove that the consumer has breached her duty of care, whereas the Online Sales and Distance Sales Directive seems to require the consumer to prove that the destruction of the goods is the result of the non-conformity. Such proof may be difficult for the consumer to provide.

The Online Sales and Distance Sales Directive does not expressly deal with the consumer's right to claim damages for damage caused by the non-conformity. The Explanatory Memorandum indicates that this matter is left to national law.[110] As was indicated above in Section 3, this is far from clear, as the Directive seems to offer an exhaustive list of remedies in Article 9. If, however, the Directive indeed leaves room for national rules on damages, it does seem likely that courts will interpret the Directive in such a way that the two-year cut-off period under Article 14 of the Directive would equally apply to a claim for damages under national law based on non-conformity. There does not appear to be a convincing argument to limit liability in this way – whereas it could be argued that there is a valid reason to exclude the consumer's right to claim repair, replacement and termination after some time in order to save the seller from the potentially far reaching consequences of these remedies, such an argument cannot reasonably made as to the statutory exclusion of the right to compensation for damage sustained after (only) two years.[111]

---

109 *Cf.* Notaries of Europe, Position Paper on the proposal for a Directive on certain aspects concerning contracts for the online and other distance sales of goods (COM(2015) 635) and a Directive on certain aspects concerning contracts for the supply of digital content (COM(2015) 634), p. 2: http://www.notaries-of-europe.eu/index.php?pageID=13390 (last visited on 15 March 2017).

110 Explanatory Memorandum, p. 3.

111 In this sense also Beale 2016, pp. 19–20.

5. DIGITAL CONTENT DIRECTIVE

5.1. SCOPE OF THE DIGITAL CONTENT DIRECTIVE

The Digital Content Directive covers the supply of digital content, irrespective of the way in which the agreement has been concluded (in or outside of a shop or at a distance) and regardless of the way in which the digital content is delivered (on a durable medium, such as a DVD, by means of a download, by way of streaming or by providing access to the consumer).[112] Moreover, the Directive is applicable both to contracts under which the supplier must enable the consumer to obtain the control over the digital content for repeated use (such as in the case of a download) and to contracts under which the supplier merely offers services (as is the case with streaming or cloud storage, but also where the supplier operates a social medium facility, such as the platforms of Twitter and Facebook). The Directive applies only where the supplier is a professional party, the other party is a consumer, and where the digital content is provided against payment of a price in money[113] or against counter-performance by the consumer in the form of the provision of data.[114]

Undoubtedly, the extension of the scope of the Digital Content Directive to certain contracts for the supply of 'free' digital content concerns the most important innovation of the Directive for legal practice. The Directive applies where the supplier requires the consumer to actively provide personal or other data in addition to such data that must be provided to the supplier in order for her to carry out the contract or to meet regulatory requirements. For example, when the supplier requests the consumer to inform the supplier of her email address in order for the supplier to send her the requested digital information via email, the provision of the email address by the consumer is necessary in order to comply with the consumer's request. In this case, the Directive *does not* apply. If the supplier, however, also uses the email address for other purposes, for example in order to target the consumer with advertising or in order to sell

---

112 Only the provisions on the supply of digital content (Art. 5 Digital Content Directive) and on the right to directly claim termination in case of a failure to deliver the digital content (Art. 11 Digital Content Directive) do not apply to the supply of digital content on a durable medium, Art. 3(3) Digital Content Directive provides. As the Online Sales and Distance Sales Directive does not indicate that in such cases that Directive is applicable if the contract is concluded at a distance, both the obligation to deliver the DVD with the digital content and the remedies for a failure to do so under Art. 18 of the Consumer Rights Directive apply. Before being able to terminate the contract, the consumer will then normally have to give notice to the seller of the DVD and to fix an additional period for delivery.

113 As far I know, this Directive for the first time explicitly indicates that 'price' is intended to mean money in exchange for the supply of digital content provided by the supplier, see Art. 2(6) Digital Content Directive.

114 See Arts. 1 and 3 Digital Content Directive.

collected email addresses to information brokers, the collection of the email address (also) has a commercial purposes, and the Directive *does* apply.[115] When a consumer creates an account with a platform for social media and to that extent agrees to transfer intellectual property rights in relation to photos and texts shared or distributed through the platform, this is considered to constitute such counter-performance.[116] The Directive also seems to apply in cases where the supplier initially does not intend to collect the consumer's data for commercial purposes, but later decides to use them for such purposes. In such case it is, however, unclear whether this later use entitles the consumer to invoke the protection of the Directive also with regard to digital content which was purchased before the supplier's later commercial use – in particular if the digital content has proven to be defective. If this would not be the case, the supplier would reap the commercial advantages of the consumer's supply of the (personal) data without suffering the consequences of the supply of non-conforming digital content – which could incentivise the supplier to claim that she did not have a commercial purpose at first and thus largely escape liability for any digital content provided until that moment. Accepting that the consumer could invoke the protection of the Directive, however, does imply that de facto the contract is classified as a digital content contract retroactively.

However, the Directive is applicable to 'free' digital content only where the consumer *actively* provides data to the supplier of the digital content. When the data is collected by the supplier, for example, by setting cookies on the consumer's computer, or when the consumer's counter-performance consists in having to tolerate advertisement, the Directive is *not* applicable.[117] The limitation of the scope of the Directive to cases where the data is gathered *explicitly* may lead to the undesirable situation that the supplier evades the applicability of the Directive by not expressly asking for the provision of the data, but by (whether or not secretively) collecting that data via cookies. In order to prevent this, the scope of the Directive needs to be expanded to include at least this situation.[118]

---

115 *Cf.* Art. 3(4) Digital Content Directive.

116 *Cf.* B. Fauvarque-Cosson, *The new proposal for harmonised rules for certain aspects concerning contracts for the supply of digital content (termination, modification of the digital content and right to terminate long term contracts), In-depth analysis*, Briefing note for the Legal Affairs Committee of the European Parliament, PE 536.495, 2016, p. 7, presented during a workshop on 17 February 2016; this paper is available at: http://www.europarl.europa.eu/committees/nl/events-workshops.html?id=20160217CHE00181 (last visited on 15 March 2017).

117 *Cf.* Art. 3(4) Digital Content Directive and recital 14 of the preamble to the Directive.

118 In this sense also Beale 2016, p. 13; V. Mak, *The new proposal for harmonised rules on certain aspects concerning contracts for the supply of digital content. In-depth analysis*, Briefing note for the Legal Affairs Committee of the European Parliament, PE 536.495, 2016, p. 9, presented during a workshop on 17 February 2016; I will refer to this paper as Mak 2016b: http://www.europarl.europa.eu/committees/nl/events-workshops.html?id=20160217CHE00181 (last visited on 15 March 2017). Amendments 31 and 35 in the Draft Report of the Committee

The notion of 'digital content' is defined broadly in Article 2(1) Digital Content Directive. It consists, in the first place, of data in digital form, which is produced and delivered in the form of video, audio, apps, games or other software. Secondly, the notion concerns the provision of a service which consists in the creation, processing or storage of data delivered in digital form by the consumer. Finally, also the supply of a service that allows a consumer to share data in digital form with other users of the service or that allows a consumer to interact with such data provided by other users of the service. The definition is intentionally broad and aims to include all types of digital content, including downloaded digital content, streamed movies, cloud storage, and social media.[119] The Directive explicitly aims to be 'future-proof'.[120]

Services that use the digital content primarily as a carrier and for which the supplier's human activity is predominant, are excluded from the scope of the Directive. The same is true for electronic communication services, services in the field of healthcare, gambling services and financial services.[121] With regard to mixed contracts, the Directive only applies to the obligations and remedies of the parties as supplier and consumer of the digital content.[122] Goods that make use of embedded software, where the digital content is functionally subordinate to the movable goods, such as the electronics and software in a car, and the software for a thermostat that can be turned on remotely with an app, fall outside the scope of the Digital Content Directive. Instead, such contracts are exclusively governed by the Online Sales and Distance Sales Directive or the Consumer

on the Internal Market and Consumer Protection of 7 November 2016 and 15 February 2017 indeed propose to extend the scope of the Directive in this sense. This draft report is available at: http://www.europarl.europa.eu/oeil/popups/ficheprocedure.do?lang=&reference=2015/0287(COD) (last visited on 15 March 2017) and will be referred to hereinafter as: Draft Report IMCO on the Digital Content Directive. See also the Opinion of the European Parliament's Committee on Civil Liberties, Justice and Home Affairs of 21 November 2016, p. 3, available at the same website. I will refer to this Opinion as: LIBE Opinion.

119 Explanatory Memorandum, p. 11; see also recital 11 of the preamble to the Digital Content Directive.

120 Mak 2016b, p. 9, doubts whether the Directive can achieve this aim, given the fact that it is intended to apply also to digital applications that currently do not even exist.

121 *Cf.* Art. 3(5) Digital Content Directive.

122 *Cf.* Art. 3(6) Digital Content Directive. Recital 12 of the preamble to the Online Sales and Distance Sales Directive offers a comparable approach to mixed contracts in which elements of a sale and of a service may be distinguished, e.g. a contract whereby a garage sells a car and agrees to maintain and service the car annually. Wendehorst rightly noes that both Directives fail to indicate what the consequences are of termination of a *part* of the contract, see C. Wendehorst, *Sale of goods and supply of digital content – two worlds apart? Why the law on sale of goods needs to respond better to the challenges of the digital age. In-depth analysis*, Briefing note for the Legal Affairs Committee of the European Parliament, PE 556.928, 2016, p. 7, presented during a workshop on 17 February 2016; this paper is available at: http://www.europarl.europa.eu/committees/nl/events-workshops.html?id=20160217CHE00181 (last visited on 15 March 2017).

Sales Directive.[123] In practice it is, however, difficult to distinguish between contracts for the supply of goods with embedded software and mixed contracts for the sale of goods and the supply of digital content. For instance, is a contract by which a laptop is sold with Windows 10 and Microsoft Office installed to be considered a mixed contract or a sales contract pertaining to goods with embedded software?[124] One could think that the distinction should be made whether or not the digital content has an independent economic significance. That is certainly the case with Microsoft Office, but already unclear with regard to Windows 10. And since both the conformity test and the remedies differ, it is rather important to classify the contract properly.[125] The development of goods and digital content that are intertwined is likely to go much further in the coming years, and it will be increasingly more difficult to make the distinction between goods with embedded software and mixed contracts. This distinction therefore jeopardises the aim of providing a 'future-proof' regulation for digital content contracts.[126] In this respect, it probably makes more sense – also with regard to future developments – that the Digital Content Directive is applicable to goods operated by embedded software, rendering the supplier liable in case of any defect in the proper functioning of the goods, unless the supplier of the digital content proves that the defect lies in the hardware of the good.[127]

Contracts that are concluded without direct human involvement, such as a refrigerator that automatically places an order at a grocery shop or a supermarket when it detects that the milk runs out, fall outside the scope of the Directive. In the preamble, in this context it noted that it is 'opportune' to address specific issues of liability related to the *Internet of Things* in a separate way.[128] That suggests that this matter is outside the scope of the Directive. However, the definition of the notion of 'digital content' is so broad that it is uncertain whether the *Internet of Things* is really outside its scope[129] – and this will all the more be the case if embedded software will be governed by the Digital Content Directive, as members of the European Parliament's Committee on the Internal Market and Consumer Protection and of the Committee on Civil Liberties,

---

123 *Cf.* recital 12 of the preamble to the Digital Content Directive. On this, see critical R. Mańko, *Contracts for supply of digital content. A legal analysis of the Commission's directive proposal. In-depth analysis*, May 2016, pp. 8–9, 12–13; this paper is prepared by the Members' Research Service, http://www.europarl.europa.eu/thinktank/en/document.html?reference=EPRS_IDA(2016)582048 (last visited on 15 March 2017). The paper will be referred to as Mańko 2016. See also Wendehorst 2016, p. 7.

124 The example is developed by Wendehorst 2016, p. 8; see critical also Mańko 2016, pp. 9, 13.

125 *Cf.* Mańko 2016, p. 14.

126 In this sense also Mańko 2016, pp. 14–15.

127 Amendments 10 and 34 Draft Report IMCO on the Digital Content Directive together propose to amend recital 12 and to add a new paragraph 3a to Article 3 of the Directive in this manner. See also LIBE Opinion, p. 6.

128 See recital 17 of the preamble to the Digital Content Directive.

129 Mak 2016b, p. 8.

Justice and Home Affairs suggest.[130] In my view, this matter should be clarified in the Directive itself and not in the recitals.

Recital 16 of the preamble to the Directive makes clear to what extent the Directive applies with regard to 3D printing. In the case of 3D printing, a consumer may obtain so-called computer-aided design (CAD) software or CAD files from a supplier of digital content, develop her own CAD file or amend an existing CAD file to her liking, and subsequently send the CAD file to a 3D printer for 3D printing.[131] According to the recital, the supply of the CAD files or the CAD software to the consumer is governed by the Directive, but the 3D printing of the goods on the basis of the CAD file sent to the 3D printer is excluded from the scope of this Directive and governed exclusively by the Online Sales and Distance Sales Directive.

The Digital Content Directive does not seem to aim at holding the *producer* of the digital content liable in case of non-conformity of the digital content. However, the wording of the Directive may very well lead to that result – and that may be a very good idea, as the supplier in many cases is not much more than an in-between person. Such direct liability of the producer seems likely when the digital content is supplied by a supplier, but is accompanied by an End User's Licence Agreement (EULA), which is submitted by the producer of the digital content. If the producer effectively forces the consumer to agree to the conclusion of the EULA and to accept the producer's terms and conditions, and requires the consumer to provide personal data, such as her email address, then it seems that the requirements of Article 3 Digital Content Directive as to the applicability of the Directive have been met. That is certainly the case if the EULA requires the producer to send regular updates and patches to remedy bugs and errors in the digital content that originally was provided by the supplier.[132] It remains to be seen, however, whether or not the contract is valid, since the consumer is more or less coerced into concluding the EULA even though she has already obtained the right to use the digital content by purchasing it from the supplier. It may very well be that under the applicable national law the consumer is entitled to avoid the EULA altogether or to invoke the unfairness of its terms. These matters have been left outside the scope of the Digital Content Directive.

Finally, it is important to note that the Directive is expressly without prejudice to the protection of individuals offered by the Data Protection Directive legislation.[133] Moreover, it does not concern provisions of general contract law,

---

130 See n 128.

131 See on this Ch. Twigg-Flesner, 'Conformity of 3D prints – Can current Sales Law cope?' in R. Schulze, D. Staudenmayer (eds.), *Digital Revolution – Challenges for Contract Law*, Baden-Baden: Nomos/Hart, 2016, p. 36.

132 In this sense also Beale 2016, p. 13.

133 Art. 3(7) Digital Content Directive. The Directive refers to the General Data Protection Regulation, i.e. Regulation (EU) 2016/679, *OJ* 2016, L 119/1. On this, see Mańko 2016, p. 6.

such as the rules on the conclusion, validity and effects of contracts in so far as these matters are not regulated in the Directive.[134] As was already mentioned with regard to the Online Sales and Distance Sales Directive, the question may arise whether in addition to a remedy for non-conformity the consumer could also invoke avoidance on the basis of mistake, or that this matter is effectively regulated in the Directive through the provisions on non-conformity. As was argued above, in Section 4.1, with regard to the Online Sales and Distance Sales Directive, this matter should be dealt with explicitly in the Digital Content Directive.

5.2. SUPPLY AND FAILURE TO SUPPLY DIGITAL CONTENT

According to Article 5(1) Digital Content Directive, the supplier must supply the digital content to the consumer or to a third party designated by her. 'Third party' in this context refers to a party that operates a physical or virtual facility through which the digital content is made available or accessible to the consumer. The notion includes an Internet host that allows for cloud storage of the digital photos produced by the supplier of the digital content, but also a platform that provides access to an online game for which the consumer has purchased, for instance, a virtual shield or other power.

The obligation to supply the digital content must be performed within 30 days, unless a shorter or longer period of time for performance is agreed between the parties, Article 5(2) provides. In practice, the parties will almost always have made a specific arrangement as to the moment of delivery: typically the parties will have agreed on immediate supply of the digital content or supply thereof within a few working days.

When the obligation to supply at the agreed moment is not met, the consumer is entitled to directly terminate the contract without prior notice of default.[135] In this respect the Digital Content Directive derogates from the corresponding provision in Article 18(2) Consumer Rights Directive. This provision indicates that for sales contracts in principle prior notice is required. A reason for the diverging approaches is not provided.[136] To complicate matters further, whereas digital content provided on a durable medium is largely governed by the Digital Content Directive, as regards the obligation to supply and the remedies for failure to supply, it is not the Digital Content Directive but the Consumer

134 Art. 3(9) Digital Content Directive.

135 See Art. 11 Digital Content Directive.

136 Amendments 689–691 Draft Report IMCO on the Digital Content Directive propose to introduce a provision similar to Article 18(2) Consumer Rights Directive. Amendments 687 and 701 together instead propose to delete Article 11 Digital Content Directive and to offer a unitary system of remedies for digital content that is either defective or not supplied.

Rights Directive that applies.[137] This means that for digital content that was to be supplied on a DVD prior notice of default is required, whereas if the digital content was to be supplied by way of a download such notice is not required.

In addition to termination, consumers can also claim damages in accordance with Article 14(1) Digital Content Directive. The Directive does not make clear whether the consumer may also simply claim performance of the contract: only damages and termination are explicitly mentioned as remedies for failure to supply the digital content. This is problematic since the Directive is based on full harmonisation. It is therefore possible that a court would find that the Digital Content Directive offers an exhaustive list of remedies – which would not be surprising given the extensive rules on the remedies for lack of conformity in its Articles 12–14 – and therefore not award specific performance. Yet, there does not seem to be a good reason to deny consumers the right to claim performance of the contract.

Another matter which deserves consideration is how a failure to provide the agreed supply of updates is to be classified: does this constitute a failure to supply the digital content within the meaning of Article 5 Digital Content Directive or should this rather be seen as non-conformity in the sense of Article 6 of the Directive?[138] This is important not only in view of the discussion above whether or not the consumer may demand the supply of the updates in case the failure to supply updates would be governed by Article 5 Digital Content Directive, but also because of the more restricted possibilities for termination for non-conformity in case the failure to supply updates would be classified as non-conformity, as will be discussed below, Section 9.

5.3. CONFORMITY OF DIGITAL CONTENT

With regard to conformity, Article 6(1) Digital Content Directive provides that the digital content must comply with the specific purposes for which the consumer has purchased it – in as far as these specific purposes have been disclosed to the supplier before the conclusion of the contract – and with the information that has been provided by the supplier before or at the conclusion of the contract.[139] This conformity test applies both to the purchase of software or games and to the supply of online services, such as a subscription to Netflix

137 See Art. 3(3) Digital Content Directive, and the definition of a sales contract in Art. 2(5) Consumer Rights Directive.

138 Fauvarque-Cosson 2016, pp. 7–8, treats this as a matter of non-conformity; I am inclined to agree with her on this. She argues, however, on p. 9 that the provisions on termination should not differ for termination because of a failure to supply and termination for non-conformity.

139 *Cf.* Art. 6(1) Digital Content Directive.

or access to an online game.[140] Moreover, unless agreed otherwise, the supplier must deliver the latest version of the digital content that was in circulation at the time of contract conclusion.[141]

The wording of Article 6(2) Digital Content Directive indicates that *objective* standards apply for the assessment as to whether the digital content conforms to the contract only if the parties have not made any specific arrangements as to what requirements the digital content has to conform with. This implies, for instance, that where the supplier had indicated for which purposes the digital content may be used, the digital content need not be fit for normal use thereof. During the symposium in Brussels,[142] Staudenmayer, acting as the representative of the European Commission, indicated that a derogation from the normal conformity rules is required in the case of digital content due to the restrictions which the holder of the intellectual property rights may have imposed on the supplier, which restrictions in turn the supplier must be allowed to pass on to the consumer. In addition, Staudenmayer argued, the supplier should be allowed to put so-called beta versions of digital content on the market. Characteristic of such beta versions is that they are still being developed and that the supplier therefore knows that the digital content will contain bugs and flaws, but does not know which bugs and flaws there will be. One could add that in the case of digital content, an objective standard often does not (yet) exist because of the often still relatively innovative character of digital content and the rapid succession of new versions and applications, or such standard is largely restricted to matters such as security or the primary functions of the digital content.[143] These objections can, however, also be accommodated by applying the objective test of Article 6(2) Digital Content Directive, according to which there is only then a lack of conformity if the digital content does not meet with what the consumer was *entitled* to expect under the agreement. Where the supplier has sufficiently clearly indicated which restrictions were imposed on him by the copyright holder and which he has to pass on, and what it means that the consumer will obtain a beta version of the digital content, this will have lowered the legitimate expectations accordingly. Moreover, the primacy of subjective over objective criteria can lead to problems: the supplier can in fact escape from the minimum requirements set by the Digital Content Directive by mentioning only very limited usage possibilities, potentially hiding that information within standard contract terms or among an abundance of other information provided to the consumer. By mentioning these limited usage

140 See also Beale 2016, p. 22, who remarks that whereas service contracts usually are characterised by obligations of means (*obligations de moyen*), the Digital Content Directive contains obligations of result (*obligations de résultat*).

141 *Cf.* Art. 6(4) Digital Content Directive.

142 For details on the conference in Brussels on 18 February 2016, see n. * above.

143 *Cf.* Mak 2016b, p. 15.

possibilities the supplier would then no longer have to vouch for the possibility to use the digital content for other, possibly more common, purposes. Moreover, in such a case the supplier would also not be bound by public statements of the producer of the digital content, unless she has repeated these statements herself, even if these statements have clearly shaped the consumer's expectations of the digital content: the compliance with such statements is part of the objective test under Article 6(2) Digital Content Directive, which does not apply if the supplier has indicated for which purposes the digital content is fit herself. It seems that on this point the Digital Content Directive has to be amended.[144]

An amendment is also needed with regard to the provision in Article 8(1) Digital Content Directive on the rights of third parties: that provision now provides that the supplier should ensure that the digital content is 'free from any right of a third party, including based on intellectual property, so that the digital content can be used in accordance with the contract'.[145] However, as far as the digital content is copyright protected, there are rights that the producer of the digital content cannot transfer to the supplier, and in turn this means that the supplier by definition cannot meet the requirements of Article 8(1). These rights pertain to personality rights (moral rights), including the inalienable right of the author of a copyright-protected work to oppose mutilations and deformities of the work.[146] The supply of copyright-protected digital content therefore by definition would lead to a lack of conformity, and would entitle the consumer to a remedy, even in those cases where the digital content could be used in accordance with the nature of the intellectual property right and therefore would not lead to mutilation or deformation of the copyright-protected work. This problem can easily be remedied by way of a textual amendment of the Article.[147]

Digital content must often be installed in order for it to function properly. Article 7 Digital Content Directive in this respect provides that the supplier is also liable for a lack of conformity resulting from the incorrect *integration* of the digital content into the digital environment of the consumer if the digital content is integrated by or under the responsibility of the supplier or if it is integrated by the consumer and the defective integration is the result of defects in the integration instructions or the absence thereof if the provision of such

---

144 In this sense also Beale 2016, pp. 20–21; Mak 2016b, p. 15; Mańko 2016, pp. 22–23. Amendments 56–60, 541, 561–563, 568–571 Draft Report IMCO on the Digital Content Directive all (in different wording) propose the recommended changes.

145 Amendments 615–618 and 620–622 Draft Report IMCO on the Digital Content Directive all aim at remedying this problem. A similar problem exists with regard to the corresponding provision of Article 7(1) Online Sales and Distance Sales Directive, but is of lesser relevance there. The most important examples for that Directive pertain to the sale of art artefacts and the sale of books.

146 *Cf.* Art. 6*bis* of the Berne Convention for the Protection of Literary and Artistic Works of 9 September 1886, as subsequently amended.

147 See also Mańko 2016, p. 5.

instructions was agreed upon between the parties. This provision is clearly based on the corresponding provisions in Article 2(5) Consumer Sales Directive and Article 6 Online Sales and Distance Sales Directive, which provisions speak of 'installation'. The term 'integration' appears to have been chosen to make clear that the provision aims at the proper functioning of the digital content in connection with the digital environment of consumers, which consists of other digital content (such as the operating system, e.g. Windows or iOS, and programs like Word), the hardware (the computer, tablet, laptop or smartphone, but also the printer), and the network connection of the consumer.[148] The definition of the notion of 'digital environment', however, does not clarify whether, for example, cloud services and other facilities operated by third parties are part of the consumer's digital environment. Yet, the fact that Article 5 Digital Content Directive explicitly acknowledges that the consumer may require the supplier to supply the digital content to such a third party suggests that this is indeed the case. In my view, this should specifically be addressed, at least in the recitals of the preamble to the Directive, since third-party services increasingly operate as an integrated part of the digital environment of the consumer. For instance, operating systems such as Windows, iOS and Android, and programs such as Word are supplied with frequent updates, and the digital content supplied by a professional supplier of digital content must also be integrated with these updates.

This points to another matter. According to Article 10(b) and (c) Digital Content Directive, the supplier is liable to the consumer for any lack of conformity which exists at the time the digital content is supplied; where the contract provides that the digital content shall be supplied over a period of time, the supplier is liable for any lack of conformity which occurs during that period. This implies that unless the parties have agreed that the supplier would provide updates, the supplier is not liable if after some time the digital content *no longer* is compatible with the consumer's digital environment.

In the case of long-term contracts, such updates by definition are part of the contract, as the digital content must remain in conformity with the contract throughout the period for which the contract is concluded.[149] For other contracts, the parties may have made explicit arrangements as to updates of the digital content.[150] Where no such agreements have been made explicitly, in my view, the consumer may nevertheless expect the supplier to ensure that she can make use of the digital content for a reasonable period of time, which period is to be determined on the basis of the circumstances of the case. The supplier's obligation, then, includes an obligation to update the digital content, free of

---

148 *Cf.* Art. 2(2) and (8) Digital Content Directive. In my view the term 'installation' could also have been used without any problems resulting from the chosen wording.

149 See Arts. 6(3) and 10(c) Digital Content Directive.

150 See Art. 6(1)(d) Digital Content Directive.

charge, in so far as this is necessary for the proper use of the digital content: if such an obligation were not imposed on the supplier, then this would imply that digital content frequently will become unusable soon after delivery.[151] This is particularly true for updates that remedy later discovered defects in the digital content, since under Article 12(1) Digital Content Directive the consumer in many cases is entitled to the supply of such updates as a remedy for the lack of conformity of the digital content.

Moreover, as a professional party of digital content, the supplier knows or ought to know that the digital environment of the consumer is subject to change. For instance, an app developer of smartphone apps knows that the operating system of a smartphone is regularly updated or upgraded. In my view, the consumer may expect to be able to update the app free of charge if soon after the supply of the digital content the operating system is updated or upgraded and as a result the app no longer properly functions. Where the supplier fails to provide such an update of the app, I believe there would be a lack of conformity, even though the defect did not yet exist at the time the digital content was supplied, since in such a case the consumer is entitled to expect an update on the basis of a (tacit) agreement in the contract.

The supplier will not have ensured that the digital content remains compatible with technical developments and with updates and upgrades of existing hardware and software that go beyond 'ordinary' updates and upgrades aimed at keeping that hardware and software fit for their ordinary purpose. Obviously, the consumer may not expect to obtain newer functionalities for the digital content that did not exist when the digital content was sold to the consumer. This means that the digital content over time will become obsolete. In such cases, the consumer will often replace the digital content with new digital content purchased from the same or another supplier and whether or not for a price in money. For these reasons, a limitation of liability for the supplier to two years after the original supply of digital content seems to be more appropriate here than is the case for the delivery of goods under the Online Sales and Distance Sales Directive.

Article 9 Digital Content Directive provides that in the case of a lack of conformity the burden of proof that the defect did not exist at the moment of delivery is on the supplier. This shift of the burden of proof is not restricted to six months (Consumer Sales Directive) or two years (Online Sales and Distance Sales Directive), but applies permanently. However, the supplier does not bear the burden of proof if she proves that the digital environment of the consumer is not compatible with the interoperability requirements and other technical requirements of the digital content and the supplier had informed the consumer before the conclusion of the contract of these requirements.

---

151 *Cf.* Beale 2016, p. 27.

This exception implies that the supplier of the digital content has an interest in obtaining information from the consumer before the conclusion of the contract regarding the consumer's digital environment, in particular in those cases where the digital content must be installed on the consumer's device (e.g. a computer or a smartphone), as the supplier is liable for defects caused by problems in the integration of the digital content in the consumer's digital environment. If the consumer has failed to provide the requested information, the reversal of the burden of proof does not apply. The consumer's duty to co-operate is restricted to providing the information that is necessary to determine the consumer's digital environment by the least intrusive technical means for the consumer. However, in my view, the supplier should only be allowed to invoke this exception if she has made it clear to the consumer why she is in need of the information, and if the consumer is not asked to provide more information than is necessary with a view to the proper performance of the contract. This approach implies, in my view, that if the supplier asks for an excessive amount of information and the consumer (possibly in reaction thereto) does not provide any information, this does not constitute a breach by the consumer of her duty to co-operate, but rather an infringement by the supplier of the consumer's privacy which the consumer may ignore. If this were be different, it would constitute an incentive for the supplier to collect in this manner information to which she is not entitled, and which the consumer in practice is forced to provide in order to conclude a contract in the first place.

A permanent reversal of the burden of proof seems to be a very heavy load for the supplier. The Explanatory Memorandum to the Directive argues that this reversal is nevertheless justified because digital content is not subject to tear and wear.[152] This is correct with regard to digital content that is not provided on a durable medium, but this is not the case for digital content supplied on a DVD or a CD. For digital content supplied in such manner it seems more fair to adopt the corresponding provision of the Consumer Sales Directive or the Online Sales and Distance Sales Directive, in which case the shift of the burden of proof would be restricted to six months or two years, respectively.[153] For other digital content contracts, the European Commission's argument appears to be convincing in so far as the supplier would only be liable if the digital content were not in conformity with the digital environment of the consumer which existed at the time of delivery, as follows from Article 10 Digital Content Directive. However, it is argued above that in many cases the consumer may in fact expect that the supplier of the digital content offers free updates to remedy a lack of conformity which occurs after the supply of the digital content as a result

152 See the Explanatory Memorandum to the Digital Content Directive, p. 12.

153 *Cf.* Art. 5(3) Consumer Sales Directive and Art. 8(3) Online Sales and Distance Sales Directive.

of updates or upgrades of other parts of the consumer's digital environment. The logical consequence of this would be that the unlimited shift of the burden of proof is restricted here to two years, as is accepted under the Online Sales and Distance Sales Directive. This has as an advantage that unnecessary differences between the two Directives are prevented. This may prevent litigation as to whether the non-conforming digital content is subordinate to the goods on which it is installed (in which case the digital content is embedded and would be classified as a sales contract) or whether the digital content has an independent economic significance (in which case the contract is a mixed contract to which also the Digital Content Directive applies).[154]

5.4. REMEDIES FOR NON-CONFORMITY OF DIGITAL CONTENT

With regard to remedies, the Digital Content Directive introduces the same hierarchy as is the case with the delivery of goods under the Consumer Sales Directive and the Online Sales and Distance Sales Directive: the consumer is first entitled to have the digital content brought into conformity with the contract; termination and – if the contract was concluded in exchange for a price in money – price reduction are available only as subsidiary remedies.[155] Similarly to the Online Sales and Distance Sales Directive, the consumer is not under a duty to notify a lack of conformity.[156]

Where the consumer invokes her right to have the digital content brought into conformity, it is for the supplier to choose the method through which she wishes to comply with the consumer's demand.[157] The supplier may, for example, provide an update or a patch or require the consumer to download a new copy of the digital content from the supplier's server or to sign up on the supplier's website for online access to the new digital content.[158] The remedy must be performed free of charge, within a reasonable period and without causing significant inconvenience to the consumer.[159] The consumer does not, however, have a right to have the digital content brought into conformity if this would be impossible, disproportionate or unlawful.[160] Since the consumer does not have the choice between repair or replacement – which in most cases would amount to the same anyway – the test to determine whether the remedy of having the

154 See above, Section 6.
155 See Art. 12(3) Digital Content Directive; see critical Mak 2016b, p. 24.
156 *Cf.* recital 9 of the preamble to the Digital Content Directive.
157 This is different from the situation under the Online Sales and Distance Sales Directive, where it is the consumer who may choose, see Art. 11 Online Sales and Distance Sales Directive.
158 See recital 36 of the preamble to the Digital Content Directive.
159 Art. 12(1) and (2) Digital Content Directive.
160 Art. 12(1) Digital Content Directive.

digital content brought into conformity would be disproportionate is amended as well: instead of comparing the costs for repair to the costs for replacement, the possible disproportionality is assessed objectively by taking into account the value that the digital content would have had if it were in conformity with the digital content, and the significance of the lack of conformity for attaining the purpose for which consumers would normally use digital content of the same description.[161] It should be noted that this reference to 'the normal purpose' of the digital content seems difficult to reconcile with the subjective conformity standard which is accepted under Article 6 Digital Content Directive. The combination of these provisions could lead to the odd result that a supplier who expressly undertakes to supply digital content enabling the consumer to use the digital content in one particular way cannot be forced to supply digital content with that functionality if the functionality would not be of interest for the normal use of the digital content, whereas on the other hand that same contractual arrangement would prevent the consumer from claiming that the digital content should be fit for normal use.

In four situations the consumer has the right to claim termination of the contract or, if the digital content was provided in exchange for a price in money, price reduction:[162]

(a) when performance is impossible, disproportionate or contrary to the law;
(b) if the supplier has failed to bring the content into conformity within a reasonable time;
(c) when performance would cause significant inconvenience for the consumer (for example, because consumers need to purchase digital content temporarily elsewhere); or
(d) when the supplier has stated that she will not bring the content into conformity, or, given the circumstances of the case, it is clear that the supplier is not willing to do so.

Termination is only allowed if the non-conformity impairs the functionality, interoperability or other core features of digital content, such as the accessibility, continuity and security of the digital content. Where the supplier claims that the lack of conformity is not serious enough to justify termination, she bears the burden of proof thereof.[163] However, if the supplier is able to prove the minor nature of the lack of conformity but simply refuses to bring the digital content into conformity even though the consumer is legally entitled to this remedy, in my view the consumer should be able to terminate the contract even

161 Art. 12(1)(a) and (b) Digital Content Directive.
162 Art. 12(3) Digital Content Directive.
163 *Cf.* Art. 12(5) Digital Content Directive.

for such minor lack of conformity.[164] If this is not the case, then in the case of non-conforming digital content that is provided in exchange for the consumer's (active) provision of data by the consumer, both the remedy of price reduction and the remedy of termination are excluded. If the supplier then refuses to cure the defect, the consumer can only claim damages, provided that she is able to prove the damage. This would in fact mean that the consumer is left without an effective remedy. If the Directive is not amended on this point, the remedies for the supply of digital content in exchange for the provision of personal information may turn out to be 'all bark and no bite'.

After termination, the supplier must return any price in money paid by the consumer within 14 days.[165] Moreover, according to Article 13(4) Digital Content Directive, the consumer is not required to compensate the supplier for any use of the digital content that had been supplied prior to termination. However, in so far as the digital content was supplied on the basis of a long-term contract, termination is possible only from the time the digital content was not (any longer) in conformity with the contract.[166] The provision of Article 13(4) implies that the consumer need not compensate the supplier for any use of the digital content supplied that originally functioned properly and only later on was found out to be defective. That, I believe, goes too far, in particular since – in contrast to the Online Sales and Distance Sales Directive – the conformity rule is limited in time only on the basis of national rules of prescription, so that the supplier could potentially be faced years later with the termination of the agreement for a lack of conformity which manifests itself only at that time.

In so far as the consumer has paid for the digital content with her data (whether or not in addition to payment of a price in money) or such data have been collected by the supplier in the course of the duration of the contract, the supplier must take all reasonable steps to prevent the further use of such data. This implies that the supplier must either delete the consumer's personal data or render it anonymous in such a way that the consumer cannot be identified by any means that is reasonably likely to be used either by the supplier or by any other person. The obligation does not go so far as to require the supplier to prevent further use by a third party of any personal data gathered and sold to third parties in accordance with data protection legislation during the duration of the digital content contract.[167]

The obligation to take reasonable steps to prevent the further use of the consumer's data applies also to any digital content provided by the *consumer*.[168]

---

164 In this sense see also Fauvarque-Cosson 2016, p. 9; Mak 2016b, p. 15.

165 Art. 13(2)(a) Digital Content Directive.

166 See Art. 13(5) Digital Content Directive.

167 *Cf.* recital 37 of the preamble to the Digital Content Directive. This implies that Art. 13(2)(b) Digital Content Directive does not stand in the way of the collection and use of personal data in the form of Big Data.

168 *Cf.* Art. 13(2)(b) Digital Content Directive.

The supplier is not required to delete the digital content that has been jointly produced by the consumer and others who continue to make use of the platform, as for instance may be the case for open-source software produced or amended by the consumer and by other users.[169] This implies, for instance, that if a consumer has put a photograph on Snapshot or on Instagram, the supplier is required to remove the photograph from her servers and to make sure that the photograph can no longer be accessed through her platform. It is, however, unclear how far the supplier's obligation goes. It seems unlikely that Snapshot or Instagram would be required to ensure that other users of the platform delete the photograph from their devices as well. But it may be that, for instance, Facebook is required to remove the photograph not only from her own servers, but also to remove the copies of the photograph on other consumers' Facebook pages. Moreover, it is uncertain whether a company such as Facebook could argue that it cannot be required to remove the digital content unless the consumer proves that *she* has originally provided the original photograph (and not obtained the photograph herself from another supplier)? Similarly, it is unclear how the supplier of a platform should deal with a post in a discussion to which other users have reacted. If the obligation to prevent the further use of the data is excluded also in these cases, then there is not much left of that obligation.

The supplier is furthermore required to offer the consumer the possibility to retrieve, free of charge, within a reasonable period and in a commonly used format, the digital content provided by the consumer (such as digital content stored in the supplier's cloud) and any data that was produced or generated by the consumer and which has been retained by the supplier.[170] This implies that the consumer should be provided with the technical means to store and use the data on her own computer or in the cloud of another provider of storage facilities. An exception applies again to digital content generated together with other users, in so far as the other users want to continue the use of the digital content.

In turn, after termination the consumer is no longer allowed to continue to use the digital content.[171] Where the digital content was not supplied on a durable medium, the consumer may comply with this requirement by deleting the copy or copies of the digital content or by rendering the copy or copies unintelligible.[172] If the digital content was supplied on a durable medium, such as a DVD or a CD, the supplier may request the consumer to return that durable medium at the supplier's expense. The consumer is required to comply with such request within 14 days from the receipt of the supplier's request.[173] The Directive

169 Examples are the CAD files discussed above, on which see Twigg-Flesner 2016, p. 36.
170 Art. 13(2)(c) Digital Content Directive.
171 *Cf.* Art. 13(2)(d) and (e)(ii) Digital Content Directive.
172 *Cf.* Art. 13(2)(d) Digital Content Directive.
173 *Cf.* Art. 13(2)(e)(i) Digital Content Directive.

does not, however, provide for a specific remedy if the consumer does not comply with his obligation to return the durable medium and not to make further use of the digital content, which implies that this is left to national general contract law.[174] It should be noted that unless the consumer is required to return the durable medium upon the supplier's request – the supplier in many cases will have no opportunity to verify whether the consumer refrains from using the digital content.[175] In this respect the additional right for the supplier to prevent the further use of the digital content herself[176] may be more useful, in particular in cases where the consumer must make use of a user account provided by the supplier.

From what is stated above it becomes clear that the obligation of the supplier to return the price becomes due before the consumer's obligation to return the durable medium, e.g. a DVD, as the latter obligation only arises if the supplier, after having been informed of the termination, requests the consumer to return the DVD, and both parties have 14 days to perform their respective obligations. The Directive does not make clear whether the consumer is entitled to withhold performance of her obligation in case the supplier has not performed her obligation on time. On the one hand, it could be argued that such a right may exist in accordance with national general contract law.[177] On the other hand, it could be argued that all rights that the consumer may have in the case of non-conformity are regulated exhaustively in Articles 10–14 Digital Content Directive and that only the consequences of the termination of the contract and the conditions governing the exercise of the right to damages are left to the Member States. In my view this should be addressed, at least in the recitals of the preamble to the Directive. The same is true with regard to the question whether the consumer is entitled to interest on the price she has paid for the digital content pending reimbursement, and more specifically whether interest becomes due as of the moment when the lack of conformity manifests, when the supplier is notified thereof, when the consumer has terminated the contract, or when the 14-day period for the repayment of the price has expired. Given the fact that the right to reimbursement arises when the contract is terminated, in my opinion the most logical moment would be the moment of termination.[178]

Unlike the Online Sales and Distance Sales Directive, the Digital Content Directive does contain a provision on damages: Article 14(1) of the Directive provides that the supplier is liable for economic damage to the digital environment of consumers caused by non-conforming digital content or

---

174 See Art. 3(9) Digital Content Directive.

175 In this sense also Mak 2016b, pp. 25–26.

176 Art. 13(3) Digital Content Directive.

177 See Art. 3(9) Digital Content Directive.

178 Fauvarque-Cosson 2016, p. 14, seems to suggest that the end of the 14-day period should be the moment when interest starts to accrue.

by a failure to supply the digital content. The provision further adds that the compensation is to bring the consumer as much as possible into the position in which she would have been if the digital content had been in conformity with the contract. National law further stipulates the conditions under which the right to damages may be exercised, paragraph (2) adds. Since the Directive is based on full harmonisation, the explicit recognition of a right to claim compensation for economic damage to the legal environment seems to imply that other grounds for damages are excluded. That indeed seems to have been the intention of the European Commission.[179] That would mean that the supplier is not liable to compensate the consumer for other forms of damage. It is, however, easy to come up with other types of damage that could justify a claim for damages. First, it would stand to reason that the consumer would have a claim for damages for the costs that she has to incur to have the digital content (temporarily) replaced or to have it repaired.[180] Secondly, non-pecuniary loss is foreseeable if, for example, digital photos or other, for the consumer valuable, memories are lost – that such loss is possible is even explicitly recognised in recital 4 of the preamble to the Directive. Nevertheless, apparently such loss need not be compensated for. Thirdly, a security bug in the digital content may cause third parties to obtain the consumer's personal data and subsequently enable them to steal money from the consumer's bank account of the consumer.[181] Although this is economic damage, it is not damage caused to the consumer's digital environment, and therefore would not have to be compensated by the supplier either – not even in the situation where the supplier *knew* of the bug and decided not to care. Finally, a lack of conformity of the digital content may even lead to personal injury. A first example is the case where the digital content is integrated into movable property and causes the movable property to malfunction and to cause personal injury. In so far as the digital content may be seen as *embedded software*, such as digital content in a car or a refrigerator, it is not the Digital Content Directive, but the Consumer Sales Directive and the Online Sales and Distance Sales Directive that apply, since ultimately the non-conformity of the movable property is at stake here[182] – and for the latter Directive it is uncertain whether a claim for damages is allowed at all.[183] It is, however, also possible that the defective digital content causes damage to the digital environment of consumers, e.g. the consumer's hardware is caused to

179 See the Explanatory Memorandum, p. 13; see also critically Beale 2016, pp. 23–24; Notaries of Europe 2016, p. 2. Instead, Mańko 2016, p. 27, argues that other losses are not covered by the Directive and therefore national law may provide compensation for such losses.

180 In this sense also Mak 2016b, p. 27.

181 See also Mak 2016b, p. 27.

182 See recital 12 of the preamble to the Digital Content Directive.

183 See above, Section 4.3.

overload. It is conceivable that in such a case the hardware causes personal injury. To give two examples: the overload may cause the computer to explode or overheat; the defective digital content may lead a pair of virtual reality glasses to cause burns or eye problems. When the manufacturer of the hardware could have been aware of the potential hazard of the hardware she will be liable on the basis of product liability, and also the seller of the hardware could be liable on the basis of non-conformity of the hardware. These parties would then in turn be able to seek redress from the supplier of the digital content. When the producer and the seller of the hardware could successfully invoke *force majeure* because the problem was caused by the digital content, and they could not be seen as having breached a duty to prevent the damage, I see no reason why in such a case the consumer should not be entitled to claim damages from the supplier of the digital content, subject to the requirements for damages under the applicable national law. In my view, the Directive needs to be amended considerably on this point.[184] Fortunately, the European Parliament seems to share this view – although not all suggested amendments are equally helpful.[185]

5.5. LONG-TERM CONTRACTS FOR THE SUPPLY OF DIGITAL CONTENT

Article 15 Digital Content Directive entitles the supplier of the digital content to change the main performance features of the digital content in case the contract is a long-term contract. This is possible subject to four conditions:

(a) the supplier must have included a clause to change the main performance features in the contract;
(b) the consumer must be expressly informed of the change a reasonable time prior to the change of the digital content and on a durable medium;
(c) the consumer must be allowed a period of at least 30 days as of the receipt of the notice to terminate the contract free of charge; and
(d) the consumer must be provided with the technical means to retrieve the digital content and other data from the servers or the cloud of the supplier after termination has taken effect.

184 In this sense also Beale 2016, pp. 23–24; Notaries of Europe 2016, p. 2.
185 See Amendments 855–870 Draft Report IMCO on the Digital Content Directive. In some cases it is just suggested to delete Article 14 – which would lead to the question whether damages are available at all, similar to the matter discussed with regard to the Online Sales and Distance Sales Directive, see above, Section 4.1. Another Amendment proposes to hold the supplier liable only in case of fault – which will be impossible for the consumer to prove.

The first three conditions appear to be a codification of the case law of the Court of Justice with regard to the assessment of the possible unfairness of clauses allowing for a change of the price.[186] In an earlier publication Luzak and I have argued that the same criteria also should apply as to the change of other contract terms[187] and to changes of the product itself.[188] The Digital Content Directive seems to confirm this by setting these conditions also in the case of modification of the digital content. The last requirement set by the Court of Justice – that the supplier should also specify in the contract on what grounds the supplier may change the price – has, however, not been retained. In my view, the European Commission has rightly chosen not to apply that condition here as well: it is difficult to predict how the technical development of digital content will proceed and therefore when and why adaptation of the main performance features may be necessary, so it would be stretching the possibilities of suppliers of digital content too far to demand them to foresee this already in their standard terms or in the contract itself.[189]

The fourth condition set by the European Commission is in line with the consequences of termination of the contract for lack of conformity and refers to the corresponding provisions.[190]

When the consumer makes use of her power to terminate the contract in case of a change of the performance features of the digital content by the supplier, the supplier must refund the consumer the price (paid in money) as far as the price pertains to the period after the change of the digital content. In addition, the supplier must refrain from (further) use of the data that the consumer has provided in exchange for the digital content, and of other data the supplier has gathered, including digital content created by the consumer. Remarkably, the exception for digital content generated by the consumer and other consumers,

186 See in particular CJEU 21 March 2013, Case C-92/11, ECLI:EU:C:2013:180 (*RWE Vertrieb AG v Verbraucherzentrale Nordrhein-Westfalen eV*), paras. 50–54; CJEU 23 October 2014, Joined Cases C-359/11 and C-400/11, ECLI:EU:C:2014:2317 (*Schulz v Technische Werke Schussental GmbH und Co KG* and *Egbringhoff v Stadtwerke Ahaus GmbH*), paras. 46–49; CJEU 26 November 2015, Case C-326/14, ECLI:EU:C:2015:782 (*Verein fur Konsumenteninformation v A1 Telekom Austria AG*), paras. 24–25.

187 M.B.M. Loos, J.A. Luzak, 'Wanted: a bigger stick. On unfair terms in consumer contracts with online service providers', *Journal of Consumer Policy* 2016/1, pp. 67–72.

188 Loos/Luzak 2016, pp. 72–74.

189 Luzak and I have argued in the same vein as to the ability of online service providers to amend their services, see Loos/Luzak 2016, p. 73.

190 It would be seem to be more logical if reference were made to the corresponding provision on termination of long-term contracts in Article 16 Digital Content Directive, which will be discussed below. However, the reference to Article 13(2)(c) Digital Content Directive could in fact point to a difference as regards the possibility of retrieving the digital content and other data for free or against payment.

expressly regulated for termination in the case of non-conformity[191] is missing here.[192]

A similar exception is also missing in the subsequent Article, which is on the supplier's right to terminate a long-term contract and on the consequences of such termination. Article 16(1) Digital Content Directive provides, first of all, that long-term contracts may be terminated at any time by the consumer from the moment when 12 months have expired from the beginning of the contract (where relevant: as subsequently extended or renewed). A corresponding right for the supplier to terminate the contract is *not* regulated, not even for cases where the digital content has become outdated and largely obsolete. The mandatory nature of the Directive[193] seems to have as a result that the supplier cannot include a contract term allowing her to terminate in such cases. She would then have to make use of a contractually agreed right to change the contract in accordance with Article 15 Digital Content Directive in order to change, for instance, the price and make the price so unattractive that the *consumer* would make use of *her* right to terminate the contract. A more straightforward right for the supplier to terminate the contract under the same conditions as those allowing her to change the performance features of the digital content seems to be preferable.

When the consumer terminates the contract, she may give notice in any form, as is the case with termination of the contract for lack of conformity. The contract then ends 14 days after the receipt of the notice.[194] The consumer is required to pay for any contract period that has already elapsed.[195] Apart from the aforementioned missing exception for digital content generated in cooperation with other consumers, the termination has the same consequences as termination for non-conformity of the digital content. The supplier also in this case must enable the consumer to retrieve the digital content and other data, but the addition that this should be made possible free of charge is missing.[196] It is unclear whether this is intentional or a drafting error – it could be argued that where the termination is attributable to the consumer the possibility to retrieve the digital content or other data need not be provided free of charge, whereas this is different if the termination was precipitated by the supplier by either not providing the digital content, by providing defective digital content, or by proposing to change the performance features of the digital content.[197]

---

191 See Art. 13(2)(b) Digital Content Directive.

192 In this sense see also FAUVARQUE-COSSON 2016, p. 15.

193 See Art. 19 Digital Content Directive.

194 Art. 16(2) Digital Content Directive.

195 Art. 16(3) Digital Content Directive.

196 FAUVARQUE-COSSON 2016, p. 15.

197 An argument in this direction could be found in the reference in Article 15(1)(d) Digital Content Directive to Article 13(2)(c) Digital Content Directive instead of to Article 16(4)(a) Digital Content Directive.

6. UNRESOLVED MATTERS

In some cases digital content and the consumer's digital environment are interdependent – the one cannot function without the other. The question is whether this must have legal consequences for contracts which, at least formally, are not interconnected. A first example is offered by satellite navigation systems and updates for roadmaps. Imagine that a consumer purchases such a system from a seller, installs it in her car, and subsequently concludes a long-term contract for updates of the roadmaps from the producer of the system. Obviously, when the satellite navigation system no longer functions or is replaced for another reason, the consumer should be able to terminate the digital content contract. Article 16 Digital Content Directive indeed offers the consumer that possibility, but only after the first year of the contract is completed. In case of a lack of conformity, the seller may be liable to compensate the consumer for the payments that become due during the remaining contract periods under national contract law, but it is uncertain whether such a claim for damages is allowed under the Online Sales and Distance Sales Directive.[198]

A second question is what happens if the consumer has sold the car on which the satellite navigation system is installed. Is the contract with the supplier of the updates automatically transferred to the new owner of the car and the satellite navigation system? If not, then the consumer would be required to pay for the remaining contract periods until she may terminate under Article 16 Digital Content Directive. This connects to a more general matter. Currently, the question on the transferability of accessory rights,[199] such as the rights under a warranty, is not dealt with under any European legal instrument. With the development of a market for second-hand goods, which are sold through online platforms, this question has gained importance as the second owner no longer is a person within the sphere of the original buyer and it is therefore unlikely that the original buyer would be willing to invoke the remedies under the warranty on behalf of the second buyer if the second buyer cannot claim these remedies herself. Even if the European legislator would shy away from direct liability of the producer[200] it could be argued there is at least a good reason to finally deal with these accessory rights.[201] First steps had been taken in the form of

---

198 See above, Section 5.

199 The same would, of course, apply with regard to the consumer's corresponding obligations (if any), such as paying a subscription price.

200 I personally believe that the European legislator should deal with such liability; in any case the arguments *against* introducing direct producer's liability are weak, see already M.B.M. Loos, *Revision of the European Consumer Acquis*, Munich: Sellier, 2008, pp. 34, 80; Loos 2010, pp. 50–51.

201 Loos 2008, pp. 33–37; M. Loos, 'Consumer sales law in the proposal for a Consumer rights directive', *European Review of Private Law* 2010/1, pp. 15–55.

the support of consumer organisations and a large number of Member States, in their comments to the Green Paper *Review of the consumer acquis*, for an automatic transfer of such rights, possibly subject to contractual modification by the seller or producer.[202] The Draft Common Frame of Reference indeed includes such a provision,[203] and the original proposal for a Consumer Rights Directive grey-listed clauses that restrict the transferability of the commercial guarantee.[204] The proposal for a Common European Sales Law, however, did not contain any proposal to include a provision on this subject, and neither do the two Directives discussed here. In my view, it is high time for the next step to be taken.

Thirdly, what happens in the case where the digital content is needed for the proper use of the purchased goods (whether the digital content is provided separately or in the form of embedded digital content) and the digital content is no longer provided by the supplier, e.g. because the supplier considers the device on which the digital content is installed to be outdated? This is not a hypothetical situation, as the Dutch case of the Dutch consumer organisation *Consumentenbond v Samsung* shows.[205] In this case, Samsung was the producer of smartphones that were sold either by Samsung itself through its own webshop or by other sellers, as well as the supplier of updates of the Android operating system installed on the smartphones. The buyers of a Samsung smartphone thus obtain a licence from Samsung to use the Android operating system and the Samsung software shell. Google frequently provides upgrades and security updates of the Android operating system, but Samsung stops providing updates to consumers once a smartphone has been on the market for two years.[206] Since a smartphone (and any computer) is subject to viruses and other security problems, this means that it is no longer safe to use the smartphone as of the moment that the updates are no longer provided. In the case of Samsung, this implied that the smartphone did not conform to

202 See Loos 2008, p. 35; Loos 2010, p. 46.

203 See Art. IV.A.-6:102(2) DCFR.

204 See Loos 2010, pp. 47, 55.

205 District Court Amsterdam 8 March 2016 (summary proceedings), ECLI:NL:RBAMS:2016:1175 (*Consumentenbond v Samsung Electronics Benelux B.V. and Samsung Electronics Co. Ltd.*). The *Consumentenbond's* claim was dismissed on procedural grounds. The *Consumentenbond* recently started substantive proceedings against Samsung, see: https://www.consumentenbond.nl/nieuws/2016/bodemprocedure-tegen-samsung-van-start (last visited on 15 March 2017).

206 See for instance Samsung's statement of May 2014 on fansite Sammobile at: http://www.sammobile.com/2014/05/08/samsung-officially-confirms-no-kitkat-for-galaxy-s-iii-gt-i9300-and-galaxy-s-iii-mini (last visited on 15 March 2017), where Samsung announced it would not provide an update for the Galaxy S III and the Galaxy S III mini, which at that time had not even been on the market for two years. The official reason for refusing to provide the update was that the RAM of these smartphones was too small to cope with the newer version of Android. This was, however, disputed on an independent technological website such as Tweakers, see: https://tweakers.net/nieuws/95894/galaxy-s3-en-s3-mini-krijgen-geen-update-naar-android-44.html (last visited on 15 March 2017).

the contract anymore. The legally relevant question then was whether the seller could be held liable for damage caused by a virus using a bug in the operating system which was not remedied by an update, since the seller was liable only for defects that already existed at the moment of delivery.[207] This might not be the case if the seller at the time of the conclusion of the contract already had informed the consumer of the fact that Samsung would only update the digital content during the first two years after the product was first put on the market, as the statement would then influence the legitimate expectations the consumer may have of the goods. This would, however, effectively severely limit the consumer's rights under the Directive.

The interrelation between the smartphone and its operating system may cause more problems. Who is liable if, at the time of delivery, the operating system was not defective, but a later update by the supplier in fact *causes* a security problem in that operating system. Since at the time of delivery the defect did not exist, it could be argued that the seller should not be liable. Moreover, if that argument were accepted, the consumer would be required to show which bug actually caused the smartphone to malfunction – which is something the average consumer would not be able to do. In my view, the solution has to be that the seller is liable for any updates provided within (at least) the two-year period by the supplier of the digital content. In turn, the seller may seek redress against his seller and, ultimately, against the supplier that has caused the problem.

A related question pertains to devices that cannot function without the embedded digital content where the supplier of the digital content simply stops supporting the digital infrastructure needed by the consumer's device. For instance, Revolv offered a device capable of communicating with light switches, garage door openers, home alarms, air conditioners, etc. By using an app on a smartphone, the device could be used remotely. The device was sold with a one-year warranty. In October 2014, Revolv was bought by Nest (which in turn is owned by Alphabet, which is also the parent company of Google), and the device was no longer offered for sale. In February 2016, Revolv announced on its website that as of 15 May 2016, the service would no longer be available, the app would not open anymore and the device would not work anymore. Since all warranties had expired, consumers were left without any contractual remedy.[208] In cases such as this, the question arises whether the consumer would be entitled to a remedy under the two new Directives. If the digital content is to be considered as subordinate to the device produced by Revolv and therefore is classified as embedded software, as a starting point only the Online Sales and Distance Sales Directive applies. During the first two years after delivery, the seller is liable for the proper functioning of the device. Where the embedded digital content or the

207 See Art. 8(1) Online Sales and Distance Sales Directive.

208 On this, see: http://www.theverge.com/2016/4/4/11362928/google-nest-revolv-shutdown-smart-home-products (last visited on 15 March 2017).

service operated by Revolv no longer functions, the seller will be liable for lack of conformity of the device as the consumer could reasonably expect the digital content to be updated and the service to be operated. When two years have passed after the device was purchased by the consumer, all remedies towards the seller are, however, lost as Article 14 Online Sales and Distance Sales Directive provides that the seller is no longer liable.

Revolv – unless it was the seller itself – will only be liable if it has concluded a *separate* digital content contract with the consumer that falls within the scope of the Digital Content Directive. In the case of embedded digital content, such a digital content contract can only have come into existence if the consumer pays Revolv a price in money for the operation of the website or for the supply of updates, or where Revolv has required the consumer to actively share his personal data when the consumer (first or later) connected to Revolv's server requesting the service or updates. In that case, Revolv is bound by the digital content contract. However, the contract may have been concluded for a determined period only; if so, the contract is terminated automatically when the agreed period has elapsed. Similarly, the contract may have been concluded for an undetermined period of time but may include a termination clause. If that clause is not unfair and the conditions for termination set out in that clause have been met, Revolv may terminate the contract by notice. In both cases, after termination Revolv would no longer be liable for any negative effects the termination of the contract might result in for the consumer.

The example of Revolv's device shows that consumers can easily be deprived of the ability to use goods with embedded digital content which technically are capable of working properly, but are rendered useless by a decision from a party they may not even have had a contract with.

7. CONCLUDING REMARKS

The two proposals for Directives discussed here will remain at the centre of attention for European private law scholars and practitioners for the coming time. In this respect, the Digital Content Directive seems to be fairly uncontroversial – of course, amendments are necessary in some respects, but overall the industry, consumer organisations, scholars and Member States seem to have welcomed the proposal and to regard its provisions fairly favourably. This Directive also has the advantage that in most Member States there is no coherent regulation for digital content contracts, whereas there certainly is a need for regulation.[209] This Directive may therefore be adopted within a relatively short period.

---

[209] The primary exception is the United Kingdom, which recently introduced legislation, see Consumer Rights Act 2015, Part 1, Chapter 3 (sections 33–47), which is dedicated to the supply of digital content. In addition, in the Netherlands the supply of digital content is

This is very different with regard to the Online Sales and Distance Sales Directive. The scope of that Directive – as long as it has not been amended following the *fitness check* of the Consumer Sales Directive – guarantees continuous abstract discussions as to the desirability of different regimes for consumer sales contracts; and the use of full harmonisation as the type of harmonisation chosen by the European Commission will lead to extensive debates as to the level of consumer protection. However, it should be noted that the current proposal does appear significantly more balanced than the original proposal for the Consumer Rights Directive was, where the minimum level of the Consumer Sales Directive and the Unfair Contract Terms Directive simply was transposed as the maximum level of protection under that proposal. With regard to the Online Sales and Distance Sales Directive, steps back in the consumer protection in one country may be levelled out by a rise in consumer protection for that country on another point, and the level of consumer protection as a whole seems to have been raised to at least the level of protection awarded in the Member States. That ultimately renders the question whether the level of consumer protection is high *enough* a (legal-)political question. This contribution does not lend itself to giving a final answer to that question. It does, however, allow for a prediction: this proposal will be the subject of prolonged and critical discussions. Acceptance of this proposal for a directive may therefore not be expected in the short run or without extensive amendments.

treated as a consumer sales contract in case the digital content is either supplied on a durable medium or is individualised and subject to the consumer's physical control (*cf.* Art. 7:5(1) and (5) BW).

PART II

PROPOSALS FOR A DIRECTIVE ON ONLINE AND DISTANCE SALES OF TANGIBLE GOODS AND FOR A DIRECTIVE ON DIGITAL CONTENT

PROPOSAL FOR A DIRECTIVE ON CERTAIN ASPECTS CONCERNING CONTRACTS FOR THE ONLINE AND OTHER DISTANCE SALES OF GOODS

Scope of Application, Definitions and Conformity

Sanne JANSEN and Sophie STIJNS*

* This contribution is up to date as at May 2016.

1. INTRODUCTION

The proposed Directive of the European Parliament and of the Council on certain aspects concerning contracts for the online and other distance sales of goods (ODSD Proposal)[1] introduces rules about conformity of goods, remedies in case of non-conformity and the modalities to exercise these remedies. In this chapter, we will only address the newly introduced definitions and the aspects concerning conformity. The level of harmonisation will be dealt with by the chapter by Straetmans and Meys in this volume.

We shall point out the differences and the similarities in comparison with the Consumer Sales Directive 1999/44/EC (CSD)[2] and the (abandoned) Regulation on a Common European Sales Law.[3] We will also compare the ODSD Proposal with the Consumer Rights Directive 2011/83/EU (CRD)[4] and national common law of contract. It is important to note, from the start of this chapter, that recital 15 ODSD Proposal states that the rules of the proposal should be applied and interpreted in a manner consistent with the rules of the CSD and the CRD (as interpreted by the case law of the Court of Justice of the European Union), a rule that will provide for more legal certainty and consistency.

1 Proposal for a directive of the European Parliament and of the Council on certain aspects concerning contracts for the online and other distance sales of goods of 9 December 2015, COM(2015) 635 final, 2015/0288 (COD).

2 Directive 1999/44/EC of the European Parliament and of the Council of 25 May 1999 on certain aspects of the sale of consumer goods and associated guarantees, *OJ* L 171, 7 July 1999, pp. 12–16.

3 Proposal for a regulation of the European Parliament and the Council on a Common European Sales Law, COM(2011) 635 final, 2011/0284 (COD). Hereafter: 'proposed regulation on a CESL' or 'CESL proposal'; if referring merely to the annex, we will use the term 'CESL'.

4 Directive 2011/83/EU of the European Parliament and of the Council of 25 October 2011 on consumer rights, amending Council Directive 93/13/EEC and Directive 1999/44/EC of the European Parliament and of the Council and repealing Council Directive 85/577/EEC and Directive 97/7/EC of the European Parliament and of the Council, *OJ* L 304, 22 November 2011, pp. 64–88.

2. SCOPE OF APPLICATION AND DEFINITIONS

2.1. SCOPE OF APPLICATION

The scope of the ODSD Proposal is restricted to *distance sales contracts* of *goods* concluded between a *seller* and a *consumer* (Article 1(1) of the ODSD Proposal). All the terms ('distance sales contract', 'contract', 'goods', 'seller' and 'consumer') used in this description of the scope of application are defined in Article 2, providing a wide range of definitions (see below, Section 2.2).

In comparison, the abandoned proposed regulation on a CESL was not only applicable to distance sales contracts but also more broadly applicable to (all kinds of) sales contracts, contracts for the supply of digital content and related service contracts.[5] The CSD is also more broadly applicable to 'the sale of consumer goods' (Article 1(1) CSD). Of course, adoption and implementation of the ODSD Proposal would mean that the distance sales contract will be excluded from the scope of application of the CSD. This is explicitly mentioned in Article 19 of the ODSD Proposal.

The description of the scope of application in Article 1(1) of the ODSD Proposal makes very clear that it has abandoned the two-track approach of the CESL (proposal) by not regulating B2B sales contracts, but only B2C sales contracts. Also C2C sales contracts are excluded because the seller has to conclude the sale contract in the sphere of his commercial or professional activities (see also below, Section 2.2.2). With regard to this last aspect, the exclusion of B2B and C2C sales contracts, the ODSD Proposal reconnects again with the CSD.[6] The exclusion of sales contracts in which there is no professional seller is to be approved, because of the basic underlying assumption of 'inequality between the contractual parties' of the ODSD Proposal.[7]

The ODSD Proposal is not applicable to distance contracts providing *services*. Nevertheless, it is always possible that a sales contract is both providing for services and the sale of goods (Article 1(2)). In this case, the ODSD Proposal is only applicable to the part relating to the sale of goods. This is the application of the so-called 'distributive' or 'cumulative' method, applying several specific regulations for different contracts simultaneously to one contract.[8] The contract will be split up and the rules of the ODSD Proposal will only apply to the sales part.

---

5 Article 5 proposed regulation on a CESL.

6 See, about the CSD, L. Serrano, 'Article 1: Scope and Definitions' in M.C. Bianca and S. Grundmann (eds.), *EU Sales Directive, Commentary*, Antwerp, Intersentia, 2002, (91) para. 60.

7 See for the same reasoning (with regard to the CSD): S. Grundmann, F. Gomez, M.G. Bridge, *et al.*, 'Introduction' in M.C. Bianca and S. Grundmann (eds.), *EU Sales Directive, Commentary*, Antwerp, Intersentia, 2002, (13) para. 91.

8 P. Brulez, *Koopovereenkomsten versus dienstenovereenkomsten: (faux) amis?*, Antwerp, Intersentia, 2015, paras. 101 *et seq.*

Secondly, the ODSD Proposal will not be applicable to any 'durable medium' incorporating digital content, if the durable medium is *exclusively* used as a carrier for the supply of the digital content to the consumer (Article 1(3)). This is a complicated way to say that it is not applicable to goods such as DVDs, CDs, etc. that solely provide digital content.[9] Of course, this exclusion is explained by the separate proposal for a Directive on certain aspects concerning contracts for the supply of *digital content* (also 'DCD Proposal' or 'Digital Content Directive Proposal') (of which the scope of application will be dealt with in the chapter by Geiregat and Steennot in this volume).[10] Conversely, the ODSD Proposal *is* applicable to goods such as household appliances or toys incorporating digital content, if the function of their digital content is secondary to the main characteristics or functionalities of the goods and if it is fully integrated in the goods.[11]

It is surprising to note that the Council of Notariats of the EU suggests in its Position Paper to clarify that all (sales) contracts concluded before a civil law notary should be excluded from the Directive's scope of application.[12] It is possible that the Council of Notariats only want to make sure that no notarial sale will ever be subject to the ODSD Proposal. We must point to the fact that the scope of application of the ODSD Proposal is restricted in any event to tangible *moveable* goods (cf. below, Section 2.2.3), whilst notarial sales will often concern immoveable goods.

Article 1(4) makes clear that the ODSD Proposal will not affect national general contract law (e.g. the rules on the formation of the contract, the validity or the effects of contracts and the consequences of the termination of the contract). This seems to imply that one can also fall back on national general contract law in case of inconsistencies, lacunae, uncertainties, etc. Recital 14 of the ODSD Proposal explains that Member States are free to regulate in more detail the aspects that are not fully harmonised by the ODSD Proposal such as limitation periods for exercising the consumer's rights, commercial guarantees, and the right of redress of the seller.

---

9 Explanatory Memorandum of the Proposal for a directive of the European Parliament and of the Council on certain aspects concerning contracts for the online and other distance sales of goods of 9 December 2015, p. 14 (hereafter: 'Explanatory Memorandum'). See also recital no. 13 ODSD Proposal (hereafter we will refer to the recitals without repeating the term 'ODSD Proposal').

10 Proposal for a directive of the European Parliament and of the Council on certain aspects concerning contracts for the supply of digital content of 9 December 2015, COM(2015) 634 final, 2015/0287 (COD).

11 Explanatory Memorandum, p. 14.

12 Position Paper of the Notaries, pp. 2–3 (explaining this difference in treatment by the obligation of notaries to provide comprehensive impartial legal information) (http://www.notaries-of-europe.eu/files/position-papers/2016/Contract-Law-CNUE-Position-Paper-11-03-16-en.pdf).

Furthermore, Article 19 excludes any applicability of the rules of the CSD.[13] This means that one cannot fall back on those rules if the rules of the new ODSD Proposal are incomplete or raise questions.[14]

It is important to note that the Explanatory Memorandum and some recitals in the preamble refer to the CRD.[15] The Memorandum even makes clear that the ODSD proposal *supplements* the CRD. Indeed, this directive has already fully harmonised certain rules about online and distance sales of goods (pre-contractual information requirements, rights of withdrawal, transfer of risk, etc.).

2.2. DEFINITIONS

Article 2 of the ODSD Proposal prescribes a list of definitions, mainly inspired by the current acquis, from the CRD or from the proposal for a Regulation on a Common European Sales Law (CESL).[16] The Memorandum explains that if definitions refer to the same concepts, they should be explained in a manner consistent with the existing acquis.[17] Recital 15 of the ODSD Proposal makes clear that the existing acquis has to be understood as the rules of the CSD and the CRD, as interpreted by the case law of the Court of Justice of the EU. In what follows, a short overview is given of the main definitions. However, we will not go into the definitions of 'commercial guarantee' (a topic that will be tackled in the chapter by Terryn and Vandemaele in this volume), 'repair' and 'free of charge' (topics that will be tackled in the chapter by Claeys and Vancoillie about the remedies).

2.2.1. Sales Contract

Contrary to the CSD,[18] the ODSD Proposal defines the concept of 'a sales contract' in Article 2(a). A sales contract is defined as:

> any contract under which the seller transfers or undertakes to transfer the ownership of goods, including goods which are to be manufactured or produced, to the consumer and the consumer pays or undertakes to pay the price thereof.

---

13 See also EPRS (European Parliamentary Research Service) Briefing document of 2016 by Rafał Mańko, PE 577.962, p. 4 (https://www.eerstekamer.nl/eu/documenteu/_briefing_van_europees_parlment_2/f=/vk1tlgwapiq8.pdf, hereafter: 'Briefing document of 2016 by Rafał Mańko, PE 577.962').

14 See also Explanatory Memorandum, p. 23.

15 See e.g. recital nos. 12, 15, 24. Explanatory Memorandum, pp. 4, 7, 14–15.

16 Explanatory Memorandum, p. 14.

17 Explanatory Memorandum, p. 14.

18 See L. Serrano, 'Article 1: Scope and Definitions' in M.C. Bianca and S. Grundmann (eds.), *EU Sales Directive, Commentary*, Antwerp, Intersentia, 2002, (91) pp. 95–96 (however,

The two most important elements are a 'transfer of ownership' by one party and 'a corresponding price' that is paid by the other party.[19]

The Council of the Notariats of the EU defends in its Position Paper that the meaning of 'undertakes to transfer' should be clarified with respect to its (potential) application to e.g. leasing contracts.[20] Will a conditional obligation to transfer the property[21] or a unilateral purchase option be sufficient to induce the application of the newly proposed Directive?

Recital 16 stresses the element of the definition that refers to so-called 'future' goods (goods that are yet to be produced or manufactured, such as a tailor-made dress).[22] These goods are also included in the scope of application of the ODSD Proposal. The insertion of this element is not surprising, since the CSD already provides for this rule in Article 1(4): 'contracts for the supply of consumer goods *to be manufactured or produced* shall also be deemed contracts of sale for the purpose of this Directive' (emphasis added).[23]

The definition of 'sale contract' differs slightly from the one in Article 2(5) CRD. There is, for example, no explicit reference to the applicability to 'future goods' under the CRD. Furthermore, the CRD refers to a 'contract having as its object both goods and services', which is not the case for the ODSD Proposal. If we compare the ODSD Proposal definition with the one in Article 2(k) of

---

everyone understands the term 'sales contract' as a synallagmatic agreement implying an exchange of goods for a corresponding price).

19 See also with regard to Art. IV.A.-1:202 DCFR: M.B.M. Loos, 'Sales Law in the DCFR', *SSRN, Centre for the Study of European Contract Law Working Paper Series No. 2010/04*, 2010, (1) p. 2 (criticises the fact that the definition does not mention that the seller has the obligation to deliver the goods in conformity with the contract). See also with regard to the proposed regulation on a CESL: R. Feltkamp and F. Vanbossele, 'The Optional Common European Sales Law: Better Buyer's Remedies for Seller's Non-Performance in Sales of Goods?', *ERPL* 2011, (873) p. 879 (also criticise the fact that the definition does not mention that the seller has the obligation to deliver the goods in conformity with the contract).

20 See Position Paper of the Council of the Notariats of the EU of 11 March 2016, p. 3 (http://www.notaries-of-europe.eu/files/position-papers/2016/Contract-Law-CNUE-Position-Paper-11-03-16-en.pdf; hereafter: 'Position Paper of the Notaries'); see, about similar problems under the CSD: L. Serrano, 'Article 1: Scope and Definitions' in M.C. Bianca and S. Grundmann (eds.), *EU Sales Directive, Commentary*, Antwerp, Intersentia, 2002, (91) paras. 10–13.

21 According to the drafters of the Principles of European Law about Sales (also 'PEL (S)') the definition of sale of goods contained in Art. 1:101 referring to sales in which ownership is to be transferred at some future time, implies its applicability in the case of retention of title clauses: E. Hondius, V. Heutger, C. Jeloschek, *et al.*, *Principles of European Law. Study Group on a European Civil Code. Sales (PEL S)*, Munich, Sellier, 2008, p. 114.

22 The following authors call these kind of contracts 'mixed-purpose contracts': R. Feltkamp and F. Vanbossele, 'The Optional Common European Sales Law: Better Buyer's Remedies for Seller's Non-Performance in Sales of Goods?', *ERPL* 2011, (873) p. 880.

23 See, about this rule extensively: L. Serrano, 'Article 1: Scope and Definitions' in M.C. Bianca and S. Grundmann (eds.), *EU Sales Directive, Commentary*, Antwerp, Intersentia, 2002, (91) para. 16. See also: S. Grundmann, F. Gomez, M.G. Bridge, *et al.*, 'Introduction' in M.C. Bianca and S. Grundmann (eds.), *EU Sales Directive, Commentary*, Antwerp, Intersentia, 2002, (13) para. 95.

the proposed regulation on a CESL, both are very similar.[24] Nevertheless, the CESL definition adds that contracts for sale on execution or otherwise involving the exercise of public authority are excluded. The ODSD Proposal also excludes the latter kind of sale contracts when defining 'goods' (see Article 2(d) ODSD Proposal, and see also below, Section 2.2.3).

2.2.2. *Consumer and Seller*

The Memorandum explains that the definition of 'consumer' stems from the current acquis.[25] It is defined in Article 2(b) as: 'any natural person who, in contracts covered by this Directive, is acting for purposes which are outside his trade business, craft or profession'.[26] This definition coincides with the one in Article 2(f) of the proposed regulation on the CESL and Article 1(2)(1) CRD. The definition of 'consumer' under the CSD is also very similar.[27] It can be said that the 'consumer' concept consists of *two* important characteristics.[28] The first main characteristic is that a consumer has to be a *natural person*. This classical point of view has often been challenged in favour of extending it to some 'weaker' moral persons (such as small or medium-sized enterprises (SMEs)).[29] The second characteristic is that he has to conclude a contract while he is acting for purposes *outside his professional or commercial activities*. This reopens the old sore about the mixed contracts problem. What if a natural person concludes a sales contract with a very small connection to his commercial or professional activities? For a very long time the leading *Gruber* case[30] – allowing a very slight connection to a professional activity (it had to be negligible) – led to debate.[31] Finally, the

---

24 Compare also with Article 1:101 PEL S (E. Hondius, V. Heutger, C. Jeloschek, *et al.*, *Principles of European Law. Study Group on a European Civil Code. Sales (PEL S)*, Munich, Sellier, 2008, pp. 113–20).

25 Explanatory Memorandum, p. 14.

26 See for the same definition Art. 2(4) DCD Proposal.

27 Replacing the word 'outside' with 'not related to'.

28 See also M. Kingisepp and A. Värv, 'The Notion of Consumer in EU Consumer Acquis and the Consumer Rights Directive – a Significant Change of Paradigm?', *Juridica international* 2011, (44) p. 44.

29 E. Hondius, 'The Notion of Consumer: European Union versus Member States', *Sydney Law Review* 2006, (89) pp. 94–95 and 98. See also J. Vannerom, 'Comments on Consumer Notion: Natural or Legal Persons and Mixed Contracts' in E. Terryn, G. Straetmans and V. Colaert (eds.), *Landmark Cases of EU Consumer Law*, Antwerp, Intersentia, 2013, (57) paras. 4–8 and 12. However, seem to understand the reasons for exclusion of legal persons with regard to the CSD: S. Grundmann, F. Gomez, M.G. Bridge, *et al.*, 'Introduction' in M.C. Bianca and S. Grundmann (eds.), *EU Sales Directive, Commentary*, Antwerp, Intersentia, 2002, (13) para. 92.

30 Case C-464/01, *Gruber v Bay Wa AG* [2001] ECR I-9049.

31 Mainly with regard to its scope of application because it dealt with procedural law: J. Vannerom, 'Comments on Consumer Notion: Natural or Legal Persons and Mixed Contracts' in E. Terryn, G. Straetmans and V. Colaert (eds.), *Landmark Cases of EU Consumer Law*, Antwerp, Intersentia, 2013, (57) para. 9.

introduction of the CRD seemed to put an end to this discussion. Although its 'consumers' definition is very brief and does not mention the issue of mixed contracts (it merely refers to contracts outside the professional or commercial activities of the natural person), recital 17 of the CRD expressly mentions the issue. If a contract is concluded partly within and partly outside one's trade and if the trade purpose is limited so as 'not to be predominant in the overall context of the contract', this person should be considered as a consumer.[32, 33] This approach implies that in the case of a mixed contract, a party will be more easily considered a consumer. However, the question remains why the drafters of the CRD have only mentioned this in the recital and not in the text of the definition. The ODSD Proposal does not reiterate this recital. It merely states in its Memorandum that the definition of 'consumer' stems from the current acquis, which might mean that it refers implicitly to recital 17 of the CRD. Consequently, we are convinced that the predominant test in recital 17 is also applicable to the ODSD Proposal.[34] It would, of course, enhance legal certainty if the drafters would expressly cross-refer to or repeat recital 17 of the CRD.

Union law does not use always the same term for the other party to a consumer contract.[35] The ODSD Proposal uses the term 'seller'. The concept of seller is extensively defined in Article 2(c) as:

> any natural person or any legal person, irrespective of whether privately or publicly owned, who is acting, including through any other person acting in his name or on his behalf, for purposes relating to his trade, business, craft or profession in relation to contracts covered by this Directive.

The two most important elements are that (1) a seller can be a physical or legal person who concludes a sales contract (2) within the sphere of his commercial or professional activities. When we compare this definition with the definitions in the CRD, we notice that the notion of 'trader' is defined in exactly the same

---

32 See about this recital: M. Kingisepp and A. Värv, 'The Notion of Consumer in EU Consumer Acquis and the Consumer Rights Directive – a Significant Change of Paradigm?', *Juridica international* 2011, (44) p. 51; J. Vannerom, 'Comments on Consumer Notion: Natural or Legal Persons and Mixed Contracts' in E. Terryn, G. Straetmans and V. Colaert (eds.), *Landmark Cases of EU Consumer Law*, Antwerp, Intersentia, 2013, (57) para. 10.

33 See also Art. I.-1:105, para 1 DCFR ('A "consumer" means any natural person who is acting primarily for purposes which are not related to his or her trade, business or profession') and M.B.M. Loos, 'Sales Law in the DCFR', *SSRN, Centre for the Study of European Contract Law Working Paper Series No. 2010/04*, 2010, (1) pp. 6–7.

34 See for similar reasoning with regard to dual-use under the proposed regulation on a CESL: C. Wendehorst, 'Art. 2 Regulation' in R. Schulze (ed.), *Common European Sales Law (CESL)*, Munich, Beck, 2012, (13) p. 20.

35 M. Ebers, 'B. The notion of "business"' in M. Ebers, H. Schulte-Nölke and C. Twigg-Flesner (eds.), *EC consumer law compendium*, Munich, Sellier, 2008, para. 1 (Common Features).

way.[36] A shorter definition of 'trader' was inserted in the proposed regulation on a CESL.[37] A similar short definition of a 'seller' was included in the CSD.[38]

2.2.3. Goods

The Explanatory Memorandum explains that the definition of 'goods' also stems from the current acquis.[39] The most important elements are that the goods must be 'tangible' and 'moveable'.[40] Indeed, Article 2(d) of the ODSD Proposal defines goods as

> any tangible movable items with the exception of
> (a) items sold by way of execution or otherwise by authority of law;[41]
> (b) water, gas, electricity, unless they are put up for sale in a limited volume or a set quantity.

This means that it can be used goods or new goods, unique (*species*) goods or serial (generic) goods, consumable or non-consumable goods, and it can also concern animals, etc. This definition implies that immovable property and intangible rights[42] are excluded from the scope of application of the ODSD Proposal.[43] The discussion that occurred about the applicability of the CSD[44]

---

36 Art. 2(2) CRD '"trader" means any natural person or any legal person, irrespective of whether privately or publicly owned, who is acting, including through any other person acting in his name or on his behalf, for purposes relating to his trade, business, craft or profession in relation to contracts covered by this Directive'.

37 Art. 2(e) proposed regulation on a CESL: '"trader" means any natural or legal person who is acting for purposes relating to that person's trade, business, craft, or profession'. See C. Wendehorst, 'Art. 2 Regulation' in R. Schulze (ed.), *Common European Sales Law (CESL)*, Munich, Beck, 2012, (13) 19 (this definition omits to explicitly include persons acting in the name or on behalf of a trader and to explicitly include legal persons owned by the public; however, there is no reason why there would be a difference in meaning).

38 Art. 1.2(c) CSD: '"seller": shall mean any natural or legal person who, under a contract, sells consumer goods in the course of his trade, business or profession'.

39 Explanatory Memorandum, p. 14.

40 For criticism (with regard to the proposed regulation on a CESL) that the term 'moveable corporeal good' is not further defined, see: R. Feltkamp and F. Vanbossele, 'The Optional Common European Sales Law: Better Buyer's Remedies for Seller's Non-Performance in Sales of Goods?', *ERPL* 2011, (873) p. 881.

41 See, for a restrictive interpretation of this exception under the CSD (which uses the same wording): L. Serrano, 'Article 1: Scope and Definitions' in M.C. Bianca and S. Grundmann (eds.), *EU Sales Directive, Commentary*, Antwerp, Intersentia, 2002, (91) paras. 37–38.

42 Such as intellectual property, personal rights (obligations) and other intangible rights.

43 See also for the same finding for the CSD: L. Serrano, 'Article 1: Scope and Definitions' in M.C. Bianca and S. Grundmann (eds.), *EU Sales Directive, Commentary*, Antwerp, Intersentia, 2002, (91) para. 30.

44 See, regarding this discussion, L. Serrano, 'Article 1: Scope and Definitions' in M.C. Bianca and S. Grundmann (eds.), *EU Sales Directive, Commentary*, Antwerp, Intersentia, 2002, (91) para. 33.

to *software* is easily solved in the ODSD Proposal. Indeed, digital content is excluded from the scope of application of the ODSD Proposal (and *is* dealt with by the DCD Proposal).[45]

The proposed definition almost coincides with the one used in the CRD.[46] It differs from the definition in the proposed regulation on a CESL with regard to the exceptions.[47] The CESL definition excludes *all* sales of electricity or *natural* gas; with regard to water and *other* types of gas they are only excluded if they are not put up for sale in a limited volume or a set quantity. The definition of consumer goods under the CSD is almost exactly the same as in the ODSD Proposal but does not offer the possibility for electricity to be recognised as goods if it is for sale in a limited volume or set quantity.[48] The CSD also provides for a possibility that the Member States may choose that the expression 'consumer goods' does not cover second-hand goods sold at public auctions where consumers have the opportunity of attending the sale in person. This exception has not been included in the ODSD Proposal, presumably because it deals only with online and other distance sales in the first place.[49]

2.2.4. Distance Sales Contract

The scope of application of the ODSD Proposal is restricted to online and other distance sales of goods. This implies that the concept of 'distance sales contracts' is a key notion which has to be defined. The term 'distance sales contract' is defined in Article 2(e) of the ODSD Proposal as

> any sales contract concluded under an organised distance scheme without the simultaneous physical presence of the seller and the consumer, with the exclusive use

---

45 Proposal for a directive of the European Parliament and of the Council on certain aspects concerning contracts for the supply of digital content of 9 December 2015, COM(2015) 634 final, 2015/0287 (COD).

46 Art. 2(3) CRD: '"goods" means any tangible movable item, with the exception of items sold by way of execution or otherwise by authority of law; water gas and electricity shall be considered as goods within the meaning of this Directive where they are put up for sale in a limited volume or a set quantity'.

47 Art. 2(h) proposed regulation on a CESL: '"goods" means any tangible movable items; it excludes: (i) electricity and natural gas; and (ii) water and other types of gas unless they are put up for sale in a limited volume or set quantity'. This definition does not mention the exclusion of 'contracts for sale on execution or otherwise involving the exercise of public authority'. But this exception is included in the definition of a 'sales contract', see above, Section 2.2.1.

48 Art. 1.2(b) CSD. Nevertheless, Serrano asserts that there is a different solution for objects that accumulate electricity (such as batteries): L. Serrano, 'Article 1: Scope and Definitions' in M.C. Bianca and S. Grundmann (eds.), *EU Sales Directive, Commentary*, Antwerp, Intersentia, 2002, (91) para. 36.

49 See about this exception under the CSD: L. Serrano, 'Article 1: Scope and Definitions' in M.C. Bianca and S. Grundmann (eds.), *EU Sales Directive, Commentary*, Antwerp, Intersentia, 2002, (91) paras. 39–40.

> of one or more means of distance communication, including via internet, up to and including the time at which the contract is concluded.

Similar definitions are used in the proposed regulation on a CESL and in the CRD.[50] The latter definitions, however, do not include an express reference to 'internet', unlike the definition under the ODSD Proposal.

2.2.5. Durable Medium

We have already indicated that the ODSD Proposal will not be applicable to any 'durable medium' incorporating digital content if the durable medium is *exclusively* used as a carrier for the supply of the digital content to the consumer (Article 1(3), see above, Section 2.1). Therefore, it is of course important to define the concept 'durable medium'. It means, according to Article 2(f) ODSD Proposal,

> any instrument which enables the consumer or the seller to store information addressed personally to him in a way accessible for future reference for a period of time adequate[51] for the purposes of the information and which allows the unchanged[52] reproduction of the information stored.[53]

We believe this definition can be understood in a quite broad way, including for example paper, CDs, DVDs, but also hard disks of laptops and computers, smartphones, USB devices, photo cameras, flashcards, etc.[54] This does not mean, in our opinion, that due to the restriction of the scope of application in Article 1(3) ODSD Proposal, all the aforementioned devices will be excluded from the scope of the Proposal if sold by way of a distance contract. Goods are

---

50 Art. 2(p) proposed regulation on a CESL (includes an additional statement that where the trader is a legal person, there must have been no simultaneous physical presence of the consumer and a natural person representing the trader: C. Wendehorst, 'Art. 2 Regulation' in R. Schulze (ed.), *Common European Sales Law (CESL)*, Munich, Beck, 2012, (13) pp. 22–23) and Art. 2(7) CRD.

51 Refers, with regard to the proposed regulation on a CESL, to a period of 10 years: C. Wendehorst, 'Art. 2 Regulation' in R. Schulze (ed.), *Common European Sales Law (CESL)*, Munich, Beck, 2012, (13) p. 28.

52 Clarifies with regard to the CESL proposal that the trader may not have any access or opportunity to change the data and that the medium must be within the sphere of the consumer: C. Wendehorst, 'Art. 2 Regulation' in R. Schulze (ed.), *Common European Sales Law (CESL)*, Munich, Beck, 2012, (13) p. 28.

53 See, for the same definition, Art. 2(11) DCD Proposal (the word 'seller' has been replaced by 'supplier'). The same definition can be found in Art. 2(t) of the proposed regulation on a CESL and in Art. 2(10) CRD.

54 See also C. Wendehorst, 'Art. 2 Regulation' in R. Schulze (ed.), *Common European Sales Law (CESL)*, Munich, Beck, 2012, (13) p. 28 (also mentions emails and text messages and excludes websites because it may be changed by the party running the website).

only excluded if the durable medium is *exclusively* used as a carrier for the supply of the digital content to the consumer. There is indeed a difference between a distance sales contract of a CD containing software (which you are buying solely for the software/digital content) and buying an iPhone with software on it, which you are not buying exclusively for the software on it.

2.2.6. Contract

Recital 17 of the ODSD Proposal states that the notion of contract should be defined to bring clarity and certainty for sellers and consumers. The recital makes clear that the chosen definition follows the common traditions of all Member States. Article 2(h) defines it as 'an agreement intended to give rise to obligations or other legal effects'.[55] The same definition was put forward in the proposed regulation on the CESL.[56] Schmidt-Kessel observes that the definition of the CESL springs from the definition in Article II.-1:101(1) of the Draft Common Frame of Reference (DCFR).[57, 58]

3. CONFORMITY

3.1. GENERAL NOTIONS

The notion of conformity explains one of the main obligations of the seller in a sales contract.[59] According to Article 4(1) ODSD Proposal, he has to deliver goods conforming to the contract. If the seller does not comply with this requirement (and if there is any 'lack of conformity' with the contract which exists at a certain moment of time), he will be liable toward the consumer (Article 8 ODSD Proposal). Also the consumer's remedies (such as repair or replacement, and, in secondary order, a price reduction or termination of the contract; see the chapter by Claeys and Vancoillie in this volume) depend upon

55 See, for the same definition, Art. 2(7) DCD Proposal.

56 Art. 2(a) of the proposed regulation on the CESL. Doubts about the relevance of this definition are expressed by: C. Wendehorst, 'Art. 2 Regulation' in R. Schulze (ed.), *Common European Sales Law (CESL)*, Munich, Beck, 2012, (13) p. 17.

57 C. Von Bar and E. Clive, *Draft Common Frame of Reference (DCFR)*, Munich, Sellier, 2009, 6v.

58 M. Schmidt-Kessel, 'Der Vorschlag der Kommission für ein Optionales Instrument – Einleitung' in M. Schmidt-Kessel (ed.), *Ein einheitliches europäisches Kaufrecht?*, Munich, Sellier, 2012, (1) p. 46 (the consequences of this definition for the CESL are 'unclear', according to this author).

59 See also about the fundamental nature of the concept of conformity under the CSD: L. Serrano, 'Article 1: Scope and Definitions' in M.C. Bianca and S. Grundmann (eds.), *EU Sales Directive, Commentary*, Antwerp, Intersentia, 2002, (91) paras. 41–43.

the establishment of a lack of conformity with the contract. If we compare the general structure of Article 4 ODSD Proposal, we must conclude that it differs from the existing CSD. The latter works with a 'presumption of conformity' if some cumulative conditions are complied with (Article 2(2) of the CSD). The ODSD Proposal only lists, in the Articles 4–7, the subjective and objective criteria which the goods must meet to be in conformity with the contract (if relevant). The CESL also lists, very similarly to the ODSD Proposal, the criteria for the conformity of the goods.[60]

The CESL, the CSD and the ODSD Proposal do not make a clear distinction between the terms 'conformity with the contract' and 'conformity of the goods'. This distinction is important to know in which situations a certain remedy can be applied. If a remedy can be applied in case of a 'non-conformity with the contract', it does not only refer to 'non-conforming goods' but also to a delay in the delivery, a delivery at the wrong place, non-delivery, etc.[61] Therefore, it is important to flesh this out and to make clear which remedy can be applied in which situation (see also below, Section 3.4).

The ODSD Proposal maintains the 'monistic' concept of 'lack of conformity with the contract' which was introduced by the CSD. A short reference to Belgian sales law is important to overcome some conceptual problems.[62] The term 'lack of conformity' has a different meaning under Belgian common sales law in comparison with consumer sales (and the ODSD Proposal).[63] Belgian general sales law provides for a dual-system, distinguishing the duty to deliver goods in conformity (Article 1604 of the Civil Code) and the duty to warranty against hidden defects (Article 1641 *et seq.* of the Civil Code). The notion of 'conformity' has a narrow meaning in Belgian common sales law. However, the same notion has a broader meaning in the CSD (and also under the ODSD Proposal).

---

60 See Arts. 99–102 CESL.

61 See e.g. about the importance of this distinction: S. Jansen, 'Price reduction as a remedy in European contract law and the consumer acquis' in A. Keirse and M. Loos (eds.), *Alternative Ways to Ius Commune. The Europeanisation of Private Law*, Antwerp, Intersentia, 2012, (169) pp. 173–74 and pp. 190–93; S. Jansen, *Prijsvermindering: remedie tot bijsturing van contracten*, Antwerp, Intersentia, 2015, paras. 340–49 (consumer sales) and paras. 414–19 (CESL).

62 See also: S. Stijns, 'De richtlijn consumentenkoop in het Belgische recht' in J. Smits (ed.), *De Richtlijn consumentenkoop in perspectief*, The Hague, Boom Juridische Uitgevers, 2003, (41) p. 59 and pp. 62–63; A. Van Oevelen, 'Het nieuwe begrip "conformiteit"' in S. Stijns and J. Stuyck (eds.), *Het nieuwe kooprecht*, Antwerp, Intersentia, 2005, (29), pp. 29–35. See after the implementation of the CSD in the Belgian Civil Code: S. Stijns, 'De consumentenkoop: actuele knelpunten' in B. Tilleman and A. Verbeke (eds.), *Knelpunten verkoop roerende goederen*, Antwerp, Intersentia, 2009, (21) pp. 37–39.

63 See for a general overview about the difference in meaning of the term 'lack of conformity' in general sales law and in consumer sales law (and pleading correctly to abolish the so-called 'dual' system in general sales law): A. Lenaerts, 'Het nieuwe begrip conformiteit in het Belgisch en het Duits kooprecht', *TBBR* 2006, (81) p. 82 *et seq.*

The two obligations (delivering in conformity and a warranty against hidden defects) have been merged into one unique obligation 'to deliver in conformity with the contract' (also called 'monism').[64]

The Explanatory Memorandum of the ODSD Proposal explains that the conformity criteria which the goods have to meet to conform to the contract can be divided into 'subjective' criteria and 'objective criteria'.[65] The subjective criteria, coinciding with what has been promised in the contract (and including pre-contractual information, forming an integral part of the contract),[66] are listed in Article 4(1) ODSD Proposal. In the absence of explicit contractual regulations, the goods must meet a set of so-called 'objective criteria' (see Article 4(2) ODSD Proposal). This means that the goods also must match the standard normally expected for goods (such as fitness for the purpose, packaging, installation instructions and normal qualities and performance capabilities). Those additional objective criteria are listed in Articles 5, 6 and 7 ODSD Proposal.

If we compare this with the CSD, we notice that the latter treats the objective and subjective conformity criteria in one and the same Article (see mainly Article 2(2) CSD).[67] Article 2(2)(a) and (b) CSD contain the subjective criteria, while Article 2(2)(c) and (d) CSD contain the objective criteria.

When comparing with the CESL, it is clear that the drafters of the ODSD Proposal try to distinguish the subjective and objective criteria (dealing with them in different articles), whereas these concepts are jumbled up in the CESL.[68] This way of presenting the conformity criteria has been heavily criticised by doctrine.[69] Some authors correctly point out that the CESL, instead of retaining

64 See also Art. 31 *et seq.* of the United Nations Convention on Contracts for the International Sale of Goods (Vienna, 1980) (also 'CISG'), applying a monistic system.

65 Explanatory Memorandum, p. 14 and recital 19 ODSD Proposal.

66 Recital 19 ODSD Proposal.

67 See about the objective and subjective criteria under the CSD: S. Grundmann, 'Article 2. Conformity with the contract' in M.C. Bianca and S. Grundmann (eds.), *EU Sales Directive, Commentary*, Antwerp, Intersentia, 2002, (117) paras. 20–29.

68 Art. 99 CESL clearly deals with the subjective conformity criteria because it indicates that the goods/digital content must have the features as stipulated by the contract. Art. 100 CESL deals with subjective (a), (c) and (f) and objective conformity criteria; see also: F. Zoll, 'Art. 99–105 CESL' in R. Schulze (ed.), *Common European Sales Law (CESL)*, Munich, Beck, 2012, (463) p. 472.

69 De Wit wonders why the drafters of the CESL have not retained the criteria set out in Art. 2(2) CSD: R. De Wit, 'Duties of Buyer and Seller. Transfer of Risk' in I. Claeys and R. Feltkamp (eds.), *The Draft Common European Sales Law: Towards an Alternative Sales Law?*, Cambridge, Intersentia, 2013, (155) para. 29. Schwenzer is confused by the 'mixed subjective/objective approach' requiring the goods to comply with the contractual standards as well as with default criteria for non-conformity: I. Schwenzer, 'The Proposed Common European Sales Law and the Convention on the International Sale of Goods', *UCC Law Journal* 2012, (457) p. 465. See also critical: H. Eidenmüller, N. Jansen, E.-M. Kieninger, *et al.*, 'The Proposal for a Regulation on a Common European Sales Law: Deficits of the Most Recent Textual Layer of European Contract Law', *The Edinburgh Law Review* 2012, (301) p. 333; R. Feltkamp and F. Vanbossele, 'The Optional Common European Sales Law: Better Buyer's Remedies for Seller's Non-Performance in Sales of Goods?', *ERPL* 2011, (873) p. 887;

the approach of the CSD, is based on Article IV.A.-2:301 DCFR.[70,71] It has to be said that the approach of the CSD and the ODSD Proposal is much more accurate in clearly distinguishing between the subjective and the objective conformity criteria.

The question arises whether or not an agreement (subjective will of the parties) can go below the standard set by the objective criteria.[72] Recital 22 ODSD Proposal stresses the importance of freedom of contract with regard to the conformity criteria, but also makes clear that it has to be balanced with the aim to achieve a high level of consumer protection. It cannot be the intention that a seller can easily circumvent liability for lack of conformity. Article 4(3) ODSD Proposal states that an agreement can *only* derogate from the mandatory rules in Articles 5 and 6 (objective criteria of conformity and incorrect installation) to the detriment of the consumer if the latter is informed about the specific condition of the goods and he has explicitly accepted this condition when concluding the contract.[73] However, it is odd that this article does not foresee the same rule for the mandatory rules in Article 7 about third party rights (legal defects).[74] The most important aim of this rule is transparency for the consumer and the prevalence of the legitimate expectations of the consumer: the seller may not 'smuggle' content into the contract of which the consumer is

O. Remien, 'Verpflichtungen des Verkäufers nach EU-Kaufrecht' in M. Schmidt-Kessel (ed.), *Ein einheitliches europäisches Kaufrecht?*, Munich, Sellier, 2012, (307) p. 319. See also about the critical assessment of the conformity criteria under the CESL: O. Remien, 'Artikel 99–105 GEK-E' in M. Schmidt-Kessel (ed.), *Der Entwurf für ein Gemeinsames Europäisches Kaufrecht. Kommentar*, Munich, Sellier, 2014, (537) p. 538.

70 R. Feltkamp and F. Vanbosselе, 'The Optional Common European Sales Law: Better Buyer's Remedies for Seller's Non-Performance in Sales of Goods?', *ERPL* 2011, (873) fns 43 and 45; O. Remien, 'Verpflichtungen des Verkäufers nach EU-Kaufrecht' in M. Schmidt-Kessel (ed.), *Ein einheitliches europäisches Kaufrecht?*, Munich, Sellier, 2012, (307) p. 318.

71 See also for a similar system: Art. 2:201–2:203 PEL (S): E. Hondius, V. Heutger, C. Jeloschek, *et al.*, *Principles of European Law. Study Group on a European Civil Code. Sales* (*PEL S*), Munich, Sellier, 2008, pp. 181–207.

72 See for the same question, with regard to the CSD: S. Grundmann, 'Article 2. Conformity With the Contract' in M.C. Bianca and S. Grundmann (eds.), *EU Sales Directive, Commentary*, Antwerp, Intersentia, 2002, (117) para. 9 ('the consumer cannot be denied the liberty of choice if meaningful information is possible and he can take his decision on an informed basis himself').

73 See also recital 22 ODSD Proposal. See for a very similar provision under the CESL: Art. 99(3) CESL (see about this CESL rule: R. De Wit, 'Duties of Buyer and Seller. Transfer of Risk' in I. Claeys and R. Feltkamp (eds.), *The Draft Common European Sales Law: Towards an Alternative Sales Law?*, Cambridge, Intersentia, 2013, (155) para. 28; C. Schuller and A. Zenefels, 'Obligations of Sellers and Buyers' in G. Dannemann and S. Vogenauer (eds.), *The Common European Sales Law in Context*, Oxford, OUP, 2013, (581) p. 596).

74 If we compare this to Art. 99.3 CESL, the latter foresees the same rule for the rules about third party rights (legal defects). But Art. 99(3) CESL forgets to mention Art. 101 CESL (incorrect installation): F. Zoll, 'Art. 99–105 CESL' in R. Schulze (ed.), *Common European Sales Law (CESL)*, Munich, Beck, 2012, (463) p. 465.

unaware (e.g. by means of non-negotiated terms).[75] If we compare this rule to Article 2(3) CSD, we notice an important difference. The CSD does not require a (derogating) *agreement* if the consumer is aware or 'could not reasonably be unaware of the lack of conformity' (or if the lack of conformity has its origin in materials supplied by the consumer).[76] If the consumer is aware or ought to be aware of a lack of conformity at the moment of the conclusion of the contract, he cannot invoke the lack of conformity or rely on the remedies for non-conformity under the CSD. This means that (possible) knowledge of any existing defects by the consumer will more easily lead to a loss of the legal warranty under the CSD than under the ODSD Proposal.[77] Perhaps this can be explained by the fact that in case of an online or distance sale the parties do not see each other or the goods? Indeed, in case of online sales knowledge of an existing defect is rather unlikely.

3.2. SUBJECTIVE CONFORMITY

Article 4(1) ODSD Proposal lists three subjective conformity criteria of the goods. As we have already mentioned, subjective conformity coincides with what has been promised in the contract, including pre-contractual information[78]

---

75 See detailed (with regard to the CESL): F. Zoll, 'Art. 99-105 CESL' in R. Schulze (ed.), *Common European Sales Law (CESL)*, Munich, Beck, 2012, (463) p. 470. See also with regard to Art. IV.A.-2:309 DCFR: M.B.M. Loos, 'Sales Law in the DCFR', *SSRN, Centre for the Study of European Contract Law Working Paper Series No. 2010/04*, 2010, (1) pp. 16–17.

76 Under the CESL, this rule is only preserved in contracts between traders: see Art. 104 CESL. F. Zoll, 'Art. 99–105 CESL' in R. Schulze (ed.), *Common European Sales Law (CESL)*, Munich, Beck, 2012, (463) pp. 486–87. Critical about the fact that the CESL only preserves this rule in contracts between traders (this rule should also apply in consumer contracts) are: R. Feltkamp and F. Vanbossele, 'The Optional Common European Sales Law: Better Buyer's Remedies for Seller's Non-Performance in Sales of Goods?', *ERPL* 2011, (873) p. 890; O. Remien, 'Verpflichtungen des Verkäufers nach EU-Kaufrecht' in M. Schmidt-Kessel (ed.), *Ein einheitliches europäisches Kaufrecht?*, Munich, Sellier, 2012, (307) pp. 323–24. Under the PEL (S) this rule is also applicable to consumer transactions; but these contracts should, according to the drafters, be treated 'with more caution': E. Hondius, V. Heutger, C. Jeloschek, *et al.*, *Principles of European Law. Study Group on a European Civil Code. Sales (PEL S)*, Munich, Sellier, 2008, p. 217. Under the DCFR the rule contained in Art. IV.A-2:307 DCFR is also applicable to consumer transactions; but these contracts should, according to the drafters, be treated 'with more caution': C. Von Bar and E. Clive, *Draft Common Frame of Reference (DCFR)*, Vol. II, Munich, Sellier, 2009, pp. 1307–08.

77 See, for the same conclusion but in a comparison between the predecessor of the CESL (proposal), the Feasibility Study (of the Expert Group on European Contract Law of 3 May 2011) and the CSD (and the CRD proposal of 8 October 2008, COM(2008) 614 final): N. Reich, 'Part III An Optional Sales Law Instrument for European Businesses and Consumers?' in H.-W. Micklitz and N. Reich (eds.), *EUI Working Papers: The Commission Proposal for a 'Regulation on a Common European Sales Law (CESL)' – Too Broad or Not Broad Enough?*, Badia Fiesolana, European University Institute, 2012, (67) p. 72.

78 Recital 19 ODSD Proposal.

forming an integral part of the contract. This means that the parties explicitly conclude an agreement about the characteristics of the goods.

Article 4(1)(a) ODSD Proposal prescribes that the goods must be of the quantity, quality and description required by the contract.[79] If the seller has shown a sample or a model to the consumer; the goods must correspond to its description and have the same quality. Grundmann clarifies, with regard to the CSD, that a *description* given by the seller must not be backed by a will to bind himself; moreover, such statements can only be expressly withdrawn or corrected by the seller before the completion of the contract.[80]

In the CESL, Article 99(1)(a) prescribes only the first part of Article 4(1)(a) ODSD Proposal. The reference to a sample or a model is provided for in Article 100(c) CESL. The CSD states in a shortened way that the goods must comply with the description given by the seller and must possess the qualities of the goods which the seller has held out to the consumer as a sample or a model.[81]

The goods must also be fit for the particular purpose the consumer meant to use them for (Article 4(1)(b) ODSD Proposal). However, the consumer must inform the seller about this specific purpose at the time of the conclusion of the contract and the seller must have accepted this. This 'particular' purpose is usually due in addition to the usual or ordinary purpose under Article 5(a) ODSD Proposal (see below, Section 3.3.1).[82] The requirement that the seller must have accepted the particular purpose of the goods is often not so important, since tacit consent is sufficient to fulfil this requirement.[83] Nevertheless, it must be noted that a tacit consent is less likely in the context of online or other distance sales. The wording of the ODSD Proposal coincides exactly with that in Article 2(2)(b) CSD.[84] It derives partially from the wording used in the CESL.[85]

---

79 If we compare this with Art. 6(1)(a) DCD Proposal, the list in the ODSD Proposal is shorter because it does not contain references to e.g. functionality and interoperability.

80 S. Grundmann, 'Article 2. Conformity with the contract' in M.C. Bianca and S. Grundmann (eds.), *EU Sales Directive, Commentary*, Antwerp, Intersentia, 2002, (117) paras. 21–22.

81 Art. 2(2)(a) CSD.

82 See similarly with regard to the CSD: S. Grundmann, 'Article 2. Conformity with the contract' in M.C. Bianca and S. Grundmann (eds.), *EU Sales Directive, Commentary*, Antwerp, Intersentia, 2002, (117) para. 24.

83 See even stronger with regard to the CSD: S. Grundmann, 'Article 2. Conformity with the contract' in M.C. Bianca and S. Grundmann (eds.), *EU Sales Directive, Commentary*, Antwerp, Intersentia, 2002, (117) para. 25.

84 Approving of this way of dealing with 'idiosyncratic purposes of the consumer': S. Grundmann, F. Gomez, M.G. Bridge, *et al.*, 'Introduction' in M.C. Bianca and S. Grundmann (eds.), *EU Sales Directive, Commentary*, Antwerp, Intersentia, 2002, (13) para. 101.

85 Art. 100(a) CESL is formulated mildly for the consumer, not requiring the acceptance of the seller and providing for an exception: goods must 'be fit for any particular purpose made known to the seller at the time of the conclusion of the contract, *except where the circumstances show that the buyer did not rely, or that it was unreasonable for the buyer to rely, on the seller's skill and judgement*' (emphasis added). The silence of the seller must be

This criterion can be illustrated by the following example: a consumer wishes to buy a vacuum cleaner to clean heavy scraps, fragments and sand at the building site of his house. If he does not choose a specialised online DIY shop but a normal household electronics web shop to buy a vacuum cleaner, he should mention this particular purpose of the goods and the seller should accept this. Not every vacuum cleaner is able to hoover sand and larger fragments.

The ODSD Proposal adopts the idea of the Article 100(f) CESL and introduces in Article 4(1)(c) pre-contractual statements as a subjective conformity criterion. According to this article the goods must possess the qualities and performance capabilities indicated in pre-contractual statements. The CSD does not phrase this idea in the same way, but puts forward that one has to take into account public statements, particularly in advertising and labelling, which are, of course, also pre-contractual statements.[86] The broad formulation under the CESL and the ODSD Proposal widens this criterion to, for example, private pre-contractual statements, taking it beyond solely public statements. Nevertheless, the ODSD Proposal does not explicitly prescribe what those 'pre-contractual statements' entail, leaving this to national law.[87]

3.3. OBJECTIVE CONFORMITY

Article 4(2) in conjunction with Articles 5, 6 and 7 ODSD Proposal makes it clear that the seller also has to comply with 'objective' criteria. We have already mentioned that this means that the goods also must match the standard normally expected for goods (cf. above, Section 3.1). These criteria are only applicable where relevant.

3.3.1. General Objective Requirements for Conformity of the Goods

Article 5 ODSD Proposal enlists some so-called general 'objective' criteria to establish the conformity of the goods. Articles 6 and 7 regulate some specific objective criteria. The word 'and' after 5(b) indicates that the general objective criteria enlisted must be met, of course where relevant, cumulatively for the goods being in conformity with the contract.

Article 5(a) ODSD Proposal prescribes that the goods must be 'fit for all purposes' for which goods with that description would normally ('ordinarily')

---

understood as consent to the particular purpose the buyer has communicated (if the seller has expressly stated that the particular purpose cannot be met by the goods, Art. 100(a) CESL will not be applicable): F. Zoll, 'Art. 99–105 CESL' in R. Schulze (ed.), *Common European Sales Law (CESL)*, Munich, Beck, 2012, (463) p. 473.

86 Art. 2(2)(d) CSD.

87 See Briefing document of 2016 by Rafał Mańko, PE 577.962, p. 5 (refers also to the so-called 'merger clause' in Art. II-4:104 DCFR).

be used (different from the particular purpose of the goods, made known by the consumer of Article 3(1)(b) ODSD Proposal, above, Section 3.2). One has to take into account the relevant market to determine the fitness for the ordinary purpose of goods.[88] The same requirement is set forth in Article 2(2)(c) CSD[89] and Article 100(b) CESL. If we come back to our example in Section 3.2, our customer will not have to warn the seller of the specific purpose he intends to use his vacuum cleaner for if he chooses an online DIY shop only selling big industrial vacuum cleaners, which are normally intended to hoover larger scraps and sand.

Article 5(b) ODSD Proposal explicitly states that, if relevant, goods are in conformity with the contract if they are delivered with the 'required accessories, packaging, installation instructions, and other instructions' that the consumer might expect to receive. The same criterion is set forth under the CESL.[90] The CESL also prescribes a subjective criterion in Article 99(1)(b) and (c) that the goods must be contained or packaged in the manner required by the contract and that the goods must be supplied along with any accessories, (installation) instructions required by the contract. The CSD, however, does not explicitly indicate this criterion at all (or whether the remedies will be applicable in case the accessories, packaging or instructions are non-conforming). We have already argued that a failure to deliver accessories could fall under the first criterion of the CSD, namely the 'description' of the goods.[91] Indeed, the delivery without accessories, adequate packaging or instructions will fall under the first (subjective) or the fourth (objective) criterion of the CSD: it would not match the 'description' or would not match the 'quality and performance which are normal in goods of the same type and which the consumer can reasonably expect'.[92] Nevertheless, it has to be applauded that the ODSD Proposal makes

---

88 See with regard to the CSD: S. Grundmann, 'Article 2. Conformity with the contract' in M.C. Bianca and S. Grundmann (eds.), *EU Sales Directive, Commentary*, Antwerp, Intersentia, 2002, (117) para. 26. With regard to the CESL, Zoll makes clear that it is not evident to qualify the 'relevant market' of goods/digital content as being of the 'same description': F. Zoll, 'Art. 99–105 CESL' in R. Schulze (ed.), *Common European Sales Law (CESL)*, Munich, Beck, 2012, (463) p. 474 (one must take into account the legitimate expectations of the buyer). Criticising, also with regard to the CESL, the open-ended notion of 'ordinary use': R. Feltkamp and F. VanbosselE, 'The Optional Common European Sales Law: Better Buyer's Remedies for Seller's Non-Performance in Sales of Goods?', *ERPL* 2011, (873) pp. 887–88.

89 Art. 2(2)(c) CSD: 'Consumer goods are presumed to be in conformity with the contract if they (c) are fit for the purposes for which goods of the same type are normally used'.

90 Art. 100(d) and (e) CESL. Art. 100(d) prescribes more extensively that the goods must be contained or packaged in the manner usual for such goods, or if there does not exist such a manner, in a manner adequate to preserve and protect those goods.

91 S. Jansen, *Prijsvermindering: remedie tot bijsturing van contracten*, Antwerp, Intersentia, 2015, para. 347.

92 See also: S. Grundmann, 'Article 2. Conformity with the contract' in M.C. Bianca and S. Grundmann (eds.), *EU Sales Directive, Commentary*, Antwerp, Intersentia, 2002, (117) para. 45 (refers to Art. 2(2)(d) CSD).

clear in its Article 5(b) that conformity of the goods requires delivery with the expected accessories, packaging and instructions.

The last general objective criterion (Article 5(c) ODSD Proposal) generally states that the goods must

> possess qualities and performance capabilities which are normal in goods of the same type and which the consumer may expect given the nature of the goods and taking into account any public statement made by or on behalf of the seller or other persons in earlier links of the chain of transactions, including the producer, unless the seller shows that: (i) the seller was not, and could not reasonably have been, aware of the statement in question; (ii) by the time of conclusion of the contract the statement had been corrected; or (iii) the decision to buy the goods could not have been influenced by the statement.

The first part of this provision of the ODSD Proposal requiring the 'qualities and performance capabilities which are normal in goods of the same type' is clearly a 'catch-all rule'.[93] The same catch-all rule is put forward in Article 2(2)(d) CSD and in Article 100(g) CESL.

The second part of this provision requires accordance with the expectations based on the goods' nature or on public statements. It is important to observe that the word 'reasonably' has been left out of Article 5(c) ODSD Proposal ('which the consumer may *expect* given the nature of the goods and taking into account any public statement') in comparison to Article 2(2)(d) CSD ('which the consumer can *reasonably expect*, given the nature of the goods and taking into account any public statements'). Perhaps the word 'reasonably' has been left out in order to avoid a wide interpretation of the criterion of 'reasonable expectations' (leading to the supremacy of objective standard-setting), while the

---

93 See for the same idea with regard to Art. 2(2)(d) CSD: S. GRUNDMANN, 'Article 2. Conformity with the contract' in M.C. BIANCA and S. GRUNDMANN (eds.), *EU Sales Directive, Commentary*, Antwerp, Intersentia, 2002, (117) para. 28; and with regard to Art. 100(g) CESL: O. REMIEN, 'Verpflichtungen des Verkäufers nach EU-Kaufrecht' in M. SCHMIDT-KESSEL (ed.), *Ein einheitliches europäisches Kaufrecht?*, Munich, Sellier, 2012, (307) p. 320; F. ZOLL, 'Art. 99–105 CESL' in R. SCHULZE (ed.), *Common European Sales Law (CESL)*, Munich, Beck, 2012, (463) p. 476. Critical with regard to the general criterion contained in Art. 100(g) CESL are: R. FELTKAMP and F. VANBOSSELE, 'The Optional Common European Sales Law: Better Buyer's Remedies for Seller's Non-Performance in Sales of Goods?', *ERPL* 2011, (873) p. 887; I. SCHWENZER, 'The Proposed Common European Sales Law and the Convention on the International Sale of Goods', *UCC Law Journal* 2012, (457) p. 465 ('How these expectations are to be assessed remains largely obscure'). See for the same idea with regard to Art. IV.A.-2:302(f) DCFR (this is a 'general sweep up rule'): C. VON BAR and E. CLIVE, *Draft Common Frame of Reference (DCFR)*, Vol. II, Munich, Sellier, 2009, p. 1286; M.B.M. LOOS, 'Sales Law in the DCFR', *SSRN, Centre for the Study of European Contract Law Working Paper Series No. 2010/04*, 2010, (1) p. 19.

expectations of the consumer should only be based on the nature of the goods and the (public) statements about the goods.[94]

Article 5(c) ODSD Proposal is very elaborate and therefore it overlaps with one of the subjective criteria, namely the pre-contractual statements[95] which become a part of the contract (see above, Section 3.2). Indeed, public statements are also pre-contractual statements. Nevertheless, the new article makes it very clear that *public* statements can also stem from persons other than the seller in earlier links of the chain of transaction (and not only the producer or his representative, as is indicated by Article 2(2)(d) CSD).[96, 97] The ODSD Proposal has thereby met Grundmann's criticism on the CSD (which merely refers to the producer and his representatives) by including the whole distribution chain.[98] The question remains whether or not non-public statements, stemming from persons other than the seller in earlier links of the chain of transaction, are also taken into account.

The ODSD Proposal sums up the same three exceptions to the rule that public statements have to be taken into account as put forward in Article 2(4) CSD.[99] The seller will have to prove the fulfilment of one of the exceptions.[100] Indeed, the seller may show that: (i) he was not, and could not reasonably have been, aware of the statement in question; (ii) by the time of conclusion of the contract the statement had been corrected; or (iii) the decision of the consumer to buy the goods could not have been influenced by the statement. Grundmann has carefully examined all three of the exceptions with regard to the CSD.[101]

---

94 *Cf.* also: S. Grundmann, 'Article 2. Conformity with the contract' in M.C. Bianca and S. Grundmann (eds.), *EU Sales Directive, Commentary*, Antwerp, Intersentia, 2002, (117) para. 31.

95 Statements must be considered to be any comment that allows the consumer to know more about the quality of the goods and do not include mere boasting about the goods; see detail with regard to the CSD: S. Grundmann, 'Article 2. Conformity with the contract' in M.C. Bianca and S. Grundmann (eds.), *EU Sales Directive, Commentary*, Antwerp, Intersentia, 2002, (117) para. 37.

96 See about this rule under the CSD: J.M. Smits, 'De richtlijn consumentenkoop en het Nederlandse recht' in J.M. Smits (ed.), *De richtlijn consumentenkoop in perspectief*, The Hague, Boom Juridische Uitgever, 2003, (1) p. 9.

97 See about the CSD: S. Grundmann, 'Article 2. Conformity with the contract' in M.C. Bianca and S. Grundmann (eds.), *EU Sales Directive, Commentary*, Antwerp, Intersentia, 2002, (117) para. 36 ('Distinguishing between public and non-public statements is important in practice only in so far as the seller is not only liable for his own but also for other persons' statements (only) if they are public').

98 S. Grundmann, 'Article 2. Conformity with the contract' in M.C. Bianca and S. Grundmann (eds.), *EU Sales Directive, Commentary*, Antwerp, Intersentia, 2002, (117) para. 39.

99 See also, for the same exceptions, Art. 6(2)(c) DCD Proposal.

100 See similarly, but with regard to the CSD: S. Grundmann, 'Article 2. Conformity with the contract' in M.C. Bianca and S. Grundmann (eds.), *EU Sales Directive, Commentary*, Antwerp, Intersentia, 2002, (117) para. 40.

101 S. Grundmann, 'Article 2. Conformity with the contract' in M.C. Bianca and S. Grundmann (eds.), *EU Sales Directive, Commentary*, Antwerp, Intersentia, 2002, (117) paras. 40–43.

According to him, the first exception will be very difficult to prove, even if it does not imply a strict liability: it is sufficient that the seller proves that he 'reasonably could not have been aware of the statement'. The second exception will be easier to prove, according to the same author, but requires that the seller makes the consumer really aware of the corrections. Exception number three will also be very difficult to prove except under the circumstances that the seller can prove that the consumer could not know of the statement at all.

The European Consumer Organisation (BEUC) suggested on 3 September 2015 in its response to the Commission that the latter should implement criteria such as 'freedom from minor defects', 'appearance and finish', 'safety' and 'durability'.[102, 103] The last criterion can be justified under the EU's objective for a 'green and circular economy' and sustainable consumption and production.[104] However, the ODSD Proposal does not refer to this specific criterion in its articles. Nevertheless, the proposed criteria can probably be categorised under the general objective criterion that the goods must have the 'expected quality and performance capability' or under the 'fitness for ordinary purposes' criterion.[105] Moreover, recital 23 of the ODSD Proposal does refer to the durability of consumer goods and makes a link with the pre-contractual statements (Article 4(4)(c) ODSD Proposal) on which a consumer may rely as to this aspect.

---

102 European Commission's public consultation on contract rules for online purchase of digital content and tangible goods, BEUC response of 3 September 2015, p. 21 (http://www.beuc.eu/publications/beuc-x-2015-077_contract_rules_for_online_purchases_of_digital_content_and_tangible_goods.pdf; hereafter: 'BEUC response').

103 Under English consumer sales law these criteria are required by statutory law (see (previous) Section 14(2B) Sale of Goods Act (1979), now included in Section 9(3) of the Consumer Rights Act 2015). See also about these criteria and the more demanding system under English law (compared to the CESL): C. Schuller and A. Zenefels, 'Obligations of Sellers and Buyers' in G. Dannemann and S. Vogenauer (eds.), *The Common European Sales Law in Context*, Oxford, OUP, 2013, (581) p. 599. See also: H. MacQueen, 'The Europeanisation of Contract Law: The Proposed Common European Sales Law' in L.A. Dimatteo, S. Saintier and K. Rowley (eds.), *Commercial Contract Law: Transatlantic Perspectives*, Cambridge, CUP, 2013, (529) between fns 100–112 (e.g. 'The proposed CESL however lacks to indicate that its concept of "purpose" extends beyond the functional to such non-functional matters as appearance and finish'). Also other EU countries refer to specific criteria such as durability, finish, safety, etc. with regard to the implementation of the CSD: H. Schulte-Nölke, C. Twigg-Flesner and M. Ebers, *EC Consumer Law Compendium*, Munich, Sellier, 2008, pp. 422–23 (see esp. Cyprus and Denmark).

104 This can also be brought in relation with the short time limit for introducing remedies, of two years as from the relevant time for establishing conformity (Art. 14 ODSD Proposal): See the EEA EFTA comment on the upcoming proposal regarding contract rules for online purchases of digital content and tangible goods of 16 November 2015, Ref. 15-7172, paras. 4.2–4.4 (http://www.efta.int/sites/default/files/documents/eea/eea-efta-comments/2015/2015-11-16-efta-comment-on-draft-eu-online-consumer-sales-law.pdf).

105 See also with regard to the CSD: S. Grundmann, 'Article 2. Conformity with the contract' in M.C. Bianca and S. Grundmann (eds.), *EU Sales Directive, Commentary*, Antwerp, Intersentia, 2002, (117) paras. 28–29.

The same question arises with regard to the so-called reasonable expectations of an ethical consumer. Does the general objective criterion that the goods must have the 'expected quality and performance capability' (Article 5(c) ODSD Proposal) imply that the goods will be produced under ethical standards (such as not violating EU labour law, international labour law standards, and human rights law)?[106] In our view, this difficult question must be addressed. A careful analysis of the price/quality ratio, public statements and policy documents of the producers might imply that consumers may reasonably expect that the bought goods are ethically sound, which would fall under the general objective criterion.

3.3.2. *Specific Objective Requirements for Conformity of the Goods*

3.3.2.1. Incorrect Installation

Article 6 ODSD Proposal equates an incorrect installation[107] or any lack of conformity from an incorrect installation to a lack of conformity of the contract of the goods in two situations: (1) if the goods were installed by the seller or under his responsibility; and (2) if the goods which had to be installed by the consumer himself, were installed by him, but the incorrect installation was due to a shortcoming in the installation instructions (so-called IKEA clause).[108] The same approach is taken in Article 101 CESL and in Article 2(5) of the CSD.[109] With regard to the shortcoming in installation instructions (if the goods have to be installed by the consumer), the instructions must be available[110] to the consumer and the shortcoming can relate to a misleading content, a high degree of difficulty, incompleteness, etc.[111]

We can suppose that a distance sales contract will not often involve installation by the seller. Nevertheless, the goods sent will often require installation by the

---

106 See for a courageous paper addressing this issue with regard to the CSD and the CESL: H. Collins, 'Conformity of Goods, the Network Society, and the Ethical Consumer', *ERPL* 2014, (619) pp. 619–40.

107 Is called 'incorrect integration' in Art. 7 DCD Proposal.

108 See also recital 20 ODSD Proposal.

109 De Wit regrets that Art. 101 CESL has not preserved the wording of Art. 2(5) CSD: R. De Wit, 'Duties of Buyer and Seller. Transfer of Risk' in I. Claeys and R. Feltkamp (eds.), *The Draft Common European Sales Law: Towards an Alternative Sales Law?*, Cambridge, Intersentia, 2013, (155) para. 32.

110 Otherwise the 'installation instructions' would be lacking, as required under Art. 5(b) ODSD Proposal.

111 F. Zoll, 'Art. 99–105 CESL' in R. Schulze (ed.), *Common European Sales Law (CESL)*, Munich, Beck, 2012, (463) pp. 478–79. See also: N. Reich, 'Part III An Optional Sales Law Instrument for European Businesses and Consumers?' in H.-W. Micklitz and N. Reich (eds.), *EUI Working Papers: The Commission Proposal for a 'Regulation on a Common European Sales Law (CESL)' – Too Broad or Not Broad Enough?*, Badia Fiesolana, European University Institute, 2012, (67) p. 73.

consumer. Correct installation instructions in understandable language will be of the utmost importance for the seller to avoid incorrect installation based on shortcomings in the installation instructions. Of course, contributory fault of a consumer who installs the goods using incorrect installation instructions must be taken into account in a proportional way.[112]

The interesting question rises whether or not it is required that the incorrect installation (due to a shortcoming in the installation instructions) is performed by the consumer himself. What if the consumer entrusts the installation to a third party (a friend, a professional etc.). Smits argues correctly, with regard to the CSD, that it does not matter who installs the goods (the consumer himself, a friend or a third party professional).[113] All rely on the (unreliable) installation instructions resulting in a lack of conformity of the goods. This means that the seller is liable for this shortcoming.

The main importance of the equation of an incorrect installation to a lack of conformity is to move forward the relevant time for establishing conformity[114] (and the starting point of the two-year period of the reversal of the burden of proof in Article 8(3) ODSD Proposal).[115] Indeed, Article 8(2) ODSD Proposal moves the relevant time for establishing (a non-)conformity with the contract to the completion of the installation or when the consumer has had a reasonable time to complete the installation.

3.3.2.2. 'Third Party Rights'

Recital 21 of the ODSD Proposal states that conformity should not only cover material defects, but also legal defects.[116] Article 7 states:

> At the time relevant for establishing the conformity with the contract as determined by Article 8, the goods must be free from any right of a third party, including based on intellectual property, so that the goods can be used in accordance with the contract.

---

[112] See also with regard to the CSD: S. Grundmann, 'Article 2. Conformity with the contract' in M.C. Bianca and S. Grundmann (eds.), *EU Sales Directive, Commentary*, Antwerp, Intersentia, 2002, (117) para. 44.

[113] J.M. Smits, 'De richtlijn consumentenkoop en het Nederlandse recht' in J.M. Smits (ed.), *De richtlijn consumentenkoop in perspectief*, The Hague, Boom Juridische Uitgever, 2003, (1) pp. 10–11. See, for a similar reasoning under the PEL (S): E. Hondius, V. Heutger, C. Jeloschek, *et al.*, *Principles of European Law. Study Group on a European Civil Code. Sales (PEL S)*, Munich, Sellier, 2008, p. 209. See, for a similar reasoning under the DCFR: C. Von Bar and E. Clive, *Draft Common Frame of Reference (DCFR)*, Vol. II, Munich, Sellier, 2009, p. 1299.

[114] See, for the same reasoning under the CESL: F. Zoll, 'Art. 99–105 CESL' in R. Schulze (ed.), *Common European Sales Law (CESL)*, Munich, Beck, 2012, (463) p. 477.

[115] See also below, para. 4.2.

[116] Under Belgian law this legal concept is known as a 'warranty against eviction'.

The term 'third party rights' is perhaps a bit confusing (see also the chapter by Geiregat and Steennot). Although Article 7 only mentions 'third party rights', which can indeed constitute a legal defect, other legal defects are also included, according to recital 21.[117] What can be considered as such 'other legal defects' (different from third party rights)? We might think about rights of the seller himself (not being a third party), and about permits, licences and concessions (which have to be granted by the competent governmental authorities).[118] The main application is, of course, the third party rights as mentioned in Article 7 ODSD Proposal. What are such third party rights? Third party rights will burden the right of ownership of the goods. One might think about pledges, a right of usufruct of a third party, intellectual property (such as mentioned by the Article itself), and contractual rights such as a lease or tenancy agreement, etc.[119] Zoll also argues, with regard to Article 102 CESL, that failure in transferring ownership falls under this article.[120] Indeed, this would mean that someone else would have the ownership of the goods and, that the goods are not free from any right of a (third) party. We can argue the same for Article 7 ODSD Proposal.

If we compare this to the rules in the CESL, we can detect Article 102 CESL, prescribing that the 'goods must be free from … any right or not obviously unfounded claim of a third party'. Article 102 CESL is much more detailed in comparison with Article 7 ODSD Proposal, because Article 102(2) CESL indicates which IP law is applicable with regard to the issue of whether goods (or digital content) are free from or cleared of such rights or claims.[121] Article 102(3) and 102(4) CESL also provide for special rules concerning the knowledge of the buyer of third party rights and claims, preventing the buyer from invoking his rights arising from a lack of conformity.[122]

---

117 'Third party rights *and other legal defects* might effectively bar the consumer from enjoying the goods in accordance with the contract when the right's holder rightfully compels the consumer to stop infringing those rights' (emphasis added).

118 See also with regard to the CESL: F. Zoll, 'Art. 99–105 CESL' in R. Schulze (ed.), *Common European Sales Law (CESL)*, Munich, Beck, 2012, (463) p. 482 (administrative restrictions).

119 See also: F. Zoll, 'Art. 99–105 CESL' in R. Schulze (ed.), *Common European Sales Law (CESL)*, Munich, Beck, 2012, (463) p. 481.

120 F. Zoll, 'Art. 99–105 CESL' in R. Schulze (ed.), *Common European Sales Law (CESL)*, Munich, Beck, 2012, (463) p. 481.

121 See detailed: R. De Wit, 'Duties of Buyer and Seller. Transfer of Risk' in I. Claeys and R. Feltkamp (eds.), *The Draft Common European Sales Law: Towards an Alternative Sales Law?*, Cambridge, Intersentia, 2013, (155) para. 34; C. Schuller and A. Zenefels, 'Obligations of Sellers and Buyers' in G. Dannemann and S. Vogenauer (eds.), *The Common European Sales Law in Context*, Oxford, OUP, 2013, (581) p. 597: F. Zoll, 'Art. 99–105 CESL' in R. Schulze (ed.), *Common European Sales Law (CESL)*, Munich, Beck, 2012, (463) pp. 483–85.

122 Art. 102(3) and (4) CESL differentiate between B2B and B2C contracts: F. Zoll, 'Art. 99–105 CESL' in R. Schulze (ed.), *Common European Sales Law (CESL)*, Munich, Beck, 2012, (463) pp. 465 and 485.

The comparison with the rules in the CSD is interesting. It is questionable whether or not the rules about conformity in the CSD also cover 'legal defects'.[123] Some authors think that this is the case.[124] However, the majority of authors consider that legal defects are not covered by the CSD.[125] The Belgian legislator made clear in the parliamentary documents that legal defects were not covered by the law implementing the aforementioned Directive.[126]

The ODSD Proposal provides a welcome clarification with regard to its applicability in the case of legal defects. However, this also means that there will be a further stratification between the general consumer sales regime (not applicable to legal defects) and consumer distance sales contracts (applicable to legal defects).

3.4. OTHER RELEVANT ISSUES REGARDING CONFORMITY

As we have already mentioned, the ODSD Proposal does not make a clear distinction between the terms 'conformity with the contract' and 'conformity of the goods' (above, Section 3.1). If, on the one hand, the 'notion of conformity' in the ODSD Proposal only refers to 'conformity of the goods', this means that the proposed Directive leaves some aspects not regulated. The concept of 'conformity of the goods' does not, according to us, refer to a *late delivery* or a

123 Remien correctly points out that defects in transfer or property, legal defects and similar questions are not addressed by the CSD: O. Remien, 'Verpflichtungen des Verkäufers nach EU-Kaufrecht' in M. Schmidt-Kessel (ed.), *Ein einheitliches europäisches Kaufrecht?*, Munich, Sellier, 2012, (307) p. 321.

124 M.C. Bianca, 'Article 3. Droits et remèdes du consommateur' in M.C. Bianca, S. Grundmann and S. Stijns (eds.), *La directive communautaire sur la vente, Commentaire*, Brussels-Paris, Bruylant-LGDJ, 2004, (179) p. 185. See also: S. Grundmann, 'Article 2. Conformity with the contract' in M.C. Bianca and S. Grundmann (eds.), *EU Sales Directive, Commentary*, Antwerp, Intersentia, 2002, (117) paras. 14–16 (hesitates with regard to 'third party rights' but ascertains that 'public law burdens on, or restrictions of, rights are treated alike with quality defects under the CSD').

125 H. Ofner, '§922' in M. Schwimann (ed.), *Schwimann ABGB Praxiskommentar, Band 4, §§859–1089, WucherG, UN-Kaufrecht*, Vienna, LexisNexis, 2005, (539) para. 3 ('legal defects' ('*Rechtsmängel*') are not covered by the Directive); M. Teneiro, 'La proposition de directive sur la vente et les garanties des biens de consommation', *REDC* 2000, (187) p. 197.

126 Explanatory Memorandum to Bill of 31 March 2004 about the supplementation of the provisions of the Civil Code about sales regarding consumer protection, *Parl. St.* First Chamber 2003–04, no. 0982/001, p. 6. See also in this regard: C. Biquet-Mathieu, 'La garantie des biens de consommation – Présentation générale' in C. Biquet-Mathieu and P. Wéry (eds.), *La nouvelle garantie des biens de consommation et son environnement légal*, Brussels, die Keure, 2005, (55) para. 6; C. Cauffman and A. Verbeke, 'Een jaar wet consumentenkoop' in B. Tilleman and A. Verbeke (eds.), *Bijzondere overeenkomsten*, Bruges, die Keure, 2005, (27) para. 14; I. Demuynck, 'De nieuwe garantieregeling voor consumptiegoederen' in K. Bernauw (ed.), *Liber Amicorum Yvette Merchiers*, Bruges, die Keure, 2001, (904) para. 28; P. Wéry, 'Les droits légaux du consommateur en cas de défaut de conformité' in C. Biquet-Mathieu and P. Wéry (eds.), *La nouvelle garantie des biens de consommation et son environnement légal*, Brussels, die Keure, 2005, (127) para. 16.

delivery at the wrong place. Furthermore, it is questionable if the aforementioned concept refers to a 'non-delivery' and a 'delivery of wrong goods' (*aliud*). If, on the other hand, the 'notion of conformity' in the ODSD Proposal refers to 'conformity of the contract', the aforementioned situations of late delivery and delivery at the wrong place will be covered. It is crucial to resolve this question to know whether or not remedies for a lack of conformity can be applied. Another tricky question is whether or not it matters that a lack of conformity is *excused*.

3.4.1. Non-Delivery, Delivery of the Wrong Goods, Late Delivery, Delivery at the Wrong Place, Delivery of Too High Quantity

As we have already argued for the (implementation of the) CSD,[127] we do consider that a non-delivery and a delivery of wrong goods can be covered by the concept of (non-)conformity of the goods. If a seller does not deliver or delivers different goods to those agreed upon, he will not be able to meet the requirement set in Article 4(1)(a) ODSD Proposal: namely that the goods shall be of the quantity, quality and description required by the contract.[128] Consequently, the seller will have breached his obligation that the goods should be in conformity with the contract.

It can also happen that a seller does not deliver the correct quantity, but instead of a shortfall in quantity, he delivers too much. Grundmann has already stated that, with regard to the CSD, it would not be within the logic of the Directive to give the seller a right to a higher price because of the delivery of an excess in quantity.[129] In our opinion this is also applicable with regard to

127 S. Jansen, *Prijsvermindering: remedie tot bijsturing van contracten*, Antwerp, Intersentia, 2015, para. 346. See for the same opinion: S. Grundmann, 'Article 2. Conformity with the contract' in M.C. Bianca and S. Grundmann (eds.), *EU Sales Directive, Commentary*, Antwerp, Intersentia, 2002, (117) para. 5 (about a complete lack of performance) and paras. 12–13 (with regard to the delivery of the wrong goods, *aliud* delivery or deviation in 'gender'). See also about this topic but with regard to the CESL: O. Remien, 'Verpflichtungen des Verkäufers nach EU-Kaufrecht' in M. Schmidt-Kessel (ed.), *Ein einheitliches europäisches Kaufrecht?*, Munich, Sellier, 2012, (307) p. 318 (an *aliud* delivery is also covered); F. Zoll, 'Art. 99–105 CESL' in R. Schulze (ed.), *Common European Sales Law (CESL)*, Munich, Beck, 2012, (463) p. 468 (an *aliud* delivery should be treated as a non-performance if this has been delivered with the 'intention to complete the performance').

128 See for a similar reasoning under the PEL (S) in case of the delivery of an *aliud* (delivery of the wrong goods): E. Hondius, V. Heutger, C. Jeloschek, *et al.*, *Principles of European Law. Study Group on a European Civil Code. Sales (PEL S)*, Munich, Sellier, 2008, p. 183. See also for a similar reasoning under the DCFR, but only with regard to the delivery of an *aliud*: C. Von Bar and E. Clive, *Draft Common Frame of Reference (DCFR)*, Vol. II, Munich, Sellier, 2009, p. 1275.

129 S. Grundmann, 'Article 2. Conformity with the contract' in M.C. Bianca and S. Grundmann (eds.), *EU Sales Directive, Commentary*, Antwerp, Intersentia, 2002, (117) para. *in fine*. See also about this issue but with regard to the CESL: F. Zoll, 'Art. 99–105 CESL' in R. Schulze (ed.), *Common European Sales Law (CESL)*, Munich, Beck, 2012, (463) pp. 466–67 (see also Art. 130 CESL).

the ODSD Proposal. Indeed, the excess delivery by the seller equates to a lack of conformity with the contract. This means that the consumer has the right to invoke a remedy under the ODSD Proposal, and not the other way around. It seems logical that if the seller wants to claim restitution of the excess in quantity, he can only do so under the condition that he will not burden or disturb the consumer. The seller will be obliged to take the excess in quantity back if the consumer requests him to do so.

A late delivery[130] and a delivery at the wrong place cannot be an example of a 'non-conformity of the *goods*'. Indeed, a late delivery or a delivery at the wrong place can be considered as non-conforming with some contractual terms (or statutory requirements) about the time of delivery and the place of delivery, but cannot be equated with a non-conformity of the goods. Conforming goods are delivered, but not at the agreed time or not at the agreed place. If the concept of conformity under the ODSD Proposal is restricted to '(non-)conformity of the goods', the remedies introduced by the ODSD Proposal will *not* be applicable. Moreover, with regard to a late delivery, it seems that the CRD regulates this aspect. Indeed, Article 18 CRD prescribes the obligation to deliver in a timely fashion and provides for the remedies in case of a late delivery. This aspect seems to be resolved. Nevertheless, there is still no harmonised solution for goods that are delivered at the wrong place. National contract law will be applicable. Therefore, it is crucial that the drafters of the ODSD Proposal clearly resolve this issue by fine-tuning the concept of 'conformity' or by indicating expressly whether the prescribed remedies are also applicable in case of a delivery at the wrong place.

3.4.2. *Lack of Conformity and* Force Majeure

The seller will be 'liable' for any lack of conformity (if the lack of conformity existed at the time as indicated in Article 8 ODSD Proposal, see below, Section 4.1). This means that a lack of conformity will imply that the consumer can invoke certain remedies (see Article 9 *et seq*. ODSD Proposal and the chapter by Claeys and Vancoillie and the chapter by Straetmans and Meys). Does this 'liability' mean that a lack of conformity must be due to an unexcused non-performance of the seller? Or can the lack of conformity also be caused by an excused non-performance (*force majeure*).

When we examine this issue in the CSD, the same difficult question arises.[131] It is clear that the consumer can invoke the remedies of the CSD in

130 See *contra* (with regard to the CSD): S. Grundmann, 'Article 2. Conformity with the contract' in M.C. Bianca and S. Grundmann (eds.), *EU Sales Directive, Commentary*, Antwerp, Intersentia, 2002, (117) para. 5.

131 See about this topic extensively: S. Jansen, *Prijsvermindering: remedie tot bijsturing van contracten*, Antwerp, Intersentia, 2015, para. 349.

the case of unexcused non-performance, but is this also the case for excused non-performance? Article 3(1) CSD states: 'The seller shall be *liable* to the consumer for *any lack of conformity* which exists *at the time the goods were delivered*' (emphasis added). The reference to 'liability' ('*aansprakelijkheid*'), might refer to 'contractual liability' and is often connected to an 'unexcused non-performance'.[132] The CSD itself does not specify anything about frustration or *force majeure* and the applicability of remedies in this regard. The French author Paisant correctly points out that the CSD is absolutely silent about this issue.[133] The French author Mathieu is of the opinion that the seller is liable, independent from the fact he is responsible for the non-performance.[134] The English author Whittaker states that all the remedies of the CSD can be invoked in case of excused and unexcused non-performances.[135] German doctrine seems to accept that the consumer can also invoke the remedies of the CSD in case of excused non-performances.[136] A complicating factor is that the liability of the seller for a lack of conformity is not expressly related to the 'passing of the risk' under the CSD.[137] Recital 14 of the CSD stipulates that any reference to the time of delivery does not imply that Member States have to change their rules about the passing of the risk. Does this mean that the CSD is not applicable to excused non-performances?[138] Or are the remedies in the event of a lack of conformity

132 See e.g. E. Dirix, B. Tilleman and P. Van Orshoven (eds.), *De Valks juridisch woordenboek*, Antwerp, Intersentia, 2004, pp. 15–16, B.A. Garner (ed.), *Black's Law Dictionary*, St. Paul, West Publishing Co., 2009, p. 997. *Cf.* also H.-W. am Zehnhoff *et al.* (eds.), *Le Docte, Legal dictionary in four languages*, Cambridge, Intersentia, 2011, p. 15.

133 G. Paisant, 'La transposition de la directive du 25 mai 1999 sur les garanties dans la vente de biens de consommation – Ordonnance du 17 février 2005', *La Semaine Juridique Edition Générale* 2005, vol. 25, I, (146) para. 33.

134 M.-L. Mathieu, 'La transposition des directives en droit français: maîtrise des mots, maîtrise sur les mots', *ERPL* 2012, (1277) p. 1302.

135 S. Whittaker, *Product Liability*, Oxford, OUP, 2005, p. 603 ('However, there is a further sense in which liability under article 2 is "strict", in that no fault in any sense (including negligence) in the seller need be shown by a buyer for "liability" to be established, and that a seller cannot escape liability by showing that a "defect of conformity" arose without fault on his part or through the fault of a third party'). Risk only passes on to the consumer on the moment of delivery (s. 20(4) Sale of Goods Act): M.G. Bridge, *The Sale of Goods*, Oxford, Clarendon Press, 2014, para. 4.09; J. Mackay, T. Cundy, S. McKeering, *et al.*, (eds.), *Halsbury's Laws of England, Sale of Goods and Supply of Services, Settlements*, Vol 91, London, Lexisnexis, 2012, para. 140.

136 S. Grundmann, 'Consumer sales – Remedies: Weber-Putz case' in E. Terryn, G. Straetmans and V. Colaert (eds.), *Landmark Cases of EU Consumer Law*, Antwerp, Intersentia, 2013, (725) p. 739.

137 See detailed about the transfer of risk in the CSD: M.C. Bianca, 'Article 3. Droits et remèdes du consommateur' in M.C. Bianca, S. Grundmann and S. Stijns (eds.), *La directive communautaire sur la vente, Commentaire*, Brussels-Paris, Bruylant-LGDJ, 2004, (179) p. 189.

138 Seems to defend this opinion (but uses the term 'fortuitous' loss): S. Grundmann, F. Gomez, M.G. Bridge, *et al.*, 'Introduction' in M.C. Bianca and S. Grundmann (eds.), *EU Sales Directive, Commentary*, Antwerp, Intersentia, 2002, (13) p. 36.

directly connected to a lack of conformity at the moment of delivery?[139] In sum, it remains very uncertain whether the CSD is also applicable in the event of an excused lack of conformity and whether remedies of the Directive can be applied under those circumstances.

Article 20 CRD *does* regulate the transfer of the risk for sales contracts where the trader *dispatches*[140] the goods to the consumer. This article prescribes that the risk passes to the consumer when he (or a third party indicated by the consumer and other than the carrier) has acquired *physical possession of the goods.*[141] As a consequence, the CRD explicitly connects the passing of the risk to the moment of delivery to the consumer (when the consumer/third party has acquired the physical possession of the goods). The implementation of this approach required a far-reaching transformation of the law in certain Member States connecting the passing of risk to the moment of the *consensus*. This means, however, that in the case where the trader delivers goods with a lack of conformity due to *force majeure*, the risk of this lack of conformity still lies with the seller (up until the transfer of risk). The trader will be *liable* for this lack of conformity (and will face claims for remedies invoked by the consumer), even if it is not his fault. After the introduction of these rules with regard to the transfer of risk, the question arose about the remedies that could be applied in case of a non-conformity due to a *force majeure* event that happened before delivery (before the transfer of risk). Would the remedies of the CSD be applicable, or the national rules on the remedies of excused non-performances?[142]

The ODSD Proposal is applicable to distance sales contracts, which means that the rules of transfer of the risk in the aforementioned Article 20 of CRD are applicable, because the seller (trader) *dispatches* the goods to the consumer (see above, Section 3.4.2). In our view, the fact that the transfer of risk only takes place at the moment of delivery (when the consumer/third party has acquired the physical possession of the goods) is a strong reason to argue that the seller will be liable for any non-conformity that happens before the transfer of risk, whether it is his fault or not. Article 8 ODSD Proposal also confirms this view by stating in 1(a) that the seller shall be *liable* for any lack of conformity with the contract which exists at the time when the consumer, or a third party indicated by the consumer and other than the carrier, has acquired physical possession of

139 *Cf.* M.C. Bianca, 'Article 3. Droits et remèdes du consommateur' in M.C. Bianca, S. Grundmann and S. Stijns (eds.), *La directive communautaire sur la vente, Commentaire*, Brussels-Paris, Bruylant-LGDJ, 2004, (179) p. 188. Seems to defend this opinion: C. Cauffman, 'De nieuwe wet op de consumentenkoop', *TPR* 2005, (787) paras. 52 and 54.

140 Rather confusing term; which will often imply, in our view, a distance contract.

141 The risk will pass to the consumer upon delivery to the carrier if the carrier was commissioned by the consumer to carry the goods and that choice was not offered by the trader.

142 See also about this issue: S. Jansen, 'Price reduction as a remedy in European contract law and the consumer acquis' in A. Keirse and M. Loos (eds.), *Alternative Ways to Ius Commune. The Europeanisation of Private Law*, Antwerp, Intersentia, 2012, (169) p. 188.

the goods.[143] This means that he is liable for any non-conformity (unexcused and excused) that exists at the moment of delivery (when the consumer/third party has acquired the physical possession of the goods).

4. RELEVANT TIME FOR ESTABLISHING CONFORMITY

4.1. GENERAL

The current CSD prescribes that the relevant time for establishing (non-) conformity with the contract is the moment of the delivery of the goods.[144] The ODSD Proposal (Article 8) provides for a more elaborate and detailed system differentiating between situations which require the installation of the goods (and whether the seller installs the goods or the consumer) and which do not require any installation of the goods, and depending on whether the carrier is chosen or not by the consumer.[145]

We have already touched upon the general rules about the relevant time for establishing conformity with the contract when examining the possibility whether the seller will also be liable for a lack of conformity in case of an excused non-performance (above, Section 3.4.2). Article 8 ODSD Proposal states that the seller shall be liable for any lack of conformity with the contract which *exists at the time* when (1) the consumer or a third party indicated by the consumer and other than the carrier has *acquired the physical possession* of the goods; or (2) the goods *are handed over* to the carrier chosen by the consumer, where that carrier was not proposed by the seller or where the seller proposes no means of carriage. The Explanatory Memorandum of the ODSD Proposal establishes also the link with the CRD.[146] The Memorandum explains that Article 8 states the time at which the conditions for the lack of conformity must be reunited in order to engage the liability of the seller for a lack of conformity. This time, according to the drafters of the Memorandum, *generally coincides with the time of the passing of risk*,[147] similarly to the CRD. The determining moment is, in principle, the moment when the consumer obtains control over the goods.

143 Or at the time the goods are handed over to the carrier chosen by the consumer, where that carrier was not proposed by the seller or where the seller proposes no means of carriage (Art. 8(1)(b) ODSD Proposal).

144 Art. 3(1) CSD. See about this rule: S. Grundmann, 'Article 2. Conformity with the contract' in M.C. Bianca and S. Grundmann (eds.), *EU Sales Directive, Commentary*, Antwerp, Intersentia, 2002, (117) para. 46.

145 Briefing document of 2016 by Rafał Mańko, PE 577.962, p. 5.

146 Explanatory Memorandum, p. 15.

147 See also Art. 105(1) CESL that explicitly links, in principle, the time to test conformity to the moment of the transfer of risk. See also e.g. O. Remien, 'Verpflichtungen des Verkäufers

One can wonder whether the rules contained in Article 8 ODSD Proposal will suffice for legal defects.[148] If the cause of the legal defect was already present *before* the relevant time for establishing conformity (i.e. the 'germs' of the legal defect were already present), the main rules of Article 8 ODSD Proposal do not seem to be problematic. But in the case of IP rights, it seems possible that a third party will make an appeal on such rights *after* the relevant time for establishing conformity with the contract. The question rises whether or not one can establish that the 'cause of the legal defect' was already present before the relevant time for establishing conformity (e.g. omission to register certain IP rights, etc.). Zoll suggests that a more relevant moment with regard to legal defects would be the time of the transfer of ownership of the goods.[149]

If the goods must be *installed* or are installed *under the control of the seller*, the completion of the installation will be considered as the moment when the consumer has acquired the physical possession of the goods (Article 8(2), first sentence ODSD Proposal).[150]

If the goods were to be *installed* by the *consumer*, the drafters take into account the reasonable time the consumer needs to install the goods (and in any case not later than 30 days after the rules prescribed by Article 8(1) ODSD Proposal) to establish the relevant time for conformity. The end of this reasonable period to install the goods shall be considered as the time when the consumer has acquired the physical possession of the goods (Article 8(2), second sentence ODSD Proposal).[151] Remien criticises (with regard to the CESL) the fact that after this 'reasonable period to install the goods', the 'relevant time' to establish (non-)conformity has elapsed.[152] He points out that when it is established that a lack of conformity results from an incorrect installation due to a shortcoming in the installation instructions *after* this reasonable period for installing the

nach EU-Kaufrecht' in M. Schmidt-Kessel (ed.), *Ein einheitliches europäisches Kaufrecht?*, Munich, Sellier, 2012, (307) p. 324; F. Zoll, 'Art. 99–105 CESL' in R. Schulze (ed.), *Common European Sales Law (CESL)*, Munich, Beck, 2012, (463) p. 488.

148 Argues (with regard to the CESL) that Art. 105 CESL does not suffice in case of legal defects: O. Remien, 'Artikel 99–105 GEK-E' in M. Schmidt-Kessel (ed.), *Der Entwurf für ein Gemeinsames Europäisches Kaufrecht. Kommentar*, Munich, Sellier, 2014, (537) p. 552. See also for this opinion: F. Zoll, 'Art. 99–105 CESL' in R. Schulze (ed.), *Common European Sales Law (CESL)*, Munich, Beck, 2012, (463) p. 488.

149 With regard to the CESL: F. Zoll, 'Art. 99–105 CESL' in R. Schulze (ed.), *Common European Sales Law (CESL)*, Munich, Beck, 2012, (463) p. 488. See also with regard to the CESL: R. Feltkamp and F. Vanbossele, 'The Optional Common European Sales Law: Better Buyer's Remedies for Seller's Non-Performance in Sales of Goods?', *ERPL* 2011, (873) 888 (the rules in Art. 102 CESL may be considered as related to an obligation of the transfer of ownership).

150 See also Art. 105(3) CESL.

151 See also Art. 105(3) CESL, which is less stringent because it does not refer to the 30-days rule and merely refers to a 'reasonable time for the consumer to install the goods'.

152 As long as the incorrect installation is due to a shortcoming in the installation instructions, this rule does not seem suitable: O. Remien, 'Artikel 99–105 GEK-E' in M. Schmidt-Kessel (ed.), *Der Entwurf für ein Gemeinsames Europäisches Kaufrecht. Kommentar*, Munich, Sellier, 2014, (537) 554.

goods, the liability of the seller will not be triggered. Nevertheless, we believe, one must take into account with regard to the ODSD Proposal that any lack of conformity which becomes apparent within two years from the 'the relevant time for establishing conformity with the contract' is *presumed* to have existed at that time. This is also the case for goods that are installed by the consumer. In this case, the period of two years starts to run from the moment the consumer has had reasonable time for the installation (but in any case not later than 30 days after the time indicated in the rules prescribed by Article 8(1) ODSD Proposal).

Also the rules about the relevant time for establishing conformity are mandatory.[153] Indeed, Article 18 ODSD Proposal prescribes that any contractual agreement that excludes or derogates from the national transposing measures to the detriment of the consumer (before the lack of conformity of the goods is made known to the seller by the consumer), shall not be binding on consumers.

4.2. REVERSAL OF THE BURDEN OF PROOF BY A PRESUMPTION: TWO-YEAR PERIOD

Taking into account the general rules concerning the allocation of the burden of proof, the burden of proving the non-conformity at the moment of delivery lies, in principle, with the buyer (the consumer). Nevertheless, already at the time of the introduction of the CSD, the Community legislator wanted to simplify the burden of proof of the consumer with regard to the 'moment of the existence of the non-conformity' in order to strengthen the functioning of the European Internal Market (consumer protection is only considered in secondary order).[154] Consequently, the CSD prescribes a presumption of non-conformity of six months in its Article 5(3):

> Unless proved otherwise, any lack of conformity which becomes apparent within *six months* of delivery of the goods shall be presumed to have existed at the time of delivery unless this presumption is incompatible with the nature of the goods or the nature of the lack of conformity (emphasis added).[155,156]

---

153 The Position Paper of the Notaries, p. 3, suggests that there will be an unwarranted fragmentation and complications in the case of mixed contracts (e.g. the sale of immovable and tangible goods; the sale of goods and the provision of services). Consequently, the Paper recommends providing for the possibility to derogate by contract from the relevant time for the assessment of (the lack of) conformity.

154 K. Sikorska, *The presumption of non-conformity in European consumer sales law*, The Hague, Eleven International Publishing, 2015, p. 50.

155 See (for the opinions) about this rule: S. Grundmann, 'Article 2. Conformity with the contract' in M.C. Bianca and S. Grundmann (eds.), *EU Sales Directive, Commentary*, Antwerp, Intersentia, 2002, (117) para. 47.

156 See also Art. 105(2) CESL; Art. 2:208 PEL (S) (E. Hondius, V. Heutger, C. Jeloschek, *et al.*, *Principles of European Law. Study Group on a European Civil Code. Sales (PEL S)*,

One of the most important new features of the ODSD Proposal – which is heavily supported by the European Consumer Organisation BEUC[157] – is that it introduces an extension of the presumption of a lack of conformity to *two years*, instead of six months, after the moment as indicated in Article 8(1) and 8(2) ODSD Proposal. Indeed, Article 8(3) ODSD Proposal states:

> Any lack of conformity with the contract which becomes apparent within two years from the time indicated in paragraphs 1 and 2 is presumed to have existed at the time indicated in paragraphs 1 and 2, unless this is incompatible with the nature of the goods or with the nature of the lack of conformity.

Some countries had already extended the period for shifting the burden of proof with regard to the CSD.[158] The Explanatory Memorandum assesses that the impact on businesses of the prolongation of the period for the shift of the burden of proof from six months to two years will not be significant.[159] Most businesses do not require today (under the consumer sales rules) from consumers that they prove the liability of the trader within the two-year legal guarantee period. There is, according to the consumer market study, a de facto reversal of the burden of proof during the entire two-year legal guarantee period.[160] Rather contradictorily to what just has been said, the Explanatory Memorandum also stresses that the alignment of the reversal of the burden of proof of two years with the legal guarantee period (see Article 14 ODSD Proposal about the time limits) will most likely lead to a higher level of consumer protection and will boost consumers' trust.[161]

On 4 June 2015 the Court of Justice rendered its long-expected judgment in *Froukje Faber v Autobedrijf Hazet ochten BV* with regard to the reversal of the burden of proof under the CSD.[162] Because the ODSD Proposal has to be explained in accordance with the current consumer acquis, this case might also

Munich, Sellier, 2008, pp. 219–21); Art. IV.A-2:308 DCFR (C. Von Bar and E. Clive, *Draft Common Frame of Reference (DCFR)*, Vol. II, Munich, Sellier, 2009, pp. 1311–12).

157 BEUC response, p. 22.

158 The Explanatory Memorandum refers to France, Portugal and Poland (p. 6). Indeed, Sikorska explains that Poland has extended this period to one year: K. Sikorska, *The presumption of non-conformity in European consumer sales law*, The Hague, Eleven International Publishing, 2015, pp. 196–202. Also the Consumer market study on the functioning of Legal and Commercial Guarantees for consumers in the EU, EU Commission, 2015, 57 (http://ec.europa.eu/consumers/consumer_evidence/market_studies/docs/legalguaranteesfinal_report_en.pdf) refers to France (two years), Portugal (two years) and Poland (one year).

159 Explanatory Memorandum, p. 12.

160 There is almost no change in the behaviour of the trader before or after the six-month period: Explanatory Memorandum, 12. See also (but implicitly): Consumer market study on the functioning of Legal and Commercial Guarantees for consumers in the EU, EU Commission, 2015, p. 58 *et seq.*

161 Explanatory Memorandum, p. 13.

162 C-497/13, *Froukje Faber v Autobedrijf Hazet Ochten BV*, ECLI:EU:C:2015:357.

have implications for the rules on the reversal of the burden of proof under the proposed Directive. The Court of Justice ruled amongst other things that Article 5(3) CSD is to be regarded as a provision of equal standing to a national rule which ranks as a rule of public policy, and that a national court must apply of its own motion any provision which transposes this rule into domestic law. It also clarified that the presumption of Article 5(3) CSD does not require the consumer to prove the *cause* of the lack of conformity or that the *origin* of the lack of conformity is due to the seller.[163]

5. (NO) NOTIFICATION OF A LACK OF CONFORMITY

The Explanatory Memorandum of the ODSD Proposal makes clear that consumers would not have the duty that they currently have under a number of national laws to notify a defect in the goods to the seller within a certain period of time from its discovery.[164] In addition, recital 25 of the ODSD Proposal states clearly that a notification obligation with regard to a lack of conformity should not be established.

Article 5(2) of the CSD provides that the Member States can introduce or maintain that the consumer must inform the seller of the lack of conformity within a period of two months from the date on which he detected such lack of conformity, in order to benefit from his rights.[165] The Belgian legislator did not provide for a binding period within which the consumer must inform the seller of a *lack of conformity* (Article 1649*quater*, §2 CC).[166] The parties may, according to this article in the Civil Code, agree upon a period, without this period being shorter than two months, as from the moment the consumer has established the lack of conformity.

The CESL only provides for a duty to examine and to notify of a lack of conformity in contracts between traders.[167] Article 121(1) CESL states the general rule that in a contract between traders the buyer must examine (or let examine) the goods within a reasonable period, not exceeding 14 days from the date of delivery of the goods.[168] Article 122 CESL requires in sales contracts between

---

163 See for a case note L. Traest, 'Ambtshalve opwerpen van de hoedanigheid van consument: een nieuw hoofdstuk in de rechtspraak van het Hof van Justitie' (note under Court of Justice 4 June 2015), *TBH* 2016, (356) pp. 356–66.

164 Explanatory Memorandum ODSD Proposal, pp. 3 and 13.

165 M. Loos, 'Consumer Sales Law in the Proposal for a Consumer Rights Directive', *ERPL* 2010, (15) p. 32.

166 See also the 19th recital of the CSD.

167 See detailed about these provisions M. Loos and H.N. Schelhaas, 'Commercial Sales: The Common European Sales Law Compared to the Vienna Sales Convention', *ERPL* 2013, (105) pp. 119–22.

168 Some detailed provisions follow in Art. 121(2) and (3) CESL.

traders that the buyer must notify the seller of the lack of conformity within a reasonable time, specifying the lack of conformity. If the buyer forgets to notify the lack of conformity within a reasonable time, he may not rely upon the lack of conformity and will lose his remedies. The notification period under Article 122 CESL starts to run as from when the goods are supplied or when the buyer discovers or ought to have discovered the lack of conformity. With regard to hidden defects, it is important to note that the buyer will in any case lose his right to rely on a lack of conformity if he does not give the seller notice of it within two years from the moment at which the goods were handed over to the buyer.

Loos has shown in a chapter about the 2008 CRD proposal his vigorous aversion to such a duty to notify of a lack of conformity by the consumer.[169] Article 28(4) of the proposed Consumer Rights Directive (which did not make it into the finally adopted Directive (CRD)) introduced the rule that the consumer is obliged to inform the seller of the lack of conformity within two months in order to be able to call upon his remedies. According to Loos, this notification duty reduces the consumer protection for a significant number of consumers in the EU. A consumer may be unaware of such a duty to notify.[170] Also the European consumer organisation BEUC rejects such an obligation to notify a defect within a certain period of time after discovery as being 'burdensome and unsubstantiated'.[171] Consumers would often be, according to this organisation, unaware of such a notification duty. In any case, sanctions due to a lack of such notification must be avoided. Loos and BEUC will probably welcome the new approach of the ODSD Proposal of banning any notification duty of the consumer with regard to a lack of conformity (for this opinion, see also the chapter by Straetmans and Meys in this volume).

Nevertheless, in our opinion, two interests have to be balanced: it is true that the lack of a duty to notify the seller about a non-conformity might result in a greater flexibility to invoke a non-conformity by the consumer (and later on, to apply remedies), but at the same time it significantly reduces the protection of the seller.[172] However, in our opinion it is essential that a creditor (consumer or not) always informs the debtor about a *lack of conformity* with the contract within

---

169 M. Loos, 'Consumer Sales Law in the Proposal for a Consumer Rights Directive', *ERPL* 2010, (15) pp. 33–34. See also detailed about the examination and notification duties under the PEL (S) and the DCFR: M.B.M. Loos, 'Sales Law in the DCFR', *SSRN, Centre for the Study of European Contract Law Working Paper Series No. 2010/04*, 2010, (1) pp. 21–25.

170 With regard to Art. III.-3:107 DCFR: C. Von Bar and E. Clive, *Draft Common Frame of Reference (DCFR)*, Vol. I, Munich, Sellier, 2009, p. 807. See also: M.B.M. Loos, 'Sales Law in the DCFR', *SSRN, Centre for the Study of European Contract Law Working Paper Series No. 2010/04*, 2010, (1) p. 24.

171 BEUC response, p. 25.

172 See about the DCFR (but about the requirement to notify remedies): I. Samoy and T. Dang Vu, 'Performance and non-performance in the DCFR' in V. Sagaert, M. Storme and E. Terryn (eds.), *The draft common frame of reference: a national and comparative perspective*, Antwerp-Oxford, Intersentia, 2011, (53) para. 69.

a reasonable period after its discovery, mainly for reasons of proof concerning the passing of risk (has the non-conformity of the goods appeared before or after the passing of risk?).[173,174] At the very least, under some circumstances, the obligation to perform one's obligations in good faith would require such a notification duty, which is clearly not the case under the current Proposal. Nevertheless, it has to be admitted that the sanction for not notifying, which is often 'losing all remedies' altogether, is quite harsh and should be mitigated.

6. CONCLUSION

Both the ODSD Proposal and the (already nationally implemented) CSD concentrate on tangible and moveable goods. Nevertheless, both directives will have an exclusive scope of application if the ODSD Proposal is adopted and implemented. Whilst the CSD would be solely applicable to face-to-face contracts, the ODSD would be limited to distance sales contracts, such as online sales. This means that distance sales contracts will be excluded from the scope of application of the CSD (Article 19 ODSD Proposal). Legal certainty will be ensured by the fact that recital 15 of the ODSD Proposal states that the rules of this proposal should be applied and interpreted in a manner consistent with the rules of the CSD and the CRD (as interpreted by the case law of the Court of Justice of the European Union).

Both set of rules regulate B2C sales contracts in a patchy way because they only regulate rules related to the conformity of the goods, the liability of the seller, the consumer's remedies in case of a lack of conformity, commercial guaranties and the right of redress of the seller. The ODSD Proposal is more complete in comparison to the CSD by introducing rules with regard for example to third party rights. Both set of rules do not affect national general contract law with regard to rules on formation, the validity or effects of contracts including the consequences of the termination of a contract (Article 1(4) ODSD Proposal).

Although one would expect that the new rules would fit into the system of the CSD – which is the case for most definitions stemming from the *acquis communautaire* – we also encountered some important differences.

A first difference is the way of regulating the requirements of the conformity of the goods (above, Section 3.1 *et seq.*). In the CSD, the conformity criteria,

---

173 See for the same opinion: R. Feltkamp and F. Vanbossele, 'The Optional Common European Sales Law: Better Buyer's Remedies for Seller's Non-Performance in Sales of Goods?', *ERPL* 2011, (873) pp. 896–97.

174 We have already established the link between the passing of risk and the relevant time for establishing conformity (cf. above, Section 4.1 *et seq.*). We also stress the important relation between the relevant time for establishing conformity and the presumption of a lack of conformity of two years (Art. 8(3) ODSD Proposal, above, Section 4.2).

objective *and* subjective, are regulated in one article. Furthermore, there is a presumption of conformity if the cumulative criteria are met (Article 2(2) CSD). The ODSD Proposal clearly distinguishes between the subjective and the objective criteria, ranging them under different articles (Articles 4–7 ODSD Proposal), without working with a 'presumption of conformity'. Nevertheless, with regard to the content, the criteria are very similar, but the ODSD Proposal is more explicit and clear (e.g. with regard to conformity with pre-contractual statements), which can only be applauded.

A second difference lies in the fact that the ODSD Proposal clearly contains a regulation for legal defects and third party rights (Article 7 and recital 21 ODSD Proposal), whilst this is not the case in the CSD, leading to legal uncertainty (above, Section 3.3.2.2).

The third and probably the most important new feature of the ODSD Proposal is that it introduces an extension of the presumption of a lack of conformity to *two years*, as opposed to six months after the moment as indicated in Article 8(1) and (2) ODSD Proposal (above, Section 4.2). Closely connected to this, we must also point at the more detailed rules of the ODSD Proposal with regard the relevant time for establishing conformity (above, Section 4.1).

We can conclude that the introduction of the ODSD Proposal would lead to further fragmentation of consumer sales law. A different legal system would apply in case of face-to-face consumer sale transactions compared to online consumer transactions, which is neither very transparent to consumers nor practicable for commercial sellers. The difference is most striking with regard to the presumption of a lack of conformity which is extended to *two years*, instead of six months. A better solution would have been to take the time to integrate online and distance sales in a revised and uniform Consumer Sales Directive.

PROPOSAL FOR A DIRECTIVE ON DIGITAL CONTENT

Scope of Application and Liability for a Lack of Conformity*

Simon GEIREGAT and Reinhard STEENNOT

* This chapter was last updated on 3 June 2016.

1. INTRODUCTION

In December 2015, the European Commission proposed a Directive on certain aspects concerning contracts for the supply of digital content.[1] The proposal is to be situated in the EU's strategy to create a digital single market[2] and aims at stimulating the digital economy.[3] To achieve this goal while ensuring a high level of consumer protection,[4] harmonising part of the law on contracts for the supply of digital content is considered necessary.[5]

1.1. SCOPE

As the title of the Proposal suggests, only some aspects of contracts for the supply of digital content are covered. According to its Article 1, the Proposal deals with (1) rules on the conformity of digital content with the contract, (2) remedies in case of lack of conformity and the modalities for the exercise of such remedies, and (3) rules on the modification of digital content and on the termination of

1 Proposal of 9 December 2015 for a Directive of the European Parliament and of the Council on certain aspects concerning contracts for the supply of digital content, COM(2015) 634 final, http://eur-lex.europa.eu/legal-content/EN/TXT/?uri=CELEX:52015PC0634 (hereinafter referred to as: the Proposal).

2 *Cf.* Communication (Commission) to the European Parliament, the Council, the European Economic and Social Committee and the Committee of the Regions, 'A Digital Single Market Strategy for Europe', COM(2015)100 final, http://eur-lex.europa.eu/legal-content/EN/TXT/?uri=CELEX:52015DC0192.

3 Recital 1 of the Proposal.

4 *Cf.* Arts. 114(3) and 169 Treaty on the Functioning of the European Union.

5 Recital 2 of the Proposal.

long-term contracts. Although not explicitly mentioned in Article 1, the Proposal also determines when and to whom the digital content has to be supplied.[6] At this point it should be mentioned that some other aspects were already fully[7] harmonised by the 2011 Consumer Rights Directive.[8] Examples thereof are the rules on pre-contractual information and the right to withdrawal.[9] The Proposal is therefore said to supplement that Directive.[10]

1.2. HARMONISATION LEVEL

EU consumer protecting directives can be based on either minimum or maximum (full) harmonisation. In case of minimum harmonisation, Member States retain the ability to adopt national provisions that offer a higher level of protection than the Directive. The only requirement thereof is that these additional protection measures are compatible with the principles of free movement of goods and services.[11] In case of maximum or full harmonisation, Member States can neither introduce nor maintain measures that offer additional protection to consumers.[12] The Directive then does not only determine the minimum of protection consumers are entitled to, but also the maximum of protection that can be offered.

The Proposal clearly pursues full harmonisation. It explicitly determines that Member States cannot maintain or introduce provisions diverging from those laid down in the proposed Directive. This precludes the enactment of both more stringent and more tolerant provisions.[13] This differs from the approach

6 Art. 5 of the Proposal. See below, at Section 3.

7 See below, at Section 1.2.

8 Directive 2011/83/EU of the European Parliament and the Council of 25 October 2011 on consumer rights, amending Council Directive 93/13/EEC and Directive 1999/44/EC of the European Parliament and of the Council and repealing Council Directive 85/577/EEC and Directive 97/7/EC of the European Parliament and of the Council, *OJ* L 304 of 22 November 2011, 64 (hereinafter referred to as: the Consumer Rights Directive).

9 *Cf.* Fact sheet (Commission) 'Digital Contracts for Europe – Question & Answer', 9 December 2015, MEMO/15/6265, http://europa.eu/rapid/press-release_MEMO-15-6265_en.htm (hereinafter referred to as: Commission Digital Contracts Q&A, MEMO/15/6265), 3 (grid). Page numbers refer to the PDF version.

10 Explanatory Memorandum accompanying the Proposal of 9 December 2015 for a Directive of the European Parliament and of the Council on Certain Aspects concerning Contracts for the Supply of Digital Content, COM(2015)634 final, http://eur-lex.europa.eu/legal-content/EN/TXT/?uri=CELEX:52015PC0634 (hereinafter referred to as: Explanatory Memorandum), 3.

11 V. Mak, 'Review of the Consumer Acquis: Towards Full Harmonization?', *ERPL* 2009, (55) 58–59; C. Twigg-Flesner, 'No Sense of Purpose or Direction? The Modernization of European Consumer Law', *ERCL* 2007, (198) 204.

12 Judgment in *VTB-VAB v Total Belgium*, C-261/07, EU:C:2009:244. C. Twigg-Flesner and D. Metcalfe, 'The proposed Consumer Rights Directive – Less Haste, More Thought?', *ERCL* 2009, (368) 371.

13 Art. 4 of the Proposal.

used in the 1999 Consumer Sales Directive.[14] The latter concerns the lack of conformity of *goods* and is based on the principle of minimum harmonisation.[15] Several recently enacted directives like the Consumer Rights Directive, however, already pursued full harmonisation. According to the Commission, full harmonisation is necessary in order to create legal certainty for professionals and to build consumer trust. Only full harmonisation will entail that professional suppliers no longer have to fear the application of more stringent laws of the consumer's state of habitual residence. Hence, they will no longer need to bear the research costs resulting from differing national laws. For consumers, full harmonisation means surety that they will receive the same protection when they obtain digital content from suppliers established in other Member States.[16]

Finally, true full harmonisation can only be realised if neither the implementing Member States, nor the contracting parties can deviate from the rules set out. Save when otherwise provided for, all rules in the Proposal therefore are mandatory law, unless and to the extent deviation is favourable to the consumer.[17]

1.3. OUTLINE

This chapter first focuses on the scope of the Proposal (Article 3). Next, it deals with supply of digital content, i.e. the questions of when and to whom the digital content are to be supplied (Article 5). The core analysis of this chapter, however, addresses the conformity requirements for digital content. That subject is split into discussions about the general conformity requirements in Article 6 on the one hand, and the specific provisions on integration (Article 7) and 'legal defects' (Article 8) on the other. The burden of proof (Article 9) and the time for (non-)conformity to be assessed will subsequently be elaborated on together with liability (Article 10). Definitions (Article 2) and Recitals are dealt with where they are relevant.

---

14 Directive 1999/44/EC of the European Parliament and of the Council of 25 May 1999 on certain aspects of the sale of consumer goods and associated guarantees, *OJ* L 171 of 7 August 1999, 12, http://eur-lex.europa.eu/legal-content/EN/TXT/?uri=CELEX:31999L0044 (hereinafter referred to as: the Consumer Sales Directive).

15 Art. 8 Consumer Sales Directive.

16 In this chapter we will not elaborate on this. Reference is made to the chapter by G. Straetmans in this volume. *Cf.* J. Smits, 'Full Harmonization of Consumer Law? A Critique on the Draft Directive on Consumer Rights', *ERPL* 2010, (5) 6–7; G. Howells and R. Schulze, 'Overview of the proposed Consumer Rights Directive' in G. Howells and R. Schulze (eds.), *Modernising and Harmonising Consumer Contract Law*, Munich, Sellier, 2009, (3) 8; P. Rott and E. Terryn, 'The Proposal for a Directive on Consumer Rights: No Single Set of Rules', *ZEuP* 2009, (456) 460–62. These authors are all quite sceptical about these arguments in the context of the Consumer Rights Directive.

17 Art. 19 of the Proposal.

2. SCOPE OF APPLICATION

Article 3 of the Proposal determines its scope of application. It determines which contracts are governed and which are excluded from its range. Furthermore, it indicates the relationship between the Proposal and other EU and national law.

2.1. CONTRACTS FOR THE SUPPLY OF DIGITAL CONTENT IN EXCHANGE FOR A PRICE OR DATA

The Proposal applies to any contract (1) where the supplier supplies digital content to the consumer or undertakes to do so, *and* (2) in exchange, a price is to be paid or the consumer actively provides counter-performance other than money in the form of personal data or any other data (emphasis added).[18] In order to fully grasp the meaning of this provision several concepts need to be addressed. Most of them are defined.

2.1.1. Digital Content

2.1.1.1. Quid?

The digital content definition is split up into three alternative descriptions. It suffices to meet one of these in order to qualify as such. Firstly, digital content can be (a) data which is produced and supplied in digital form, for example video, audio applications, digital games and any other software. Secondly, it may also be (b) a service allowing the creation, processing or storage of data in digital form, where such data is provided by the consumer. Lastly, it might also be (c) a service allowing sharing of and any other interaction with data in digital form provided by other users of the service.[19]

– *Data in digital form*

The first part of the definition resembles the digital content concept in the Consumer Rights Directive.[20] Pursuant to that Directive, the term *only* relates to data which are produced *and* supplied in digital form.[21] The Proposal's very definition non-exhaustively specifies that it includes, inter alia, video, audio,

18 Art. 3(1) of the Proposal.

19 Art. 2(1) of the Proposal.

20 On the digital content concept in Belgian law transposing the Consumer Rights Directive, see H. Jacquemin, 'La protection du consommateur de contenus numériques', *DCCR* 2015, ed. 3–4, (5) (hereinafter referred to as: J. Jacquemin, *Contenus numériques*) 11–12, para. 7.

21 Art. 2(11) Consumer Rights Directive.

applications, digital games and 'any other software', such as downloadable apps.[22] Needless to say that this first part of the definition does not solely envisage 'computer programs', a more narrowly definable term.[23] E-books, for example, also come under this category, whereas paper-printed books bought online do not, for they are not supplied in digital form.[24]

– *Services*

The Commission did not confine itself to copy-pasting the existing definition and adding some examples. Digital content should be understood in a broad(er) sense. It encompasses all types of digital content so as to be 'future-proof' in a 'technologically fast changing market'.[25] Therefore, digital content additionally indicates two types of *services*. These services should either allow (1) the creation, processing or storage of data in digital form, where the data have been provided by the consumer, or allow (2) sharing of and any other interaction with data in digital form provided by other users of the service.[26] This is the first time that these *services* have been qualified as digital content.

The second category of services 'allowing for sharing of [or] interaction with data in digital form provided by other users' seems quite clear. Facebook, Twitter and Instagram are prime examples thereof. The first category of services may, by contrast, require some explanation. First, it calls for emphasis that it only governs the creation, processing or storage of *data provided by the consumer.* The Preamble explains that 'data *generated* by consumers' comprises a wide range of examples. These include digital images, video and audio files, blogs, discussion forums, text-based collaboration formats, posts, chats, 'tweets', logs, podcasting, content created on mobile devices, content created in the context of online virtual environments, ratings and collections of links referring to online content.[27] Hence, the service should allow the consumer to do any of the following: to create data, to process data, or to store data in digital form. Examples include the consumer's possibility to make a digital photo-album or to store data in the cloud.

Services that merely 'provide access' clearly are outside the digital content definition. In addition, the Proposal expressly excludes its application to the 'Internet of Things'[28] and to data which are necessary for the interaction between

---

22 Art. 2(1)(a) of the Proposal.

23 In copyright law, authors usually define it something like 'an ordered set of self-executable instructions'. *Cf.* D. Davidson, 'Protecting Computer Software: a Comprehensive Analysis', *Jurimetrics Journal* 1983, (337) 340–41, who distinguishes software from a computer program.

24 *Cf.* in addition J. Jacquemin, *Contenus numériques*, 5, para. 1.

25 Recital 11 of the Proposal. *Cf.* Explanatory Memorandum, 11.

26 Art. 2(1)(a) and (b) of the Proposal.

27 Recital 15 of the Proposal.

28 The Internet of Things is generally defined as an 'infrastructure of networked physical objects'. Whereas the old, common internet allowed people and things to be interconnected,

machines.[29] Lastly, 3D printing services are also out of the Proposal's range, except for the supply of visual modelling files that precedes actual printing and physical delivery of the printed goods.[30]

2.1.1.2. Irrelevance of the Incorporating Medium

The Proposal's scope in principle[31] also covers 'every durable medium incorporating digital content in such a way that the goods function exclusively as a carrier of the digital content'.[32] 'Durable medium' is to be read as 'tangible medium'.[33] It encompasses DVDs, CDs, CD-ROMs and data sticks. As a result, it is safe to conclude that the medium used to transmit the digital content is not relevant. It does not matter whether the digital content is downloaded, streamed or supplied on a tangible medium. Moreover, it is irrelevant whether digital content supplied on a tangible medium, is sold as part of a distance sale or face-to-face.

As such, the same rules will apply to inter alia downloaded music and movie files (e.g. MP3 or MPEG files), streamed music and video (e.g. Spotify or Netflix) and to music and films incorporated in a traditional CD or DVD. In the latter case it will additionally be irrelevant whether the CD or DVD was bought online or in a local store. By contrast different contract law will govern the plummeting number of CD *supplies* for one thing, and the reviving number of vinyl (LP) *sales* for another. This is because content is stored on CDs in a *digital* form, while LP fabrication makes use of *analogue* groove modulation.

The Proposal no longer distinguishes digital content supplied on a tangible medium from content supplied otherwise, as far as the legal guarantee for conformity is concerned.[34] Consequently, it might herald[35] the end of a major deficit in consumer protection law.[36] At the moment it is completely unclear to

---

the Internet of Things allows devices ('smart objects') to interact and collaborate without immediate human intervention. W. Keith Robinson, 'Patent Law and Challenges for the Internet of Things', *Wake Forest J. Bus. & Intell. Prop. L.* 2014–15, (655) 661.

29 Recital 17 of the Proposal.

30 Recital 16, last phrase, of the Proposal.

31 Contrary to that rule, the provisions on the supply (Arts. 5 and 11 of the Proposal) are excluded. *Cf.* below, at Section 3.

32 Art. 3(3) of the Proposal.

33 A durable medium is defined in Art. 2(11) of the Proposal as 'any instrument which enables the consumer or the supplier to store information addressed personally to that person in a way accessible for future reference for a period of time adequate for the purposes of the information and which allows the unchanged reproduction of the information stored'. The concept of a durable medium is traditionally used in the context of information requirements. (*Cf.* Arts. 2(10), 7 and 8 Consumer Rights Directive.) It cannot be used in the context at issue. It should (and will) be replaced by 'tangible medium'.

34 The Consumer Rights Directive by contrast still makes that distinction. It is highly relevant to the withdrawal right.

35 However, see below, at Section 3.

36 J. Jacquemin, *Contenus numériques*, 20–21, para. 16; N. Helberger, L. Guibault, M. Loos, C. Mak, L. Pessers and B. van der Sloot, *Digital Consumers and the Law. Towards*

what extent consumer sales law applies to digital content that is not supplied on a durable medium. Moreover, doubts persist as to whether standard software can be considered goods, subject to consumer sales law. This is true even if it is supplied on a tangible medium.[37] Hence, unarguably, uniform legal guarantee rules for digital content have the potential of increasing legal certainty and consumer protection. Prerequisite to that aim is that these rules' substance is clear enough and sufficiently consumer-friendly.

The Proposal applies to goods incorporating digital content in such a way that the goods function '*exclusively* as a carrier of the digital content' (emphasis added).[38] This first of all means that different rules will apply when a consumer buys a movie on a DVD or a CD containing classical music on the one hand, and an empty DVD or CD for data storage on the other. In the former situation, the rules on digital content apply, in the latter they do not.

In the second place, the Proposal will not apply to digital content that is embedded in goods in such a way that 'it operates as an integral part of the goods and its functions are subordinate to the main functionalities of the goods'.[39] The consequences of that finding must be borne in mind. Every present-day car, for instance, contains software. Nevertheless the traditional consumer sales rules apply if the car does not function properly. Cars do not fit into the digital content definition. The Proposal's regime is thus not activated, not even if the lack of conformity is due to the software included in the car.[40]

2.1.2. In Exchange for a Price or the Active Provision of (Personal) Data

Not every supply of digital content comes within the Proposal's scope. It additionally requires that the consumer either needs to pay a price *or* has to actively provide counter-performance other than money in the form of personal data or any other data (emphasis added).[41] Contracts providing other or no counter-performances are not covered. Hence, the Proposal does not merely apply to all 'exchange' contracts[42] that deal with digital content, and *a fortiori* not to the supply of content free of charge.[43]

---

a Cohesive European Framework, Alphen aan den Rijn, Kluwer, 2013 (hereinafter referred to as: N. Helberger *et al.*, *Digital Consumers*), 3 and 17–18.

37 N. Helberger *et al.*, *Digital Consumers*, 21.

38 Art. 3(3) of the Proposal.

39 Recital 11 of the Proposal.

40 See, however, below, at Section 2.4.

41 Art. 3(1) of the Proposal.

42 Meaning *contrat d'échange* in the broadest sense (Art. 1702 French Civil Code; Art. 1702 Belgian Civil Code), including *swaps* and *barter agreements*.

43 J. Sénéchal, 'The Diversity of the Services provided by Online Platforms and the Specificity of the Counter-performance of these Services – A Double Challenge for European and National Contract Law', *EuCML* 2016, (39) (hereinafter referred to as: J. Sénéchal, *Double Challenge*) 44. *Cf.* (on the exclusion of contracts without counter-performance) J. Jacquemin, *Contenus numériques*, 13–14, para. 9.

2.1.2.1. Price

'Price' is defined as 'money that is due [by the consumer] in exchange for digital content supplied'.[44] The concept of money, however, is not defined. In our view it is to include all kinds of money and not solely legal tender.[45] This is a logical conclusion for various reasons. First, it is true that legal tender in one Member State does not necessarily constitute legal tender in another. Second, a restrictive interpretation of the money concept would limit the Proposal's scope. It would for that matter be unacceptable if the Proposal were not to be applicable if the consumer for instance pays by electronic money. Taking into account the function of the definition at hand, one could even argue that Bitcoin and other virtual currency comes under it. Finally, the method of payment is irrelevant. Pay-per-download, pay-per-bundle, pay-per-use, flat access fees and subscription fees are all covered.

2.1.2.2. Provision of Data

The consumer does not have to be bound to pay money. The Proposal equally applies if the consumer's counter-performance takes the form of the provision of data. Accordingly, the Commission recognises that information about individuals often has a value comparable to money within our digital economy.[46] Consumer-provided data can be used for reselling or for targeted advertising.[47] Or, as Axel Voss[48] restated: 'if you are not paying for it, you're the currency'.[49]

Many contracts would escape the Proposal's field of application, if it were limited to contracts exchanging digital content for money. In practice digital content is often supplied in exchange for other counter-performances, consisting of access to personal data or other data.[50] Many social media make use of that business model. Conversely, using diverging approaches based on the nature of the counter-performance might amount to a discrimination between business

---

44 Art. 2(6) of the Proposal.

45 Legal tender is any official medium of payment recognized by law that can be used by a debtor to terminate his contractual obligation to pay (i.e. to extinguish his debt), or to meet a financial obligation.

46 N. Helberger *et al.*, *Digital Consumers*, 162–63 and 165–66; J. Sénéchal, *Double Challenge*, 43.

47 N. Helberger *et al.*, *Digital Consumers*, 5.

48 Member of the European Parliament; Vice-Chair of the JURI Committee on Legal Affairs.

49 The original expression 'If you are not paying for it, you're not the customer; you're the product being sold' presumably stems from Andrew Lewis. *Cf.* G. Magalhães Martins and J.V. Rozatti Longhi, 'Internet Service Providers' Liability for Personal Damages on Social Network Websites', *US-China L. Rev.* 2014, (286) 286.

50 *Cf.* M. Loos, 'The Regulation of Digital Content B2C Contracts in CESL', *euvr* 2014, (146) (hereinafter referred to as: M. Loos, *Digital Content B2C in CESL*) 148.

models. It could even entail an unjustified incentive for businesses to shift towards offering digital content against data.[51] In sum, simply changing business models would suffice to escape the proposed regime. Besides, paying a price surely is not a prerequisite for nonconformity of the digital content to impact on a consumer's economic interests.

– *Conditions*

The Proposal only covers content-for-data contracts if two cumulative conditions are met. First, the supplier has to *request* the data. Second, the consumer is to *actively provide* the data to the supplier, either directly or indirectly. The concepts of 'requesting' and 'actively providing' are undefined. A Recital explains that active provision of data by the consumer can for example take place through individual registration or on the basis of a contract which allows access to consumers' data, which can include photos.[52]

The Preamble furthermore specifies that the Proposal does not relate to situations where the supplier merely *collects* information, even if that is personal data. Gathering IP addresses for example is insufficient. The same is true for collecting other automatically generated information such as information collected and transmitted by a cookie. The acceptance by the consumer of a cookie, is not considered an active provision of data by the consumer. Likewise, there is no active provision when a consumer is to endure advertisements exclusively to gain access to the digital content.[53] Hence, unskippable commercials preceding YouTube videos are excluded from the intended counter-performance.[54]

In our view there is a thin line between requesting and collecting data. Similarly, it may prove difficult to tell active from inactive provision of data by the consumer. The use of these non-defined concepts undoubtedly will create discussions when determining the exact scope of the Proposal. Legal certainty is perhaps better served if the rules are applied whenever the supplier collects data, irrespective of the active provision thereof by the consumer.

– *Exemptions*

Some noticeable situations are excluded from the concept of counter-performance by data provision. The Proposal does not apply to the extend the collection of the consumer's *personal* data is *strictly necessary* for the performance of the contract.[55] The consumer might for instance disclose his geographical location to ascertain the proper functioning of a mobile application, like a

51 Recital 13 of the Proposal.
52 Recital 14, 1st phrase, of the Proposal.
53 Recital 14, 3rd phrase, of the Proposal.
54 That finding is regrettable. *Cf.* M. Loos, *Digital Content B2C in CESL*, 148.
55 Art. 3(4), 1st phrase, of the Proposal.

navigation app.[56] Or, he could insert data on his weight and height in order for an app to calculate his BMI. The provision of these data will as such not entail application of the Proposal. The same holds true when personal data are *strictly necessary* to meet legal requirements.[57] Figure the consumer's registration is required by law for security and identification purposes.

The Proposal will however again be applicable if the supplier further processes the exempted personal data in a way which is incompatible with the original purpose,[58] i.e. either performance of the contract or meeting legal requirements. Imagine for instance that the consumer-provided weight and height data are afterwards sold to third parties and/or used for targeted advertising. It is doubtful however whether this explicit prohibition will suffice to exclude all abuses of the exemption for personal data that is strictly necessary for the contract. Most of the time it will be for the supplier to determine what data are 'necessary'. Hence, changing business model could lead to the requalification of certain data as 'necessary for the contract'. As a result, a supplier can easily circumvent the scope of application of the Proposal. He could, for instance, send download links to email addresses instead of allowing online downloads directly from his website. The consumer's email address consequently becomes data necessary for the performance of the contract.

An additional exemption is laid down with regard to data, other than personal data. This exception applies if the supplier requests the consumer to provide data for the purpose of ensuring that the digital content is in conformity with the contract, or of meeting legal requirements. The exemption's effect is, however, limited by the requirement that the supplier does not use that data for commercial purposes.[59]

A closer look reveals that Article 3(4) substantially distinguishes between personal and other data actively provided by the consumer. For the exemption to apply, personal data should be *strictly necessary* for the performance of the contract. That wording implies that the supplier cannot execute the contract without these data. Other data by contrast have to be provided *for the purpose of ensuring* that the digital content is in conformity with the contract. In addition, personal data cannot be used for any further processing in *any way incompatible* with the original purpose. Other data by contrast cannot be used for *commercial* purposes.[60]

The concept of personal data is not defined in the Proposal. A definition can, however, be found in data protection law, where personal data is generally

56 Recital 14, 2nd phrase, of the Proposal.
57 Art. 3(4), 1st phrase, of the Proposal.
58 Art. 3(4), 1st phrase, *in fine*, of the Proposal.
59 Art. 3(4), 2nd phrase, of the Proposal.
60 See above.

described as 'any information which relates to an identified or identifiable natural person'.[61] The exact boundaries of the term are additionally set by the Article 29 Working Party on the Protection of Individuals with regard to the Processing of Personal Data. Both objective and subjective information about a person in whatever capacity may be considered as personal data, irrespective of the technical medium on which it is contained. It is not necessary that these data immediately allow for an identification of the natural person. It is sufficient that an identification is possible on the basis of means that can reasonably be expected to be used when trying to identify a natural person.[62]

The concept of personal data has a very broad meaning.[63] This should be borne in mind when determining the applicable rules. Still, a lot of data relating to individuals will be considered 'other' data. Illustrations of other than personal data include photos and videos that do not allow their viewer to identify a natural person. General email addresses like info@domain.com constitute another example. Certain technical information provided by consumers also qualifies as non-personal data. Imagine a consumer's online acquisition of a computer program. Say the consumer indicates on the supplier's website that he uses Microsoft Windows 10 64-bit as an operating system. This kind of data does not allow the supplier to identify the consumer. Lots of other people use that operating system. The provision of this information certainly is necessary for the digital content to be in conformity with the contract. If the consumer does not provide it, then the supplier will be unable to supply a computer program version that is interoperable.[64]

2.1.3. Contract for Supply

The Proposal applies to contracts for the supply of digital content. The existence of a *contract* thus is prerequisite. That term is defined as 'an agreement intended to give rise to obligations or other legal effects'.[65] Hence, if the Proposal is enacted, EU consumer law will have an express,[66] autonomous meaning of the contract

---

61 Art. 2(a) Directive 95/46/EC of the European Parliament and of the Council of 24 October 1995 on the protection of individuals with regard to the processing of personal data and on the free movement of such data, *OJ* L 281 of 23 November 1995, 31 (hereinafter referred to as: Data Protection Directive).

62 Article 29 Data Protection Working Party, Opinion 4/2007 on the concept of personal data, 01248/07/EN - WP 136, http://ec.europa.eu/justice/data-protection/article-29/documentation/opinion-recommendation/files/2007/wp136_en.pdf (hereinafter referred to as: Article 29 WP Opinion 4/2007).

63 *Cf.* Article 29 WP Opinion 4/2007, 4.

64 See below, at Section 4.1.2.1. (Interoperability and functionality).

65 Art. 2(7) of the Proposal.

66 Since the enactment of the Unfair Terms Directive (Council Directive 93/13/EEC of 5 April 1993 on unfair terms in consumer contracts, *OJ* L 95 of 21 April 1993, 29) however, it was already argued that 'contract' was to be deemed an EU autonomous concept, because it often

concept. Its meaning is intended to encompass a broad scope and for example includes pre-contractual agreements like service level agreements.[67] The substance of the definition is hardly surprising. It largely corresponds to the definition used in the Draft Common Frame of Reference (DCFR)[68] and it is identical to that in the Common European Sales Law (CESL) Proposal.[69] Moreover, it seems compatible with Belgian law[70] and with old[71] and new[72] French contract law.

The contract's object needs to encompass the supply of digital content. 'Supply' is defined as 'providing access to digital content or making digital content available'.[73] That wording calls up the law on lease contracts.[74] It is of no relevance which techniques are used to allow the consumer to gain access, or to make the content available. The temporary or permanent nature of the supply is equally irrelevant. The only relevant issue is whether the contract's purpose consists in allowing the consumer to make 'use' of the digital content in exchange for a counter-performance.

Finally, it deserves mentioning that the Proposal applies irrespective of the legal nature of the contract. It does not matter whether the contract qualifies as a sale[75] or a service agreement, or even as a lease contract.

---

determines the scope of consumer protection rules. *Cf.* P. Cambie, *Onrechtmatige bedingen*, Brussels, Larcier, 2009, 56, para. 66.

67 *Cf.* Recital 18 of the Proposal.

68 Art. II.-1:101 DCFR. The DCFR is published by C. von Bar and E. Clive (eds.), *Principles, Definitions and Model Rules of European Private Law – Draft Common Frame of Reference (DCFR)* – Full Edition, I, Munich, Sellier, 2009 and http://ec.europa.eu/justice/contract/files/european-private-law_en.pdf.

69 Art. 2(a) of the Proposal of 11 October 2011 for a Regulation of the European Parliament and of the Council on a Common European Sales Law, COM(2011) 635 final, http://eur-lex.europa.eu/legal-content/EN/TXT/?uri=CELEX:52011PC0635 (hereinafter referred to as: CESL Proposal).

70 Art. 1101 Belgian Civil Code. *Cf.* R. Dekkers, A. Verbeke, N. Carette, K. Vanhove and G. Baeteman, *Handboek burgerlijk recht, III, Verbintenissen – Bewijsleer – Gebruikelijke contracten*, Antwerp, Intersentia, 2007, 8, para. 11; R. Vandeputte, *De overeenkomst*, Brussels, Larcier, 1977, 11.

71 *Cf.* J. Ghestin and I. Marchessaux-Van Melle, 'Les contrats d'adhésion et les clauses abusives en droit français et en droit européens (rapport français)' in J. Ghestin and M. Fontaine (eds.), *La protection de la partie faible dans les rapports contractuels. Comparaisons franco-belges*, Paris, L.G.D.J., 1996, (1) 4–7, paras. 4–9; B. Petit and S. Rouxel, 'Art. 1101 à 1108-2 – Contrats et obligations – Définition et classification des contrats' in *JurisClasseur Civil Code* 2013, para. 2.

72 Art. 1101 French Civil Code, as replaced by Art. 2 Act ('ordonnance') no 2016-131 of 10 February 2016 'portant réforme du droit des contrats, du regime général et de la preuve des obligations', *Journal Officiel* 11 February 2016, which entered into force on 1 October 2016.

73 Art. 2(11) of the Proposal.

74 J. Sénéchal, *Double Challenge*, 42.

75 J. Sénéchal, *Double Challenge*, 44.

2.1.4. *Consumers and Suppliers*

Ratione personae the application of the Directive is limited to contracts concluded between a *supplier* and a *consumer*.[76] Both concepts are defined.

2.1.4.1. Consumer

A consumer means 'every natural person who is acting for purposes which are outside that person's business, trade, craft or profession'.[77] This has become a standard definition in EU consumer law.[78] We therefore limit ourselves to reiterating that the expertise of the party to whom digital content is supplied is not relevant to determine whether a natural person can be qualified a consumer.[79] Even if a person is a digital content expert, he can still be a consumer. As soon as a natural person acquires digital content for private purposes, he is a consumer. The meaning of 'private purposes' will not be assessed in this chapter. We note, however, that it is regrettable that the EU legislator did not seize the opportunity to clarify the issue of so-called 'mixed purpose' transactions. The Proposal, in addition, nowhere states that the consumer concept should be interpreted in conformity with prior EU legislation. The parallel Online and Distance Sales of Goods Directive Proposal, by contrast, expressly provides that suggestion.[80]

The Proposal intends only to protect consumers. As a result, small and medium-sized enterprises purchasing digital content for their businesses will not be able to invoke that protection. For that matter it is irrelevant whether these businesses are legal persons or natural persons, and whether they have or lack digital expertise. The Commission stated that the protection of SMEs will be dealt with in later proposals.[81]

2.1.4.2. Supplier

The professional party involved is the supplier. That term is to mean every natural or legal person who is acting for purposes relating to that person's trade,

---

76 Art. 3(1) of the Proposal.

77 Art. 2(4) of the Proposal.

78 *Cf.* inter alia Art. 2(b) Unfair Terms Directive; Art. 2(a) Consumer Sales Directive; Art. 2(1) Consumer Rights Directive; Art. 2(f) of the Annex to CESL Proposal.

79 *Cf.* judgment in *Costea v SC Volksbank România SA*, C-110/14, EU:C:2015:538, where the CJEU held that a lawyer was to be considered a consumer, as he had concluded a mortgage credit agreement for private purposes.

80 *Cf.* Recital 15 of the Proposal of 9 December 2015 for a Directive of the European Parliament and of the Council on certain aspects concerning contracts for the online and other distance sales of goods, COM(2015)635 final, http://eur-lex.europa.eu/legal-content/EN/TXT/?uri=CELEX:52015PC0635 (hereinafter referred to as: Online and Distance Sales Directive Proposal).

81 Explanatory Memorandum, 11 (on Article 3).

business, craft or profession. It is irrelevant whether that person is privately or publicly owned. A person can still be considered a supplier if he acts through any other person who acts in his name or on his behalf.[82]

Traditionally, the concept of supplier is used to indicate that only persons acting in the course of their business have to meet the requirements laid down in EU consumer protection law. That is also true for this Proposal. Whoever supplies digital content to consumers on an occasional basis will not be subject to the Proposal, for he acts outside his trade or profession. A person who sells some DVDs of his personal collection cannot be considered a supplier of digital content. The reverse is true, by contrast, if one purchases DVDs on a large scale and intends to resell them. In practice, however, qualification will not always be easy.

In a digital environment it might prove difficult to ascertain at what exact point amateur sellers turn into professional suppliers within the meaning of the Proposal.[83] When they do, they can be held liable for any lack of conformity. Imagine an amateur who funds his blog through advertisements or a person who develops an app which can only be downloaded in exchange for a micropayment, i.e. a small price. To determine whether such individual has become a supplier, several interconnected criteria can be used. These include the organisational level, the offered amount of digital content, his turnover, the presence of a profit motive, the impression generated towards consumers.[84] A student who enables consumers to download an application he made as a homework assignment clearly will not be considered a supplier. By contrast, an IT expert continuously developing and selling applications through a well-developed and commercial-looking website and realising a turnover of thousands of euros will. It is not clear, however, where exactly on the spectrum the line is to be drawn.

In addition, persons do not necessarily (only) supply content they created themselves.[85] Suppose that a consumer uses a virtual platform like the Apple App Store or Google Play to purchase and download an app on his smartphone. Or imagine the consumer purchases a disk containing installable software, be it online or in a local store. Who is the supplier?[86] Is it the person with whom the consumer concludes the agreement? Or is it the person who has created the digital content or who is entitled to the intellectual property rights, i.e. a software developer or a right-holder? This is a paramount question. The supplier is the one liable in case of failure to supply the digital content and in case of lack

---

82 Art. 2(3) of the Proposal.

83 N. Helberger *et al.*, *Digital Consumers*, 8.

84 *Cf.* N. Helberger *et al.*, *Digital Consumers*, 45–51.

85 N. Helberger *et al.*, *Digital Consumers*, 6.

86 *Cf.* C. Busch, H. Schulte-Nölke, A. Wiewiórowska-Domagalska and F. Zoll, 'The Rise of the Platform Economy: A New Challenge for EU Consumer Law?', *EuCML* 2016, (3) (hereinafter referred to as: C. Busch *et al.*, *The Rise of the Platform Economy*) 7–8.

of conformity.[87] Pursuant to the Proposal, the consumer can only seek redress against a supplier.

A plain interpretation of the Proposal leads to the conclusion that only the immediate co-contracting party of the consumer[88] qualifies as the supplier.[89] First, this view is in line with Article 3(1), where it states the supplier is *contractually* obliged to supply the digital content. Moreover, Article 5(1) prescribes obligations the supplier is to meet *when performing the contract.* Article 11, furthermore, allows the consumer to terminate *the contract* if the supplier has failed to accordingly supply the digital content. Finally, Article 17 assumes that a supplier is held liable for failure to supply or for a lack of conformity. If that failure or lack results from an act or omission by (a) person(s) in earlier 'links' of the chain of transactions, the supplier is entitled to pursue remedies against that person(s).[90] This right of redress makes no sense if a party other than the direct contractual partner of the consumer was to be considered the supplier. Suppose, for the sake of the argument, that it were true that the consumer instead had to address another person than his immediate co-contracting party (*quod non*). An obligation of that kind would utterly erode the consumer protection aim pursued by the Proposal.

Some digital content requires the consumer to conclude so-called end-user licence agreements (EULAs). This is true for example for installable computer programs.[91] Our conclusions above can be extrapolated to that phenomenon. Hence, the person with whom the consumer has concluded the EULA can only be considered supplier if he at the same time actually *supplies* the digital content. Suppose a consumer purchases a Microsoft Office software pack in a local store. In that case the storekeeper will be considered the supplier. It is irrelevant to the current Proposal that the local storekeeper has no impact whatsoever on the conformity of the software pack, which presumably he cannot even test himself. The Proposal does not touch upon licence agreements or intellectual property in general.[92] The Commission chose to disregard EULAs concluded between a consumer and a professional licensor who is *not* the supplier. Overall the latter has a much stronger economical position than the supplier, though. The question therefore arises whether the current approach is justified. If the local storekeeper is held liable towards the consumer, he will encounter serious difficulties to recover his losses.[93]

---

87 Art. 10 of the Proposal. See below, at Section 5.3.

88 J. Sénéchal, *Double Challenge*, 42.

89 *Cf.* H. Schulte-Nölke's finding, as summarised in M. Hönisch, 'Conference Report: New Rules for Contracts in the Digital Single Market. What's in it for Consumers and Businesses in Europe? – Vienna, 21–22 January 2016', *EuCML* 2016, (68) (hereinafter referred to as: M. Hönisch, *Vienna Conference Report*) 69.

90 See the chapter by B. Keirsbilck in this volume.

91 N. Helberger *et al.*, *Digital Consumers*, 3.

92 Recital 21 of the Proposal.

93 This point of criticism is further elaborated on in Section 5.4.2, below.

2.2. SUPPLY OF DIGITAL PRODUCTS DEVELOPED ACCORDING TO THE CONSUMER'S SPECIFICATIONS

Contracts for the supply of 'digital products developed according to the consumer's specifications' are also subject to the Proposal.[94] Presumably, the phrase 'digital products' is to be read as digital content'.[95] To put it differently, the scope of application includes digital content which is tailor-made, i.e. created in accordance with the consumer's specific requests.[96] Software designed on the consumer's demand, digital photos taken as per instructions, 3D modelling files made according to specifications,[97] as well as customised databases, make good examples. The CESL Proposal already endorsed this approach.[98] It is justified by the fact that consumers should have the same remedies for digital content lacking conformity with the contract, irrespective of the way the content was developed.

2.3. EXCLUDED CONTRACTS

Certain contracts for the supply of digital content are explicitly excluded from the scope of application of the Proposal.[99] A first exclusion concerns 'services performed with a predominant element of human intervention by the supplier where the digital format is used mainly as a carrier'.[100] The underlying idea is that the Proposal applies only to those services whose main subject-matter is providing digital content.[101] Therefore, it should not apply to services which the supplier personally supplies and where the digital means are only used for access or delivery purposes.[102]

A translation service is quoted as an example. Imagine a professional translator makes a translation on a consumer's request. The former emails the translated document to the consumer. The translator thus only uses digital means to produce the output of his service. As a result, the Proposal does not apply. The opposite is true when the consumer for example downloads a

94 Art. 3(2) of the Proposal.

95 Recital 16, 2nd phrase, of the Proposal only mentions *content*, not *products*.

96 Recital 16, 2nd phrase, of the Proposal.

97 *Cf.* Recital 16, last phrase, of the Proposal. See above, at Section 2.1.1.1 (Services).

98 Arg. ex Art. 2(j) of the Annex to the CESL Proposal. *Cf.* I. Claeys, 'CESL tools: issues settled, matters addressed, rules, principles, objectives and all its provisions' in I. Claeys and R. Feltkamp (eds.), *The Draft Common European Sales Law: Towards an Alternative Sales Law? A Belgian Perspective*, Cambridge – Antwerp – Portland, Intersentia, 2013, (17) 22, para. 7.

99 Art. 3(5) of the Proposal.

100 Art. 3(5)(a) of the Proposal.

101 Recital 19, 1st phrase, of the Proposal.

102 Recital 19, 2nd phrase, of the Proposal.

translation app for travel use, or if he purchases a dictionary e-book. The same reasoning applies when the consumer obtains advice. Suppose he contacts a legal counsel to get legal expert opinion. The Proposal does not apply, simply because the legal advice is sent to the consumer by email. On the other hand, the situation is different when the consumer completes an online questionnaire that instantaneously produces advice in digital format. Insofar as a price was due or data were to be actively provided in exchange, the Proposal then applies.

Financial services are often provided by electronic means. Nonetheless they are explicitly excluded from the Proposal's scope.[103] This holds water as far as the actual provision of financial services is concerned. No solid arguments can explain however why the Proposal should not apply to digital content supplied by financial institutions. Imagine that a financial institution places an app at its clients' disposal. That app can be used to initiate financial transactions, such as credit transfers. Obviously, those credit transactions do not come within the Proposal's scope, albeit that they are digitally initiated and executed. Specific law deals with the liability of the parties involved, should the transfer be executed incorrectly. By contrast, the Proposal should be applicable to the conformity of the app itself. There is no valid reason to exclude this app from that scope. The fact is that there are no similar specific rules that address, for example, the malfunctioning of apps that are designed to initiate financial transactions.

Gambling services are also excluded from the Proposal's scope.[104] They are defined as services which involve wagering a stake with monetary value in games of chance, including those with an element of skill, such as lotteries, casino games, poker games and betting transactions, by electronic means and at the individual request of a recipient. Concerning those services, the observations about financial services hold similarly true. Only the actual gambling services should escape the Proposal.

The Proposal will furthermore not govern electronic communication services.[105] Those are defined as 'services normally provided for remuneration which consist wholly or mainly in the conveyance of signals on electronic communications networks, including telecommunications services and transmission services in networks used for broadcasting'. The definition, however, covers neither 'services providing, or exercising editorial control over, content transmitted using electronic communications networks and services'[106] nor 'information society services … which do not consist wholly or mainly in

103 Art. 5(e) of the Proposal.
104 Art. 3(5)(d) of the Proposal.
105 Art. 3(5)(b) of the Proposal.
106 Art. 2(c) Directive 2002/21/EC of the European Parliament and of the Council of 7 March 2002 on a common regulatory framework for electronic communications networks and services (Framework Directive), *OJ* L 108 of 24 April 2002, 33 (hereinafter referred to as: Framework Directive).

the conveyance of signals on electronic communications networks'.[107] Examples of electronic communication services include SMS and call services provided over a mobile network, or services provided by Skype, WhatsApp and Facebook Messenger. This at least is true insofar as their providers do not exercise 'editorial control'. Again, one should *mutatis mutandis* take into account the observations with regard to financial services.[108] It seems logical to exclude the actual peer-to-peer communications where those services are used. There is, however, no valid reason simply not to apply the Proposal to all contracts that to some extent deal with software like Skype and WhatsApp.

Finally, certain healthcare services are excluded. This notably is the case for 'health services provided by health professionals to patients to assess, maintain or restore their state of health, including the prescription, dispensation and provision of medicinal products and medical devices'.[109] If a medical practitioner therefore uses digital content to monitor for example the heart rate of a patient, this does not entail the applicability of the Proposal.

2.4. MIXED CONTRACTS

Where a contract includes elements in addition to the supply of digital content, the Proposal only applies to the obligations and remedies of the parties as supplier and consumer of the digital content.[110] In other words, mixed contracts are split into that part concerning digital content and the remaining part. Only the former part is governed by the Proposal. The Preamble assists in visualising that partition. The Proposal, for instance, only applies to digital content if

---

107 Art. 2(c), *in fine*, Framework Directive read jointly with Art. 1 Directive 98/34/EC of the European Parliament and the Council of 22 June 1998 laying down a procedure for the provision of information in the field of technical standards and regulations and of rules on Information Society services, *OJ* L 204 of 21 July 1998, 37, which was repealed, which results in the reference to Art. 1 reading as referring to Art. 1(1)(b) Directive (EU) 2015/1535 of the European Parliament and of the Council of 9 September 2015 laying down a procedure for the provision of information in the field of technical regulations and of rules on Information Society services, *OJ* L 241 of 17 September 2015, 1 (arg. ex Art. 10 of the latter Directive). Information society services are defined as 'any service normally provided for remuneration, at a distance (i.e. without the parties being simultaneously present), by electronic means (i.e. sent initially and received at its destination by means of electronic equipment for the processing (including digital compression) and storage of data, and entirely transmitted, conveyed and received by wire, by radio, by optical means or by other electromagnetic means) and at the individual request of a recipient of services (i.e. provided through the transmission of data on individual request)'.

108 See above, in the current Section.

109 Art. 3(5)(c) of the Proposal, read jointly with Art. 3(a) Directive 2011/24/EU of the European Parliament and of the Council of 9 March 2011 on the application of patients' rights in cross-border healthcare, *OJ* L 88 of 4 April 2011, 45.

110 Art. 3(6) of the Proposal.

the supplier offers that content in combination with other services, such as telecommunication services or the provision of goods. This is true provided that these other goods do not merely function as a carrier of the digital content.[111]

On the one hand the Proposal spells out that it only applies to the digital content part of mixed contracts. On the other hand, it determines that it is applicable to 'any [tangible] medium incorporating digital content [*only* if] the durable medium has been used *exclusively* as a carrier of the digital content' (emphasis added).[112] How do these two provisions interrelate? According to Recital 11 the Proposal is inapplicable 'to digital content which is embedded in goods in such a way that it operates as an integral part of the goods and its functions are subordinate to the *main* functionalities of the goods' (emphasis added).[113] Consequently, a distinction has to be made between two categories of situations. On the one hand, there are *goods* in which digital content is integrated and where the functions of the digital content are subordinate to the main functionalities of the goods. On the other hand, there are goods where the digital content is not integrated with the goods or where the content's functions are not subordinate to the main functionalities of the goods. Contracts regarding the former type of goods are entirely excluded from the Proposal's scope. The regime on consumer sales of goods applies to them. To the latter category of contracts, the aforementioned division into a digital content part and the remaining part must be applied. Issues relating to digital content are governed by the Proposal, other issues are not.

An example should demystify the intended partition. Imagine a consumer purchases a smart TV. The TV itself is considered goods. It is therefore excluded from the Proposal. Instead, it comes under traditional consumer sales law. Smart TVs, however, contain digital content. That embedded digital content is an integral part of the TV. Its functions are subordinate to the main functionalities of the TV, i.e. allowing viewers to watch channels. Hence, the Proposal does not apply. Suppose by contrast that the consumer not only purchases the smart TV. Simultaneously, he subscribes to gain access to an on-demand movie streaming service like Netflix. A distinction is to be made between the smart TV sale and the contract for the supply of that digital content. The Proposal (only) applies to the latter contract. The same reasoning can likewise be applied to any other *smart device*. These devices are in principle not governed by the Proposal.[114]

However, inevitably situations will arise where a clear-cut partition into a digital content part and a remaining part is impossible. What about for instance embedded navigation software simultaneously ordered when buying a car?

---

111 Recital 20, 1st phrase, of the Proposal.

112 Art. 3(3) of the Proposal. See above, at Section 2.1.1.2.

113 Recital 11, last phrase, of the Proposal.

114 *Cf.* C. Wendehorst's conclusion, as mentioned in M. Hönisch, *Vienna Conference Report*, 69.

Undoubtedly that software is an integral part of the car. But is it subordinate to the main functionalities of the car? A car's most important functionality is to allow people to be (safely) transported. The embedded navigation software is useless without the car. Hence, we are inclined to conclude that the Proposal is not applicable to the navigation software, even though it constitutes digital content. The rights and remedies of the Proposal thus are inapplicable. The consumer for example cannot benefit from the unlimited term for lack of conformity to become apparent.[115]

Other examples are even more illustrative of the qualification issues that may arise. PCs, laptops, smartphones and GPS devices today are sold with (a lot of) digital content embedded into them. To name but a few examples, the former three contain an operating system like Microsoft Windows 10 or Google Android 6.0, and a web browser such as Windows Internet Explorer. In addition, it is plausible that for example Microsoft Office is pre-installed on certain devices. Nonetheless, in the current Proposal they are excluded from the scope of application. The consumer sale of these devices will, in principle, be entirely governed by the Consumer Sales Directive.

The unconditional subjection of PCs, smartphones and the like to sales law will prove to be problematic. The aforementioned line of reasoning leads to unequal treatment.[116] Imagine the consumer buys a device without any pre-installed operating system, or at least with the intention to replace the embedded operating system by another. If he then purchases that operating software separately, he enjoys the rights and remedies of the Proposal.[117] These include the unlimited guarantee period. Consumers who, by contrast, use the embedded operating system will only benefit from the two-year guarantee period in consumer sales law.[118] This is all the more paradoxical, as a consumer who installs an operating system himself usually is more specialised and therefore more attentive to nonconformity.[119] The same conclusions are true for other pre-installed digital content, such as Microsoft Office.

The Commission worried that it would be 'difficult to explain to the consumer' that a different regime applies for a scratch on a music CD on the one hand, and a data error within the CD on the other.[120] They therefore abandoned that 'more legally clean solution'. Instead, they opted for a regime that treats digital content-related and other lack of conformity in the same way, provided that the goods

---

115 See below, at Section 5.2.2.

116 *Cf.* J. Jacquemin, *Contenus numériques*, 20, para. 16.

117 That is true, even if it is supplied on a durable medium like a CD-ROM, pursuant to Art. 3(3) of the Proposal.

118 Art. 5(1) Consumer Sales Directive.

119 However, it should be recalled that a contracting party's expertise level is irrelevant to determine his qualification as consumer. *Cf.* above, at Section 2.1.4.1.

120 *Cf.* G. Spindler's paraphrased statement in M. Hönisch, *Vienna Conference Report*, 68.

at issue are used 'exclusively as a carrier of the digital content'.[121] However, the aforementioned examples show that the issue is actually not resolved. It is merely relocated to contracts on goods that are inter alia carriers of digital content.

The application of the same conformity rules to digital content and goods is one solution worth consideration. It may, however, prove difficult or undesirable to enact criteria appropriate to both contract types. Alternatively, in our opinion the Proposal's applicability to goods containing digital content could be logically rephrased as follows. First, one would need to ascertain whether the good (i.e. the medium) has an economic value that is more than marginal in comparison with the content.[122] Such is the case for music CDs, movie DVDs, software CD-ROMs etc. If, however, the goods' value exceeds a marginal part of the digital content's value, then the contract needs to be split up. Conformity of the goods is governed by traditional sales law, irrespective of its function as carrier/medium of content. Conformity of the digital content is governed by the Proposal, irrespective of its potential subordinate role. The same reasoning should apply if multiple, separable units of digital content are incorporated into one good. This will for example be the case for most PCs. In such circumstances, sales law should govern the good, whereas each of the digital content units should be individually governed by the Proposal.

2.5. RELATION TO OTHER LAW

As far as the relation to other instruments is concerned, the Proposal auto-qualifies as *lex generalis*. If any of the Proposal's provisions conflicts with sector-specific or subject-specific provisions in other EU instruments, indeed the provision of that other instrument takes precedence.[123] As such, acts on telecommunications law, audio-visual law and on copyright law prevail over the Proposal. In general acts on these subjects will not conflict with the proposed provisions, for they deal with other issues. Telecommunications law for one does not govern the supply of digital content itself, but rather the transport of such content through electronic communication services.[124]

The Proposal furthermore explicitly restates that it is without prejudice to two branches of law. First, it does not affect the protection of individuals with regard to the processing of personal data.[125] Consequently, all safeguards

---

121 Art. 3(3) of the Proposal.

122 This presumably is what is expressed by Art. 3(3) of the Proposal.

123 Art. 3(7) of the Proposal.

124 *Cf.* N. Helberger, M. Loos, L. Guibault, C. Mak and L. Pessers, 'Digital Content Contracts for Consumers', *J Consum Policy* 2013, (37) (hereinafter referred to as: N. Helberger *et al.*, *Digital Content Contracts*) 19.

125 Art. 3(8) of the Proposal.

granted by the Data Protection Directive and the e-Privacy Directive,[126] for instance undoubtedly remain applicable. Second, the Proposal does not affect national general contract laws, such as rules on formation, the validity or effects of contracts, including the consequences of the termination of a contract.[127]

3. SUPPLY

Article 5 of the Proposal lays down to whom the digital content must be supplied and at what point in time the supply of the digital content has to take place. Attention is drawn to the fact that these provisions do not apply to digital content supplied on a tangible medium,[128] like movie DVDs and music CDs. This makes sense because the Consumer Rights Directive already governs the delivery (supply) of goods that incorporate digital content.[129]

3.1. RECIPIENT

To properly execute his contractual obligations, the supplier is to supply the digital content either to the consumer,[130] or to a third party. In the latter case, it is required that the third party 'operates a physical or virtual facility making the digital content available to the consumer or allowing the consumer to access it and which has been chosen by the consumer for receiving the digital content'.[131] Internet providers seem to be meeting those criteria. The legislator's choice to allow the supplier to supply the content to someone other than the consumer, is justified. The supplier is in principle not responsible for acts or omissions of an internet provider or an electronic platform manager that the consumer has selected in order to receive the digital content.[132] Indeed, it is logical that the supplier is not to be held liable solely because something goes wrong at the consumer's internet or telecom provider. The supplier has no influence on the provider chosen by the consumer.

The acceptability of this rule on supply, however, largely depends on the burden of proof as far as the actual supply is concerned. The consumer cannot

126 Directive 2002/58/EC of the European Parliament and of the Council of 12 July 2002 concerning the processing of personal data and the protection of privacy in the electronic communications sector, *OJ* L 201 of 31 July 2002, 37.
127 Art. 3(9) of the Proposal.
128 Art. 3(3) read jointly with Art. 5 of the Proposal. The sanctions to Article 5 (spelled out in Article 11) are likewise excluded from the scope.
129 *Cf.* Recital 12, 3rd phrase, of the Proposal. See below, at Section 3.2.
130 Art. 5(1)(a) of the Proposal.
131 Art. 5(1)(b) of the Proposal.
132 Recital 23, 2nd phrase, of the Proposal.

reasonably be expected to prove that the content was supplied neither to him in person, *nor to his provider*. Such a requirement would entail a very burdensome obligation to prove two negatives, i.e. a double *probatio diabolica*. The original Proposal is silent about the burden of proof with regard to the act of supplying.[133] Hence, the issue has to be solved according to the national law applicable to the contract. In Belgian contract law, it is up to the person who claims to have executed his obligations to prove the veracity of that claim.[134] Belgian law thus requires the supplier to prove that the digital content is supplied either to the consumer or to a third party that meets the cited criteria.

3.2. TIME OF SUPPLY

The supplier has to supply the digital content immediately after concluding the contract. This is true unless the parties have agreed otherwise.[135] The supply is deemed to take place, either when the digital content is supplied to the consumer himself, or when it is supplied to the chosen third party that meets the aforementioned[136] criteria. Only the earliest of both events is taken into account.[137]

This rule is clearly different from the correspondent provision in the Consumer Rights Directive. As far as the sale of goods is concerned, that Directive determines that 'the trader shall deliver the goods by transferring the physical possession or control of the goods to the consumer without undue delay, but not later than thirty days from the conclusion of the contract', except as otherwise agreed on.[138] That rule still applies to the sale of CDs, DVDs or other tangible media that only function as a carrier of digital content.[139] That is only logical, since an immediate delivery is not always possible, for instance if a CD or DVD is bought online.

Should the supplier fail to supply the digital content in accordance with Article 5, then the consumer is entitled to terminate the contract immediately.[140] This contrasts with the regime pursuant to the Consumer Rights Directive. According to the latter Directive,[141] the consumer in principle first has to call

133 Art. 9 of the Proposal only deals with the burden of proof as conformity (Arts. 6–8) is concerned.
134 Art. 1315 Belgian Civil Code.
135 Art. 5(2), 1st phrase, of the Proposal.
136 See above, at Section 3.1.
137 Art. 5(2), 2nd phrase, of the Proposal.
138 Art. 18(1) Consumer Rights Directive.
139 Art. 3(3) of the Proposal. See above, at Section 3.
140 Art. 11 of the Proposal.
141 Art. 18(2) Consumer Rights Directive.

upon his professional co-contracting party to make the delivery within an additional period of time appropriate to the circumstances.[142]

4. CONFORMITY

The rules on conformity of digital content constitute the heart of the Proposal. Article 6 spells out an elaborate set of rules with regard to conformity in general. The next two, shorter, articles provide additional rules for very specific conformity issues.

4.1. GENERAL CONFORMITY REQUIREMENTS

Article 6 primarily provides for the general conditions that need to be met in order for digital content to conform with the contract. In the first place, the conformity assessment is concentrated on the contract. Only in the second place do general default rules on conformity apply.

4.1.1. Preliminary Remarks

Article 6(1) of the Proposal determines the conditions for the supplied digital content to be in conformity with the contract. Insofar as they are relevant, several requirements have to be met simultaneously. In particular, digital content has to be:

> (a) of the quantity, quality, duration and version and shall possess functionality, interoperability and other performance features such as accessibility, continuity and security, *as required by the contract* including in any pre-contractual information which forms integral part of the contract; (b) fit for any particular purpose for which the consumer requires it and which the consumer made known to the supplier *at the time of the conclusion of the contract* and which the supplier accepted; (c) supplied along with any instructions and customer assistance *as stipulated by the contract*; and (d) updated *as stipulated by the contract* (emphasis added).

These criteria are elaborated on below.

4.1.1.1. Subjective and Objective Criteria

Preliminarily, it must be stressed that the conformity of digital content primarily depends on the contract. It is up to the parties to determine what quality,

[142] These sanctions are not elaborated on in this chapter. Arts. 11 and 13 of the Proposal are dealt with in the chapter of I. Claeys and J. Vancoillie, in this volume.

functionality and performance features the digital content should possess and for what purposes it ought to be fit. The Proposal lays down subjective instead of objective criteria to determine whether or not conformity is lacking. Hence, the proposed conformity criteria are not mandatory law. They are instead left to party autonomy.

Only in the second place does the Proposal lay down that the digital content must be fit for the purposes for which digital content of the same description *would normally be used*.[143] Specifically, that standard becomes effective to the extent that the contract fails to stipulate the requirements for the digital content where relevant, or fails to do so in a clear and comprehensive manner. If one of these two situations occurs, the fitness-for-purpose assessment takes into account the 'functionality, interoperability[144] and other performance features such as accessibility, continuity and security'.[145] To put things differently, (only) if the parties do not agree on the digital content's requirements, the Proposal determines which requirements that content must meet. Hence, only in the absence of clear and comprehensive criteria in the contract does the Proposal provide for objective criteria.

In sum, the objective criteria of Article 6(2) can be deviated from by contract pursuant to Article 6(1). The Proposal is silent as to the modalities and formalities of the contract in which such deviations should be laid down. Contracts are, however, broadly defined.[146] As a result, the Proposal cannot be read as requiring deviations from the objective standard for instance to be expressly stipulated, in writing, individually negotiated or to be laid down in a particular typeface. Standard terms and conditions and other unilaterally-drafted or pre-formulated contracts thus can also deviate from the default objective criteria.

4.1.1.2. Criticism

This two-step regime proposed by the Commission completely differs from the approach that was used in the 1999 Consumer Sales Directive. In the latter Directive, most conformity conditions are objective criteria. Pursuant thereto, a set of minimum requirements are to be met *in any case*. This sharply contrasts with the current Proposal. A justification for the diverging approach is provided for in the Preamble. It states that '[i]n order to promote innovation in the Digital Single Market and cater for technological developments reflected in the fast-changing characteristics of digital content', digital content should, above all, be 'in conformity with what is agreed in the contract'.[147]

143 Art. 6(2), introductory phrase, of the Proposal.
144 See below, at Section 4.1.2.1 (Interoperability and functionality).
145 Art. 6(2), introductory phrase, of the Proposal.
146 Art. 2(7) of the Proposal. See above, at Section 2.1.3.
147 Recital 24 of the Proposal.

The argument of fast technological changes as a reason for subjective criteria is hardly convincing.[148] We believe that innovation and technological developments do not prevent the articulation of a set of minimum requirements for digital content.[149] Such requirements should reflect consumers' legitimate expectations. These expectations should always be met, for they can be considered essential in all circumstances. Moreover, it is highly doubtful whether it makes sense to elaborate rules on the conformity of digital content, if in the end everything is left to party autonomy. This particularly holds true if one takes into account that party autonomy is most often a fiction in consumer contracts, especially[150] in contracts for the supply of digital content. The weak bargaining position of consumers is precisely one of the problems that consumer contract law tries to remedy.[151] In reality consumers often do not read the lengthy texts determining the exact scope of the digital content supplied.[152] Most of them will even lack the expertise to fully understand what is spelled out in these texts. Therefore, the Proposal generates the risk that party autonomy is (ab)used by the supplier to minimise his obligations in respect of the digital content to be supplied.

It has been argued that the use of objective criteria alone would be incompatible with the common practice of so-called *beta versions*. In short, beta versions are early versions of software that are not ready to be marketed, because they most probably still contain errors. They are supplied to *beta testers*, i.e. people who actively report software issues that need to be solved. These beta testers tend to volunteer to provide this service free of charge and in exchange get benefits like being among the first users of new software. In our opinion, introducing objective criteria to assess conformity would not affect this practice. Clearly, the concrete interpretation of those criteria would differ from interpretation of the criteria used for software that is ready to be marketed. The quality a user can expect from beta versions is usually much lower than the

---

148 *Cf.* N. Helberger *et al.*, *Digital Content Contracts*, 50–51.

149 *Cf.* C. Twigg-Flesner's suggestion summarised in M. Hönisch, *Vienna Conference Report*, 69.

150 N. Helberger *et al.*, *Digital Content Contracts*, 51; J. Jacquemin, *Contenus numériques*, 7, para. 3.

151 *Cf.* inter alia (on other consumer contract instruments) judgment in *Océano Grupo Editorial SA v Murciano Quintero and Others*, Joined cases C-240/98–C-244/98, EU:C:2000:346, para. 25; judgment in *Mostaza Claro*, C-168/05, EU:C:2006:675, para. 25; judgment in *Caja de Ahorros y Monte de Piedad*, C-484/08, EU:C:2010:309, para. 27; judgment in *Pannon GSM Zrt. v Erzsebet Sustikne Gyorfi*, C-243/08, EU:C:2009:350, para. 22; judgment in *Asturcom*, C-40/08, EU:C:2009:615, para. 29; judgment in *Pereničová*, C-453/10, EU:C:2012:144, para. 27; judgment in *Banco Español de Crédito*, C-618/10, EU:C:2012:349, para. 39; judgment in *Banif Plus Bank*, C-472/11, EU:C:2013:88, para. 19; judgment in *Brusse*, C-488/11, EU:C:2013:341, para. 31; judgment in *Birutė Šiba v Arūnas Devėnas*, C-537/13, EU:C:2015:14, para. 22. *Cf.* H. Schulte-Nölke, C. Twigg-Flesner and M. Ebers, *EC Consumer Law Compendium – Comparative Analysis*, Munich, European Communities, 2008, 338.

152 N. Helberger *et al.*, *Digital Content Contracts*, 49–50.

quality to be expected from a released final version of the same software.[153] The only prerequisite for such a lowered standard would be clear communication. The consumer should (be able to) understand that the contract relates to a beta version. In conclusion, the mere existence of beta version release practices does not justify an overall choice to apply subjective criteria to all digital content.

4.1.1.3. Transparency Requirement

The objective criteria can only be deviated from by contract, if those deviations are stipulated 'in a clear and comprehensive manner'.[154] If the supplier violates that transparency requirement, the Proposal specifically spells out that the objective criteria shall apply instead of the subjective criteria. Hence, it is of utmost importance to determine under what circumstances a clause is sufficiently transparent.

In our view, analogic references are to be made to the case law developed by the Court of Justice of the EU. The Court has already laid down various requirements with regard to transparency of consumer contracts. Earlier EU legislation already required professional co-contracting parties to draft terms 'in plain and intelligible language'.[155] With regard thereto, the Court held that this rule not only requires that the terms are grammatically understandable by the average[156] consumer; it should even raise the consumer to a position where he has clear and intelligible criteria at his disposal, so as to evaluate the economic consequences for him that derive from the contract he is about to conclude.[157] Applied to the Proposal, this implies that the conformity requirements for digital content should be drafted in a way that an average consumer is able to understand their meaning. Moreover, 'clear' implies that a consumer does not need to go through a bundle of pages before he is able to determine the requirements the digital content at hand should meet.[158]

4.1.2. Subjective Criteria

Article 6(1) spells out four main conformity requirements for digital content, provided the requirements for the digital content at issue are stipulated in a clear

---

153 N. Helberger *et al.*, *Digital Content Contracts*, 53.

154 Art. 6(2), introductory phrase, of the Proposal.

155 Art. 5, 1st phrase, Unfair Terms Directive.

156 Judgment in *Kásler*, C-26/13, EU:C:2014:282, para. 72; judgment in *Matei*, C-143/13, EU:C:2015:127, para. 75; judgment in *Van Hove*, C-92/14, EU:C:2015:262, para. 47; judgment in *Bucura*, C-348/14, EU:C:2015:447, para. 56.

157 Judgment in *RWE Vertrieb*, C-92/11, EU:C:2013:180; judgment in *Kásler*, C-26/13, EU:C:2014:282.

158 On the transparency requirement, see inter alia S. Geiregat, 'Nietigheid en "meest gunstige interpretatie": de remedies bij onrechtmatige bedingen in consumentenovereenkomsten in het licht van de rechtspraak van het Hof van Justitie', *TPR* 2016, (97) 154–163, paras. 87–100.

and comprehensive manner. The content needs to possess the features agreed on; it has to be fit for purpose; it should be supplied along with instructions as stipulated; and it should be updated if the contract provides for that.

4.1.2.1. Performance Features

The digital content has to be 'of the quantity, quality, duration and version and shall possess functionality, interoperability and other performance features such as accessibility, continuity and security, as required by the contract'.[159]

– *Benchmark: contract and pre-contractual statements*

The content's performance features have to be assessed in relation to the contract. The EU legislator expressly added that the reference to 'the contract' is to be understood as including 'any pre-contractual information which forms an integral part of the contract'.[160] Undoubtedly, the latter encompasses statements made by the supplier before the contract was concluded. Such statements can thus result in the supplier's liability for a lack of conformity. Moreover, it should be borne in mind that statements made in the pre-contractual phase that are not in conformity with the contract are misleading. Consequently, they can be considered an unfair commercial practice.[161]

By contrast it is less clear whether a lack of conformity can result from misleading statements made by other persons in earlier links of the chain of transactions. Can the supplier, for instance, be held liable because of faulty statements in the advertisements of a content producer or a platform service provider?[162] As to that, the provision on the 'default' objective criteria[163] explicitly mentions that such third party statements have to be taken into account when assessing the supplier's liability for non-conformity.[164] The Consumer Sales Directive and the Online and Distance Sales of Goods Directive Proposal[165] provide for similar rules.[166] The Proposal on digital content does not. This leads

159 Art. 6(1)(a) of the Proposal.

160 Art. 6(1)(a), *in fine*, of the Proposal.

161 This is true insofar as the incorrect information deceives or is likely to deceive the average consumer and simultaneously is likely to cause the consumer to take a transactional decision that he would not have taken otherwise. *Cf.* Art. 6 Directive 2005/29/EC of the European Parliament and of the Council of 11 May 2005 concerning unfair business-to-consumer commercial practices in the internal market and amending Council Directive 84/450/EEC, Directives 97/7/EC, 98/27/EC and 2002/65/EC of the European Parliament and of the Council and Regulation (EC) No 2006/2004 of the European Parliament and of the Council, *OJ* L 149 of 11 June 2005, 22 (hereinafter referred to as: the Unfair Commercial Practices Directive); judgment in *Trento Sviluppo and Centrale Adriatica*, C-281/12, EU:C:2013:859.

162 C. Busch *et al.*, *The Rise of the Platform Economy*, 6.

163 Art. 6(2) of the Proposal. *Cf.* above, at Section 4.1.1.1.

164 Art. 6(2)(c) of the Proposal.

165 Art. 5(c) Online and Distance Sales Directive Proposal.

166 Art. 2(2)(d) Consumer Sales Directive.

to the conclusion that there are two possible situations. In a first scenario, the contract does not contain all necessary information. In that event, one needs to fall back on the objective criteria in Article 6(2). Public statements made by other persons in earlier links of the chain of transactions are to be taken into account. A second hypothesis assumes that the contract *does* contain all relevant information. Then third party public statements cannot be considered when asserting conformity. The latter finding, however, does not preclude that those statements might be qualified as unfair commercial practices by the third party, for instance because they are misleading.[167]

– *Required performance features*

The required performance features are (rather unusually) listed in the following terms: quantity, quality, duration, version, functionality, interoperability, accessibility, continuity and security. No additional clarification is needed for most of these criteria. It is for instance quite obvious that digital content should actually be supplied in the amount mentioned in the contract and that it should be of the agreed quality. Similarly to the duration of supply, these criteria do not seem to add much to default contract law: the content should be as agreed on. Furthermore, 'accessibility' should be interpreted as a broad concept that is useful as a catch-all requirement.[168] On the other hand, some of the features might require some additional explanation. Functionality, interoperability and security notably are further elaborated on in the next few paragraphs.

• *Interoperability and functionality*

Interoperability is defined by the Proposal as 'the ability of digital content to perform all its functionalities in interaction with a concrete digital environment'. This term is not new and is rightfully considered important to consumers.[169] It has already made an entry in the Consumer Rights Directive[170] and way back in the Directives on the legal protection on computer programs.[171] The concept

---

167 *Cf.* Arts. 2(d), 5, 6 and 7 Unfair Commercial Practices Directive. Addressing the remedies for such practices would exceed the scope of this chapter.

168 *Cf.* N. Helberger *et al.*, *Digital Consumers*, 10–12. According to these authors access(ibility) includes inter alia compatibility.

169 N. Helberger *et al.*, *Digital Consumers*, 93.

170 Recital 19, Art. 5(1)(h) and Art. 6(1)(s) Consumer Rights Directive.

171 Recital 12 of Council Directive 91/250/EEC (repealed) of 14 May 1991 on the legal protection of computer programs, *OJ* L 122 of 17 May 1991, 42; Recital 10 Directive 2009/24/EC of the European Parliament and of the council of 23 April 2009 on the legal protection of computer programs, *OJ* L 111 of 5 May 2009, 16. In both instruments, interoperability is defined as 'the ability to exchange information and mutually to use the information which has been exchanged'. The definitions in the Consumer Rights Directive and the Proposal seem more 'consumer-oriented'.

therefore is not expected to give rise to heavy debates,[172] the more so because it is considered dynamic.[173]

For this chapter, it suffices to cite some examples of interoperability. The question of interoperability mainly arises when *application software* (also called 'apps') needs to be embedded in an *operating system*. A word processor like Microsoft Word for instance needs to be installed e.g. on a Microsoft Windows PC or on an Apple Mac PC. For the word processor to be able to function, it should be apt to 'work together with' (hence *inter-operate*) either the consumer's Windows edition or his Mac edition. Because these two systems work very differently, a Mac version of Microsoft Word will be of no use to a consumer who has a Windows PC. The purchased software is not *interoperable* with the consumer's operating system. Likewise, a mobile app like the Angry Birds game can be purchased for use either on an Apple iPhone, on a Google Android device or on a Windows Phone. Apps that work on one type of device will not automatically work on another. Interoperability can furthermore equally describe the relation between for example the firmware[174] of a device and the operating system, between a particular computer program and its plug-ins or between a file (e-book, music file, etc.) and an application program. Recital 26 of the Proposal provides additional examples.

Surprisingly, the Directive's *body* does not define *functionality*; the Preamble does however. Indeed, functionality generally refers to 'the ways in which digital content can be used'. It should include 'the absence or presence of any technical restriction', inter alia DRM[175] protection[176] or regional coding.[177] According to some eminent authors in the field, the term also includes 'the use of tracking software, such as cookies, watermark or personal identifiers, as well as the use of restrictive technologies that are used for other purposes than protecting copyrights'.[178] The definition is expected not to provoke any more discussions than the aforementioned one. It was used before in the Consumer Rights Directive[179] and should be applauded for its simplicity.

---

172 On the concept of *digital environment*, see below, at Section 4.2.2.1.

173 N. Helberger *et al.*, *Digital Content Contracts*, 48.

174 I.e. the permanent software programmed into the memory of a device.

175 I.e. digital rights management, which can be subscribed as 'technology that protects content against unauthorised access, monitors the use of content, or enforces restrictions on what users can do with the content'. E. Scheirer, 'Content Out of Control', *The Forrester Report* September 2000, (1) 2. *Cf.* M. Fallenböck, 'From Anticircumvention Provisions to Intermediary Liability: Digital Rights Management Legislation in Europe and the U.S.', *MR-Int* 2004, (11) 11.

176 N. Helberger *et al.*, *Digital Consumers*, 13–14.

177 Recital 26, last phrase, of the Proposal.

178 N. Helberger *et al.*, *Digital Consumers*, 64; N. Helberger *et al.*, *Digital Content Contracts*, 49.

179 Recital 19, 7th phrase and Arts. 5(1)(g) and 6(1)(r) Consumer Rights Directive.

The interoperability definition redirects to 'functionalities'. This might come as a surprise, as contractual conformity pursuant to Article 6 requires digital content to possess both interoperability and functionality. This however is not a pleonasm. *Functionality* is a more absolute term. Software, for instance, either has a certain functionality or has not. A word processing program can either allow the colour of a text to be changed or cannot. *Interoperability* is relative. Suppose a word processor has got the functionality of allowing different text colours. If it is installed on the most recent Windows computer, it can be used to apply colour to a text. But when the program is installed either on a Mac, or on a Windows version of 10 years ago, it appears the button to change the colour does not work. Behold a computer program that in theory has a certain functionality, but proves to lack interoperability with the consumer's digital environment.

Addressing the topics of functionality and interoperability should be praised. If the consumer can legitimately expect that his purchased digital content can fully operate in his digital environment, then it should do so. The Consumer Rights Directive already addresses one aspect of functionality and interoperability in business-to-consumer relations. It requires the professional party to provide the consumer with any relevant information on 'the functionality, including applicable technical protection measures, of digital content'.[180] In addition it requires information on the 'interoperability of digital content with regard to hardware and software that the trader is aware of or can reasonably expected to have been aware of'.[181] This is true unless that information is 'already apparent from the context'.[182] This rule applies to *any* contract concluded between a trader and a consumer.[183] Omitting this information may in some circumstances be considered an unfair commercial practice. By contrast, such an omission has as yet had no direct repercussions on (any) contracts subsequently concluded, unless provided for by national law.[184] The present Proposal will supply the necessary 'teeth' to effectively tackle false interoperability promises and to enforce legitimate expectations if consumers enter into a contract (at least partly) due to these promises.

---

180 Art. 5(2) in combination with Art. 5(1)(g) and (Art. 6(2) in combination with Art. 6(1)(r) Consumer Rights Directive, with regard to contracts other than distance or off-premises contracts resp. distance and off-premises contracts. In Belgian law these provisions were transposed in Art. VI.2, 8° (general rule for contracts), Art. VI.45, §1, 18° (distance contracts) and Art. VI.64, §1, 17° (off-premises contracts) Economic Law Code.

181 Art. 5(2) in combination with Art. 5(1)(h) and (Art. 6(2) in combination with Art. 6(1)(s) Consumer Rights Directive. In Belgian law: Art. VI.2, 9° (general rule for contracts), Art. VI.45, §1, 19° (distance contracts) and Art. VI.64, §1, 18° (off-premises contracts) Economic Law Code.

182 Art. 5(1), introductory phrase, Consumer Rights Directive.

183 Art. 3(1), 1st phrase, Consumer Rights Directive.

184 *Quod non*, in Belgium. *Cf.* R. Steennot and E. Terryn, 'De nieuwe bepalingen uit Boek VI van het Wetboek Economisch Recht: een eerste commentaar', *DCCR* 2014, (3) 16–17, paras. 24 and 34–35, para. 62.

However, a remarkable difference between the Consumer Rights Directive and the Proposal should not go unnoticed. The former Directive limits the information duties to interoperability which the professional party concerned 'is aware of or can reasonably be expected to have been aware of'.[185] This important nuance is omitted in the Proposal. As a result, the supplier will even bear the consequences of interoperability issues he was not supposed to know.[186] Hence, if the provision is enacted as it is, it might entail considerable unwanted effects for suppliers that are not the producers of the digital content they supply.

- *Security*

The Commission appears to set great store by the security of digital content. This can be derived from the Preamble.[187] In particular, 'a high level of … security' is deemed 'essential across the [EU]'. We agree that the security of digital content is a noble and pressing concern.[188] Consumers should be allowed to expect to a reasonable extent that purchased content does not increase their vulnerability to third party threats. Because of that finding, it is all the more surprising that the Proposal does not provide for objective security minima.[189] Why should there, for instance, not be a general duty[190] to supply digital content free of viruses and Trojan horses?[191] It is also surprising that the consumer's expected share in his own security is nowhere addressed. Is it for instance not reasonable to expect him to always install the most recently updated version available?[192]

4.1.2.2. Fit for Purpose

The second main conformity requirement is that digital content should be 'fit for any particular purpose for which the consumer requires it and which the consumer made known to the supplier at the time of the conclusion of the contract and which the supplier accepted'.[193] Self-evidently this requirement can

185 Art. 5(1)(h), *in fine*, and Art. 6(1)(s), *in fine*, Consumer Rights Directive.

186 *Cf.* M. Loos, *Digital Content B2C in CESL*, 155–56, who lists some situations where it is justified for the supplier to be liable for ignorance about a lack of interoperability.

187 Recital 27 of the Proposal.

188 N. Helberger *et al.*, *Digital Consumers*, 16–17; N. Helberger *et al.*, *Digital Content Contracts*, 41–42 and 52–53.

189 See above, at Section 4.1.1.2.

190 N. Helberger *et al.*, *Digital Consumers*, 107.

191 A *Trojan horse* (or *Trojan*) is a piece of software hidden in seemingly innocent digital content, that forces its way into a computer when that content is installed, settles there and subsequently can cause damage. K. De Schepper and F. Verbruggen, 'De bescherming van het zakengeheim in het strafrecht: cavalerie of calvarie?' in B. Allemeersch, K. Andries, G.L. Ballon, K. De Schepper, D. D'hooghe, N. Kiekens and F. Verbruggen, *Zakengeheim in Recht en onderneming*, Bruges, die Keure, 2012, (131) 161, para. 51.

192 N. Helberger *et al.*, *Digital Content Contracts*, 53.

193 Art. 6(1)(b) of the Proposal.

only be applied if the consumer informs the supplier of the particular purposes, at the latest at the time of conclusion of the contract. What is more, however, the supplier has to accept that the digital content is fit for these purposes.

Three remarks must be made. First, on many occasions the circumstances in which the contract is concluded do not allow the consumer to communicate about particular purposes. Second, it is the consumer who needs to ensure that he can prove that the supplier has ascertained that the digital content is fit for the expressed purposes. Finally, we wonder whether this requirement has any actual additional value to the aforementioned obligation to supply content that possesses the performance features *determined by the contract.*[194] Obviously this fit-for-purpose requirement is inspired by the list of conformity criteria in the Consumer Sales Directive.[195] Conformity in that Directive is generally assessed by means of objective criteria. It is therefore useful to include an additional requirement that deals with the situation where the consumer wants to use the good for particular purposes. By contrast, such a conformity criterion does not make much sense when conformity is generally assessed by means of subjective criteria.[196]

4.1.2.3. Instructions and Assistance Included

In order for the digital content to be in conformity, it must be supplied along with any instructions and customer assistance as stipulated by the contract.[197] Hence, it is up to the parties to agree on which instructions and assistance the supplier needs to supply. By extension, the contract can easily state that the consumer is entitled to no instructions or assistance whatsoever.[198]

4.1.2.4. Updates

Finally, the digital content has to be updated as stipulated by the contract.[199] This requirement is to be distinguished from the right to obtain the latest version, which is elaborated on below.[200] Once again, regrettably[201] parties can agree that no updates whatsoever are to be provided. If the contract is silent with regard to this issue, then the necessity of updates has to be assessed by means of the objective criteria in Article 6(2).

---

194 Art. 6(1)(a) of the Proposal.
195 Art. 2(2)(b) Consumer Sales Directive.
196 *Cf.* the findings in N. Helberger *et al.*, *Digital Consumers*, 90.
197 Art. 6(1)(c) of the Proposal.
198 Where lack of conformity due to shortcomings in instructions (or due to absence of instructions) is concerned, see below, at Section 4.2.2.2 (Integration instructions).
199 Art. 6(1)(d) of the Proposal.
200 See at Section 4.2.1.
201 N. Helberger *et al.*, *Digital Consumers*, 103.

4.1.3. Objective Criteria

The situation is different if the contract does not stipulate the requirements for digital content, or at least does not do so 'in a clear and comprehensible manner'.[202] In that event, the objective criteria apply. This entails that the digital content has to be fit for the purposes for which digital content of the same description would normally be used including its functionality, interoperability and other performance features such as accessibility, continuity and security.[203] To put it differently, the absence of clear provisions in the contract on (certain) aspects of the digital content leads to a shift of the expectations that need to be met. Regard is then no longer paid to the parties' wishes. Instead, the (lack of) conformity is assessed on the basis of what (average) consumers can legitimately expect when similar digital content is supplied.[204]

The performance features that are assessed when the objective criteria apply are equal to the features listed with regard to the subjective criteria. Insofar as the used terminology is not prima facie clear, it was elaborated on above.[205] Nonetheless, expectations are that it will not prove easy to determine what actual features a consumer is in practice entitled to expect with regard to concrete digital content.[206]

Three main elements should be taken into account when objective criteria are used to assess conformity. These elements include the consumer's counter-performance, the existence of standards, codes of conduct and good practices, as well as public statements.[207]

4.1.3.1. Consumer's Counter-Performance

First of all, in assessing the objective conformity, one has to take into account 'whether the digital content is supplied in exchange for a price or other counter-performance than money'.[208] The fact that the consumer's counter-performance consists of the active provision of (personal) data instead of money, does not prevent the applicability of the Proposal.[209] By contrast, it seems that it does have an effect when determining the conformity of digital content.[210] This at least is true if the contract does not clearly and comprehensively determine the requirements for its conformity.

---

202 See above, at Section 4.1.1.3.
203 Art. 6(2) of the Proposal.
204 *Cf.* (on the CESL Proposal) M. Loos, *Digital Content B2C in CESL*, 155.
205 See above, at Section 4.1.2.1 (Required performance features).
206 *Cf. in extenso*, N. Helberger *et al.*, *Digital Consumers*, 84–107, 111 and 178.
207 Art. 6(2)(a)–(c) of the Proposal.
208 Art. 6(2)(a) of the Proposal.
209 Art. 3(1) of the Proposal. See below, at Section 2.1.2.
210 *Cf.* M. Loos, *Digital Content B2C in CESL*, 148.

It is doubtful whether this provision per se means that a consumer's expectations of digital content are to be lowered in all cases where (personal) data is provided as a counter-performance. Sometimes personal data have the same economic value as money. Is it for instance justifiable to distinguish between personal data that can be used for targeted advertising on the one hand, and micropayment on the other? It is advisable to state in more general wording that the economic value of the counter-performance must be taken into account when determining conformity. A restatement of that kind would better match the Proposal's rationales.[211]

4.1.3.2. Standards, Codes of Conduct and Good Practice

Secondly, 'where relevant, existing international technical standards' have to be taken into account when assessing conformity on the basis of objective criteria. In the absence of such technical standards, 'applicable industry codes of conduct and good practices' should be paid attention to.[212] The Recitals in this context state that the Commission may consider the promotion of the development of international and European standards and the drawing up of a code of conduct by trade associations and other representative organisations that could support the uniform implementation of the Directive.[213] Actions of that kind might indeed prove necessary, as the availability of standards on digital content seems rather limited[214] in spite of their importance to determine expectations.[215]

4.1.3.3. Public Statements

Finally, 'any public statement made by or on behalf of the supplier or other persons in earlier links of the chain of transactions' must be taken into account.[216] The criterion used is identical to the one incorporated in the Consumer Sales Directive.[217] However, there is an important difference. In that Directive this criterion is automatically applicable and cannot be derogated from. In the Proposal, that is not the case: the criterion only applies if the contract does not clearly and comprehensively lay down the digital content's conformity requirements.

Basically this criterion implies the inclusion in the contract of public statements like the ones made in advertisements. This is true even when the

211 *Cf.* our findings above, at Section 2.1.2.2.
212 Art. 6(2)(b) of the Proposal.
213 Recital 28 of the Proposal.
214 N. Helberger *et al.*, *Digital Consumers*, 4 and 57–58; M. Loos, *Digital Content B2C in CESL*, 155.
215 N. Helberger *et al.*, *Digital Content Contracts*, 51.
216 Art. 6(2)(c), introductory phrase, of the Proposal.
217 Art. 2(2)(d) Consumer Sales Directive.

statements were not made by the supplier, but instead by other persons in earlier links of the chain of transactions. The impact of such third party statements to the consumer's expectations is not to be underestimated.[218] Companies that have developed and/or produced the digital content constitute prime examples of third parties that issue statements. Platform service providers can most probably also qualify as 'other persons in earlier links of the chain of transactions'.[219] The supplier can, however, escape liability for third party public statements. To do so, he needs to prove that one of three alternative criteria is true. First, he could show that he was not aware of the statement in question, and could not reasonably have been so.[220] Second, he may prove that the statement was corrected by the time of conclusion of the contract.[221] Third, the supplier could demonstrate that the decision to acquire the digital content could not have been influenced by the statement.[222] The same exceptions are found in the Consumer Sales Directive.

4.2. SPECIFIC CONFORMITY REQUIREMENTS

Besides the extensive general conformity rules in Article 6(1) and (2), the Proposal contains three more specific conformity requirements. First, Article 6(4) establishes a limited right to the latest version. Second, Article 7 addresses the incorrect integration of digital content. Third, Article 8 lays down that third party rights should not hinder the consumer's use of the digital content. A lack of compliance with any of these rules, per se entails the presence of a lack of conformity.[223] Consequently, the Proposal's remedies will apply.

4.2.1. Right to the Latest Version

Consumers are only expressly granted a right to updates if the supply contract says so.[224] By contrast, the Proposal provides a default right for the consumer to obtain the most recent version of the digital content he purchased.[225] The recentness of the digital content is to be assessed at the time of conclusion of the contract,[226] so the mere development of newer, better versions of the content does not imply non-conformity.[227] Contractual agreements may, however, deviate from this 'right to the latest version'.

---

218 N. Helberger *et al.*, *Digital Consumers*, 89–90.
219 C. Busch *et al.*, *The Rise of the Platform Economy*, 6.
220 Art. 6(2)(c)(i) of the Proposal.
221 Art. 6(2)(c)(ii) of the Proposal.
222 Art. 6(2)(c)(iii) of the Proposal.
223 Art. 6(5) of the Proposal. *Cf.* Recital 31, 1st phrase, of the Proposal.
224 Art. 6(1)(d) of the Proposal. See above, at Section 4.1.2.4.
225 Art. 6(4) of the Proposal.
226 *Cf.* N. Helberger *et al.*, *Digital Consumers*, 102–103.
227 N. Helberger *et al.*, *Digital Consumers*, 110.

The wording of this provision leaves some questions unanswered. First, it does not take into account the economic practices with regard to digital content versions. The recentness of a content version is a relative matter. It should be assessed in relation to the concrete market the content is released onto. The most recent version of a computer program could be different in one country from another. In addition, account must be taken of the digital environment it will be used in. The latest version on the market could be different for a Microsoft Windows PC and for an Apple Mac device.

Second, the recentness of the version is assessed at the moment of contract conclusion. Consequently, this right to the latest version adds little protection to long-term contracts. It is tempting to think that lack of protection is overcome by the aforementioned[228] right to updates.[229] That is a fallacy however. In the first place, it was pointed out that a right to updates in principle only exists if the contract provides for one, while the latest-version right is granted unless otherwise provided for. Hence, the consumer is in a better starting position if he is entitled to the latest version. In the second place, there still is less protection even if a consumer is entitled to an update right. That is true because such a right does not per se entail a right to the latest version of the digital content. Imagine that a consumer purchases a software pack including a word processor, a slideshow creator and a spreadsheet program, like Microsoft Office Home and Student 2016. Say the consumer receives weekly security updates for 20 years in accordance with the licence agreement. Every seven days, some recently discovered security breaches in the programs are fixed by automatically downloaded pieces of software. By contrast, the consumer is not entitled to the latest version of the software pack. In the year 2026, he might still receive security updates as new threats are identified and cleared away. He is, however, in no way entitled to the new 2026 version of the software pack. This makes sense, because a one-off purchase was at issue. On the other hand, suppose the consumer paid for a similar software pack to be supplied 'as a service', like Microsoft Office 365 for Students. In exchange for annual fees he receives one-year licence codes to access ('unlock') that software pack. If he then pays his renewal fee again in 2026, is it justified that he is still merely entitled to a 2016 version that is enhanced by 10 years of security updates? Should he not be entitled to the 2026 version without terminating the long-term contract and concluding a new one, possibly involving additional costs? In brief, the EU legislator may want to consider providing consumers with a limited right to receive the latest version of the digital content for a 'reasonable' period[230] in the case of long-term contracts.

---

228 See above, at Sections 4.1.2.4 and 4.2.1.

229 Art. 6(1)(d) of the Proposal.

230 *Cf.* N. Helberger *et al.*, *Digital Consumers*, 103 and 108.

4.2.2. *Integration*

Some digital content requires additional actions before it can be used by the consumer in accordance with its intended purposes. A dishwasher can only be used if it is plumbed into the water supply. A pile of floor tiles can only be used after they are laid. Similarly, one generally is only able to use a word processor or a PC game after it is properly installed on a computer. Throughout this installation process, things might not always go as expected. Consequently, an object of a business-to-consumer transaction might no longer conform with the contract, in spite of the fact that it did conform at the time of supply. The front panel could break off while a dishwasher is being fit into the cabinet. A floor tile might break to pieces.

Against that background the Proposal sets some rules on installation mishaps. Very similar solutions are found in both the parallel Proposal for an Online and Distance Sales of Goods Directive[231] and in the 1999 Consumer Sales Directive.[232] The terminology used, however, is slightly different. Both the Online and Distance Sales Directive Proposal and the Consumer Sales Directive mention the *installation* of purchased goods. That concept is not explicitly defined. The Proposal on digital content on the other hand addresses the *integration* of digital content and provides a definition.

4.2.2.1. Definition

Integration is defined by the Proposal as 'linking together different components of a digital environment to act as a coordinated whole in conformity with its intended purpose'.[233] On a closer look, it appears that this definition does not differ much from how one would describe the 'installation' of consumer goods. Installing a dishwasher, too, for instance means linking together different components (the dishwasher, the cupboard, the front panel, the skirting-board, etc.) of [a kitchen] to act as a coordinated whole in conformity with its intended purpose. The only aspect distinguishing *installation* from *integration* thus is the 'digital environment'.

The Proposal defines *digital environment* as 'hardware, digital content and any network connection to the extent that they are within the control of the user'. The Recitals do not provide additional information on this concept. Nor can inspiration for interpretation be drawn from recently enacted British law on the B2C supply of digital content, for the 2015 Consumer Rights Act omits the

231 Art. 7 of the Online and Distance Sales Directive Proposal.
232 Art. 2(5) Consumer Sales Directive. In Belgium, this provision was transposed in Art. 1649*ter*, §4, Belgian Civil Code.
233 Art. 2(2) of the Proposal.

concept.[234] This leads to the conclusion that the definition is to be understood in a literal but broad way. One's *digital environment* simply is *any* hardware, *any* digital content[235] and *any* network connection a person has the factual power to control.

There's something odd about both the *integration* and the *digital environment* concepts. With regard to the latter, it is surprising that the definition is built around 'the user' instead of 'the consumer'. Needless to state that the undefined 'user' is a far broader concept than the well-defined[236] 'consumer' notion. This, however, bears no consequences for the scope of the Proposal. Only the consumer's environment is covered by the substantive provisions of the Proposal,[237] in spite of the generic references to *any* user's environment in the definition.[238]

As far as *integration* is concerned, it is someway remarkable that the Commission has preferred the latter term to *installation*. '*Installing* digital content', firstly, is more closely related to the common language used with regard to digital content.[239] It can likewise be found in case law[240] and in the CESL Proposal.[241] Therefore, using *installation* (and its derivatives) could facilitate the consumer's understanding of his rights. More convincing even is that the general use of *installation* would lead to identical terminology in sales law of (non-digital) goods[242] and in the law on the supply of digital content. Parallel conclusions could easier be made in case law and doctrine, and law makers could more easily enact norms applying to both types of consumer contracts.

The meaning of *integration* is likely not to cause insuperable difficulties. Still, some examples could be of use. After downloading a game or computer

---

234 *Cf.* Consumer Rights Act 2015 (UK), ss 33–47.

235 On this term, see above, at Section 2.1.1.1.

236 Art. 2(4) of the Proposal. See above, at Section 2.1.4.1.

237 Recitals 32, 33, 40 and 44, Art. 7, introductory phrase, and Arts. 9(2), 9(3) and 14(1) of the Proposal.

238 Arts. 2(2), 2(5) and 2(9) of the Proposal.

239 *Cf.* C.A. den Boon, D. Geeraerts and R. Hendrickx (eds.), *Dikke Van Dale Online*, Utrecht, Van Dale Uitgevers, 2015, www.vandale.be, at '*installeren*'; A. Gabrielli (ed.), *Grande dizionario Hoepli italiano*, Milan, Hoepli, 2011, www.hoepli.it, at '*installare*'; Laurousse (ed.), *Dictionnaire de français*, www.larousse.fr/dictionnaires/francais-monolingue, at '*installer*'; X, *Merriam-Webster*, www.merriam-webster.com, at '*install*'.

240 Examples of the use of '*installation*' (and its translations) of digital content in case law are endless. A random sample of some supreme courts' decisions mentioning the term is given: Cass. (FR) 9 December 2015, no 14-87.835, 5530, FR:CCASS:2015:CR05503; Cass. (FR) 19 January 2016, no 14-21.670, 14-21.671, 71, FR:CCASS:2016:CO00071; HR (NL) 27 April 2012, no 10/03890, NL:HR:2012:BV1299; HR (NL) 13 February 2015, no 13/00975, NL:HR:2015:285; BGH (DE) 4 March 2004, no III ZR 96/03, *MMR* 2004, 308; BGH (DE) 11 December 2014, no I ZR 8/13, *NJW-RR* 2015, 1138; Cass (BE) 26 April 2012, no AR C.11.0393.N, *ICIP* 2012, 265 (note), *Pas.* 2012, 929.

241 *Cf.* Arts. 99(1)(c), 100(e), 101(1)(b) and 105(3) of the Annex to the CESL Proposal.

242 Art. 7 of the Online and Distance Sales Directive Proposal and Art. 2(5) Consumer Sales Directive.

program, clicking on the downloaded file will usually open up an installation wizard window. Step by step, this installation software guides the user through the installation process. From downloading 'til the moment when the game or program is ready for use, *integration* pursuant to the Proposal is taking place. The same is true from the insertion in a disk tray of an installation CD containing such a game or program, until the moment it can be used.

Finally, one should beware not to confuse *integration* with the aforementioned concept of *interoperability*.[243] The former word relates to a set of *acts* necessary to make a digital asset actually work as it is supposed to be. Interoperability, by contrast, indicates whether or not it is *technically possible* to make a certain digital asset work as it should.

4.2.2.2. Conditions for Equating Integration Mishaps to Lack of Conformity

The Proposal establishes two alternative situations in which the risk of mishaps during the *integration* (or installation) has to be borne by the supplier. Both are also found in the Online and Distance Sales of Goods Directive Proposal[244] and in the Consumer Sales Directive.[245] The rationale for equating these circumstances to a lack of conformity, is that in both situations the reasons for incorrect integration are deemed to be 'in the sphere of the supplier'.[246] If during such an integration process the content becomes non-conforming, remedies will apply as if the content lacked conformity from the start. This is the case (1) if the content is integrated either by the supplier himself or under his responsibility. The same applies (2) if the consumer performs the integration in accordance with faulty instructions.

– *Integration by the supplier or under his responsibility*

First, in some cases the (incorrect) integration is directly carried out by the supplier or 'under his responsibility'. It is fairly easy to imagine examples thereof. A consumer for example hands over his laptop to the local software shop. The shop's IT specialist installs the programs purchased by the consumer. The consumer calls for his laptop the day after. Similarly, the IT specialist could come around to the consumer's residence and install the lot there. Anyhow, it is clear that it would make no sense to differentiate between the situation where the IT specialist strictly is the consumer's co-contracting party for the supply of the content on the one hand, and the case where he is an employee of that party or an independent specialist hired by that party on the other hand. Therefore,

243 See above, at Section 4.1.2.1 (Interoperability and functionality).
244 Art. 7 of the Online and Distance Sales Directive Proposal.
245 Art. 2(5) Consumer Sales Directive.
246 Explanatory Memorandum, 12 (on Article 7).

it must be welcomed that the Proposal equates a supplier who integrates the content himself to someone who does so 'under his responsibility'.

The integration of digital content is sometimes carried out at a distance. The installing IT specialist could for instance use a remote access tool to integrate the purchased digital content on a consumer's device. There seems to be no reason to exclude this type of integration from the envisaged scope. The assessment, however, will have a different outcome if the digital content is supplied together with self-executable installation software. That is the case when for example an installation wizard is launched after the installation CD-ROM is inserted or an installation file is opened. Even if such an installation program is created by the supplier of the digital content, still we reckon that situation cannot be classified as integration 'under the supplier's responsibility'. The Preamble clarifies that *responsibility* should be read as *control*.[247] As a consequence, Article 7(a) should only apply to those cases in which the supplier (in person or through someone acting under his control) can actually control the full integration process, including the parts of the digital environment essential to that process. Nevertheless, this in no way precludes that the installation program at issue fulfils the criteria of Article 7(b).[248]

Finally, there is a noticeable difference between the present twin proposals[249] on the one side and the Consumer Sales Directive on the other. The former both do not attach any importance to the question whether or not the installation/integration duty for the supplier 'forms part of the contract of sale [or supply]' itself.[250] From a consumer's perspective this constitutes a rise in protection. Should the Proposal be enacted, no debate could arise as to the inclusion of the integration/installation service in the digital content supply contract.

– *Integration by the consumer following instructions*

The second described situation is the so-called IKEA clause[251] or DIY provision. Pursuant to Article 7(b) the lack of conformity due to an incorrect installation shall have the same effects as a lack of conformity with the contract. This is true only if the digital content

> was intended to be integrated by the consumer and the incorrect integration was due to *shortcomings in the integration instructions* where those instructions were supplied

[247] Recital 30, 2nd phrase, *medio*, of the Proposal.

[248] See below, at Section 4.2.2.2 (Integration instructions).

[249] *Cf.* Art. 6(a) of the Online and Distance Sales Directive Proposal, which reeds *mutatis mutandis* the same as Art. 7(a) of the Proposal.

[250] Art. 2(5), 1st phrase, Consumer Sales Directive. *Cf.* (on the transposing Belgian law) R. Steennot and S. Dejonge, *Handboek Consumentenbescherming en Handelspraktijken*, Antwerp, Interentia, 2007, 529, para. 1060.

[251] R. De Wit, 'Duties of Buyer and Seller. Transfer of risk' in I. Claeys and R. Feltkamp (eds.), *The Draft Common European Sales Law: Towards an Alternative Sales Law? A Belgian*

in accordance with point (c) of Article 6(1) or should have been supplied in accordance with Article 6(2) (emphasis added).

It should be noted that the proposed DIY provision does not require the digital content to be integrated by the consumer himself.[252] Article 7(b) only demands that the content is *intended* to be integrated by the latter. This differs from a literal reading of the 1999 Consumer Sales Directive[253] and should be applauded.[254] There is no reason why the protection against lack of conformity should for example not be extended to the case where the contracting consumer allows a family member or friend to install some photo editor software on his computer.

- *Integration instructions*

Not all lack of conformity that result from integration flaws gives rise to the remedies in the Proposal. For that to be true, shortcomings have to be established in the integration instructions.[255] In other words, the mere fact that the person who integrates the digital content follows the faulty instructions provided should ipso facto lead to a lack of conformity. Hence, as a principle the existence of *integration instructions* is a prerequisite for the DIY provision.

Perhaps the most obvious example springing to mind is the case where an owner's manual, user guide or instructions for use are supplied on paper, together with the content. In a digitalised world, however, hard copies are rarely still provided with digital content. Instructions could instead be supplied in a digital file that comes along with the supplied content. This also falls within the provision here discussed. Websites containing installation (*integration*) instructions furthermore are increasingly used. As nothing is mentioned about the techniques used for the instructions, online versions in principle also fall within the scope of the provision at issue. An important prerequisite for Article 7(b) to apply however, is that the instructing webpages are somehow 'supplied along [with the digital content]'. In our opinion, that condition will be met if a supplier explicitly refers to a specific webpage, for instance by sending a hyperlink. By contrast, a supplier's general reference to a search engine will not suffice. But what if he verbally advises the consumer to 'look it up on the developer's website'? Clearly, it is highly uncertain in what circumstances the DIY provision will or will not apply to websites.

Perspective, Cambridge – Antwerp – Portland, Intersentia, 2013, (155) (hereinafter referred to as: R. De Wit, *Duties. Risk* [*in the CESL*]), 171, para. 32.

252 The same is true for Art. 101(1)(b) of the Annex to the CESL Proposal.

253 Art. 2(5), 2nd phrase, Consumer Sales Directive requires that 'the product, intended to be installed by the consumer, is *installed by* the consumer' (emphasis added).

254 R. Steennot, 'Art. 1649ter BW' in *Comm.Bijz.Ov.* I, 2015, issue 101, 16, para. 23. *Contra* (presumably, and with regard to the homologous CESL Proposal): R. De Wit, *Duties. Risk* [*in the CESL*], 171, para. 32.

255 Art. 7(b), *medio*, of the Proposal.

The aforementioned[256] step-by-step wizard program guiding users through the installation process of digital content, in our opinion falls within the intended ambit. The installation software itself might already be present on a device, at least partially. Nonetheless it cannot be used to actually install (*integrate*) the digital content if some triggers and/or parts were not 'supplied along' with that content.

To avoid confusion, it should be made clear that generally speaking the DIY provision cannot apply to (online or offline) 'how-to' manuals or to the help section included in the digital content (if any). These are also 'instructions' and might be 'supplied along' with the content. Nonetheless, these instructions relate to how the digital content should be *used*. They do not necessarily provide for information on the integration of it. If they contain errors, Article 7(b) in principle will not apply. Depending on the circumstances, however, these errors might be relevant for the assessment of conformity pursuant to the general rule in Article 6.

Some uncertainties are furthermore inherent in Article 7(b). Discussions are notably to be expected with regard to integration instructions made or supplied by anyone other than the supplier. This will often be the case. Although digital content may sometimes be supplied directly by its producer to the consumer, in many cases this content will be subject to a (long) supply chain. In the current Proposal, only the direct co-contracting party of the consumer (i.e. the supplier)[257] can be held liable for faulty instructions.[258] That is, without prejudice to the former's right to redress based on national law.[259] Is it fair that for example the local computer store bears the risks and costs of faulty instructions provided by Adobe, Microsoft or Apple, in the knowledge that the store cannot change anything to these instructions?

Another uncertainty arises when the use of acquired digital content requires prior installation of other content, like software. This likewise is not an unusual event. When acquiring access to an online film streaming service, a consumer might have to install a certain browser and a specific video player (e.g. Adobe Flash Player) or plug-in. Some software might need additional software like Oracle Java, Microsoft Silverlight, Microsoft Visual C++, etc. Similarly, to be able to open a program's instruction manual or help section, downloading a PDF viewer is sometimes needed. All of these constitute digital content provided by third parties. Is the consumer still acting within the scope of Article 7(b) when downloading and installing that content? Should the supplier bear the

---

256 See above, at Sections 4.2.2.1 and 4.2.2.2 (Integration by the supplier or under his responsibility).

257 See above, at Section 2.1.4.2.

258 Art. 10(b) read jointly with Art. 7(b) of the Proposal.

259 Art. 17 of the Proposal. With regard thereto, see the chapter by B. Keirsbilck in this volume.

initial risks (and costs) if actions with regard to that content lead to a lack of conformity of the digital content originally acquired?

- *Absence of integration instructions*

The provision under discussion here contains a regrettable formulation of the rule applicable if no installation instructions are 'supplied along with' the content. It deals with 'shortcomings in the ... instructions, where those instructions were supplied in accordance with [Article 6(1)(c)] or should have been supplied in accordance with Article 6(2)'.[260]

Literally interpreted, the supplier could simply set aside the application of Article 7(b) by clearly and comprehensively stipulating in the consumer contract that no instructions are to be supplied.[261] If, on the other hand, the contract does not contain anything about integration instructions or if these instructions are not stipulated in a transparent way, one should ask whether integration instructions *should have been* supplied. Assuming this is the case, a *very* literal interpretation asks whether the lack of conformity is a consequence of instructions that should have been supplied (but were not). This of course makes no sense: what legal obligation could there be to provide instructions that contain errors?

Pursuant to a functional interpretation however, Article 7(b) can be read as equating non-conformity due to faulty instructions with non-conformity resulting from a lack of instructions. By contrast, it would amount to an inacceptable interpretation *contra legem* if we were to read that Article 6 prevents contracting parties from stipulating that there is no obligation to provide for instructions. Therefore, we propose to interpret or reformulate Article 7(b) as such:

> and the incorrect integration was (i) due to shortcomings in the integration instructions provided, if the supplier has provided integration instructions; or (ii) due to *the lack of* clear and comprehensive *instructions* the supplier should have supplied, taking into account the factors mentioned in Article 6(2)(a), (b) and (c).

In that wording, it is clear that shortcomings due to a lack of instructions are in any event covered by the DIY provision.

Lastly, suppose a lack of instructions can indeed lead to non-conformity. The consequences of accepting that interpretation might have a noticeable effect on the suppliers' obligations. If a supplier offers digital content products that could be wrongly used in the absence of instructions, Article 7(b) might indirectly

260 Art. 7(b), *in fine*, of the Proposal.

261 Art. 7(b) read jointly with Art. 6(2) (which only applies if 'the contract does not stipulate ... in a clear and comprehensive manner') and Art. 6(1)(c) (pursuant to which the supply of instructions is due 'as stipulated by the contract') of the Proposal.

give rise to a positive obligation for that supplier to actively provide correct integration instructions. This may result in a reverse of business plans.

4.2.2.3. Non-Conformity that Arises

It is more or less clear in which cases mishaps during integration are covered by paragraphs (a) and (b) of Article 7. However, it should be pointed out that the scope of Article 7 is strongly limited because of the fact that *a lack of conformity* must arise from the integration process. Hence, the remedies in the Proposal only apply when the digital content *itself* degrades in some way. In a sense, Article 7 thus only postpones the moment when conformity is to be assessed.[262]

Imagine that a consumer purchases a word processor at a local enterprise. The enterprise's IT specialist agrees to install this software on the consumer's laptop right away. During this 'integration' process, the laptop crashes and all of the consumer's data are irretrievably lost. The software, however, can still be used. It can be downloaded from the producer's website again onto another computer, because the licence key is not yet used. This case is *not* covered by the Directive.[263] Depending on the circumstances, the consumer could invoke the enterprise's liability for contractual breach or negligent act. If, however, the installation software was to blame, damages could be obtained from the software producer[264] pursuant to product liability law.[265] When applying EU product liability law however, account should be taken of the EUR 500 minimum threshold.[266] Often the consumer's damage will not exceed that amount.

Instead, Article 7 only applies if the digital content itself can no longer 'do what it has to do'. Some examples can be imagined. If digital content is to be installed (integrated) on a computer or smartphone, it is not unthinkable that the installation software itself crashes. The main content might then nevertheless be able to perform all promised functions; it simply cannot be accessed by the consumer and therefore does not conform. CDs or DVDs could constitute

---

262 See below, at Section 5.2.1.1.

263 *Cf.* Art. 14(1), 1st phrase, of the Proposal, pursuant to which consumers are only entitled to damages in case of 'economic damage to [his] digital environment *caused by a lack of conformity* or a failure to supply' (emphasis added). It should be noted however Article 14 was expected to be left out of the legislative project at the time this chapter was finished.

264 D. Verhoeven, 'Productveiligheid en productaansprakelijkheid: krachtlijnen en toekomstperspectieven' in G. Straetmans and R. Steennot (eds.), *Wetboek Economisch Recht en de bescherming van de consument*, Antwerp – Cambridge, Intersentia, 2015, (193) 211–13, paras. 22–23.

265 *Cf.* Directive 85/374/EEC of the Council of 25 July 1985 on the approximation of the laws, regulations and administrative provisions of the Member States concerning liability for defective products, *OJ* L 210 of 7 August 1985, 29 (hereinafter referred to as: Product Liability Directive).

266 Art. 9, 1st paragraph, (b) Product Liability Directive.

another illustration. Say a CD or DVD reads that it can be used on any disk player whatsoever. But when used on the consumer's player this turns out not to be true. The disk is irrecoverably broken and the content is unreadable. Therefore, it does not conform (any more).

In a final example we assume that the installation and downloading of required additional software also falls within the process of integration.[267] Imagine that *in casu* Adobe Flash Player needs to be installed to use the acquired digital content. The installation wizard requires the consumer to download that software before the installation of the content can continue. This pre-installation, however, keeps failing. Because of that, the consumer can never use the acquired digital content on his intended device, although the supplier may have stated that he would be able to do so. Thus, the digital content is not 'fit for purpose'[268] and as such does not conform. Is the Proposal applicable to that situation as well?

The given examples show that lack of conformity resulting from incorrect integration is theoretically possible. Nonetheless today digital content is often offered online. If the content producer is repeatedly notified about installation errors, often he will provide a repaired version at short notice. The EU legislator to some extent codified that practice in Article 12(2).[269] The moment of assessing conformity can consequently be delayed for 'a reasonable time' starting from the moment when he is informed about the lack of conformity.

4.2.3. *Third Party Rights*

Despite its clear purpose on the face, Article 8 is probably the Proposal's prize blunder from a legal jargon perspective. On its current reading it obliges the supplier to supply the content 'free of any right of a third party, including based on intellectual property'.[270] Most likely it will soon be redrafted. The meaning of this provision ought to be clear from a consumer's perspective: the consumer should be able to fully enjoy the benefits of the supplied digital content. He should be left out of any discussion his professional co-contracting party has with third parties, 'so that the digital content can be used in accordance with the contract'.[271]

It is notable that the EU legislator uses the term 'legal defects' (*défauts juridiques*) to indicate any interference with the consumer's use by 'unwanted' third party rights (or claims). This term contrasts with all of the situations of non-conformity in Articles 6 and 7, collectively called 'material defects'.[272] This

267 See above, at Section 4.2.2.2 (Integration instructions).
268 Art. 6(1)(b) of the Proposal.
269 See the chapter by I. Claeys and J. Vancoillie, in this volume.
270 Arts. 8(1) and (2) of the Proposal.
271 Art. 8(1), *in fine*, and Art. 8(2), *in fine*, of the Proposal.
272 Recital 31, 1st phrase, of the Proposal.

wording sounds a bit odd. First, it might have been more consistent to refer to a 'defect in title'.[273] Second, it is rather confusing to use the word 'defect' to refer to a third party's legitimate claim or title. The terminology is more concise than 'no third party rights interference right' though, so we will maintain it below.

The provision distinguishes two points in time at which this 'legal defect prohibition' plays a part. Paragraph 1 of Article 8 lays down the general rule that always applies when digital content is supplied: legal defects should be absent at the moment of delivery of the content. In paragraph 2 the legislator adds that digital content supplied over a certain period of time should be free of legal defects during the full supply period. The distinction between one-off and *long-term* digital content supply contracts, for the purposes of assessing conformity, thus is in keeping with Article 6(3)[274] and the Proposal's rationales.[275]

4.2.3.1. Interpreting Article 8

– *Literal interpretation*

The original version of Article 8 is poorly drafted, for it would at least be utterly unnecessary and very burdensome (if not plainly impossible), for a supplier to comply with it. The literal text demands the supplied digital content to be 'free of' any rights that do not belong to either the supplier or the consumer. Hence, the content should, inter alia, be 'copyright-free',[276] so that requirement will be used as an example. From an IP perspective, requiring 'copyright-free content' is nonsense. If the conditions for copyright protection are fulfilled, then the author is entitled to his rights *ipso jure* (*de plein droit*). The author's rights in some EU countries like Belgium,[277] France[278] and Germany[279] include *moral rights*. These are inalienable and cannot be waived. Some of the author's economic rights are

---

273 This wording is used in references to the analogous Arts. 41 and 42 CISG. *Cf.* I. Schwenzer, 'Conformity of the Goods and Third Party Claims' in I. Schwenzer (ed.), *Commentary on the UN Convention on the International Sale of Goods (CISG)*, Oxford, Oxford University Press, 2010, (568) (hereinafter referred to as: I. Schwenzer, *Conformity* [*in the CISG*]) 648, para. 1.

274 See below, at Section 5.2.1.2.

275 Recital 29, 1st and 2nd phrases, of the Proposal.

276 *Cf.* Recital 31, last phrase, of the Proposal.

277 E.g. Art. XI.165, §2, Economic Law Code (as installed by Art. 3 Act of 19 April 2014 'portant insertion du livre XI "Propriété intellectuelle" dans le Code de droit économique, et portant insertion des dispositions propres au livre XI dans les livres I, XV et XVII du même Code', *Moniteur Belge*, 12 June 2014).

278 E.g. Art. L. 121-1, third paragraph, Code de la propriété intellectuelle (as inserted by Art. 1, Act no 92-597 of 1 July 1992 'relative au Code de la propriété intellectuelle (partie Législative)', *Journal Officiel*, 3 July 1992).

279 E.g. §§12, 13 and 14 Act of 9 September 1965 'über Urheberrecht und verwandte Schutzrechte', *Bundesgesetzblatt* I 16 September 1965, 1273 (hereinafter referred to as: Urheberrechtsgesetz). In Germany, however, *all* authors' rights are unalienable pursuant to §29 Urheberrechtsgesetz.

furthermore made unwaivable by means of an EU Directive.[280] In summary, it is legally impossible to 'free' protected content from all of its copyright protection.

Applying a less strictly literal understanding to Article 8, the supplier is obliged to acquire all third party rights that are waivable. This is legally possible, but would be unnecessarily burdensome for the supplier. It is easy to grasp that movie or music providers like Netflix or iTunes will never find the willingness of big film or music producers like MGM or Sony Music to transfer all of the exploitation rights on their movies or songs. Requiring this would herald the end of many intermediaries supplying digital content. Hence, most probably the EU legislator does not require such comprehensive transfer. Where copyright is concerned, Article 8 should at most be interpreted as requiring the supplier to obtain licences necessary to make use of protected content in the usual fashion.

Another issue is left open, even when creatively interpreting Article 8 as a mere obligation to obtain all prerequisite agreements for 'consumer use' of the digital content. What if the supplier in good faith believes that he has all required permissions, while later it becomes clear that was not the case? Let us take a fee-based online movie platform like Netflix. This supplier supplies a certain movie in a digital format, which the consumer can (or rather, needs to) reproduce to watch. The supplier agreed on this supply type with the alleged copyright holder, the movie company. Four months later a random person shows up and claims that he wrote the movie script and did not transfer his rights. A court confirms his authorship over the work. As a result, inter alia, the consumer should have had his permission to reproduce his movie. The risk of 'unexpected' third parties showing up demonstrates that it is ex ante factually unfeasible to have absolute certainty that no third party rights will interfere with the consumer's use.

– *Previous appearances*

The wording of Article 8 originally stems from the Convention on the International Sale of Goods (CISG),[281] which does not apply to consumer contracts.[282] An obligation to supply objects 'free of third party rights' also shows up in prior EU instruments, like the DCFR[283] and the Proposal for a Common European Sales Law[284] (of which the adoption procedure was postponed

280 E.g. Art. 1 Directive 2001/84/EC of the European Parliament and of the Council of 27 September 2001 on the resale right for the benefit of the author of an original work of art, *OJ* L 272 of 13 October 2001, 32 and Art. 5 Directive 2006/115/EC of the European Parliament and of the Council of 12 December 2006 on rental right and lending right and on certain rights related to copyright in the field of intellectual property, *OJ* L 376 of 27 December 2006, 28.

281 Arts. 41 and 42 UN Vienna Convention on Contracts for the International Sale of Goods of 11 April 1980, *United Nations Treaty Series*, vol. 1489, I-25567 (hereinafter referred to as: CISG).

282 Art. 2(a) CISG.

283 Arts. IV.A.-2:305 and 306 DCFR.

284 Art. 102 of the Annex to the CESL Proposal.

sine die[285]). The CESL contains more precise provisions than the current Proposal and the DCFR. It not only prescribes that the contract's object has to be free 'of rights', but likewise free of any 'not obviously unfounded claim of a third party'. Probably that nuance was added in an attempt, inter alia, to overcome the situation described above in the previous paragraph.

4.2.3.2. Third Party Rights in General versus Intellectual Property Rights

The CISG, the DCFR and the CESL all have distinctive regimes for third party rights in general (*sensu stricto*) on the one hand, and intellectual property rights on the other. The general third party rules are more stringent than the specific IP rules.[286] The Proposal in hand does not differentiate; all 'third party rights' *sensu lato* are governed by the same principles.

– *Third party rights in general*

Third party rights other than IP rights will probably not entail either more issues or different issues than is the case under current general, consumer and international sales law. Imagine a professional seller (supplier) sells a CD containing digital content to a consumer. Later it turns out the seller was entitled neither to own nor to sell the CD. The true owner (a third party) claims the recovery of his CD. Who is entitled to what and what happens to the consumer sale contract? These issues are not specific to digital content. The same principles apply to other movables sold without a title. Therefore, this topic is not further elaborated on in this chapter.[287]

– *Intellectual property rights*

With regard to intellectual property rights, the CESL Proposal limits the extent of the legal defect provision to the territory where the consumer will (or could) use the content.[288] The supplier furthermore gets off if he neither was nor should have been aware of the rights or claims concerned.[289] He is likewise discharged if the consumer knew of the rights or claims at the time of conclusion of the contract.[290] *Mutatis mutandis* the CISG contains very similar limits to liability. In addition, however, it restricts the seller's duty if the legal defect arises from the need to meet the specifications communicated by the buyer.[291] Regrettably, these essential nuances were omitted from the current Proposal.

---

285 Commission Work Programme 2015, Annex 2 COM(2014)910 final, 12, para. 60.

286 I. Schwenzer, *Conformity* [*in the CISG*], 648, para. 1.

287 Reference should instead be made to the chapter by S. Jansen and S. Stijns, in this volume.

288 Art. 102(2)(a) of the Annex to the CESL Proposal. *Cf.* Art. 42(1)(a) and (b) CISG.

289 Art. 102(2)(b) of the Annex to the CESL Proposal. *Cf.* Art. 42(1), introductory phrase, *medio*, CISG.

290 Art. 102(4) of the Annex to the CESL Proposal. *Cf.* Art. 42(2)(a) CISG.

291 Art. 42(2)(b) CISG.

4.2.3.3. Transposing Article 8

When implementing and applying the legal defect provision in Belgian law, we suggest it that it is classified as a mandatory form of *porte-fort* of the supplier.

– *Porte-fort*

A *porte-fort* promise clause can be best described as a contractual clause whereby a contracting party gives an undertaking to his co-contracting party that he will persuade a third party to give a certain undertaking.[292] As *porte-fort* entails a so-called obligation to achieve a result, the former essentially *guarantees* that the third party will in fact be persuaded. In the event that this subsequently does not happen, the party promising *porte-fort* will be liable for breach of contract. He thus will need to reimburse his co-contracting party.[293]

Article 8 of the Proposal should be read as neither more nor less than a mandatory *porte-fort* clause that cannot be stipulated away in a professional-to-consumer contract on the supply of digital content.[294] The supplier should *guarantee* that he has all prerequisite legal bases to enable the consumer to perform all acts necessary for him to 'consume' the digital content in accordance with Article 6 of the Proposal. These legal bases can include contractual agreements like IP licences, as well as legal exceptions (if any). To achieve that result, the supplier could correspondingly limit the acts the consumer can perform with the supplied content and should make these limitations clear to him before the contract for supply is concluded.[295]

– *Open questions*

Suppose that the supplier violates his obligation pursuant to Article 8 because he does not hold the rights required for the consumer to use the content. The consumer subsequently encounters a third party claim. In that event, the

292 Art. 1120 Belgian Civil Code.

293 H. De Page, *Traité élémentaire de droit civil belge*, II, Brussels, Bruylant, 1964, 705; E. Dirix, B. Tilleman and P. Van Orshoven, *De Valks juridisch woordenboek*, Antwerp, Intersentia, 2001, 299; I. Samoy and D. Leroy, 'Sterkmaking: gevreesd en bemind' in A. De Boeck, S. Stijns and R. Van Ransbeeck (eds.), *Positie van de derde in het privaat vermogensrecht*, Bruges, die Keure, 2012, (199) 204, para. 7; S. Stijns, *Verbintenissenrecht*, Bruges, die Keure, 265, para. 332; B. Tilleman, 'Sterkmaking' in P. Van Orshoven, K. Geens, R. Lesaffer and B. Steen (eds.), *Ad amicissimum amici scripsimus, Vriendenboek Raf Verstegen*, Bruges, die Keure, 2004, 292; W. Van Gerven and S. Covemaeker, *Verbintenissenrecht*, Leuven, Acco, 2006, 231. *Cf.* M. Fontaine, '"Best Efforts", "Reasonable Care", "Due Diligence" and Industry Standards in International Agreements', *IBLJ* 1988, (983) 1001.

294 Art. 19 of the Proposal.

295 The supplier's obligation to provide information inter alia on these limitations of use could be derived from the information requirements in Art. 5(2) in combination with with Art. 5(1)(g) (consumer contracts in general) and Art. 6(2) in combination with Art. 6(1)(r) (distance and off-premises consumer contracts) Consumer Rights Directive.

consumer has an explicit legal basis in (the national law transposing) Article 8 in order to invoke the sanction regime installed by the Directive. Thus far the effects of the legal defect rule are clear. But is there more to it?

- *Impact on the third party–consumer relationship*

First, it should be set straight that Article 8 cannot be interpreted to such an extent that the supplier can be held liable every time the consumer infringes a third party right. The supplier has to guarantee to the consumer that third parties will not spoil his content 'consumption'. However, he should not hold the consumer harmless whenever the latter is summoned by a third party.

Second, imagine that a third party brings an action for infringement against the consumer. The action is based on certain acts that the consumer could only perform because of the supplier. What should the supplier then do? A first hypothesis is that the third party claim is justified. The consumer, for instance, downloaded a movie he obtained from the seller. He did not know that this seller had no licence allowing for reproductions. Supposedly the consumer could lawfully assume that the supplier had obtained the required authorisation for this act. The supplier could reasonably expect that the consumer would perform such an act. What should the supplier do? Is he obliged to intervene in all negotiations and law suits between the parties? Should he take the place of the consumer in all civil cases? If he holds the consumer harmless anyway, then can the third party hold the supplier liable and if so, does this discharge the consumer from his debts? Are these questions to be answered differently if the supplier neither knew nor should have known that there was a third party right not taken into account?[296] All of these issues are not addressed in the Proposal.

The second hypothesis starts from the circumstance that the third party claim was ill-founded. A court, for instance, holds that a work is not copyright-protected because it lacks originality. In brief, a person's claim to be recognised as an author fails. Neither the consumer nor the supplier has infringed any third party right. Should these proceedings and other consumer costs still be financed by the supplier?

- *Impact on the supplier–third party relationship*

Thirdly, does Article 8 entail an obligation for the supplier to make certain contractual arrangements with these right-holders, including the professionals who are in their turn 'the supplier's suppliers'? More specifically, should the supplier persuade these right-holders to give an undertaking that they will not sue the *consumer* for infringing their rights, if they can also point their claims at the *supplier*? An obligation of that kind could provoke devastating effects for small enterprises that act as a supplier. Their bargaining position vis-à-vis giant

[296] See above, at Section 4.2.3.1 (Literal interpretation).

right-holders will never be strong enough for them to be able to alter a contract to such an extent.

- *Impact on the third party's rights*

Fourthly and in connection with the previous paragraph, what are the potential consequences of Article 8 for the 'third party right-holders' at stake, including copyright holders? Save if otherwise stipulated, who can they direct their claims to? Should we arrive at the conclusion that these right-holders can no longer sue consumers for infringing their rights, when these rights were present at the time the related content was supplied to the consumer by the supplier? Can or should they instead sue the supplier (first)? None of these drastic options are justified. Why would a third party have to suffer negative effects of a contract regarding content he has justified claims to? It should be brought to mind this third party *by definition* is not involved in that contract.[297] Summing up, third parties should endure no direct negative effects of this provision.[298] The Preamble confirms this, but only as to intellectual property rights.[299]

- *Expected use of the digital content*

Finally, questions arise as to the limitation of the obligation to supply 'freed' content to the extent 'that the digital content can be used in accordance with the contract'. Clearly the interpretation of this limitation is important for the scope of Article 8. The key question is what kind of actions the consumer can expect to be allowed to perform. The expectations that need to be taken into account will depend on whether a clearly and comprehensively drafted contract applies to the supply. If that is true, Article 8 should be read as referring to the concrete co-contracting consumer.[300] Otherwise, the reasonable expectations of the average consumer are to be taken into account.[301] It could, however, prove very difficult[302] to ascertain these reasonable expectations in practice.[303]

4.2.3.4. Comparison: Online and Distance Sales of Goods Directive Proposal

Disregarding the unfortunate wording of the rule, it must finally be applauded that the EU legislator did not fail to incorporate a similar provision on 'legal

297 *Cf.* I. Schwenzer, *Conformity [in the CISG]*, 661–62, para. 3.
298 With regard to the right of redress (Art. 17 of the Proposal), see, however, the chapter by B. Keirsbilck, below.
299 Recital 21 of the Proposal.
300 Arg. ex Article 6(1) of the Proposal.
301 Arg. ex Article 6(1) of the Proposal.
302 See N. Helberger *et al.*, *Digital Content Contracts*, 44–47 for interesting and concise findings on this regard.
303 See above, at Section 4.1.3.

defects' in the parallel Proposal for an Online and Distance Sales of Goods Directive.[304] Similar issues might arise with regard to *goods* being ('physically') delivered to consumers. IP law is not at all specific to 'the digital world', and neither are third party rights in general. Copyright, design and trademark law, for instance, may equally apply to a chair bought by a consumer. The risks of an infringement by a consumer in such cases might be lower, but that is not the situation covered by the proposals. They only address the existence of hindering 'legal defects' at the time of supply. So, in our opinion there is no valid reason for the professional co-contracting party ('seller')[305] in those cases not to compensate the consumer, if the latter gets summoned by a third party.

5. CONFORMITY ASSESSMENT: TIME, LIABILITY AND PROOF

Both Articles 9 and 10 in essence provide rules on the assessment of the lack of conformity (if any) with the contract. Article 10 of the Proposal is entitled 'liability of the supplier'. In spite of that, together with Article 6(3) it constitutes the only provision that is related to the time limit issues as regards the supply of digital content. Article 9 on the other hand provides for specific rules on the parties' burden to prove conformity or the lack of it. All of these aspects will be discussed in this section.

5.1. SITUATIONS GIVING RISE TO REMEDIES

Pursuant to Article 10, the supplier can in essence be held liable by the consumer in two sets of circumstances. That is, either if the digital content is not supplied at all,[306] or if it (is supplied and) is affected by a lack of conformity.[307] This short enumeration of liability cases is surprising. It hardly corresponds to the parallel provision in the Online and Distance Sales of Goods Directive Proposal.[308] Firstly, that provision clarifies that liability can arise equally from not supplying to the consumer himself[309] as from not supplying to a third party (carrier) chosen by the consumer.[310] In combination with Article 5[311] of

304 Art. 7 of the Online and Distance Sales of Goods Proposal.
305 Art. 2(c) of the Online and Distance Sales of Goods Proposal.
306 Art. 10(a) of the Proposal.
307 Art. 10(b) and (c) of the Proposal.
308 Art. 8 of the Online and Distance Sales of Goods Proposal.
309 Art. 8(1)(a) of the Online and Distance Sales of Goods Proposal.
310 Art. 8(1)(b) of the Online and Distance Sales of Goods Proposal.
311 Art. 5(1) of the Proposal differentiates between (a) supplying to the consumer and (b) to, inter alia, 'a third party ... allowing the consumer to access [the digital content] and which has been chosen by the consumer'. See above, at Section 3.1.

Proposal on digital content, however, both situations are ultimately covered by Article 10 as well. Secondly and even more surprisingly, the Proposal under consideration omits any express confirmation of the supplier's liability in the two discussed cases of lack of conformity arising during the *integration of the digital content*. Again, however, this omission is overcome by Article 7, which equates integration-based non-conformities to lack of conformity in general.[312] Nevertheless, the absence of all of these clarifications is regrettable for the consequent lack of predictability and comprehensiveness.

Furthermore, it should not go unnoticed that the provision under consideration draws a distinction between the supplier's duty to supply on the one hand, and his duty to trade in goods that conform with the consumer contract on the other.[313] A similar diverging approach is currently used with regard to consumer sales law. The Consumer Sales Directive notably only harmonises the conformity issue. Rules on the delivery of consumer goods are, by contrast, harmonised by the Consumer Rights Directive.[314] Similarly to the latter Directive,[315] the Proposal at hand will allow the consumer to hold the supplier liable in case of non-delivery.[316]

5.2. TIME-RELATED RULES

The law on the sale of goods shows that multiple time-related rules may apply, including time bars as well as provisions temporarily shifting the burden of proof. First, the moment of assessing the existence of a lack of conformity should be set.[317] Next, there is a time frame during which this lack of conformity should become apparent in order to fall within the scope of the remedies.[318] Furthermore there might be a period during which the apparent lack of conformity is presumed (*iuris tantum*) to have existed at the former moment.[319] There also might be a maximum term for the affected party to react to the discovery of the lack of conformity.[320] When remedies are furthermore put into practice, additional

312 Art. 7, introductory phrase, read jointly with Art. 6, read jointly with Art. 10(a) or (b) of the Proposal.

313 *Cf.* Recital 34, 1st phrase, of the Proposal.

314 Art. 18 Consumer Rights Directive, which does not apply to 'digital content which is not supplied on tangible medium' pursuant to its Art. 17(1), *in fine*. This fits with Art. 10(a), read jointly with Art. 5 of the Proposal, as 'durable medi[a] incorporating digital content' are excluded from the application of Art. 5 pursuant to Art. 3(3) of the Proposal.

315 Art. 18(4) Consumer Rights Directive.

316 See above, at Section 3.

317 *Cf.* e.g. Art. 3(1), or Art. 3(1) read jointly with Art. 2(5) Consumer Sales Directive: 'at the time the goods were delivered'.

318 *Cf.* e.g. Art. 5(1), 1st phrase, Consumer Sales Directive: 'within two years as from delivery'.

319 *Cf.* e.g. Art. 5(3) Consumer Sales Directive: 'within six months of delivery of the goods'.

320 *Cf.* e.g. Art. 5(2), 1st paragraph, Consumer Sales Directive: 'within a period of two months from the date on which he detected [the] lack of conformity'.

time bars could apply, like terms for the supplying party to act by e.g. repairing or replacing the contract's subject-matter[321] or for the affected party to react by for example sending back the goods.[322] Finally, it is conceivable[323] that procedural or general 'common' law (*droit commun*) provides for generally applicable time limits that cause obligations, rights and claims of parties to expire.[324]

Time limits with regard to remedies (if any) will be dealt with in another chapter in this volume. Additional time limits stemming from national law will likewise not be discussed here, as they exceed this section's aim. Instead, we will respectively address the moment conformity is assessed, the point in time when the lack of conformity shows up and the period during which the burden of proof is reversed. In the (perhaps vain) hope of achieving some comprehensiveness, reference will finally be made to the maximum time for the consumer to inform the supplier about the lack of conformity that arose.

5.2.1. *Time to Assess Conformity*

The presence or absence of digital content's conformity with the contract is principally assessed as at the moment it is supplied.[325] Any lack of conformity arising after that point in time generally is not to be borne by the supplier. This logical keynote is equally present in the Consumer Sales Directive[326] and in the parallel Proposal on goods.[327]

In two situations, the moment to assess conformity is postponed. First the two cases of non-conformity resulting from integration should be brought to mind. Second, long-term contracts entail long-term conformity duties.

5.2.1.1. Postponement in Case of Integration 'in the Supplier's Sphere'

The first case in which the conformity assessment is delayed, occurs when the digital content has to be *integrated* into the consumer's digital environment. This is true at least if additional conditions are met. As was discussed above,[328]

---

321 *Cf.* e.g. Art. 9(2) of the Online and Distance Sales of Goods Proposal: 'within a reasonable time'.

322 *Cf.* e.g. Art. 13(b) of the Online and Distance Sales of Goods Proposal: 'in any event not later than 14 days'.

323 It should not go unnoticed at this point that the Belgian legislator chose not to apply the general time limit for obligations (see the footnote below) to lack of conformity of consumer goods. Instead, Art. 1649*quater*, §3, Belgian Civil Code provides for a specific rule. R. Steennot, 'Art. 1649quater BW' in *Comm.Bijz.Ov.* I, 2015, issue 101, 12–13, para. 13.

324 *Cf.* e.g. Art. 2262*bis*, §1, 1st paragraph, Belgian Civil Code, setting a 10-year limit as *lex generalis* principle for, inter alia, contractual obligations, starting from the due date.

325 Art. 10(b) of the Proposal.

326 Art. 3(1) Consumer Sales Directive.

327 Art. 8(1) of the Online and Distance Sales of Goods Proposal.

328 See above at Section 4.2.2 and esp. Section 4.2.2.3.

conformity is tested later, either if the integration operation was performed by the supplier or under his responsibility,[329] or if the consumer integrated the content in accordance with faulty integration instructions supplied by the supplier.[330]

If such an integration 'in the supplier's sphere' takes place, the new time to assess conformity will logically be the moment the integration process is finished. This will be true if the digital content is ready for use as intended. It will be up to the courts to decide when this legal fact has taken place. With regard to the integration performed by/under the responsibility of the supplier, ascertaining that time is unlikely to cause heavy debates.

If the consumer on the other hand is to perform the integration himself, two surprising findings cannot be left unnoted. First, the Proposal does not contain a time limit for the consumer to perform the integration operation. Such a limit, by contrast, *is* present in the Online and Distance Sales of Goods Directive Proposal.[331] Secondly, there is no restriction as to the number of times the supplier is obliged to enable integration that does not lead to a lack of conformity of the content. The flawless integration obligation is not expressly limited to the *first* time the consumer integrates the digital content in his 'digital environment'. Can we therefore conclude that any lack of conformity arising from faulty installation instructions at whatever point in time will entail that the consumer is entitled to invoke the Proposal's remedies, even if he (re)installs (integrates) the acquired content for the umpteenth time? This would place an (unduly) heavy burden on the supplier, as the consumer theoretically could decide to integrate the digital content at any given moment.

In conclusion, in both scenarios the conformity obligation of the supplier can be unlimitedly extended in time. Hence, either specific time rules should be incorporated in the Proposal, or some 'reasonable time test' like the abuse of law doctrine[332] should apply.

5.2.1.2. Postponement in Case of Long-Term Supply Contract

The point in time to assess contractual conformity is furthermore delayed when the contract provides that the digital content shall be supplied over a period of

329 Art. 7(a) of the Proposal.

330 Art. 7(b) of the Proposal.

331 Art. 8(2), 2nd phrase, of the Online and Distance Sales of Goods Proposal: 'the time when the consumer had reasonable time for the installation but in any case not later than 30 days after [the date of supply]'.

332 *Cf.* L. Cadiet and P. le Tourneau, 'Abus de droit' in *Répertoire de droit civil*, 2015, at '*abus de droit*', www.dalloz.fr, para. 8; A. Lenaerts, 'The General Principle of the Prohibition of Abuse of Rights: A Critical Position on Its Role in a Codified European Contract Law', *ERPL* 2010, (1121) 1122; A. Van Oevelen, 'Woord vooraf' in J. Rozie, S. Rutten and A. Van Oevelen (eds.), *Rechtsmisbruik*, Antwerp – Cambridge, Intersentia, 2015, (v) v.

time.[333] In that event, the content should conform throughout the full duration of the contract.[334] Within the scope of that provision, it is not necessary for the contract to be concluded for a definite period of time. If the contract is concluded for an indefinite period, it will be up to the supplier to terminate the agreement, should he no longer be able to ensure the conformity of the digital content. Only in that way can he avoid liability for lack of conformity.

This provision sharply contrasts with the conformity assessment rules in the law on the sale of goods. Pursuant to these rules, the seller usually can only be held liable if there is a lack of conformity at the time of delivery of the goods. By the rule in the current Proposal, the EU legislator supposedly wanted to match a lessor's duty to see that property can be fully enjoyed by the lessee.[335] A provision of that kind is characteristic of the law on lease contracts.[336]

It is important that this provision has a mandatory nature and can therefore not be derogated from by the contract. As a result, one should distinguish between two aspects subject to assessment. On the one hand, there is conformity as such. This can be agreed upon. On the other hand, there is the obligation to guarantee the agreed conformity throughout the full duration during which digital content is supplied. The latter obligation cannot be derogated from.

It is easy to imagine concrete examples of long-term contracts for the supply of digital content. A social network and an online gaming account in exchange for the provision of data make two illustrations. Access to a cloud service or to an online movie database like Netflix, paid for monthly, make two more examples. Despite these obvious illustrations, classifying a digital content supply contract as either one-off or *long-term* will not always be easy. This issue will be elaborated on below.[337]

5.2.2. *Time for the Lack of Conformity to Become Apparent*

Unlike the Consumer Sales Directive[338] and the Online and Distance Sales of Goods Directive Proposal,[339] the Proposal at issue does not mention a two-year (or any other) time frame during which the lack of conformity needs to become apparent for the remedies to be applicable.

The absence of a time provision is the result of a deliberate choice of the EU legislator.[340] It is formally justified by the nature of digital content: by using

333 Arts. 6(3) and 10(c) of the Proposal.
334 Art. 6(3) and Recital 34 of the Proposal.
335 *Cf.* M. Loos, *Digital Content B2C in CESL*, 147.
336 *Cf.* e.g. Art. 1719, 3° Belgian Civil Code; Art. 1719, 3° French Civil Code; Arts. 7:203 and 7:206(1) Dutch Civil Code. See above, at Section 2.1.3.
337 See below, at Section 6.2.
338 Art. 5(1), 1st phrase, Consumer Sales Directive.
339 Art. 14, 1st phrase, of the Online and Distance Sales of Goods Proposal.
340 *Cf.* Commission Digital Contracts Q&A, MEMO/15/6265, 2.

content, its value does not decline to the same extent as it does for goods. The intention not to have a time bar is confirmed by the Proposal's Preamble, which states that

> [b]y fully harmonising all requirements related to the topics regulated by this Directive, it precludes Member States, within its scope of application, from providing any further formal or substantive requirements, such as a *period during which the lack of conformity has to become apparent* (emphasis added).[341]

This observation has far-reaching consequences. Suppliers might still need to make accounting provision for rightful claims made by consumers, years and years after the supply of digital content. Strikingly, this is the case for one-off contracts. This will require suppliers to keep track of performed transactions for a long time. Expectations therefore are that a time limit similar to that in the Online and Distance Sales of Goods Directive Proposal will be inserted in the course of the legislative process. However, one must bear in mind an important difference. Specifically, the Preamble confirms that 'Member States should remain free to rely on national prescription rules in order to ensure legal certainty in relation to claims based on the lack of conformity of digital content'.[342] As a result, attention is due to the importance of national law that causes obligations, rights and claims of parties to extinct. Diverging starting points and terms may apply depending on the law applicable.

5.2.3. *Time of Reversal of the Burden of Proof*

Current EU consumer sales law provides for a minimum term of six months from the delivery date during which the burden of proof of the lack of conformity is reversed in favour of the consumer.[343] The Proposal on digital content goes further. It principally reverses the burden of proof without limits as to duration.[344] That newly outlined regime is explained below.[345] As a rationale, the Explanatory Memorandum to the Proposal explains 'digital content is not subject to wear and tear'.[346] This generalisation is, however, highly questionable, as the Proposal's scope includes, inter alia, CDs and DVDs.[347]

---

341 Recital 9 of the Proposal.
342 Recital 43, last phrase, of the Proposal.
343 Art. 5(3) Consumer Sales Directive.
344 Explanatory Memorandum, 12. *Cf.* Art. 9(1) and Recital 32, 3rd phrase, of the Proposal.
345 See below, at Section 5.4.
346 Explanatory Memorandum, 12.
347 Recital 12, 1st phrase, of the Proposal.

5.2.4. *Time to Notify the Supplier of a Lack of Conformity*

The Proposal, finally, does not require the consumer to notify the supplier of a lack of conformity within a specific time frame. The Consumer Sales Directive, by contrast, allowed Member States to lay down a maximum notification term of two months as from the date the lack of conformity was detected.[348] The Proposal's Preamble furthermore clarifies that national law can under no circumstance introduce a similar notification obligation.[349] Conversely, nothing is stated about the possibility of the contracting parties doing so.[350] The results of these findings will, however, be dealt with elsewhere in this volume.[351]

5.3. LIABILITY

Assuming that a lack of conformity is found, Article 10 of the Proposal spells out that the supplier should be considered liable. In other words, the positive obligation to supply digital content in conformity with the contract lies entirely upon the supplier. In some cases this can be perfectly justified, especially with regard to digital content, though this might not always be the case. The latter finding was already touched upon above.[352] It will be further elaborated on at the end of this chapter.[353]

5.4. BURDEN OF PROOF

It was pointed out above that the burden of proof with regard to the supply will not be harmonised.[354] Only the burden of proof of (non-)conformity is regulated. Pursuant to the Proposal, it shall not be for the consumer to prove a lack of conformity. Instead, 'in case of a dispute it should be for the supplier to prove that the digital content is in conformity with the contract, unless the supplier proves that the consumer's digital environment is not compatible with the digital content'.[355] One should, however, take care in interpreting these rules on the proof of non-conformity.

---

348 Art. 5(2), 1st subparagraph, Consumer Sales Directive. The Belgian legislator partly made use of this possibility by allowing parties to stipulate a maximum notification term, as long as that term does not exceed two months (Art. 1649*quater*, §2, Belgian Civil Code).

349 Recital 9 of the Proposal.

350 A functional interpretation of Art. 4 (full harmonisation) and Art. 19 (mandatory nature of the rules) of the Proposal however leads to the prima facie conclusion that the contracting parties neither can insert a notification period.

351 See the chapter by I. Claeys and J. Vancoillie in this volume.

352 See above, at Section 2.1.4.2.

353 See below, at Section 6.4.

354 See above, at Section 3.1.

355 Recital 32 of the Proposal.

5.4.1. *Who Proves What?*

For one thing, the consumer will have to prove that *something is wrong* about the digital content he acquired. This is nowhere mentioned in the Proposal, but is self-evident.[356] The consumer should only be entitled to remedies for lack of conformity if he can put his finger on the aspect he deems is not 'working properly'.[357] It will be up to the courts to confirm that finding.

It is only in the next phase the reversal of the burden of proof sets in. After the lack of conformity is established, the Proposal assumes it was already present at the time it should have been, notably at the supply date or at one of the two later moments explicitly laid down.[358] As a result, it is up to the supplier to prove that the lack of conformity was *not* present at the relevant time.

5.4.1.1. Reversing the Burden of Proof (Again)

Article 9 should be understood as allowing the supplier to refute this presumption in two ways. First, the presumption is reputable *iuris tantum*, meaning that the supplier can use all available means to prove that the digital content was in conformity at the time given. He could, for instance, invoke declarations made by the consumer on the conformity, or retrieve indications of (mis)use through technical means. It will be for the courts to decide whether this proof suffices.

Secondly, paragraph 2 of Article 9 'cancels' the reversal of the burden of proof in one specific circumstance. This notably is the case if the supplier shows that the consumer's digital environment[359] is incompatible with the digital content's technical requirements, including the interoperability.[360] In that event, however, the supplier additionally needs to prove that he provided pre-contractual information about those requirements to the consumer. Only if both conditions are met, will it once again be for the *consumer* to prove the non-conformity existed at the time of the aforementioned moment.[361] If the latter cannot, then the courts have to accept that the content did conform with the contract when it was supplied (or integrated).

Hence, the supplier should make sure that he proves that the two conditions were fulfilled. He himself is on the one hand responsible for providing the mentioned information. Therefore, it is up to him to make sure evidence of this

---

356 This can, however, be derived from the Commission Digital Contracts Q&A, MEMO/15/6265, 2: '*If* the digital content is defective, it will not be up to the consumer to prove that the defect existed' (emphasis added).

357 *Cf.* (on the CESL Proposal) M. Loos, *Digital Content B2C in CESL*, 155.

358 See above, at Section 5.2.1.

359 On the *digital environment* concept, see above, at Section 4.2.2.1.

360 On the *interoperability* concept, see above, at Section 4.1.2.1 (Interoperability and functionality).

361 Recital 32, last phrase, of the Proposal.

action is created and can later be produced in court. On the other hand, it is difficult to see how the supplier could provide evidence of a technical issue that relates to the consumer's digital environment, if there is no incentive for the consumer to help the supplier to establish the truth.

5.4.1.2. Proving Incompatibility of the Consumer's Digital Environment

To remedy the fact that the consumer holds the key to reversing the burden of proof again, the Proposal obliges the consumer to cooperate with the supplier in order 'to determine the consumer's digital environment'.[362] As an excessive use of that cooperation duty by the supplier could involve far-reaching consequences for the consumer, it is limited by some safeguards.

– *Safeguards for the consumer*

As a main guarantee, the supplier is only allowed to assess the environment's suitability for the content by using 'the technically available means which are the least intrusive for the consumer'.[363] The Recitals complete this line of reasoning by adding that the assessment

> may often be done for instance by providing the supplier with automatically generated incident reports or details of the consumer's internet connection. Only in exceptional and duly justified circumstances where with the best use of all other means there is no other way possible, this may also be done by allowing virtual access to the consumer's digital environment.[364]

How one should picture this in practice is left to our imagination. Is the supplier entitled to briefly peek at the consumer's computer while the latter is using it? Can the consumer be forced to transfer the control over his smartphone to the supplier? How can reports on the consumer's internet consumption prove the suitability of his digital environment for particular content and at the same not intrude upon the consumer's private life? When are circumstances 'exceptional and duly justified'? What is 'virtual access'; does that encompass all access *to* the consumer's 'virtual' digital assets, or simply access by virtual *means*, like remote access?

The Commission appears to take things quite easily where it proposes to merely provide that the consumer should cooperate 'without prejudice to the fundamental rights to the protection of private life, including confidentiality of communications, and the protection of personal data of the consumer'.[365]

---

362 Art. 9(3), 1st phrase, of the Proposal.
363 Art. 9(3), 2nd phrase, of the Proposal.
364 Recital 33, 1st phrase, *in fine*, and 2nd phrase, of the Proposal.
365 Recital 33, 1st phrase, initial part, of the Proposal. *Cf.* Art. 3(8) of the Proposal.

Moreover, the accompanying Memorandum states that the EU instruments on the processing of personal data are 'fully applicable'.[366] By contrast, however, the legislator omits any reference to the rights to privacy and data protection[367] in the (very short) section on the Proposal's impact on fundamental rights[368] in the Memorandum. It should therefore be advised that more research is conducted on the Proposal's impact on privacy and data protection law.

– *Consumer does not comply*

For the sake of the argument, suppose that minimally intrusive means were available to assess (non-)conformity of the consumer's digital environment. If the consumer then does not cooperate, the Proposal imposes a sanction on him. The burden of proof then notably is shifted to him again.[369] Hence, he can still try to prove that a lack of conformity was present at the relevant time. This, however, will be very burdensome, not least because the consumer's refusal to cooperate could give raise to suspicion as to the merits of his claim.

5.4.2. *Rationales*

The reversal of the burden of proof is motivated by the assumption that

> [d]ue to the specific nature of digital content with its high complexity as well as the supplier's better knowledge and access to knowhow, technical information and high-tech assistance, it is the supplier who is in a better position than the consumer to know the reasons for the digital content not being in conformity with the contract. The supplier is also in a better position to assess whether the lack of conformity with the contract is due to incompatibility of the consumer's digital environment with the technical requirements for the digital content.[370]

That basic assumption is highly questionable. Of course it might be true that the supplier's knowledge on the digital content and on digital environments will often exceed that of the consumer. Sometimes, however, the latter will be more specialised, particularly when it comes to his own concrete digital environment. Many advanced users are, for instance, well aware of the applications they have installed on their devices. A general assumption that the supplier always has more concrete technical knowledge than the consumer, thus in the first place is problematic due to the existence of lots of more specialised consumers.

366 Explanatory Memorandum, 4.
367 Arts. 7 and 8 Charter of Fundamental Rights of the EU.
368 Explanatory Memorandum, 10.
369 Art. 9(3), last phrase, and Recital 33, last phrase, of the Proposal.
370 Recital 32, 1st and 2nd phrase, of the Proposal.

More importantly however, the quoted presumption passes over the many European small business owners. Often small to medium-sized enterprises[371] involved in retailing digital content will lack highly specialised knowledge on all content they are willing to supply. As such, the local bookshop owner selling some movies on DVD and some games for game consoles like Sony PlayStation cannot reasonably be expected to have at its disposal the same amount of expertise as multinationals like the DVD-issuing movie company or Sony Interactive Entertainment. Hence, the truth of the knowledge assumption is in the second place even more doubtful because of the presence of technically less educated retailers.

Should *all* retail companies really be expected to know *all* technical details about *all* of the digital content they sell, irrespective of their size and the variety of products they offer?[372] Admittedly, it is appealing to be convinced by the counter-argument that all of these enterprises should simply reach agreements on the issues with their suppliers. Often, however, they are in more or less the same weak bargaining position as the consumer.[373] As such they are in fact squeezed between the stringent consumer protection rules on one side, and inescapable contractual duties on the other.

Excessive enactment of consumer protection legislation can just as much pose a threat to economies and consumer welfare as its absence. Eliminating the middle man limits the number of sales channels for digital content. As a result, producers' market power can increase and the risk of abuse becomes real. Hence, consumers literally pay the price for their protection.

6. UNSOLVED ISSUES

The Proposal addresses a fair number of aspects regarding the supply of digital content to consumers. If it is to be passed on its current reading, it will unquestionably provide answers to some of the prime uncertainties in digital content transactions. A lot of issues will remain unsolved, however. Generally speaking, it looks like the Proposal is 'missing the bigger picture'.

---

371 *Cf.* Explanatory Memorandum, 2, where it is stated that '[t]he purpose of [the Proposal] is to create a business-friendly environment and make it easier for businesses, especially SMEs, to sell cross-border'.

372 That stated, attention is to be drawn to the fallacy at Explanatory Memorandum, 2. There a false dilemma is used to persuade the reader that either all obligations equally apply to supplying SMEs, or SMEs are fully exempted from the Proposal, entailing that consumers cannot benefit from any protection whatsoever when contracting with SMEs. Multiple compromises can, however, be imagined.

373 See above, at Section 2.1.4.2.

6.1. LEGAL STATUS *ERGA OMNES* OF DIGITAL CONTENT

First, the Proposal *as such* will be insufficient to regulate the legal *status* of 'digital assets' (or digital 'goods' if you like) in a general way. The need for legal certainty regarding that status is obvious if one looks 'beyond' this first contract through which the supplied digital content reaches the recipient it is intended to be used by, viz the consumer. Can the consumer for instance *resell* the digital content he paid for access to?[374] And if so, can he split up the content and sell it to several persons? What law would apply to such contract? Would this entail legal obligations for the original supplier? Would he only be authorised to pass on the content to another consumer? Is he or should he be entitled to pass on his right to access to the content as a whole?

It is a common misconception that these issues can be tackled solely by intellectual property law and by copyright in particular. IP law does not 'automatically' apply to everything in a digital environment.[375] IP mainly concerns the outcome of a creative mental human activity,[376] which led part of the doctrine to describe IP rights' objects as 'intangible'.[377] Digital content, confusingly, is also sometimes referred to as 'intangible'.[378] They are, however, two different kinds of 'intangibility': incontestably 'an idea' or 'a creative expression' legally cannot be fitted into the same category as 'an e-book' or 'a Netflix account'. In short, IP law is not digital property law.

Perhaps the time has come to install a European property-law-like regime for digital content. Lots of legal issues arise from the absence of *erga omnes* rules that provide for rights and obligations *in rem* with regard to digital content. This creates a legal vacuum.[379] Digital content is generally said not to be *goods*[380] and thus cannot be subject to ownership or to property law in general, nor is it covered by sales law. Its carrying medium (a hard disk, CD, DVD, etc.) conversely is goods. Often the supply of digital content is qualified as a *service*.[381] But this type of service in general largely differs from most other services: a digital

374 *Cf.* judgment in *UsedSoft*, C-128/11, EU:C:2012:407 and its vast aftermath in doctrine.

375 The Preamble suggests that this error of reasoning also underlies odd Article 8. In recital 31, 3rd phrase, of the Proposal, the legislator errs in considering that digital content 'by its nature, is subject to intellectual property rights'.

376 A. Kur and T. Dreier, *European Intellectual Property Law: Text, Cases and Materials*, Cheltenham, Edward Elgar, 2013 (hereinafter referred to as: A. Kur and T. Dreier, *European IP*), 2.

377 A. Kur and T. Dreier, *European IP*, 2; A. Lucas, H.J. Lucas and A. Lucas-Schloetter, *Traité de la propriété littéraire et artistique*, Paris, LexisNexis, 2012, 34–38, paras. 28–29.

378 E.g. M. Lehmann, 'Contrat et immatériel. Rapport général' in Bruylant and LB2V (eds.), *L'immatériel. Journées espagnoles*, Brussels, Larcier/Bruylant, 2015, (341) 350.

379 *Cf.* N. Helberger *et al.*, *Digital Content Contracts*, 42–43; M. Loos, *Digital Content B2C in CESL*, 147.

380 *Cf.* e.g. the juxtaposition of 'goods' and 'services' in Recital 12 of the Proposal.

381 *Contra*: Recital 19 Consumer Rights Directive. *Cf.* J. Jacquemin, *Contenus numériques*, 16, para. 13.

content service leaves its customer with *something* (s)he can reuse, while other services are ephemeral.[382]

The Proposal already addresses the goods-*versus*-services matter to some extent. The definition of the scope in itself entails that specific rules will apply for digital content consumer contracts. These rules are different from the rules governing consumer contracts on both the sale of goods and the provision of services. If the Proposal is to be adopted, it could therefore become a first small but significant step[383] towards a proper comprehensive regime governing digital content.

6.2. ONE-OFF VERSUS LONG-TERM CONTRACTS

Secondly, the non-ephemeral character of digital content supplies has another complicating consequence. It was pointed out[384] that the Proposal for various purposes distinguishes one-off contracts from contracts that stipulate that digital content will be supplied over a period of time.[385] The time span during which the conformity obligation should be met and assessed, is one example. In our opinion however, it might not always be easy to correctly determine how a given contract is to be classified. Some cases are clear. Buying an old-school PC game on a CD-ROM will be a one-off contract. Conformity will therefore only be assessed at the time of supply. Acquiring access to a social network account or to a cloud service[386] undoubtedly establishes a long-term contract and *ditto* conformity obligations. But what to do with a paid-for application program that is rightfully downloaded onto a user's hard drive but automatically gets patches and updates every time the computer is connected to the internet? The payment, download and first installation were all one-off events, but due to the updates a contractual 'connection' persists. The user will constitute one party to that contract. It is questionable, however, who will be his co-contracting party. Must the supplier be classified as such? Updates are commonly provided directly by the developer. Hence, it would be more logical to conclude that the latter qualifies as the consumer's co-contracting party.

6.3. NEW PLATFORM ECONOMY

Thirdly, the Proposal omits law on digital content contracts concluded business-to-business (B2B) and consumer-to-consumer (C2C), and even on contracts

382 *Cf.* the divergent use of 'service' in Recitals 12 and 20 *versus* Recital 19 of the Proposal.
383 *Cf.* Lord J. Thomas' conclusion, as restated in M. Hönisch, *Vienna Conference Report*, 69.
384 See e.g. above, at Sections 4.2.3 and 5.2.1.2.
385 See inter alia Recital 29 and Arts. 6(4), 8(2), 13(5), 15(1) and 16 of the Proposal.
386 Recital 29, 2nd phrase, of the Proposal.

where the consumer is the party bound to supply the digital content. Especially the fact that digital content supplies by consumers to either other consumers or a professional party are not covered might create a great deal of uncertainty. The present-day internet infrastructure facilitates rapid and cheap exchanges of data and promotes a sharing economy. PC and mobile applications and games are for instance designed by a creative IT student on one side of the world and are downloaded by whatever natural person on the other side of the world. Often these apps can be obtained for free (with ads) or in exchange for a very low price (ad-free version). Exchange of this digital content often requires the use of an intermediate platform[387] like Google Play, Windows Store or the Apple App Store.

The correctness of classifying platform managers like Google, Microsoft or Apple as 'suppliers' of the content in those cases, is highly questionable.[388] Undoubtedly, there might be a contract concluded between the platform owner and the consumer.[389] However, are the former not merely internet platform service providers?[390] More logically, the aforementioned IT student is expected to qualify as the consumer's co-contracting party as far as the supply of digital content is concerned.[391] The current Proposal does not cover issues relating to the complex legal structures involved in digital platforms. That finding is regrettable, for legal uncertainties may restrain the potential of the digital platform market.

6.4. FORGETTING ABOUT THE SUPPLY CHAIN

In the section about the burden of proof[392] it was elucidated that the Proposal seems to be overlooking the smaller-scale retailer of digital content. The supplier is expected to have a vast amount of technical knowledge at his disposal, which not always seems reasonable. The analysis of other rules in the Proposal led to similar conclusions. It was touched upon that all suppliers are (unreasonably) presumed to be interoperability experts.[393]

Furthermore, it was pointed out that the supplier will often have no choice but to endure situations that are presented to him as an unalterable fact. As such

387 *Cf.* D. Možina, 'Retail Business, Platform Services and Information Duties', *EuCML* 2016, (25) (hereinafter referred to as: D. Možina, *Retail business*) 25.

388 J. Sénéchal, *Double Challenge*, 42. C. Busch *et al.*, *The Rise of the Platform Economy*, 5 therefore recommend that EU legislation should require the platform service provider to actively clarify its role to consumers.

389 D. Možina, *Retail business*, 25–26.

390 M. Loos, 'Standard terms for the use of the Apple App Store and the Google Play Store', *EuCML* 2016, (10) 10.

391 See above, at Section 2.1.4.2.

392 See notably above, at Section 5.4.2.

393 See above, at Section 4.1.2.1 (Interoperability and functionality).

he will often not be in a position to create or change installation (integration) instructions. Nevertheless, suppliers need to bear the consequences of third parties' choices to provide (correct) instructions. Similarly, there is no unambiguous solution in the case where additional third party content has to be installed as a prerequisite for use of the acquired content.[394] Finally, the consequences of Article 8 on 'legal defects' should be brought to mind.[395]

In general, it seems as if the EU legislator assumes that most of the digital content is supplied directly by its producer to the consumer. In reality however, a whole chain of suppliers is situated between those actors. In the current Proposal the consumer can turn to the supplier to raise non-conformity of digital content for an unlimited term.[396] If he does so after years have passed, he will still benefit from the reversal of the burden of proof.[397] Assuming that the retailing supplier is unable to prove that the non-conformity only arose after the supply date, the remedies apply. That supplier will by contrast not be able to benefit from the reversed burden of proof in relation to the previous link in the sales chain, namely his supplier. As a result, that retailer has to bear the costs of the non-conformity, while the producers remain untouched.[398] Needless to say that outlook will hardly appeal to potentially new retailers and there will barely be an incentive for producers to adapt their behaviour.

The Commission's Q&A press release denounces the 'untapped potential of cross-border e-commerce in the EU', explaining that '[o]nly 12% of EU retailers sell online to consumers in other EU countries'.[399] It claims the Proposal will lead to 'more competitive prices'.[400] In addition, the Explanatory Memorandum states that competition will increase and that a win-win situation for businesses and consumer will emerge.[401] In the light of what was argued above, it is, however, doubtful whether the Proposal will actually reach the goals the Commission promises.

6.5. FINDING

It is regrettable that at least some of these issues are not dealt with in the Proposal. However, it is clear that finding solutions for all of this would underestimate the required time and work as well as the need for political compromises.

394 See above, at Section 4.2.2.2 (Integration instructions).
395 See above, at Section 4.2.3.1 (Literal interpretation).
396 See above, at Sections 5.2.2 and 5.2.4.
397 See above, at Section 5.2.3.
398 *Cf.* the comments made by C. Wendehorst, as summarised in M. Hönisch, *Vienna Conference Report*, 69.
399 Commission Digital Contracts Q&A, MEMO/15/6265, 1. *Cf.* Explanatory Memorandum, 2.
400 Commission Digital Contracts Q&A, MEMO/15/6265, 2.
401 Explanatory Memorandum, 9.

An exaggerated scope could raise the risk of the Proposal being rejected. The Commission apparently learned from the past[402] and therefore chose an approach that involves a so-called 'targeted and focused set of fully harmonised rules'.[403] It only focuses on the essential 'mandatory consumer EU contract rights' which are 'identified as trade barriers'.[404] A modest tenor might indeed decrease the likelihood of the Proposal to fail.[405]

7. CONCLUSIONS

By this Proposal, the EU legislator takes a promising new step towards a proper legal framework for the digital world. It has a broad scope of application. That scope pivots on the threefold definition of digital content, which includes both data and services. Digital content is governed by the Proposal as soon as it constitutes the object of a supplier-to-consumer contract where the consumer pays a price or actively provides data in exchange. It is irrelevant whether the content is supplied on a tangible medium, whether it is tailor-made and whether the contract is classified as sale, as a service agreement or as another contract type. All of these simplifications are to be welcomed. Similarly, the equation of actively provided data to money must be applauded. Nonetheless, a number of clarifications or adaptations are necessary to enhance legal certainty. It should, inter alia, be clarified what circumstances constitute an 'active provision' and how the circumvention of the rules through the exemptions can be avoided. In addition, it should not go unnoted that the Proposal contradictorily does distinguish between money and data when ascertaining conformity. The scope of some of the excluded contracts furthermore needs an express limitation. Last but not least, the Proposal should include logical rules on mixed contracts that do not lead to discriminatory situations. There is no valid reason why software on a CD-ROM is assimilated to a software download, while other rules apply to the same software that is pre-installed in a device.

Rights, obligations and remedies in the current Proposal are only fit for two-party relations between consumers and suppliers. The drafters apparently assume that digital content is (mostly) supplied directly from its developer to its consumer and that the professional nature of the consumer's counterparty is

402 Communication (Commission) to the European Parliament, the Council and the European Economic and Social Committee 'Digital contracts for Europe – Unleashing the potential of e-commerce', COM(2015)633 final, http://eur-lex.europa.eu/legal-content/EN/TXT/?uri=consil:ST_15261_2015_INIT (hereinafter referred to as: 'Commission Digital Contracts Communication, COM(2015)633 final'), 6, para. 3; Explanatory Memorandum, 2. In both documents express references are made to the (failed) CESL Proposal.

403 Explanatory Memorandum, 2.

404 Explanatory Memorandum, 6.

405 *Cf.* Commission Digital Contracts Communication, COM(2015)633 final, 6.

always clear. These assumptions are problematic for numerous reasons. It is not always possible for the consumer to ascertain the identity of his counterparty. Furthermore, the rising use of platform service providers and the long-time frequent use of end-user licence agreements are ignored. In addition, it is unreasonable to always expect intermediaries to have full technical knowledge on the content they supply, let alone to be able and entitled to alter the content so that it conforms. More generally speaking, it seems the EU legislator disregards the existence of the supply chain. The Proposal could, inter alia, have detrimental effects on small enterprises, that are squeezed between consumer law and producers' bargaining power.

The act of supplying digital content is only governed by the Proposal if the content is not supplied on a tangible medium. In the opposite case, the Consumer Rights Directive applies. The supplier has fulfilled his supply obligation when the good arrives with the consumer or at a specific third party. That supply should in principle take place immediately after the conclusion of the contract, on pain of the immediate termination of the contract. We found that the burden of proof of the supply is not harmonised and therefore depends on national law.

The conformity provisions constitute the Proposal's core. Deplorably, however, the proposed regime in principle merely guarantees conformity with the contract by imposing subjective criteria. Objective safeguards only apply if contractual provisions are absent or non-transparent. The reasons given for that regime are unconvincing; it undermines the whole idea of consumer law. Next, the subjective and objective criteria both refer to the same list of performance features. Courts will need to interpret the scope of these features. If subjective criteria apply, the Proposal needs additional requirements to be met. Unfortunately, all of these requirements can be stipulated away by the supplier. Again, the result is an instrument that adds little protection. This contrasts with our findings as to previous EU consumer contract instruments.[406] Often the latter give shape to consumer protection rules with high potential, but lack effective remedies. The Proposal at issue on the other hand is a tiger that presumably does have teeth,[407] but unfortunately it barely has any body.

Some specific mandatory conformity requirements are added to the general rule. Both of them pursue praiseworthy aims but deserve to be redrafted. The provision on integration is analogous to the long-standing rules on the installation of goods, but laudably requires neither that the installation process is part of the supply contract, nor that the consumer himself integrates the

406 *Cf.* inter alia A. De Franceschi, 'The EU Digital Single Market Strategy in Light of the Consumer Rights Directive: The "Button Solution" for Internet Cost Traps and the Need for a More Systematic Approach', *EuMCL* 2015, (144) 145 and 148 (on the Consumer Rights Directive).

407 An analysis of the remedies in the Proposal however is the subject of the chapter by I. Claeys and J. Vancoillie, in this volume.

digital content. Clarifications are due with regard to non-conformity arising from integration instructions (or the absence thereof). Article 8 on 'legal defects' should furthermore be provided with a lot of nuances. It should be classified as an obligatory *porte-fort* clause by which the supplier guarantees that he has all required legal bases to enable the consumer to make use of the digital content.

Multiple time-related rules can be inferred from the Proposal. In principle, conformity will be assessed on the moment of supply. It is assessed on a later point in time, however, either if the supplier has to bear the risks involved in integration, or if a long-term supply contract is at hand. We however argued that in general it will not always be easy to determine whether a contractual relation concerning digital content is one-off or long-term. In its current wording it is furthermore of no relevance at what moment the lack of conformity becomes apparent and there is no time limit for the consumer to notify the supplier. The Proposal, however, will not affect national-law time bars that cause obligations, rights or claims to expire.

The burden of proof is only regulated as far as conformity is concerned. If the consumer can proof there is a lack of conformity, then that lack is deemed to have been present at the time of supply. This inversion of the burden of proof is drafted to have no limitation in time. The reasons cited to justify this unlimited shift are unconvincing. The supplier can reverse the burden of proof to the consumer if he can prove that the consumer's digital environment is incompatible with the content rather than the other way around. The consumer has to cooperate in order to ascertain whether this is the case, on pain of the burden of proof being shifted to him again. Issues may arise as to the means allowed to verify compatibility of the consumer's digital environment, and as to the impact thereof on the consumer's privacy and data protection rights.

Finally, we found that the enactment of a Directive with the scope at hand would only entail solutions for the tip of the iceberg of legal issues arising from the digital world. A comprehensive legal regime on a status *erga omnes* for digital assets is probably far off. Nonetheless, the Proposal may be a first and essential step towards the future. It confirms the need for specific rules on digital content and will be the outcome of a delicate balancing exercise around political willingness, simplicity, a demand for comprehensiveness, etc.

REMEDIES, MODIFICATION OF DIGITAL CONTENT AND RIGHT TO TERMINATE LONG-TERM DIGITAL CONTENT CONTRACTS

Ignace Claeys and Jonas Vancoillie

1. INTRODUCTION

In an ideal world, contracting parties should know their contractual rights and obligations with sufficient certainty and without prohibitive cost. We all know that the reality is often different. Parties either incur additional costs to determine their legal position, or they accept the risk of not knowing the ins and outs of their legal position (and sometimes they can still invoke mistake or some other remedy for not having been sufficiently informed when concluding the contract). This is true for domestic transactions and even more so for cross-border contracts. Those active on the market in the European Union (EU), both businesses and consumers, are confronted not with a single contract law regime but with at least[1] as many contract law regimes as there are Member States. Evidently, many concepts, principles and rules of contract law are quite similar across the borders of the EU Member States, and the EU institutions have created uniform contract law rules in an incremental way through various sets of legal instruments, such as regulations and directives, and also through the case law of the Court of Justice. Those rules are, however, mostly limited in scope and are

1 When not taking into account intra-state differences, such as Scottish versus English contract law.

mainly restricted to business-to-consumer (B2C) transactions. Persons active on the EU market (and, *a fortiori*, those active internationally) are therefore forced to include the effects of the variety of national contract law regimes in their legal risk assessments. While large companies spend money on comparative exercises, for example by preparing long questionnaires on issues of national contract law regimes, most small and medium-sized enterprises (SMEs) and consumers do not have the financial means to perform such exercises and therefore either take the legal risk involved or refrain from engaging in a particular activity.

Starting in the 1980s, these transaction costs led to the establishing of various sets of definitions, rules and principles in European contract law (and beyond). Contract law specialists like to denominate those sets by their abbreviations, the main ones being the PECL,[2] the DCFR,[3] and the CESL.[4] While the former two sets were mainly academic exercises, the Common European Sales Law (CESL) was a directive proposed in 2011 by the previous European Commission. It was conceived as a set of contract law rules that parties could opt to employ (hence its description as an optional instrument), in which event otherwise applicable national rules would no longer apply to the topics covered by the CESL. It was, however, withdrawn by the current European Commission in late 2014.[5] Although the CESL covered a specific subset of contracts only (mainly sales contracts), it covered many issues of general contract law such as the formation and validity of contracts, and it had rules for both business-to-business (B2B) and B2C transactions. Apparently, the time was deemed not to be ripe for such a broad initiative.[6]

The proposed Directive concerning contracts for the online and other distance sales of goods (ODSD)[7] and Directive concerning contracts for the

---

2 O. Lando and H. Beale (eds.), *Principles of European Contract Law, Parts I and II*, prepared by the Commission on European Contract Law, The Hague, Kluwer Law International, 2000.

3 C. von Bar, E. Clive and H. Schulte-Nölke, *Principles, Definitions and Model Rules of European Private Law. Draft Common Frame of Reference (DCFR). Outline Edition*, prepared by the Study Group on a European Civil Code and the Research Group on EC Private Law (Acquis Group), Munich, Sellier, 2009. Book I sets out general provisions, followed by Book II on contracts and other juridical acts, Book III on obligations and corresponding rights, and Book IV on specific contracts and the rights and obligations arising from them (in which the rules on sales can be found in Part A).

4 Proposal for a Regulation of the European Parliament and of the Council on a Common European Sales Law, COM(2011) 635 final, http://eur-lex.europa.eu/legal-content/EN/TXT/?uri=CELEX%3A52011PC0635 (hereinafter referred to as: CESL).

5 Annex to the Communication from the Commission to the European Parliament, the Council, the European Economic and Social Committee and the Committee of the Regions Commission Work Programme 2015. A New Start, Annex 2, COM(2014) 910 final, http://ec.europa.eu/atwork/pdf/cwp_2015_withdrawals_en.pdf.

6 For a recent historical overview of European contract law, see R. Schulze, 'The New Shape of European Contract Law', *EuCML* 2015/4, 139–44.

7 Proposal of 9 December 2015 for a Directive of the European Parliament and of the Council on certain aspects concerning contracts for the online and other distance sales of

supply of digital content (DCD)[8] launched on 9 December 2015 are a renewed attempt to harmonise certain aspects of contract law within the EU. This time, the European Commission wishes to focus on removing the main legal obstacles to realising a single digital market. The proposed directives were produced in the context of the Digital Single Market Strategy adopted by the European Commission on 6 May 2015.[9] The two proposed directives therefore have a much narrower scope than the CESL originally had.[10] They are limited to some rules for distance purchases (e.g. online, telephone or mail) of goods and the supply of digital content (such as 'music, movies, apps, games, films, cloud storage services or broadcasts of sport events'[11]). The Commission repeatedly encourages a focus on removing the 'uncertainty about key contractual rights',[12] or, in more detail on,

> harmonising at Union level only those targeted, key mandatory consumer EU contractual rights which are essential in cross-border online transactions, and which have been identified as barriers to trade by stakeholders and are necessary to build consumer trust when buying online abroad.[13]

---

goods, COM(2015) 635 final, http://eur-lex.europa.eu/legal-content/EN/TXT/?uri=COM%3A2015%3A635%3AFIN (hereinafter referred to as: ODSD).

8 Proposal of 9 December 2015 for a Directive of the European Parliament and of the Council on certain aspects concerning contracts for the supply of digital content, COM(2015) 634 final, http://eur-lex.europa.eu/legal-content/EN/TXT/?uri=CELEX:52015PC0634 (hereinafter referred to as: DCD).

9 Communication from the Commission to the European Parliament, the Council, the European Economic and Social Committee and the Committee of the Regions. A Digital Single Market Strategy for Europe, COM(2015) 192 final, http://eur-lex.europa.eu/legal-content/EN/TXT/?qid=1447773803386&uri=CELEX%3A52015DC0192 (hereinafter referred to as: Digital Single Market Strategy).

10 The European Parliament's Committee for Legal Affairs (JURI) proposed to limit the scope of the CESL to distance contracts, notably online contracts. See Memo of the European Commission, 'Optional European Sales Law: Commission proposal backed by European Parliament committee', MEMO/13/792, http://europa.eu/rapid/press-release_MEMO-13-792_en.htm. The European Parliament supported this. See: European Parliament legislative resolution of 26 February 2014 on the proposal for a regulation of the European Parliament and of the Council on a Common European Sales Law, P7_TA(2014)0159, http://www.europarl.europa.eu/sides/getDoc.do?pubRef=-//EP//TEXT+TA+P7-TA-2014-0159+0+DOC+XML+V0//EN. For the response of the European Law Institute, see: Statement of the European Law Institute on the Proposal for a Regulation on a Common European Sales Law, COM(2011) 635 final. 1st Supplement: Response to the EP Legislative Resolution of 26 February 2014, http://www.europeanlawinstitute.eu/fileadmin/user_upload/p_eli/Publications/CESL_1st_Supplement.pdf.

11 Explanatory Memorandum accompanying Proposal of 9 December 2015 for a Directive of the European Parliament and of the Council on certain aspects concerning contracts for the online and other distance sales of goods, COM(2015) 635 final, http://eur-lex.europa.eu/legal-content/EN/TXT/?uri=COM%3A2015%3A635%3AFIN (hereinafter referred to as: Explanatory Memorandum DCD), 3.

12 E.g. Recital 7 ODSD.

13 Explanatory Memorandum DCD, 6.

In other words, not all legal aspects of distance purchases of goods or the supply of digital content are covered. The proposed directives are also limited to B2C relations. No rules are provided for B2B relations, nor for C2C (consumer to consumer) or P2P (peer to peer) relations. The proposals are also limited to the relationship between a seller and a purchaser and therefore do not cover relations between a producer and the ultimate consumer in a chain of contracts.

The digital revolution is rapidly transforming our economy and our society in general.[14] E-commerce is growing steadily. Businesses increasingly offer goods and digital content online and across borders to consumers. According to the European Commission, however, cross-border e-commerce is not realising its full potential. The patchwork of national consumer laws is said to make these cross-border transactions unnecessarily complicated, and to discourage consumers and businesses from engaging in e-commerce.[15] When goods purchased by a consumer via the web from an online shop established in another EU Member State prove to be defective, the differences in consumer laws among Member States are believed to adversely affect consumer confidence when purchasing cross-border.[16] When it comes to digital content contracts, consumers may be confronted with an even higher level of uncertainty. So far, many EU Member States have refrained from specifically regulating digital content contracts. It is not even certain to which specific type of contract those contracts belong (e.g. sale, service, rental). The lack of a clear contractual framework for such contracts is said to contribute to the erosion of consumer protection and legal fragmentation.[17] Not only consumers, but also businesses (in particular SMEs) are faced with additional costs caused by the lack of a uniform or clear contractual framework when selling goods online or offering digital content. Businesses must take into account different national consumer laws when selling goods cross-border and might not even know which rules at all are applicable when offering digital content to consumers.[18]

The editors of this book have asked us to analyse the remedies under both the ODSD and the DCD, as well as the specific provisions of the CDS on modification of digital content and termination of long-term contracts. With our analysis, we

---

14 For other examples, see R. Schulze and D. Staudenmayer (eds.), *Digital Revolution: Challenges for Contract Law in Practice*, Baden-Baden, Nomos, 2016.

15 Digital Single Market Strategy, 3–4.

16 Recital 7 ODSD; Commission Staff Working Document Impact Assessment accompanying the document Proposals for Directives of the European Parliament and of the Council (1) on certain aspects concerning contracts for the supply of digital content and (2) on certain aspects concerning contracts for the online and other distance sales of goods, SWD(2015) 274 final, 2, http://eur-lex.europa.eu/legal-content/EN/TXT/PDF/?uri=CELEX:52015SC0274R(01)&from=EN (hereinafter referred to as: Impact Assessment), 13–16; Digital Single Market Strategy, 4.

17 Recitals 4–7 DCD; Impact Assessment, 13; Digital Single Market Strategy, 4.

18 Recital 6 ODSD; Recitals 3 and 5–6 DCD; Impact Assessment, 10–13.

would be happy to achieve two goals. By systematically comparing the proposed rules of the ODSD and the DCD with existing Belgian consumer and contract law, we first want to assess the potential impact of these proposals on Belgian law.[19] The second goal is to consider whether the proposed rules are apt to satisfy the Commission's stated objectives of providing a high level of consumer protection and increasing legal certainty in such a way that the key legal barriers to e-commerce are removed.

The chapter is presented in three sections. In the first section, as an introduction, we provide a brief overview of the background to and the essential characteristics of the ODSD and DCD (topics which, for the most part, are dealt with further by other chapters of this volume). In the second section, we analyse the remedies which would be made available to consumers under the two proposals. In the third section, we address two specific provisions of the DCD regarding modification of digital content as well as termination of long-term contracts. In the conclusion we summarise our findings and offer some recommendations for amending the two proposals on the topics covered by this chapter.

2. BACKGROUND AND ESSENTIAL CHARACTERISTICS OF THE PROPOSALS

The 1999 Consumer Sales Directive[20] (CSD) already harmonised some aspects of contracts for the sale of consumer goods. Under Belgian law, this Directive was implemented in the Civil Code (CC) in article 1649*bis* onward.[21] These rules are applicable to the sale of consumer goods by a professional seller to a consumer.[22] The European Commission has now proposed two additional consumer rights directives.

---

19 For an analysis of the proposals from a United Kingdom perspective, see: H. Beale, 'Scope of application and general approach of the new rules for contracts in the digital environment. In-depth analysis', *Workshop for the JURI Committee*, PE 536.493, Brussels, Policy Department C: Citizens' Rights and Constitutional Affairs, European Parliament, 2015.

20 Directive 1999/44/EC of the European Parliament and of the Council of 25 May 1999 on certain aspects of the sale of consumer goods and associated guarantees, *OJ* L 171, 7 August 1999, 12, http://eur-lex.europa.eu/legal-content/EN/TXT/?uri=CELEX:31999L0044 (hereinafter referred to as: CSD).

21 C. Cauffman, 'De nieuwe wet op de consumentenkoop', *TPR* 2005, 787–861; L. Peeters, 'De nieuwe wetgeving voor consumentenkoop ... (eindelijk) in het BW', *RW* 2004–05, 411–56. S. Stijns and J. Stuyck (eds.), *Het nieuwe kooprecht. De wet van 1 september 2004 betreffende de bescherming van de consumenten bij verkoop van consumptiegoederen*, Antwerp, Intersentia, 2005.

22 Article 1649*bis*, §1 CC; Article 1 CSD.

The first proposal, the ODSD, is applicable to[23] contracts for the online and distance sale of tangible goods[24] concluded between a consumer[25] and a professional seller.[26] The ODSD takes the CSD as a starting point and holds to the main provisions of the CSD.[27] Nevertheless, the ODSD is not a mere copy of the CSD. Several rules are supplemented and clarified in the new proposal. Moreover, the ODSD also introduces rules which diverge from those in the CSD. For example, unlike the CSD,[28] the ODSD allows consumers to terminate the contract in the case of a minor lack of conformity.[29] The ODSD also supplements the 2011 Consumer Rights Directive,[30] which fully harmonised certain rules for distance sales of goods, such as pre-contractual information requirements and the right of withdrawal.[31]

The second proposal, the DCD, covers contracts where the supplier[32] supplies digital content[33] to a consumer[34] in exchange for a price[35] or another

---

23 Article 1(1) ODSD.

24 'Goods' is defined in Article 2(d) ODSD as 'any tangible movable items with the exception of (a) items sold by way of execution or otherwise by authority of law; (b) water, gas and electricity unless they are put up for sale in a limited volume or a set quantity'.

25 A 'consumer' is defined in Article 2(b) ODSD as 'any natural person who, in contracts covered by this Directive, is acting for purposes which are outside his trade, business, craft or profession'.

26 A 'seller' is defined in Article 2(c) ODSD as 'any natural person or any legal person, irrespective of whether privately or publicly owned, who is acting, including through any other person acting in his name or on his behalf, for purposes relating to his trade, business, craft or profession in relation to contracts covered by this Directive'.

27 Explanatory Memorandum accompanying the Proposal of 9 December 2015 for a Directive of the European Parliament and of the Council on certain aspects concerning contracts for the supply of digital content, COM(2015) 634 final, http://eur-lex.europa.eu/legal-content/EN/TXT/?uri=CELEX:52015PC0634 (hereinafter referred to as: Explanatory Memorandum ODSD), 3.

28 Article 3(6) CSD.

29 Below, Section 3.1.3.3.

30 Directive 2011/83/EU of the European Parliament and the Council of 25 October 2011 on consumer rights, amending Council Directive 93/13/EEC and Directive 1999/44/EC of the European Parliament and of the Council and repealing Council Directive 85/577/EEC and Directive 97/7/EC of the European Parliament and of the Council, OJ L 304, 22 November 2011, 64, http://eur-lex.europa.eu/legal-content/EN/TXT/?uri=CELEX:32011L0083 (hereinafter referred to as: CRD).

31 Explanatory Memorandum ODSD, 4.

32 A 'supplier' is defined in Article 2(3) DCD and has the same definition as 'seller' in the ODSD, n 26 above.

33 'Digital content' is defined in Article 2(1) DCD and means '(a) data which is produced and supplied in digital form, for example video, audio, applications, digital games and any other software, (b) a service allowing the creation, processing or storage of data in digital form, where such data is provided by the consumer, and (c) a service allowing sharing of and any other interaction with data in digital form provided by other users of the service'.

34 A 'consumer' is defined in Article 2(4) and thus in the same way as in the ODSD, n 25 above.

35 'Price' is defined in Article 2(6) DCD as 'money that is due in exchange for digital content supplied'.

counter-performance in the form of data.[36] As is the case with the ODSD, this proposal also supplements the CRD, which already fully harmonised some other features.[37] Besides this, there are only very few specific rules for digital content contracts in the national legislation of EU Member States, including Belgium. The existing legal regime in the EU for digital content contracts is considered to be vague and ambiguous. The current proposal intends to provide coherent consumer rights for digital content contracts.[38]

The target of both the ODSD and the DCD is limited.[39] The European Commission has chosen to target only the key issues which have been identified as the main barriers to both traders and consumers in cross-border transactions[40] (e.g. conformity and remedies in case of lack of such conformity[41]). Since the proposals only lay down rules for specific key areas, they do not affect the national contract laws of the EU Member States in areas not regulated by the proposals, such as the validity of the contract and limitation periods.[42] Below we present an overview of the areas covered and the areas not covered by the two proposals in order to put these proposals in the right perspective (the grey cells indicate the areas covered by the proposals).

Table 1. Aspects covered and aspects not covered by the ODSD and the DCD

	ODSD	DCD
Formation and validity of the contract	N	N
Interpretation of the contract	N	N
Delivery/supply	N	Y (Article 5)
Conformity with the contract	Y (Articles 4–6 & 8)	Y (Articles 6–7 & 9)
Free of third party rights	Y (Article 7)	Y (Article 8)
Seller's/supplier's remedies	N	N
Consumer's remedies for failure to deliver/supply	N	Y (Articles 11 & 14)
Consumer's remedies for non-conformity	Y (Articles 9–13), but without rules on damages	Y (Articles 12–14), including a rule on damages
Guarantee period	Y (Article 14)	Y (Recital 43: no restricted guarantee period)

(continued)

36 Article 3(1) DCD.
37 Explanatory Memorandum DCD, 3.
38 Explanatory Memorandum DCD, 2–3 and 5.
39 This is elaborated on in the chapter by R. Steennot and S. Geiregat in this volume.
40 Explanatory Memorandum ODSD, 7; Explanatory Memorandum DCD, 6.
41 Commission Staff Working Document Impact Assessment, SWD(2015) 274, Brussels, 9 December 2015, 10–13 and 14–15.
42 Recital 14 ODSD; Recital 10 DCD.

Table 1 *continued*

	ODSD	DCD
Termination of long-term contracts	N	Y (Article 16)
Interest	N	N
Passing of risk	N	N
Modification of the goods/content	N	Y (Article 14)
Commercial guarantees	Y (Article 14)	N
Right of redress	Y (Article 16)	Y (Article 17)
***Force majeure* & hardship**	N	N
Prescription/Limitation	N	N
Enforcement and compliance	Y (Article 17)	Y (Article 18)

Key: N = not covered; Y = yes, covered

In addition, the proposals only cover B2C transactions. The proposals do not cover B2B or C2C (or P2P) transactions. However, they do not make any distinction based on whether the transaction is cross-border or purely domestic.

The consumer contract law rules in both proposals are of a mandatory nature.[43] The parties may not include contractual clauses which, to the detriment of the consumer, exclude the application of the rules in the proposals or derogate from or vary their effects before the lack of conformity is brought to the seller's or supplier's attention by the consumer. For instance, the consumer will not be bound by general terms and conditions which limit the consumer's remedies in case of non-conformity compared to the regime set out in the proposals. However, once the consumer brings the lack of conformity to the attention of the seller or supplier, the parties regain their freedom to agree on terms which derogate from the rules in the proposals. A deviating term will not be binding as long as the consumer is unaware of the fact that the goods or the digital content is tainted by a lack of conformity or, more precisely, as long as the consumer has not brought the lack of conformity to the seller's or supplier's attention (it is not specified how this should occur).

Unlike the CSD, which is a minimum harmonisation directive, both the ODSD and the DCD are maximum harmonisation instruments ensuring uniform consumer law rules within the EU. Member States will not be allowed to introduce or maintain laws that diverge from the provisions contained in the proposals. This may result in a decrease in consumer protection with respect to certain aspects in some EU Member States, because national provisions cannot offer a higher level of consumer protection than the proposals. EU Member States may be required to remove certain rights that consumers have under existing law if those rights are not included in the proposals.

43 Article 18 ODSD; Article 19 DCD.

While the CSD has already been criticised for its fragmentary nature,[44] the new proposals add another set of consumer law rules to the existing consumer acquis by providing specific rules for distance sales contracts and digital content contracts. This approach will result in further fragmentation of existing consumer law.[45] The new rules on distance contracts will slightly diverge from those for face-to-face sales, generally without adequate justification (and the recitals give the impression that the Commission is well aware of this). The question should be raised whether a more uniform approach should be the preferred option, even if

> omni-channel businesses could actually cope with possible transitional differences between the online and face-to-face sales regimes for goods by applying the respective higher standards to all of their sales and thus operating under a single business model.[46]

Both the ODSD and the DCD contain a provision on enforcement, requiring EU Member States to ensure that adequate and effective means exist to ensure compliance with the proposed Directives.[47] More specifically, the proposals require the Member States to ensure that (i) public bodies or their representatives and/or (ii) consumer organisations having a legitimate interest in protecting consumers, and/or (iii) professional organisations having a legitimate interest in acting, may take action before courts (or before administrative bodies) to ensure that businesses comply with the obligations under these proposals.[48] Such a provision is not new; it can also be found, for example, in the CRD[49] and the CSD.[50]

In Belgian law,[51] a collective redress action has been recently introduced for the benefit of consumers when a business breaches one of its contractual obligations or violates one of the statutes exhaustively listed in article XVII.37 of the Code of Economic Law. Strictly speaking, no modification of the list of statutes would be necessary, because the liability of the seller/supplier to the consumer is contractual in nature. Moreover, the list of statutes in article XVII.37 includes Book VI (and Book XIV) of the same Code regarding

44 S. Stijns, 'De remedies van de koper bij niet-conformiteit' in S. Stijns and J. Stuyck (eds.), n 21 above, 53–54 and 67–68.

45 J. Smits, 'The new proposal for harmonised rules for the online sales of tangible goods: conformity, lack of conformity and remedies. In depth analysis', *Workshop for the JURI Committee*, PE 536.492, Brussels, Policy Department C: Citizens' Rights and Constitutional Affairs, European Parliament, 2015, 8.

46 Explanatory Memorandum ODSD, 12.

47 Article 17(1) ODSD; Article 18(1) DCD.

48 Article 17(2) ODSD; Article 18(2) DCD.

49 Article 23 CRD.

50 Article 23 CSD.

51 Article XVII.36 of the Code of Economic Law.

market practices and consumer protection.[52] If the Belgian legislator implements the proposed directives in Book VI, no amendment of article XVII.37 is necessary. If the implementation occurs otherwise (through a reform of the Civil Code or a self-standing statute), article XVII.37 could be amended in order to include the rules under the statute implementing the proposed directives in the list of statutes (as the law of 1 September 2004 on the protection of consumers in the event of a sale of consumer goods is also expressly listed).

3. THE CONSUMER'S REMEDIES

It is time to analyse the various remedies, first under the ODSD and then under the DCD.

3.1. REMEDIES IN ONLINE AND DISTANCE SALES

3.1.1. General Characteristics

3.1.1.1. Hierarchy of Remedies for the Lack of Conformity

The ODSD provides remedies only for the lack of conformity of the goods with the contract.[53] The proposal does not deal with the consumer's remedies in the event of other types of non-performance, such as failure to deliver the goods (unlike the DCD). The remedies for these other types of non-performance are dealt with in general contract law or other existing specific (consumer) sales law. For example, failure to deliver goods in time is currently regulated by article VI.43 of the Belgian Code of Economic Law.[54] In principle, unless the parties have agreed otherwise, the seller is obliged to deliver the goods immediately and in any event not later than 30 days as from the conclusion of the contract. If the seller has failed to deliver the goods within those 30 days or the term agreed, the consumer must, as a rule, call upon him to make the delivery within an additional and appropriate period of time (*Nachfrist*).[55] If the seller still fails to deliver the goods within that additional period of time, the consumer has the right to terminate the contract.

---

52 Book VI of the Belgian Code of Economic Law.

53 The requirements for conformity are set out in Article 5 ODSD, which is analysed in the chapter by S. Stijns and S. Jansen in this volume.

54 Implementation of Article 18 of the CRD.

55 This rule is not applicable to sales contracts where the seller has refused to deliver the goods, or where timely delivery was essential. In these cases, the consumer has the right to terminate the contract immediately (see article VI.43, §2, second subparagraph of the Belgian Code of Economic Law).

Furthermore, the ODSD only provides for remedies in the event of a breach by a *seller*. It does not set out any remedies a seller may have if a *consumer* breaches the contract (e.g. when a consumer does not pay). The proposal only intends to harmonise the consumer's remedies if defective goods have been delivered. The ODSD thus remains in line with the CSD, which also only lays down the consumer's remedies in case of non-conformity.

The legal regime for the consumer's remedies in the ODSD is characterised by a hierarchy of remedies which is in essence a two-step remedy system.[56] In the event that delivered goods are defective, the consumer has the initial right to have those goods repaired or replaced. Repair and replacement are the so-called 'primary' remedies available to the consumer before he has the right to invoke the other remedies of price reduction and termination. The ODSD thus grants the seller a right to cure or an additional opportunity to bring the goods into conformity with the contract. Only if the seller does not repair or replace the defective goods as required by the ODSD is the consumer entitled to have the price reduced or to terminate the contract. Price reduction and termination are the so-called 'secondary' remedies.

The hierarchy of remedies is not new. It has its origin in the CSD and has been implemented in Belgian consumer sales law.[57] Despite criticism that repair and replacement are impractical remedies in an international context,[58] the hierarchy of remedies was maintained in the ODSD. Repair and replacement should help to preserve the contractual relationship whenever possible and appropriate (*favor contractus*). They should also encourage sustainable consumption and contribute to greater durability of products.[59] The two-step remedy system is also the result of balancing the consumer's rights and the seller's interests. The consumer should give the seller a second chance to properly perform the contract before invoking the more severe remedies of price reduction or termination.

The ODSD further specifies that a consumer is not entitled to a remedy to the extent that he himself contributed to the lack of conformity or its effects.[60] Although this provision takes away all remedies from the consumer, it lacks clarity regarding the extent to which the consumer must have contributed to the lack of conformity or its effects.

---

56 J. Smits, 'The new proposal for harmonised rules for the online sales of tangible goods: conformity, lack of conformity and remedies. In depth analysis', *Workshop for the JURI Committee*, PE 536.492, Brussels, Policy Department C: Citizens' Rights and Constitutional Affairs, European Parliament, 2015, 11.

57 Article 1649*quinquies* CC; Article 3 CSD.

58 M. Loos, 'Consumer sales law in the proposal for a consumer rights directive', *European Review of Private Law* 2010-11, 37.

59 Recital 26 ODSD.

60 Article 9(5) ODSD.

This provision, if adopted, would diminish consumer rights. Belgian consumer sales law does not contain that rule as such. Evidently, according to article 1649*quater*, §1, subparagraph 1 CC,[61] a seller is only liable for a non-conformity which exists at the time the goods were delivered. If it is established that the non-conformity exists only at a later moment in time, the seller will not be liable for it. However, this is not the same as saying that the consumer has no remedies if he has somehow contributed to the lack of conformity.

According to article 1649*quinquies*, §1, subparagraph 2 CC, the fact that the damage has increased due to the consumer's use of the good, after he has or should have observed the defect, should be taken into account (without any explanation as to how this should be taken into account). This is generally considered to be an application of the duty to mitigate damages.[62] Again, this is not the same as radically denying all remedies to the consumer by reason of his 'contribution' to the non-conformity or its effects, as is currently proposed in the ODSD.

3.1.1.2. No Notification Duty

Existing Belgian consumer sales law provides that the seller and the consumer can agree on a certain period within which the consumer has the duty to notify a lack of conformity to the seller.[63] This contractual notification period cannot be shorter than two months from the date on which the consumer discovered the defect. Contracts between a consumer and a seller often stipulate that the consumer forfeits the right to claim if he fails to notify a lack of conformity within the contractual time limit.[64] The CSD expressly allows Member States to provide such a notification period in their national law.[65] Such notification duty evidently aims to protect sellers against late claims which are difficult to verify or dispute because of the lapse of time.[66]

The ODSD, however, prohibits Member States from maintaining such a notification period for distance sales contracts. According to the proposal,

61 Article 3(1) CSD.

62 R. Steennot, 'Commentaar bij art. 1649bis–1649octies BW (Inl.)' in *Bijzondere overeenkomsten. Artikelsgewijze commentaar met overzicht van rechtspraak en rechtsleer*, Kluwer, 2015, para. 101, 95; S. Stijns, 'De remedies van de koper bij niet-conformiteit' in S. Stijns and J. Stuyck (eds.), n 21 above, 57.

63 Article 1649quater, §2 CC; A. Verbeke, 'De termijnen' in S. Stijns and J. Stuyck (eds.), n 21 above, 94–97.

64 R. Steennot, n 62 above, 66.

65 Article 5(2) CSD.

66 J. Smits, n 56 above, 15; M. Loos, 'Consumer sales law in the proposal for a Consumer rights directive', *ERPL* 2010–11 and http://ssrn.com/abstract=1425036, 15–16.

a notification period is not justified, because consumers can lose well-substantiated claims for remedies because they were not aware of this notification duty, especially where the law of another Member State applies.[67] This prohibition does not result from a specific provision of the ODSD, but it is mentioned in a recital. That should suffice, given the maximum harmonisation of the ODSD.

Since EU Member States will no longer be allowed to maintain the requirement for consumers to notify the seller of a non-conformity by a certain deadline, a seller will not be able to validly include such time limits in a contract with a consumer for online or other distance sales of goods. The abolition of the notification duty is a clear example of increased consumer protection. However, the balance seems to swing in the opposite direction in that it may overly limit the responsibilities of consumers and impose an unreasonable burden on the sellers.[68] Policy-wise, it may be more acceptable if a somewhat longer or maximum time limit is provided by the legislator for a notification, since the legislator now incentivises stale claims. In any case, we do not see any justification for treating distance sales differently from face-to-face sales with respect to a time limit for notification of non-conformity of goods.

3.1.1.3. Two-Year Guarantee Period

Current Belgian consumer sales law provides in article 1649*quater*, §1 CC[69] that a seller can be held liable by a consumer for any lack of conformity that becomes apparent within two years of delivery. However, when a lack of conformity appears after the lapse of this two-year period, the consumer is not necessarily left without a remedy. Article 1649*quater*, §1 CC stipulates that after the lapse of this two-year period, the warranty rules of article 1641 ff. CC for latent or hidden defects become applicable. A consumer can therefore hold the seller liable for latent defects that became apparent after the expiry of the two-year period.[70] Even though the CSD itself does not contain such a rule for latent defects, the Belgian legislator was allowed to provide such additional protection, as the CSD is a 'minimum harmonisation' instrument, allowing national laws to offer a higher level of consumer protection.

---

67 Recital 25 ODSD.

68 See also in the context of the CESL: R. Feltkamp and F. Vanbossele, 'Remedies under the optional Common European Sales Law – a good alternative for Belgian sales law?' in I. Claeys and R. Feltkamp, *The Draft Common European Sales Law: towards an alternative sales law?*, Antwerp, Intersentia, 228.

69 Article 5(1) CSD.

70 Court of Appeal of Mons 6 April 1998, *JT* 1998, 574; R. Steennot, n 62 above, 64; S. Stijns, 'De remedies van de koper bij niet-conformiteit' in S. Stijns and J. Stuyck (eds.), n 21 above, 78–80.

For online and distance contracts, consumers may lose the right to hold the seller liable after two years have elapsed since delivery if the ODSD is to be adopted in its current version. Article 14 ODSD adopts the CSD rule that a consumer is entitled to a remedy for a lack of conformity where the defect becomes apparent within two years after delivery. Recital 32 describes these two years as 'the period during which the seller is held liable for any lack of conformity which exists at the time when the consumer acquires the physical possession of goods'. This suggests that a consumer purchasing at a distance can no longer invoke any remedies (including damages) for a lack of conformity that appears once the two-year period has expired.[71] Member States are not allowed to provide additional consumer protection measures, since the proposal pursues maximum harmonisation for distance sales. The result is that consumers purchasing at a distance will not be able to hold the seller liable for hidden defects that become apparent after the two-year period. These consumers will only be able to hold the seller liable after the expiry of this period if the sales contract contains a commercial guarantee which is valid longer than the statutory guarantee period of two years.

Consumer protection would seriously diminish if consumers purchasing at a distance can no longer rely on the general latent defect rules in order to hold the seller liable for defects that become apparent after the two-year period. This is especially relevant for durable goods that society can reasonably expect to last longer than two years (such as cars, furniture or washing machines) or for defects that take some time before they become apparent.[72]

It is, of course, a truism to say that limiting the liability of a seller to the two-year guarantee period simplifies sales law and avoids a considerable burden for the seller.[73] It is, however, highly questionable whether such a blunt rule contributes to the durable development of society. If the lifespan of goods should be more than two years, as in the example of a washing machine (which we may well expect for the sake of future generations), the statutory remedies for a lack of conformity should be available for a longer time. The proposed rule seriously undermines the idea of durability and sustainable consumption which the Commission repeatedly describes as important throughout the proposal.[74]

---

71 H. Beale, n 19 above, 19.

72 H. Beale, n 19 above, 19; J. Smits, n 56 above, 11–12; B. Tilleman, *Overeenkomsten. Deel 2. Bijzondere overeenkomsten. A. Verkoop. Deel 2. Gevolgen van de koop*, Mechelen, Kluwer, 2012, 604.

73 A. Verbeke, 'De termijnen' in S. Stijns and J. Stuyck (eds.), n 21 above, 91–92; S. Stijns, 'De remedies van de koper bij niet-conformiteit' in S. Stijns and J. Stuyck (eds.), n 21 above, 79–80.

74 Recitals 23 and 26 ODSD; Explanatory Memorandum ODSD, 13. Compare with Article 37 of the Charter of Fundamental Rights of the European Union, as well as Article 3(3) and (5) of the Treaty on European Union.

That being said, it is not utterly impossible for a consumer purchasing at a distance to hold a seller liable after the lapse of the two-year period. The consumer might be able to rely on the Belgian Product Liability Law[75] in order to hold liable a seller who is also the producer or importer, although that law is limited in scope (e.g. liability only where the goods do not provide the safety which a person is entitled to expect)[76] and the damages recoverable under that specific law are limited as well. Moreover, the seller is sometimes more accessible than the producer or the importer.[77]

Again, needless to say, the sales channel should not be a criterion for making a distinction in this regard. Whether a purchase is concluded face-to-face or at a distance, this should not make a difference in relation to the rule applicable after the lapse of the two-year legal guarantee. If the ODSD is accepted, it is therefore to be expected that the liability for latent defects after the lapse of the two-year guarantee period now accepted under the Belgian CC will soon disappear for lack of justification.

According to article 1649*quater*, §1, subparagraph 2 CC, the two-year period during which the seller is liable for non-conforming goods is suspended for the duration of the time needed for repair or replacement.

However, the ODSD does not provide any grounds for suspension of the two-year time period. Therefore, it seems that the suspension during repair or replacement will no longer be applicable in the case of distance sales contracts. This would not only result in a decrease in the level of consumer protection, but it would again create a distinction between face-to-face sales and distance sales without any justifiable reason.

Current Belgian law provides an exception to the two-year time limit during which the seller is liable for non-conforming goods. Article 1649*quater*, §1, subparagraph 3 CC stipulates that the seller and the consumer may agree on a shorter time period, with a minimum of one year, in the case of a contract for the sale of second-hand goods.[78]

This might also change with the ODSD. The current proposal does not stipulate any differing time limits for second-hand goods, even though there are good reasons to allow a shorter time period for the liability of the seller for lack of conformity in the case of second-hand goods. The expectations of consumers are different in relation to second-hand goods.

And again, in this regard as well, it is hard to justify a distinction based on whether a sale is concluded face-to-face or at a distance.

---

75 Law of 25 February 1991 concerning liability for defective products. This law implements Directive 85/374/EEC of 25 July 1985 on the approximation of the laws, regulations and administrative provisions of the Member States concerning liability for defective products, OJ L 210, 7 August 1985, 29–33.

76 Article 5 of the Belgian Product Liability Law.

77 H. Beale, n 19 above, 20.

78 Article 7(1) CSD expressly allows Member States to stipulate such a provision.

3.1.2. *Repair or Replacement as Primary Remedies for Non-Conformity*

If delivered goods are not in conformity with the contract, the consumer has the right under the ODSD to have the goods brought into conformity with the contract by the seller.[79] In principle, the consumer has the right to choose between having the goods repaired[80] or replaced.[81] Nonetheless, the possibility for the consumer to choose freely between repair and replacement is subject to two limitations.

First, the consumer loses the right to choose between the two remedies if one of the remedies is impossible or unlawful. For example, it would most often be impossible to replace a unique and original art painting. While current Belgian consumer sales law also provides for the exception of an impossible remedy, the unlawfulness exception is not expressly mentioned in article 1649*quinquies*, §2 CC,[82] although it is arguably encompassed by the impossibility criterion. However, Belgian legal scholars usually interpret the criterion of impossibility as a material impossibility.[83] The addition of unlawfulness is therefore useful to prevent an overly restrictive interpretation of the exception to the consumer's right to choose between repair and replacement.

Secondly, the choice between repair and replacement is also not available where one of those options would imply disproportionate costs for the seller compared to the other option. In order to determine whether one of the remedies imposes disproportionate costs on the seller in a given case, all the circumstances must be taken into account. The ODSD expressly refers to the following circumstances: the value the goods would have had if they had been in conformity with the contract; the significance of the lack of conformity; and whether the alternative remedy would cause no significant inconvenience to the consumer.[84] According to a recital in the ODSD, it may, for example, be disproportionate to demand the replacement of goods with a minor scratch that could easily be repaired.[85] The exception of disproportionality does not deviate from existing Belgian consumer sales law, as it is already provided for in article 1649*quinquies*, §2 CC.[86]

---

79 Article 9(1) ODSD.

80 'Repair' is defined in Article 2(i) ODSD as 'in the event of lack of conformity, bringing goods into conformity with the contract'.

81 'Replacement' is not defined in the ODSD.

82 The exception of unlawfulness is also not expressly mentioned in the CSD.

83 B. Tilleman, n 72 above, 613–14; C. Cauffman, 'De nieuwe wet op de consumentenkoop', *TPR* 2009, 826; I. Demuynck, 'De nieuwe wet op de consumentenkoop voor consumptiegoederen' in *Liber amicorum Yvette Merchiers*, Bruges, die Keure, 2001, 888; S. Beyaert, 'Consumentenkoop' in I. Claeys (ed.), *Contractenrecht in beweging*, Mechelen, Kluwer, 2004, 53.

84 Article 11 ODSD.

85 Recital 27 ODSD.

86 Article 3(3) CSD.

According to Article 9(2) ODSD – and in line with current Belgian consumer sales law[87] – repair or replacement must be completed within a reasonable time and without any significant inconvenience to the consumer, taking account of the nature of the goods and the purpose for which the consumer required the goods. It is understandable that the drafters of the proposal preferred to use the vague 'reasonable time' standard instead of well-defined time limits, because such assessment greatly depends on the specific circumstances. For example, the replacement of a unique customised good will understandably take longer than the replacement of mass-produced goods.

The proposal (like the CSD) does not expressly stipulate whether the seller has the right to perform repeated repair or replacement (as consumers may experience in practice), or has only one opportunity. The recitals do indicate that the consumer is not required to accept any further attempts by the seller to repair or replace the non-conforming goods in relation to the same lack of conformity once a reasonable time has expired.[88] It seems that the seller will only have the right to perform repeated repair or replacement if these subsequent attempts do not cause significant inconvenience to the consumer and are still within a reasonable time.

Both current Belgian consumer sales law and the proposed ODSD stipulate that repair or replacement must be free of charge.[89] Where the non-conforming goods are being replaced by the seller, the seller must take back those goods at his own expense. Parties can only agree otherwise *after* the lack of conformity has been brought to the seller's attention by the consumer.[90] This means that a seller cannot bindingly impose all or some expenses of replacement on the consumer at the time of concluding the sales contract, e.g. by means of a clause in the contractual terms and conditions.

In the past, questions arose in the scenario where the consumer discovers non-conformity of goods only after their installation (e.g. a kitchen). This situation is not expressly dealt with in the CSD or in Belgian consumer sales law, but it has been addressed in a decision of the Court of Justice. In the *Weber* and *Putz* cases, the Court determined that the seller's obligation to replace the goods implies that the seller must either remove the installed goods himself and install the replacement goods at the same spot, or else bear the cost of removal and installation of the replacement goods by the consumer or a third party. The Court clarified that this obligation exists regardless of whether the seller was obliged under the contract of sale to install the consumer goods originally purchased.[91] However, the Court also eased this obligation on the seller by ruling

87 Article 1649*quinquies*, §2 CC.

88 Recital 28 ODSD.

89 Article 9(1) ODSD.

90 Article 10(1) ODSD (wording in line with Article 18 ODSD).

91 CJEU 6 June 2011, Joined Cases C-65/09 and 87/09, ECLI:EU:C:2011:396, *Weber v Jürgen Wittmer and Ingrid Putz v Medianess Electronics GmbH*, ECR 2011, I-5257.

that when replacement, as the only possible remedy, involves disproportionate costs because of the need to remove the non-conforming installed goods and install the replacement goods, the CSD does not preclude the consumer's right to reimbursement of the cost of removing the defective goods and installing the replacement goods from being limited, where necessary, to an amount proportionate to the value the goods would have had if there were no lack of conformity and taking into account the significance of the lack of conformity. Such limitation is considered to leave intact the consumer's right to seek replacement of the non-conforming goods.[92] The Court does not clarify how this 'proportionate' amount should be calculated.[93]

Unlike the CSD and current Belgian consumer sales law, the ODSD expressly deals with the scenario of installed goods. Article 10(2) ODSD follows the case law of the Court of Justice: if the non-conforming goods were already installed, the seller is obliged to remove them and install the replacement goods, or to commission a third party to do so, at his own expense. However, the consumer can only exercise this right on the condition that he had installed the non-conforming goods in a manner consistent with their nature and purpose. However, the ODSD does not include the Court's nuance of limiting the consumer's right to reimbursement of the costs of replacement (removal and installation of replacement goods) to a proportionate amount. It therefore seems that the consumer will have a right to full reimbursement of these costs.

Furthermore, the proposed ODSD clarifies that the consumer does not have to pay for the use which he made of the replaced goods prior to the replacement.[94] This also is a codification of the case law of the Court of Justice.[95]

According to Article 9(4) ODSD, the consumer is entitled to withhold payment until the goods are brought into conformity.[96] The right to withhold payment (*exceptio non adimpleti contractus*) is not expressly laid down in current Belgian consumer sales law, but is available on the basis of general contract law for reciprocal contracts such as sales contracts. A consumer in a sales contract can withhold payment under Belgian law[97] under the following conditions: the seller has failed to perform as agreed; the consumer is not obliged to pay first (before seller's performance is due); the consumer has notified the seller of the

---

92 Ibid, para. 74.

93 J. Luzak, 'Who should bear the risk of the removal of the non-conforming goods? Joined cases C-65/09 and C-87/09 (Weber and Putz)', *Journal of European Consumer and Market Law* 2012, 39; J. Luzak, 'A storm in a teacup? On consumers' remedies for non-conforming goods after Weber and Putz', *Centre for the Study of European Contract Law Working Paper Series No. 2015-04*, http://ssrn.com/abstract=2591301, 4.

94 Article 10(3) ODSD.

95 CJEU 17 April 2008, Case C-404/06, ECLI:EU:C:2008:231, *Quelle AG v Bundesverband der Verbraucherzentralen und Verbraucherverbände*, ECR 2008, I-2685.

96 Article 9(4) ODSD.

97 R. Steennot, n 62 above, 18.

breach; the breach of the seller is not caused by the consumer; and the consumer acts in good faith.[98]

The ODSD does not stipulate these conditions but simply states that the consumer is entitled to withhold payment of any outstanding part of the price until the seller has brought the goods into conformity. The conditions of national law for withholding payment cannot simply be transplanted into the condition provided in the ODSD. This does not mean that case law of the Court of Justice would simply ignore any further requirement for withholding payment, but the requirements will have to be uniform for the EU given the maximum harmonisation by the ODSD.

3.1.3. Price Reduction or Termination as Secondary Remedies for Non-Conformity

3.1.3.1. Principles

If the lack of conformity is not or cannot be remedied through repair or replacement, the consumer is entitled to invoke the secondary remedies. More precisely, the consumer is entitled to a price reduction or termination of the contract in the four situations described below.

First of all, the consumer is entitled to invoke a secondary remedy where repair and[99] replacement are impossible or unlawful. Repair and replacement would be impossible where a consumer purchased a unique painting which the seller had claimed was painted by a well-known artist. Afterwards, the consumer finds out that the painting was painted by another artist. Replacement is not available as a remedy, as the well-known artist never painted the picture. Repair and replacement may also be unlawful. For example, a consumer orders certain medicines but the seller delivers the wrong ones. In the meantime, a ban is issued on selling the medicine purchased because that medicine represented a severe threat to health. For obvious reasons, it is unlawful (and legally impossible) for the seller to replace the wrongfully delivered medicines with the ordered but now banned medicines.

Secondly, the consumer is entitled to ask for a price reduction or to terminate the contract where the seller did not complete repair or replacement within a reasonable time. Once the seller has failed to *successfully* remedy the defect within a reasonable time, the consumer is no longer obliged to accept any further attempts by the seller to remedy the same lack of conformity.[100] This is

---

98 W. van Gerven and A. van Oevelen, *Verbintenissenrecht*, Leuven, Acco, 2015, 210–13.

99 Note, however, that Article 9(3)(a) regrettably uses the word 'or' instead of 'and'. It is however doubtful that the secondary remedies would come into play as soon as *one* of the primary remedies is not available. In this sense, Article 3(5) of the CSD also states that the consumer may require a price reduction or termination of the contract if the consumer is entitled to *neither* repair *nor* replacement.

100 Recital 28 ODSD.

important, because it may well occur rather frequently that goods that have been repaired break down again a short time after repair.

Thirdly, price reduction and termination are also available where repair and[101] replacement would cause significant inconvenience to the consumer. For example, repeated repair and replacement could be considered as causing too much inconvenience to the consumer.

Fourthly, the seller has declared, or it is equally clear from the circumstances, that the seller will not bring the goods into conformity with the contract within a reasonable time. For example, a consumer received a defective tablet computer and the seller states that, due to supply issues, it will take a few months to replace the tablet.

Article 9(3) ODSD does not deny the right of the consumer to demand repair or replacement in the event that these two primary remedies would impose disproportionate costs on the seller compared to the secondary remedies of price reduction or termination.[102] This approach is in line with the *Weber* and *Putz* cases, in which the Court of Justice determined that national law cannot provide that the seller has the right to refuse to replace goods not in conformity (where repair was impossible) on the ground that replacement imposes costs on him which are disproportionate.[103]

The ODSD contains an express provision stating that the consumer has the right to choose between repair and replacement. Such an explicit provision cannot be found for the choice between termination and price reduction. However, it may be derived from Article 9(3) of the ODSD according to which the consumer is entitled to a price reduction or termination, which seems to imply that the consumer may choose. This interpretation would be in line with the current interpretation of the CSD in Belgium.[104] It would, however, be clearer if the consumer's choice between termination and price reduction were expressly stipulated.

3.1.3.2. Price Reduction

The consumer is entitled to a price reduction in the event of non-conformity by way of secondary remedy. The ODSD expressly determines the standard for

---

[101] A similar comment can be made with regard to the first situation; see n 99 above.

[102] Unlike Article 12(1) DCD, according to which the consumer is not entitled to have the digital content brought into conformity with the contract if this is disproportionate (meaning if this remedy imposes unreasonable costs on the supplier). Below, Section 3.2.4.1.

[103] CJEU 6 June 2011, Joined Cases C-65/09 and 87/09, ECLI:EU:C:2011:396, *Gebruder Weber v Jürgen Wittmer* and *Ingrid Putz v Medianess Electronics GmbH*, ECR 2011, I-5257; R. Steennot, n 62 above, 84–85.

[104] R. Steennot, n 62 above, 87. However, the consumer may lose the right to terminate the contract if the consumer acted in a way that is irreconcilable with the right to terminate (Court of First Instance of Antwerp, 11 April 2008, *RW* 2010–11, 115).

calculating the reduction in price. Article 12 ODSD stipulates that the price reduction shall be proportionate to the decrease in value of the goods received compared to the value which conforming goods would have had. Under current Belgian consumer sales law, we do not have such an explicit criterion for the calculation of the price reduction,[105] but scholars generally accept that the price reduction should be proportionate to the decrease in value.[106]

The proposal does not clarify who should determine the price reduction. In practice, much will depend on whether or not the consumer already paid the purchase price. In most scenarios, the consumer will already have paid the purchase price. The seller may offer to grant a certain discount, which the consumer either accepts or otherwise will have to contest (in court, if necessary). Where the consumer had not yet paid the purchase price, the consumer could at least partly withhold payment and pay only the reduced price. It would then be up to the seller to claim payment in court if he believes the price reduction applied by the consumer is higher than the difference between the value of the delivered goods and the value of the goods if they were in conformity with the contract.[107]

3.1.3.3. Termination

As indicated above, termination is another secondary remedy provided by the ODSD. This is also consistent with current Belgian consumer sales law. What is new is that the ODSD expressly regulates the conditions and effects of termination. This will result in some important changes compared with current Belgian consumer law. Again, there is no reason not to provide rules for face-to-face sales that are equivalent to those set for distance sales.

– *When and how can a consumer terminate the contract?*

Under current Belgian consumer sales law, a consumer who received non-conforming goods does not have the right to terminate if the lack of conformity is only minor.[108] The consumer must establish that the non-conformity is sufficiently serious in order to justify termination.[109] The ODSD, however,

105 Under article 1649*quinquies*, §3 CC, a consumer may require 'an appropriate reduction of the price'. There are no guidelines on when a price reduction is appropriate.

106 R. Steennot, n 62 above, 86; B. Tilleman, n 72 above, 629.

107 R. Feltkamp and F. Vanbossele, 'Remedies under the optional Common European Sales Law' in I. Claeys and R. Feltkamp (eds.), *The Draft Common European Sales Law: towards an alternative sales law?*, Antwerp, Intersentia, 2013, 239.

108 Article 1649*quinquies*, §3, subparagraph 2 CC.

109 R. Steennot, n 62 above, 87; S. Stijns, 'De remedies van de koper bij niet-conformiteit' in S. Stijns and J. Stuyck (eds.), n 21 above, 77.

allows the consumer to terminate the contract for any lack of conformity, even in the case of minor non-conformity.[110]

This would be an important change, resulting in a higher level of consumer protection. It is said to be a strong incentive for the seller to take the necessary steps in order to bring goods with even small defects into conformity with the contract by repair or replacement. However, in the scenario that repair and replacement are not feasible, it is questionable whether the consumer has the right to choose between price reduction and termination. In that scenario, the seller cannot hypothetically be incentivised to remedy small non-conformities by repair or replacement, although it may give a better incentive to sell goods that are without non-conformities in the first place.

Another major change the ODSD brings when compared to Belgian consumer sales law is the method of exercising the right to terminate. The CSD does not specify the formal requirements for exercising the right to terminate the contract in case of non-conformity of the delivered goods. Belgian consumer sales law also remains silent with respect to this issue. General Belgian contract law therefore applies, which means that a consumer must claim termination on the basis of article 1184 CC. In principle, the consumer has to claim termination of the contract in court.[111] Unless the parties have agreed to a termination clause, a party can only unilaterally consider a contract to be terminated in exceptional circumstances, viz. where the trust between the parties has completely disappeared or in the event of urgency.[112]

However, the ODSD, if adopted, would introduce extrajudicial or unilateral termination as a rule for online and distance consumer sales contracts in Belgian law. Article 13(1) ODSD allows the consumer to unilaterally terminate the agreement by notice given by any means. The consumer would no longer be required to apply to a court in order to have the contract terminated. A simple notice would suffice (e.g. using an online form or a customer service email). No other formal requirements are imposed. Of course, it should be taken into account that termination is a secondary remedy which cannot be invoked before

110 Explanatory Memorandum ODSD, 15; Recital 29 ODSD.

111 Article 1184, third paragraph CC; B. Tilleman, n 72 above, 628; R. Steennot, n 62 above, 89; S. Stijns, 'De remedies van de koper bij niet-conformiteit' in S. Stijns and J. Stuyck (eds.), n 21 above, 74.

112 S. Stijns, *De gerechtelijke en de buitengerechtelijke ontbinding van overeenkomsten – Onderzoek van het Belgisch recht getoetst aan het Franse en het Nederlandse recht*, Antwerp, Maklu, 1994; W. Van Gerven and A. Van Oevelen, n 98 above, 197–98.

Certain legal scholars are of the opinion that the Belgian Court of Cassation accepted the principle of extrajudicial termination in two decisions of 2 May 2002 (Cass. 2 May 2002, *RW* 2002–03, 501; *TBBR* 2003, 337). However, the decisions are ambiguous, to say the least. See concerning the different views among legal scholars: I. Claeys, 'Ontbinding en nietigheid van overeenkomsten: rechterlijke tussenkomst altijd vereist?' in I. Claeys (ed.), *Contractenrecht in beweging*, Gandaius 6, Kluwer, 2004, 181 ff; W. Van Gerven and A. Van Oevelen, n 98 above, 198–202.

the seller is given the opportunity to repair or replace the defective good (if possible and lawful).

Allowing extrajudicial termination for consumers has two important advantages. First, requiring consumers to start court proceedings erodes the practical usefulness of this remedy for consumers. An easy way of terminating the contract guarantees the effectiveness of this right and consequently increases consumer protection.[113] Secondly, the ODSD provision regulating termination does away with a fundamental difference among EU legal systems. Since the CSD does not deal with this aspect, termination of a consumer sales contract is currently subject to different conditions in different EU Member States.[114] The ODSD does away with this difference, albeit only with regard to distance sales between businesses and consumers.

– *Partial termination, accessory goods and linked contracts*

The current Belgian legislative rules on consumer sales do not contain an explicit rule on partial termination. General contract law does not offer a clear-cut rule either on partial termination.[115] It is usually assumed that, in principle, the consumer cannot partially terminate the agreement.[116]

The ODSD does not allow partial termination of distance sales contracts without any restrictions. The consumer's right to terminate is limited to partial termination of those contracts where the lack of conformity relates to only some, and not all, of the delivered goods. The consumer may, as a rule, terminate the contract only in relation to the non-conforming goods. However, where the consumer has purchased a main item and acquired (by purchase or otherwise) accessory goods and the main item is defective, the consumer also has the right to terminate the contract in relation to the conforming accessory goods.[117]

This explicit provision on partial termination is a useful addition to the current consumer sales law. It prevents consumers from abusing their right of termination in the case of conforming goods. Nonetheless, the proposal ignores the fact that the consumer may purchase digital content as an accessory to the non-conforming goods. For instance, a consumer may purchase a new computer together with a package of software (such as an office tool or an anti-virus program) from the same trader by means of a single contract.[118] The question

113 H. Beale, n 19 above, 17.

114 M. Loos, 'Consumer sales law in the proposal for a Consumer Rights Directive', *ERPL* 2010–11 and http://ssrn.com/abstract=1425036, 21–22.

115 For further details, see T. Tanghe, *Gedeeltelijke ontbinding en vernietiging van overeenkomsten*, Antwerp, Intersentia, 2015.

116 B. Tilleman, n 72 above, 629; P. Wéry, 'Les droits légaux du consommateur en cas de défaut de conformité' in C. Bisquet and P. Wéry, *La nouvelle garantie des biens de consommation et son environnement légal*, Bruges, la Charte, 2005, 154.

117 Article 13(2) ODSD; Recital 29 ODSD.

118 If the sale of the goods is considered to be a contract separate from the supply of the digital content, the two contracts are linked. This is dealt with below, Section 3.1.3.3.

then arises what should happen with the contract for the supply of digital content when the delivered computer is not in conformity with the contract and the consumer has the right to terminate the contract for the sale of the goods. We know that Article 13(2) ODSD provides that the consumer may terminate the contract in relation to both non-conforming goods and the *goods* acquired as an accessory to the non-conforming goods. However, software and other digital content are not goods within the meaning of the ODSD.[119] Therefore, as long as the digital content conforms to the contract, the consumer will not be able to terminate the contract in relation to the accessory digital content on the basis of the ODSD. There is no convincing reason to allow consumers to terminate a contract for both the non-conforming goods and also for accessory *goods* (although they are in conformity) but not for accessory *digital content*. It may, however, be argued that the ODSD does not provide for partial termination in relation to *digital content* acquired with goods by way of a single contract. There is only a rule on partial termination where a contract for the sale of multiple *goods* is concluded. Therefore, where a contract for the sale of goods combined with supply of digital content is being terminated on the basis of the ODSD, it can be argued that this should cover the entire contract, including the digital content purchased as an accessory to the goods.

Closely related to the issue of accessory goods purchased in one contract is the topic of linked contracts. Article 13(2) ODSD states that the consumer may terminate *the contract* in relation to the non-conforming goods and any goods acquired as an accessory to the non-conforming goods. This provision seems to refer only to the situation where the accessory goods were delivered under one and the same contract. A consumer could also conclude one contract for the purchase of goods and another separate contract for the purchase of accessory goods with the same seller. Such linked contracts are not clearly regulated in the proposal.[120]

It seems that these issues are not even covered by the ODSD and will remain to be regulated by the national laws of the EU Member States,[121] although Belgian law does not yet have clear-cut rules on these issues.

---

119 Goods are defined in Article 2(d) ODSD as 'any tangible movable items'.

120 The question arises when there are actual multiple contracts. Multiple instruments (documents) could be considered as being part of the same contract. See E. Dirix, 'De meerpartijenovereenkomst', *TPR* 1983, 774–75. However, in Belgian law, it is unclear how to determine whether these multiple instruments qualify as one contract or more than one contract. See T. Thange, *Gedeeltelijke ontbinding en vernietiging van overeenkomsten*, Intersentia, Antwerp, 2015, 48–50.

121 It would not be convincing to argue that national law cannot deal with this issue because the effects of termination are covered by the proposed Directive. Recital 30 of the ODSD states that the proposal only prescribes the *main* effects of the right of termination.

– *Effects of termination*

Both the ODSD and Belgian law adopt the rule that when a contract is terminated, each party has to be put in the position they would have been in in the absence of the contract.[122] This means that the parties must return what they have received in the performance of the contract. Article 13(3) ODSD harmonises the main effects of termination, in particular the rules on restitution in the event of termination.[123] This is not true for the CSD (as implemented in article 1649*quinquies* CC), which does not regulate the effects of termination.

According to Article 13(3)(a) ODSD, the seller must reimburse the price paid. He is obliged to do so without undue delay and in any event no later than 14 days from receipt of the termination notice. The seller also bears the costs of reimbursement (such as the bank charges for the wire transfer of the money). The ODSD does not provide any rules on late payment interest.

The effect of partial termination on the reimbursement of the price is also not entirely clear. Article 13(3)(a) ODSD simply stipulates that where the consumer terminates a contract as a whole or in relation to only some of the goods delivered, the seller shall reimburse the consumer the price paid. This wording gives the (hopefully wrong) impression that the seller must reimburse the full price even though the contract is only partially terminated. It should be clarified that where the contract is only partially terminated, the seller must only reimburse part of the price in relation to the non-conforming goods.

Pursuant to Article 13(3)(b) ODSD, the consumer must return the goods to the seller without undue delay and in any event no later than 14 days from sending the notice of termination. The seller is obliged to bear the costs of returning the goods. This obligation is important, because these costs often represent a significant barrier for consumers wishing to exercise their termination right.

It is worth noting the different wording used in the proposal in the provisions on the return of the goods in the event of a *replacement* on the one hand and in the event of *termination* on the other hand. Article 10(1) ODSD, dealing with replacement of goods, stipulates that 'the seller shall take back the replaced goods at the seller's expense'. By contrast, Article 13(3)(b) ODSD, dealing with restitution after termination for non-conformity, stipulates that 'the consumer shall return, at the seller's expense, to the seller the goods'. When the legislator uses different wording, the assumption usually is that this was done for a reason, certainly if the different wording stems from the same legal instrument. The different wording gives the impression that, in the event of replacement, it is up to the seller to take the initiative for organising the return of the goods, whereas

[122] B. Van Den Bergh, 'De (terugwerkende kracht van de) rechtsgevolgen na gerechtelijke ontbinding wegens wanprestatie: confectie of maatwerk?' (annotation to Cass. 8 February 2010), *RW* 2011–12, 648–52.

[123] Recital 30 ODSD.

this obligation rests on the shoulders of the consumer in the event of termination for non-conformity. At first sight, the practical importance of this difference in wording is rather limited, because in both events the costs of returning the goods are in any case clearly to be borne by the seller.

Nevertheless, in practice, the consumer has the obligation to return the non-conforming goods within a possibly shorter period (no later than 14 days after *sending* the termination notice) than the period for the seller to reimburse the purchase price (no later than 14 days after *receipt* of the termination notice). If the withholding-of-payment remedy is available to the seller,[124] the seller may wait until he has received the goods. This effect may not necessarily incentivise cross-border B2C transactions.

Article 13(3)(c) ODSD applies when the non-conforming goods cannot be returned in kind because they are destroyed or lost. The consumer then has to pay the seller the monetary value which the non-conforming goods would have had at the moment of restitution. This clear rule deserves approval, as it is uncertain whether current Belgian law takes into account the value at the time of receipt of the goods or the value at the time of restitution.[125]

Furthermore, the ODSD clarifies that the consumer does not have to pay the monetary value of the goods when they are destroyed or lost *because of* a lack of conformity. The provision is so formulated that the consumer has the burden of proof in that regard. For example, if a consumer purchases a toaster from an online retailer which bursts into flames because of non-conformity, the consumer has the right to be reimbursed and evidently has no obligation to pay the retailer the value of the toaster.

Existing Belgian consumer sales law provides that, when reimbursing the price of the goods to the consumer because of termination due to non-conformity, the amount reimbursed should be reduced taking into account the use the consumer had of the goods since delivery.[126] In other words, in case of termination because of lack of conformity, the consumer must pay for the use he had before termination.

The ODSD, by contrast, does not impose such a duty on the consumer to pay for the use of the goods before termination for lack of conformity. Pursuant to Article 13(3)(d) ODSD, the consumer is only liable for the decrease in value to the extent that this decrease exceeds depreciation through regular use. This

---

124 This should be the case, since the ODSD only regulates the right of the consumer to withhold the payment of the price in Article 9(4) ODSD; for other situations, the remedy is left to national law.

125 J. Baeck, 'Restitution under the CESL proposal: to be revised …' in I. Claeys and R. Feltkamp (eds.), *The Draft Common European Sales Law: towards an alternative sales law?*, Antwerp, Intersentia, 2013, 285.

126 Article 1649*quinquies*, §3, subparagraph 3 CC.

sum cannot exceed the price paid for the goods either.[127] In other words, the consumer cannot be obliged to pay for the decrease in value due to normal use.

– *Smart goods*

The ODSD and the DCD do not clearly regulate hybrid products consisting of tangible goods embedded with digital content.[128] Even though these so-called 'smart goods' are increasingly becoming part of our daily life (such as smart TVs, smart electricity meters, smart watches and connected household devices), the current proposals seem to ignore this by providing two separate regimes for the sale of tangible goods and the supply of digital content. At first sight, the proposals seem to imply that smart goods are solely governed by the ODSD, stipulating that this proposal is applicable to

> digital content integrated in goods such as household appliances or toys where the digital content is embedded in such a way that its functions are subordinate to the main functionalities of the goods and it operates as an integral part of the goods,

while the DCD is not applicable to such digital content.[129] However, for many goods, it will be very difficult to assess whether or not the embedded digital content is subordinate to the main functionalities of the goods.[130]

Assuming only the ODSD is applicable to smart goods, it is regrettable that the Commission seems to ignore the fact that such goods incorporate digital content, even if the digital content is subordinate to the main functions of the goods. This is certainly reflected in the remedies, in particular the effects of termination. For example, a consumer may have the right to terminate the contract for the sale of a fitness tracker watch because the watch delivered was the wrong colour. In accordance with Article 13 ODSD, the seller is obliged to reimburse the price paid and the consumer must return the watch. However, the ODSD nowhere obliges the seller to refrain from using possible data stored on the watch. Such an obligation is provided for in the DCD when a contract for the supply of digital content is terminated.[131] It is not clear to us why the obligation of the supplier of digital content in the DCD to refrain from further use of the data provided, as well as the consumer's right to retrieve that data, should not

---

127 Article 13(3)(d) ODSD.

128 See concerning this in detail: C. Wendehorst, 'Sale of goods and supply of digital content – two worlds apart? In-depth analysis', *Workshop for the JURI Committee*, PE 556.928, Brussels, Policy Department C: Citizens' Rights and Constitutional Affairs, European Parliament, 2015.
The scope of the DCD and the ODSD respectively are elaborated on in the chapter by R. Steennot and S. Geiregat and the chapter by S. Stijns and S. Jansen in this volume.

129 Recital 13 ODSD; Recital 11 DCD; C. Wendehorst, n 128 above, 7.

130 This is elaborated on in the chapter by R. Steennot and S. Geiregat in this volume.

131 Below, Section. 3.2.4.3.

be applicable to this situation, presumably governed by the ODSD. Such a rule should also apply to goods embedded with digital content that is subordinate to the main functionalities of the goods.[132]

3.1.4. *Damages?*

When one talks in terms of 'remedies', one thinks of damages. Nevertheless, the ODSD does not include damages as a remedy.

The CSD does not cover damages either. As a minimum harmonisation instrument, it leaves damages as an additional measure within the competence of EU Member States. Belgian law, in article 1649*quinquies*, §1 CC, does provide that the consumer has the right to claim damages as an additional remedy.

Given the maximum harmonisation of the ODSD, one might conclude that damages are no longer available. It is particularly awkward not to see any reference to damages in the recitals or the memorandum. It is most likely that the European Commission intends to still leave damages as a matter for national law. Since the issue of damages is not dealt with in any way in the ODSD, national general contract law should not be affected.[133] However, it would be advisable to expressly mention in the recitals that the Directive does not affect the national rules on damages of the Member States, in order to remove all doubt.

3.2. REMEDIES IN THE DIGITAL CONTENT DIRECTIVE

The DCD provides for remedies in case the digital content is not supplied at all or the digital content is not in conformity with the contract. To a large extent, the remedies regime of the DCD is in line with the rules of the ODSD. However, the rules of the two proposals are certainly not identical. The rules applicable to tangible goods had to be tweaked and supplemented, taking into account the unique characteristics of digital content ('its high complexity as well as the supplier's better knowledge and access to know how, technical information and high-tech assistance'[134]).

3.2.1. *General Characteristics*

The DCD will have a profound effect on Belgian consumer law. As already noted, current Belgian consumer sales law as governed by article 1649*bis* ff. CC is only applicable to the sale of consumer goods by a seller to a consumer.[135] There are

132 C. Wendehorst, n 128 above, 20.
133 Article 1(4) ODSD.
134 Recital 32 DCD.
135 Article 1649*bis*, §1 CC.

two important restrictions arising from this definition, resulting in the exclusion of a substantial part of consumer contracts for the supply of digital content from the scope of Belgian consumer sales law.

- The first restriction arises from the definition of 'consumer goods'. Consumer goods are defined as tangible, movable items.[136] With respect to digital content, a distinction is usually made according to whether or not the digital content was provided on a durable medium. Digital content provided on a durable medium, such as a USB stick, is considered to be consumer goods.[137] Although uncertain, digital content is probably not considered to be consumer goods under Belgian law if it is not supplied on a durable medium, for example when it is downloaded directly from the internet.[138]
- A second restriction stems from the term 'sale'. This concept is not defined in the CSD or in article 1649*bis* CC. In its ordinary contract law meaning, a contract is a sale if one party (the seller) undertakes to transfer the property title of an item to another party (the purchaser), who undertakes to pay a price.[139] This definition excludes a substantial number of contracts for the supply of digital content for two reasons. First, the consumer will often not pay a price in money but provides another counter-performance, often personal data.[140] Such contracts are usually not considered to be sales contracts. Secondly, there is often no transfer of ownership of the digital content. The so-called 'purchaser' (a better term is 'user') often only obtains a licence from the so-called 'seller' (a better term is 'supplier') to use the digital content.[141]

---

136 Article 1649*bis*, §2, 3° CC.

137 C. Caufmann and A. Verbeke, 'Een jaar Wet Consumentenkoop' in *Bijzondere overeenkomsten*, Bruges, die Keure, 2005, 29; R. Steennot, 'Commentaar bij art. 1649bis-1649octies BW (Inl.)' in *Bijzondere overeenkomsten. Artikelsgewijze commentaar met overzicht van rechtspraak en rechtsleer*, 2015, para. 101, 28; B. Tilleman, n 72 above, 581. See also Recital 19 CRD.

138 R. Steennot, n 137 above, 28; B. Tilleman, n 72 above, 581–82. The same is true for the UK and many other EU Member States, see: H. Beale, 'Scope of application and general approach of the new rules for contracts in the digital environment. In-depth analysis', *Workshop for the JURI Committee*, PE 536.493, Brussels, Policy Department C: Citizens' Rights and Constitutional Affairs, European Parliament, 2015, 7.

139 C. Caufmann and A. Verbeke, n 137 above, 28; S. Stijns, 'De consumentenkoop: actuele knelpunten' in *Knelpunten verkoop roerende goederen*, Antwerp, Intersentia, 2009, 27; R. Steennot, n 137 above, 29. In Article IV.A.-1:202 DCFR, a contract for the sale of goods is defined as 'a contract under which one party, the seller, undertakes to another party, the buyer, to transfer the ownership of the goods to the buyer, or to a third person, either immediately on conclusion of the contract or at some future time, and the buyer undertakes to pay the price.'

140 M. Loos, N. Helberger, L. Guibault and C. Mak, 'The regulation of digital content contracts in the optional instrument of contract law', *ERPL* 2010–11, 750.

141 H. Beale, n 19 above, 7.

In the parliamentary records for the Belgian law implementing the CRD, it is expressly stated that digital content which is not supplied on a durable medium should be considered as a service.[142] In the light of this view, a consumer cannot invoke the specific remedies of current consumer sales law in case of non-conforming digital content that is not supplied on a durable medium, but rather has to rely on general contract law, unless one could speak of a *sui generis* contract to which the remedies for sales contracts might be applied *mutatis mutandis*,[143] as is now also envisaged to a large extent with the DCD.

Belgium does not yet have specific national legislation on contracts for the supply of digital content (this is also the case in the majority of the EU Member States[144]). As a consequence, it is unclear which rights and obligations consumers and suppliers have with a contract for digital content.

The lack of specific rules for digital content contracts does not mean that consumers have no legal protection whatsoever when concluding a contract for the supply of digital content. In principle, consumers might rely on rules of general contract, rules applicable to some specific types of contract, or consumer law, if a supplier breaches the contract. Nonetheless, the current legal situation needs clarification. In practice, it is unclear which specific rules govern a digital content contract and which rights consumers have against the supplier of digital content. Moreover, the existing general contract law rules, as well as the traditional consumer law rules, are not always suited to contracts for the supply of digital content.[145] The specific nature of digital content makes the application of general contract law rules difficult in some areas. One example, which we will discuss in more detail below, is the obligation to return the benefits of a contract if terminated due to a party's breach of contract. Returning tangible goods is rather easy, but how does one return something intangible such as digital content?

Therefore, a comprehensive set of rules specifically designed for contracts involving digital content would be a welcome change. The DCD regulates certain aspects regarding contracts for the supply of digital content[146] to consumers,

---

142 *Parliamentary works of the Chamber*, Doc. 53, 3018/001, 16.

143 The specific rules for nominated contracts might be applied analogously to comparable sui generis contracts. See W. van Gerven and A. van Oevelen, n 98 above, 63–64.

144 Commission Staff Working Document Impact Assessment, SWD(2015) 274, Brussels, 9 December 2015, 9.

145 H. Beale, n 19 above, 7; M. Loos, N. Helberger, L. Guibault, C. Mak, L. Pessers, K. Cseres, B. van der Sloot and R. Tigner, *Analysis of the applicable legal frameworks and suggestions for the contours of a model system of consumer protection in relation to digital content contracts. Final report: Comparative analysis, law & economics analysis, assessment and development of recommendations for possible future rules on digital content contracts*, http://ec.europa.eu/justice/consumer-marketing/files/legal_report_final_30_august_2011.pdf, 278.

146 Article 2(1) DCD defines digital content as: '(a) data which is produced and supplied in digital form, for example video, audio, applications, digital games and any other software,

irrespective of whether a price is paid or another form of counter-performance is provided by the consumer and irrespective of whether or not the ownership of the digital content is transferred to the consumer. Filling this gap in the current law would serve to increase consumer protection by clarifying the consumer's rights and obligations and would therefore also increase legal certainty.

Like the ODSD, the DCD sets out a hierarchical remedies regime for the consumer in case of non-conformity with the contract.[147] Unlike the ODSD, the DCD also stipulates which remedies the consumer has in the event that the supplier fails to supply. The DCD does not deal with other types of breaches of contract besides lack of conformity and failure to supply. Nor does it touch upon remedies available to the supplier if the consumer should breach the contract.

The DCD provides for a hierarchy of remedies similar to that of the ODSD regime. As a first step, the consumer has the right to have the digital content brought into conformity with the contract. This is the mirror image of repair or replacement of non-conforming goods under the ODSD. As a second step, the consumer can exercise the right to price reduction, or – in case of non-conformity relating to the main performance features – to terminate the contract.

The DCD does not provide for a notification period which the consumer must respect once having detected a lack of conformity. Taking into account that the DCD is a full harmonisation instrument containing mandatory rules, contracting parties will not be able to include such a notification period in their contract in a binding or enforceable way.

Unlike the ODSD, the DCD does not stipulate any time limits during which a supplier can be held liable for a lack of conformity. The DCD does not deviate from general Belgian sales law on this point. According to the drafters of the DCD, this is justified by the fact that digital content is not subject to wear and tear while being used and is often supplied over a limited period of time.[148] The only time period that should be taken into account with respect to claims based on the lack of conformity of digital content is the national law's prescription period(s). Article 2262*bis*, §1, subparagraph 1 CC provides a prescription period of 10 years for contractual claims starting from when the claim is due. It seems that the short period applicable in Belgian general sales law for claiming a remedy for latent defects would not apply.

(b) a service allowing the creation, processing or storage of data in digital form, where such data is provided by the consumer, and (c) a service allowing sharing of and any other interaction with data in digital form provided by other users of the service'. The definition of digital content is elaborated on in the chapter by R. Steennot and S. Geiregat in this volume.

147 Conformity of the digital content with the contract is set out in Article 6 DCD. This is elaborated on in in the chapter by R. Steennot and S. Geiregat in this volume.

148 Recital 43 DCD.

3.2.2. *Remedies in the Event of Failure to Supply*

Unlike the ODSD, the DCD sets out the consumer's remedy in the event that a supplier fails to supply altogether. The recitals of the proposal explain that interruptions of supply, making the content unavailable over a short period of time, should be treated as a case of non-conformity with the contract and not as a failure to supply.[149] This implies that a consumer will not have the right to terminate the contract immediately in case of interruptions and outages with, for example, an email service or an online game.

The supplier is obliged to supply the digital content immediately after the conclusion of the contract, unless the parties have agreed otherwise.[150] According to Article 11 DCD, if the supplier fails to deliver the digital content immediately or within the agreed delivery time, the consumer has the right to terminate the contract immediately by giving notice. It is remarkable that there is no requirement of prior notice ('*ingebrekestelling*'/'*sommation*') before the consumer has the power to exercise the right to terminate. The effects of termination are discussed below.[151]

In addition to the right to terminate, given the wording in Article 14 DCD, the consumer can claim damages in the event of failure to supply the digital content (see below[152]).

The provision of Article 11 DCD is highly reprovable, since without any further explanation it seems to exclude a primary remedy for breaches of contract, viz. specific performance of the contract. The fact that Article 11 is captioned 'Remedy for the failure to supply' at least gives the impression that termination is the sole remedy for failure to supply (albeit that the damages remedy is also provided in Article 14 DCD) and that the European Commission does not want to give any further space for the specific performance remedy in case of failure of supply. In any event, it speaks for itself that this should be made clear before the final vote.

As discussed above, the DCD is of a mandatory nature. However, Article 19 states that a contractual term cannot bindingly exclude the application of the proposal or derogate or vary from it 'before the lack of conformity with the contract is brought to the supplier's attention by the consumer'. This provision does not take into account the situation where there is no lack of conformity but a failure to supply. Article 19 DCD should be amended so that it also refers to the situation of failure to supply.

---

149 Recital 35 DCD.
150 Article 5(2) DCD.
151 Below, Section 3.2.4.3.
152 Article 14 DCD; below, Section 3.2.5.

3.2.3. *Having the Digital Content Brought into Conformity as a Primary Remedy for Non-Conformity*

If the digital content is not in conformity with the contract, the consumer is entitled to have the content brought into conformity with the contract.[153] This is the primary remedy for the consumer in the event of a lack of conformity, just as repair and replacement are the primary remedies under the ODSD.[154] This means that the consumer must grant the supplier the opportunity to perform the contract, unless this is impossible, unlawful or disproportionate.

The method of bringing the digital content into conformity with the contract will depend on the technical characteristics of the digital content, and it is up to the supplier to select the appropriate method. For example, the supplier could provide the consumer with a new copy of the content or issue an update.[155]

The supplier must bring the digital content into conformity free of charge. If, for instance, the supplier has to develop an update in order to fix the digital content, the costs thereof cannot be charged to the consumer.

The consumer cannot exercise this remedy if bringing the digital content into conformity with the contract is impossible, unlawful or disproportionate. The DCD explains that this remedy is deemed disproportionate where the costs it imposes on the supplier are unreasonable. To determine whether the costs are unreasonable, one should take into account (i) the value the digital content would have if it were in conformity with the contract and (ii) the significance of the lack of conformity with the contract for attaining the purpose for which digital content of the same description would normally be used.[156]

Article 12(2) DCD explains that the supplier must bring the digital content into conformity within a reasonable time and without significant inconvenience to the consumer, this time taking account of the nature of the digital content and the purpose for which the consumer required the digital content.[157] Like the ODSD, the DCD does not establish a fixed deadline for the supplier to bring the digital content into conformity with the contract. This would not be appropriate given the diversity of digital content.[158] For example, a supplier who streams a soccer game in real time online will have very little time to bring the content into conformity if the consumer does not have access to the live stream due to technical issues caused by the supplier.

Unlike the ODSD, the DCD proposal does not give the consumer the right to withhold payment until the digital content is brought into conformity with

153 Article 12(1), paragraph 1 DCD.
154 Above, Section 3.1.2.
155 Recital 35 DCD.
156 Article 12(1), paragraph 2 DCD.
157 Article 12(2) DCD.
158 Recital 36 DCD.

the contract. It is true that, in many cases, such a right to withhold payment would not be useful, because generally the consumer pays directly (e.g. using online banking or a credit card) and only receives the digital content after successful payment. A right to withhold payment would nevertheless be useful in the situation where the digital content is supplied over time. For example, if a consumer pays a monthly fee to use certain software and a bug becomes apparent after a few months, the consumer's right to withhold payment of the monthly subscription fee until the software is fixed seems to be a reasonable remedy.

The question is whether a consumer could still rely on general contract law in order to withhold payment. Much will depend on whether the DCD exhaustively lists the consumer's remedies in case of non-conformity, in which case national law cannot provide additional remedies because the DCD is a maximum harmonisation instrument. This approach could find some support by pointing out that the ODSD expressly allows the withholding of payment, while the DCD does not stipulate such a rule. Since the two proposals were adopted simultaneously by the Commission and the text differs, one would assume that the text difference is intentional and suggests that the consumer cannot withhold payment in the case of a digital content contract. It is hard to see any justification for this. We would therefore rather favour the idea that general contract law applies because that aspect is not dealt with in the DCD. The legislator should in any event make its intentions in this regard clear before the final vote.

3.2.4. Price Reduction or Termination as Secondary Remedies for Non-Conformity

3.2.4.1. Principles

By way of secondary remedies, the consumer can demand to have the price reduced or the contract terminated. These remedies can be invoked where:

- the remedy to bring the digital content into conformity is impossible, unlawful or disproportionate;
- the primary remedy would cause significant inconvenience to the consumer;
- the supplier has not completed the primary remedy within a reasonable time; or
- the supplier has declared, or it is equally clear from the circumstances, that the supplier will not bring the digital content into conformity with the contract.[159]

[159] Article 12(3) DCD.

3.2.4.2. Price Reduction

Where the digital content is supplied in exchange for the payment of a price, the consumer is entitled to a price reduction as a secondary remedy.[160] The price reduction must be proportionate to the decrease in value of the received non-conforming digital content compared to the value of conforming digital content.[161]

A reduction in price will be a useful remedy where the digital content has some flaws but the consumer wishes to continue to use it nonetheless (e.g. when the consumer receives less cloud storage capacity than set out in the cloud computing contract). If the consumer does not wish to use the non-conforming digital content, he will generally prefer to terminate the contract.

3.2.4.3. Termination

– *When and how can a consumer terminate the contract?*

Like the ODSD, the DCD also introduces the remedy of unilateral termination for contracts for the supply of digital content. The consumer is not required to start court proceedings to claim termination.[162] As mentioned previously, this is an important change compared to current Belgian law (article 1184 CC).

Not all forms of lack of conformity can justify termination. The right of the consumer to terminate the contract is limited to those cases where the lack of conformity with the contract impairs functionality, interoperability and other main performance features of the digital content.[163] However, the supplier has the burden of proof that the lack of conformity does not impair functionality, interoperability and other main performance features. This seems to be a severe burden of proof for the supplier. According to the Conseil des barreaux européens (CCBE), it is not adequate to put the burden of proof on the shoulders of the supplier unless the consumer is required to substantiate his claim beforehand.[164] Article 13(1) DCD does not expressly require the consumer to substantiate the grounds on which he is exercising the right to terminate, but simply requires the consumer to give notice to the supplier without specifying the content of such

---

[160] Article 12(3) DCD.

[161] Article 12(4) DCD.

[162] B. Fauvarque-Cosson, 'The new proposal for harmonised rules for certain aspects concerning contracts for the supply of digital content. In depth analysis', *Workshop for the JURI Committee*, PE 536.495, Brussels, Policy Department C: Citizens' Rights and Constitutional Affairs, European Parliament, 2015, 13.

[163] Article 12(5) DCD.

[164] Council of Bars and Law Societies of Europe, *CCBE position concerning contract rules for online purchases of goods and digital content*, COM(2015) 634 and 635, 18 March 2016, http://www.ccbe.eu/index.php?id=33 (consultation 22 April 2016).

notice. However, in the light of general principles of law in the Member States, it seems only reasonable to require justification in the notice of termination for non-conformity. In order to avoid all doubt, the proposal could clarify that the consumer should at least indicate in the termination notice what the lack of conformity entails.

The requirement that the non-conformity impairs the main performance features of the digital content is somewhat remarkable as the ODSD, by contrast, expressly allows the consumer to terminate the contract even when the defect is only minor.[165]

The question arises which remedy the consumer can invoke when confronted with a supplier who is unwilling or unable to fix a lack of conformity which is considered to be rather annoying but does not impair functionality, interoperability or other main performance features (and for which a primary remedy is not available). If the consumer has paid a price for the digital content, he can demand a price reduction. However, if the digital content was provided in exchange for any other counter-performance, it seems that the consumer has no remedy whatsoever. This is particularly worrying because the hypothesis is one of non-conformity. Either there is conformity or there is non-conformity, in which event an effective remedy should be available.

– *Effects of termination*

Existing Belgian law does not contain specific rules on the effects of termination of a contract for the supply of digital content. Therefore, principles of general contract law should be applied, implying that, as a general rule, termination has a retroactive effect and each party is obliged to return the benefits it received under the contract.

However, effective restitution is more complicated for digital content than in the case of tangible goods. For example, if a consumer purchases a book from an online retailer and he receives the wrong book, the consumer must send the book back to the retailer in case of termination. In the case of an e-book as well, under general principles of Belgian law, the consumer has to return the e-book in case of termination. Unlike tangible goods, however, digital content cannot physically be given back to the supplier. General contract law principles are clearly inadequate to deal with restitution in the case of digital content contracts.[166]

The intention of the DCD drafters to clarify the rules on restitution in cases of termination of digital content contracts can only be welcomed. The other effects of termination of the contract which are not regulated by the DCD are

165 Above, Section 3.1.3.3.

166 M. Loos, N. Helberger, L. Guibault, C. Mak, L. Pessers, K. Cseres, B. van der Sloot and R. Tigner, n 145 above, 230.

not covered by the proposal, and Member States remain free to regulate these in their national law (such as through additional damages[167] or the discharge of contractual obligations which parties still had to perform).[168]

Where the consumer paid a price for the digital content, the supplier must reimburse the price paid without undue delay and in any event no later than 14 days from receipt of the notice.[169] This is no different from the ODSD.

The situation is more complicated where the consumer did not pay a price but provided another form of counter-performance. In that case, the consumer 'pays' with personal and other data rather than with money. This data could have been provided directly (e.g. when the consumer fills in his personal information in an online form) or indirectly (e.g. via cookies). In these situations, there is no price paid to be reimbursed, but the DCD does deal with the effect of termination on the collected data.

The supplier is obliged to take all measures which could be expected in order to refrain from the use of the counter-performance (data) other than money provided by the consumer, as well as any other data collected by the supplier in relation to the supply of the digital content.[170] This includes any content provided by the consumer. For example, once the user of a social network has cancelled his account, the provider of the social network site cannot retain the pictures and other information that the user uploaded. However, if the content was generated jointly with other consumers who make use of it, the supplier is entitled to continue to use it.[171]

The obligation of the supplier to refrain from using the data provided by the consumer might prove to be unworkable in certain cases, for example where the data has been processed.[172] Once data is processed it may be no longer possible to track and identify all the retained data of an individual consumer. In such a case, the supplier will have to rely on the rule that he must only take measures 'which could be expected' and argue that he cannot reasonably be expected to refrain from the use of processed data. This is supported by the recitals, which clarify that, in the case of personal data, the obligation to refrain from using the data means that

> the supplier should take all measures in order to comply with the data protection rules by deleting it *or rendering it anonymous in such a way that the consumer cannot be identified* by any means likely reasonably to be used either by the supplier or by any other person (emphasis added).[173]

---

167 Below, Section 3.2.5.
168 Recital 10 DCD.
169 Article 12(2)(a) DCD.
170 Article 13(2)(b) DCD.
171 Ibid; Recital 38 DCD.
172 B. Fauvarque-Cosson, n 162 above, 15.
173 Recital 37 DCD.

In other words, once personal data is processed in such a way that it is no longer possible to identify the consumer, the supplier does not have to take further measures in relation to this data.

When data has been passed on to a third party, the question could be raised whether the supplier has to take certain steps so that the third party will also refrain from making further use of the consumer's data. The recitals clarify that, without prejudice to Directive 95/46/EC,[174] the supplier should not be obliged to undertake any measures regarding data lawfully provided to third parties in the course of the contract for the supply of digital content.[175] It seems reasonable that if a consumer has given his consent to the supplier for the sale of his data to third parties, and to the extent that the rules on data protection have been respected, it cannot be expected that the supplier should take measures to forbid the 'buyer' of the data from making any further use of it. This could be realised by severing the supply consent from the consent to further commercialise the data.

In any case, it is not clear how far the obligation to take measures to refrain from use of the data extends and we can only make an educated guess. These issues also make it clear that, more generally, the legal status of data should be urgently worked out.

The supplier of digital content must allow the consumer to retrieve all content provided by the consumer and any data produced or generated by the consumer's use of the digital content. In order to do so, the supplier must provide the consumer with all technical means to retrieve the content or data.[176]

This obligation is not limited to data which the supplier was obliged to retain under the contract, but also covers all data actually retained in relation to the contract.[177] This could include, for example, additional data that was collected through cookies and retained.

The consumer has the right to retrieve this content free of charge, without significant inconvenience and within a reasonable time.[178] However, the recitals specify a justifiable exception to the 'free of charge' obligation of the supplier: costs generated by the consumer's own digital environment, such as the cost of

---

174 Directive 95/46/EC of the European Parliament and of the Council of 24 October 1995 on the protection of individuals with regard to the processing of personal data and on the free movement of such data, http://eur-lex.europa.eu/LexUriServ/LexUriServ.do?uri=CELEX:31995L0046:en:HTML. This Directive will be replaced by Regulation (EU) 2016/679 of the European Parliament and of the Council of 27 April 2016 on the protection of natural persons with regard to the processing of personal data and on the free movement of such data, and repealing Directive 95/46/EC, http://eur-lex.europa.eu/legal-content/EN/TXT/?uri=uriserv:OJ.L_.2016.119.01.0001.01.ENG&toc=OJ:L:2016:119:TOC (hereafter: 'General Data Protection Regulation').

175 Recital 37 DCD.

176 Article 13(2)(c) DCD.

177 Recital 39 DCD.

178 Article 13(2)(c) DCD.

a network connection, are not included, as they are not specifically linked to the retrieval of the data.[179]

Consumers should also be able to retrieve their data in a commonly used data format. The format of the retrieved data is a classic exit issue. The supplier's obligation should avoid lock-in effects caused by the possible lack of interoperability between different suppliers' platforms. However, 'a commonly used data format' is a vague term. For instance, if a consumer switches to another cloud service, he wants his data in a commonly used electronic format that allows him to send the data to another provider. However, although a PDF is arguably a common format, it is not a format allowing the transfer of the data to another system. It would be useful if the proposal could specify that the data format should allow further (reasonably expected) use by the consumer. The General Data Protection Regulation notably sets the more stringent requirements that the data format, apart from being a commonly used format, should also be structured and machine-readable.[180]

The obligation for the supplier to allow consumers to retrieve content and data makes sense in many situations. For example, a consumer will evidently want to retrieve data stored on a cloud computing service when he terminates the contract with that service. However, three important observations should be made:

- First of all, not all platforms support the retrieval of data. For example, a consumer may generate content in an online game (e.g. a structure that was built in Minecraft).[181] This content cannot exist independently from that game. The proposal, however, does not nuance the obligation of the supplier to provide the consumer with the technical means to retrieve all content provided, so as to limit it to cases where this would not be technically possible, or at least not without excessive costs for the supplier.
- Secondly, the supplier's obligation is described in very broad terms. The consumer must not only be able to retrieve the content provided, but also all data produced or generated through the consumer's use of the digital content to the extent that data has been retained by the supplier. It should be questioned whether this will always be practically possible.[182] Can a supplier of digital

179 Recital 40 DCD.

180 Article 20(1) General Data Protection Regulation.

181 UK Interactive Entertainment, *Ukie response to BIS call for evidence on Draft Directive on the Online Sale of Digital Content*, 19 February 2016, http://ukie.org.uk/sites/default/files/cms/docs/Ukie%20response%20to%20BIS%20call%20for%20views%20on%20draft%20EU%20directive%20on%20the%20online%20sale%20of%20digital%20content.pdf, 9.

182 European Digital Media Association, *EDIMA feedback on proposed Directive on certain aspects concerning contracts for the supply of digital content*, 15 April 2016, http://www.europeandigitalmediaassociation.org/pdfs/latest_news/EDiMA%20feedback%20on%20proposed%20directive%20on%20contract%20rules%20digital%20content.pdf (consultation 21 April 2016).

content always track and identify all the retained data of a user? What if this data has been retained but has been processed in a larger pool of data and is no longer individually identifiable? Whereas the goal of the Digital Agenda is to develop the digital market and economy, one might ask whether the DCD is not running counter to the goals expressed.

- Finally, even though the provision clearly states that other *data* produced or generated through the consumer's use must only be retrievable to the extent it has been retained by the supplier, this nuance probably does not relate to the *content* provided by the consumer. It is also unclear whether the distinction between content and data was made on purpose when providing that

> the supplier shall provide the consumer with technical means to retrieve all content provided by the consumer and any other data produced or generated through the consumer's use of the digital content to the extent that data has been retained by the supplier.

Where the digital content was provided on a durable medium, the consumer must return the durable medium at the request and expense of the supplier. The consumer must do so without undue delay, and no later than 14 days from receipt of the supplier's request. There is a notable distinction here compared with the restitution of goods by the consumer when terminating a contract governed by the ODSD. In the latter situation, the consumer must automatically return the goods no later than 14 days from sending the notice of termination.[183] In the case of a digital content contract, by contrast, the consumer must only return the durable medium when requested by the supplier (and no later than 14 days from the supplier's request). This may be attributed to the fact that the supplier will often not consider it useful to have the consumer return the durable medium, as it has no resale value in most cases. Also, the return of the durable medium will often not prevent the consumer from making further use of the digital content itself once it is installed on a device.

Besides returning the durable medium at the request of the supplier, the consumer is also obliged to delete any usable copy of the digital content, render it unintelligible or refrain from using it or making it available to third parties.[184] If the digital content was not supplied on a durable medium, the consumer is not required to return anything tangible to the supplier, but the consumer is again obliged to refrain from using the digital content (by deleting it or rendering it unintelligible) or making it available to third parties.[185] For example, if a consumer purchased a movie on a DVD, he must not only return the DVD but also delete any copies of the movie saved on his computer.

183 Article 13(3)(b) ODSD.
184 Article 13(2)(e) DCD.
185 Article 13(2)(d) DCD.

However, it will often be virtually impossible to monitor whether the consumer actually refrains from making further use of the digital content or whether the consumer has rendered it unusable.[186] For example, when a consumer has downloaded software (for offline use), a supplier often cannot simply cut off access to it, as it has been transferred to the consumer's computer. It is then up to the consumer to delete the software on his own initiative, and the supplier has no easy means of verifying whether the consumer has done so.[187]

M. Loos suggests charging the consumer a price for the value of the benefit that he enjoys by keeping the digital content (except for contracts where counter-performance consists of data, in which case a stipulation could exempt the consumer from paying for the value of the benefit, as it would be illogical to demand payment only upon termination).[188] No such rule is proposed by the Commission. Consumer protection clearly took precedence over the interests of the industry; rightly so, in our opinion, because it is not self-evident to charge for possible use by a customer of digital content which, hypothetically, has been found not to be in conformity with the contract. That value may often be close to nil. It may be more useful if the proposal includes a rule that, if a consumer keeps using the software after termination, he has to pay for it,[189] thus guarding against unjustified enrichment.

The above problem does not occur in those cases where the supplier himself can prevent any further use of the digital content by the consumer, for example by blocking his access or disabling his account (e.g. blocking a consumer's video streaming account). The proposals expressly give the supplier the right to do this.[190] However, this right of the supplier must be clearly balanced with the consumer's right to retrieve his data. A supplier should not be allowed to block the consumer's access before the consumer has been able to retrieve his data, unless the supplier has continued to transfer the data to the consumer afterwards for a reasonable time. For example, if a consumer terminates a cloud storage agreement, the supplier should not be allowed to block the consumer's access to

186 V. Mak, 'The new proposal for harmonised rules on certain aspects concerning contracts for the supply of digital content. In depth analysis', *Workshop for the JURI Committee*, PE 536.494, Brussels, Policy Department C: Citizens' Rights and Constitutional Affairs, European Parliament, 2015, 25–26.

187 B. Fauvarque-Cosson, n 162 above, 16; M. Loos, N. Helberger, L. Guibault, C. Mak, L. Pessers, K. Cseres, B. van der Sloot and R. Tigner, *Analysis of the applicable legal frameworks and suggestions for the contours of a model system of consumer protection in relation to digital content contracts. Final report: Comparative analysis, law & economics analysis, assessment and development of recommendations for possible future rules on digital content contracts*, http://ec.europa.eu/justice/consumer-marketing/files/legal_report_final_30_august_2011.pdf, 126.

188 M. Loos, N. Helberger, L. Guibault, C. Mak, L. Pessers, K. Cseres, B. van der Sloot and R. Tigner, n 187 above, 230–31.

189 V. Mak, n 186 above, 26.

190 Article 13(3) DCD.

the cloud storage before the consumer has been able to retrieve the content he stored there, unless the supplier has been transferring the content afterwards for a reasonable time.

Article 13(4) DCD expressly states that the consumer is not liable for any use made of the digital content in the period prior to the termination of the contract for non-conformity. This rule was probably copied from the ODSD, which stipulates that a consumer cannot be charged for using non-conforming goods prior to the termination of the contract. However, this rule will often not be equitable in the case of contracts for digital content with continuing performance, which we will discuss in detail below.[191]

The DCD remains silent on what happens when the consumer makes use of the digital content *after* termination (especially where the supplier could not block the consumer's access). The consumer is prohibited from using the digital content after termination, but, as we discussed above, it is often difficult to monitor this.

– *Partial termination*

As we explained above, as a rule, the supplier is obliged to reimburse the consumer the price paid if the contract for digital content is terminated for non-conformity. This rule in the DCD is no different from restitution in Belgian general contract law, where termination for non-conformity is considered to have a retroactive effect (termination *ex tunc*). However, the retroactive effect of termination in Belgian contract law generally does not apply in the case of contracts with continuing performance.[192] For such contracts, restitution for the past is not due and the effects of termination only relate to the performance that was not yet due at the time of termination (termination *ex nunc*).[193]

The proposal provides for a rule with a similar effect where the digital content has been supplied in exchange for a price and extends over a period of time. However, this is not done by making a distinction between termination with or without retroactive effect, but by introducing the functionally equivalent concept of partial termination.[194] According to Article 13(5) DCD, the consumer can only terminate the contract in relation to that part of the period of time when the digital content has not been in conformity with the contract.[195]

In the case of partial termination, Article 13(6) DCD clarifies that the supplier is only required to reimburse that part of the price paid which corresponds to

191 Below, Section 3.2.4.3.

192 A typical example is a rental agreement, where one party rents goods and pays monthly rent.

193 B. Van Den Bergh, 'De (terugwerkende kracht van de) rechtsgevolgen na gerechtelijke ontbinding wegens wanprestatie' (annotation to Cass. 8 February 2010), *RW* 2011–12, 650.

194 According to some legal scholars, termination without retroactive effect can be characterised as partial termination. See: T. Thange, n 120 above, 44–46.

195 Article 13(5) DCD.

the period of time when the digital content was not in conformity with the contract.[196] Also, the supplier does not have to refrain from making use of the content or data provided by or through the consumer in relation to the period during which the digital content was in conformity with the contract.[197] Partial termination is not available where the digital content is provided against non-monetary counter-performance, because it would be impossible to apportion a counter-performance other than money.[198]

An example of partial termination is where a user pays a monthly subscription fee in order to access an online newspaper. After a few months, a glitch in the supplier's digital content appears which makes it impossible for the user to read the newspaper. If the user terminates his subscription because of this non-conformity, he cannot reclaim the subscription fees paid for the months when the digital content was working properly in conformity with the contract.

At first sight, this is stating the obvious, because Article 13(5) and (6) seem to hold a fair balance between the interests of the consumer and the interests of the supplier. However, these provisions could result in inequitable situations where a contract with continuing performance is being terminated some time after it was entered into, even though the non-conformity existed at the time of delivery but the consumer simply had not yet discovered the defect.

For example, a consumer pays a monthly fee to use certain software on his computer operating on Microsoft Windows. After a few months, the consumer switches to an Apple MacBook and discovers that the software is not compatible with the different operating system used on this laptop, even though the contract expressly, but mistakenly, stipulated otherwise. The supplier informs the consumer that the software is inoperable with Apple's operating system. The consumer decides to terminate the contract for non-conformity. As discussed above, the DCD provides that the consumer can only terminate the contract in relation to the period of time during which the software was not in conformity with the contract. However, theoretically speaking, the software has always been non-conforming, as it was incompatible with an Apple MacBook from the start, but the consumer simply had not discovered this yet. Moreover, Article 13(4) DCD expressly states that the consumer is not required to pay for any use made of the digital content in the period prior to termination. As a result, it seems that the supplier must reimburse all the monthly payments made by the consumer for the previous months. This cannot be considered equitable, as the consumer was able to use, and did in fact use, the software during those months.

196 Article 13(6) DCD.
197 Article 13(6) DCD.
198 Recital 42 DCD.

- *Accessory digital content and linked contracts*

The DCD is silent on the issue of accessory digital content when terminating a contract for the supply of digital content.[199] For example, a consumer acquires music player software for which he pays a monthly subscription price and subsequently purchases downloadable music files from the same trader. After a while, the music player software is updated and as a result it is no longer in conformity with the contract. The consumer subsequently exercises his right to terminate the contract. As a result, the consumer no longer has access to the music player, but this also means that he can no longer play the music files he has downloaded. What happens with regard to the price paid for those music files? There are two possible approaches.

The first approach is that the supply of the music player software and the supply of the music files would both be construed as being part of one single contract. Even if such construction were feasible, it would then still not be clear whether the consumer has the right to reimbursement of the price paid for the music files. Article 13(5) DCD states that when the digital content is supplied over a period of time, the consumer may terminate the contract only in relation to that part of the period of time where the digital content was not in conformity with the contract. The music files were purchased when the music player was still in conformity. However, the consumer expects to use the music files for a long period of time, not just at the time of purchase, and now he can no longer use them.

The second approach is that the contract for the supply of the music player and the contract for the supply of the music files are considered to be separate but linked contracts.[200] Since the DCD remains silent on the topic of the effects of termination on linked contracts,[201] the applicable national law would have to be analysed to determine the rights and obligations of the parties.

3.2.5. *Damages*

It is very surprising that, unlike the ODSD, the DCD contains a rule concerning the right to damages. Damages are defined in Article 2(5) DCD as a sum of money to which consumers may be entitled as compensation for economic damage to their digital environment. Article 14 DCD, captioned 'Right to damages', states that the supplier shall be liable to the consumer for any economic damage to the digital environment of the consumer caused by a lack of conformity with the contract or a failure to supply the digital content.

---

199 Contrary to the DCD, which deals with the effect of termination in relation to the goods accessory to the non-conforming goods. Above, Section 3.1.3.3.

200 M. Loos, N. Helberger, L. Guibault, C. Mak, L. Pessers, K. Cseres, B. van der Sloot and R. Tigner, n 187 above, 133.

201 The same is true for the ODSD, above, Section 3.1.3.3.

As the right to damages is not included in the hierarchy of remedies, it seems to be available in addition to each of the other remedies available under the DCD (bringing into conformity, price reduction and termination;[202] in case of failure to supply, termination[203]).

Damages must put the consumer as closely as possible in the position he would have been in if the digital content had been duly supplied and had been in conformity with the contract, as stated in Article 14(1) DCD. This type of damages is generally known as compensation for the expectation or positive interest of the consumer.

The proposal does not lay down detailed conditions for the exercise of the right to damages, but leaves this expressly to the EU Member States.[204] However, national laws cannot introduce rules that would further restrict the right to damages compared to what is set out in the proposal. For instance, the recitals explain that discounts on prices for future supplies of digital content will 'not necessarily' put the consumer as closely as possible in the position he would have been in if the supplied digital content had been in conformity with the contract.[205] Evidently, it is possible that a consumer will accept such a discount by way of compensation once he has brought the lack of conformity to the supplier's attention.

Under existing Belgian general contract and consumer law, there are several restrictions on contractual limitations of liability. Based on general contract law principles, a clause for the limitation of liability is invalid if (i) it limits liability for intent, (ii) it is contrary to public policy or a mandatory law or (iii) it renders the subject-matter of the contract futile. Additional restrictions exist for limitation of liability clauses in consumer contracts. In particular, a limitation for liability clause can be invalid under the rules on unfair terms in consumer contracts.[206] Article VI.83, 13° of the Belgian Code of Economic Law, for example, prohibits businesses from excluding their liability towards a consumer for wilful intent, gross negligence or their liability for non-performance of one of their main obligations. Article VI.83, 25° of the same Code prohibits a business from excluding or limiting its statutory liability in the event of the death of a consumer or personal injury to the latter resulting from an act or omission of that business.

---

202 Articles 12–13 DCD.

203 Article 11 DCD.

204 Article 14(2) DCD.

205 Recital 44 DCD.

206 Article VI.82 ff. and Article XIV.49 ff. of the Code of Economic Law. See also: M. Loos and J. Luzak, 'Wanted: a bigger stick. On unfair terms in consumer contracts with online service providers', *Journal of Consumer Policy* 2016, vol. 39, 79–81; X, 'Discussion paper on Unfair Contract Terms in Cloud Computing Service Contracts', Expert Group on Cloud Computing Contracts, 5–6 March 2014, 9, http://ec.europa.eu/justice/contract/files/expert_groups/discussion_paper_unfair_contract_terms_en.pdf (consultation 23 April 2016); X, 'Working paper on liability for non-performance including remedies', Expert Group on Cloud Computing Contracts, 11–12 December 2014, 1–2, http://ec.europa.eu/justice/contract/files/expert_groups/liability_working_paper_en.pdf (consultation 23 April 2016).

The DCD further restricts the supplier's ability to limit its liability for non-conformity (and for failure to supply). It gives the consumer a clear right to demand compensation for damage to his digital environment caused by a lack of conformity or a failure to supply. A supplier will not be able to limit or exclude this liability, as this would be contrary to mandatory law. Only once the lack of conformity is brought to the supplier's attention by the consumer[207] could a different contractual arrangement be made between the supplier and the consumer.

Taking into account that the DCD is based on maximum harmonisation, other restrictions in national law on the liability of the supplier for damage to the consumer's digital environment should not be applicable. Therefore, it seems that a supplier will not be able to escape this liability by showing that it was impossible for the supplier to discover the defect (*onoverwinnelijke onwetendheid*[208]). Article 14 DCD does not provide for any exception to the supplier's liability for economic damage to the consumer's digital environment caused by a lack of conformity or failure to supply. It is not up to national law to provide additional requirements or exceptions to a rule aimed at maximum harmonisation.

However, the current provision raises serious concerns. It is striking that the proposal defines the right to damages very narrowly.[209] There are three cumulative conditions to be met in order for the damage suffered to be eligible for compensation under the DCD: (i) *economic* damage, (ii) caused by a *lack of conformity* with the contract or a *failure to supply*, (iii) to the consumer's *digital environment*. Article 2(8) DCD defines 'digital environment' as hardware, digital content and any network connection to the extent that they are within the control of the user.[210]

While the proposal expressly states that it is up to the EU Member States to lay down detailed rules for the exercise of the right to damages, national laws are, in principle, not allowed to expand the right to damages, because the proposal is a full harmonisation directive prohibiting the Member States from introducing more stringent or less stringent provisions.[211] The Explanatory Memorandum states that 'Article 14 establishes a right to damages *restricted to cases* where damage has been done to the digital content and hardware of the consumer' (emphasis added).[212] This might be interpreted in such way that

207 Article 19 DCD.

208 Belgian Court of Cassation 6 October 1961, *Pas.* 1962, I, 152, *RGAR* 1962, no. 6905, annotated by R. Dalcq, *RW* 1961–62, 783, with opinion of Advocate-General F. Dumon; Belgian Court of Cassation 7 May 1977, *RCJB* 1979, 162, annotated by M. Fallon.

209 V. Mak, n 186 above, 26.

210 See for more detail the chapter by R. Steennot and S. Geiregat in this volume.

211 Article 4 DCD.

212 Explanatory Memorandum DCD, 13. The question is whether this ambiguous recital means that the right to damages is restricted to damage done to the digital environment, or whether Article 14 is restricted to that type of damage and does not regulate other types of damage.

other types of damage are not eligible for compensation. As a result, the right to damages would be very limited, and damage such as loss of enjoyment, damage to property and personal injury would not be eligible for compensation.

There are many examples imaginable where a user of digital content suffers damage which would not be eligible for compensation under the DCD. For instance, what if a bug in an app or social media allows a hacker to steal a user's private photos and publish them on the internet, resulting in moral (and possible economic) damage? Or what if digital content contains spyware which allows third parties to retrieve users' passwords and PIN numbers, giving hackers access to the users' bank accounts?[213]

The restriction of the consumer's right to damages for non-conformity of the digital content could result in a lower degree of consumer protection compared to current Belgian law. There seems to be no good reason to give the supplier immunity for losses other than losses to the consumer's digital environment.[214] There is no reason why the European legislator should exempt the digital content industry from types of damage other than damage to the consumer's digital environment. This would give rise to an unjustified benefit for digital businesses compared to other businesses.

It seems therefore unreasonable to interpret Article 14 DCD in such a way that suppliers of digital content cannot be held liable for any damage other than damage to the consumer's digital environment. Instead, it is more likely that the Commission intends to provide for a type of liability that the supplier cannot escape, and that liability for other losses is not covered by the DCD. As a result, the proposal should not affect national laws for these other types of losses suffered by a consumer. Nonetheless, the current proposal should definitely be amended in order to clarify this and to avoid an unreasonable and even discriminatory interpretation. All ambiguity should be removed.

It should still be observed that it is doubtful that the specific product liability legislation that applies to tangible movable goods only would give a right to damages in the case of digital content that is not materialised on a durable medium.[215]

---

213 Examples taken from V. Mak, n 186 above, 27.

214 H. Beale, n 19 above, 24.

215 Software materialised on a durable medium is considered to be a product under the Product Liability Directive, according to the Commission (PB. C. 8 May 1989, afl. 114/42, question no. 706/88 by G. De Vries) and Belgian legislative history (*Parl.St.* Kamer 1990–91, no 1262/5, 5; *contra* D. Van De Gehuchte 'Productaansprakelijkheid in België' in *Efficiënt Ondernemen nr. 5*, Ghent, Mys & Breesch, 2000, 36–37).

It is, however, uncertain whether software not materialised on any medium (e.g. offered online) can also be considered as a product (T. Vansweevelt, 'De Wet van 25 februari 1991 inzake productenaansprakelijkheid', *TBBR* 1992, 106; M. Fallon, 'La loi du 25 février 1991 relative à la reponsabilité du fait des produits défectueux', *JT* 1991, 470; D. Van De Gehuchte above, 36–37; J. Verlinden, 'Twintig jaar productaansprakelijkheid, een stand van zaken'

To the extent that the Product Liability Law is applicable, limitation of liability is not permitted.[216] However, this law has a narrow scope (e.g. a product is considered defective only where it does not provide the safety which a person is entitled to expect)[217] and the damages that are recoverable under that specific law are limited to (i) personal injuries and moral damage and (ii) damage to goods, other than the defective goods themselves, used mainly for private use and exceeding the threshold of EUR 500.[218]

3.3. CONCLUSION ON THE PROPOSED REMEDIES REGIMES

3.3.1. *Overview of the Specific Rules on Remedies in Belgian Consumer Sales Law (Implementing CSD) Compared to the Proposed Remedies Regimes*

With the increased fragmentation of legal rules applicable to remedies for non-conformity, it is useful to put the various regimes side by side in a matrix. The overview below is only a scheme which should be combined with the definitions and the text of the rules, as explained in the text. Where there is a decrease or a risk of decrease in consumer protection, the cell is highlighted in grey.

Table 2. Comparison between Belgian consumer sales law, the ODSD and the DCD

	1649*bis* ff. Belgian CC (consumer sales)	**ODSD**	**DCD**
GENERAL			
Scope[219]	Sale of consumer goods by a seller to a consumer	Distance sales contracts between sellers and consumers	Contracts for the supply of digital content to consumers
AVAILABLE REMEDIES			
Remedies for failure to deliver/ supply	No specific rule, except right to terminate after granting seller an additional period of time to deliver[220]	No specific rule	Right to terminate immediately + damages (for economic damage to the digital environment of the consumer)

(continued)

in M. Debqene and P. Soens (eds.), *Aansprakelijkheidsrecht. Actuele tendensen*, Brussels, De Boeck & Larcier, 2005, 35; D. Wuyts, 'Productaansprakelijkheid: een Richtlijn voor (n)iets?', *TBBR* 2008, 10; B. Tilleman, n 72 above, 653; T. Vansweevelt and B. Weyts, *Handboek buitencontractueel aansprakelijkheidsrecht*, Antwerp, Intersentia, 2009, para. 792).

216 Article 10 of the Product Liability Law.

217 Article 5 of the Product Liability Law.

218 Article 11 of the Product Liability Law.

219 This is elaborated on in the chapter by R. Steennot and S. Geiregat in this volume.

220 Article VI.43 Code of Economic Law.

Table 2 *continued*

	1649*bis* ff. Belgian CC (consumer sales)	**ODSD**	**DCD**
Hierarchy of remedies for non-conformity	*Primary remedies:* Repair or replacement *Secondary remedies:* Price reduction or termination	*Primary remedies:* Repair or replacement *Secondary remedies:* Price reduction or termination	*Primary remedy:* Bringing the content into conformity *Secondary remedies:* Price reduction (where relevant) or termination
CONSUMER'S CONTRIBUTION TO THE LACK OF CONFORMITY			
Consumer's contribution to the lack of conformity	The circumstance that the damage increased due to the consumer's use of the goods should be taken into account (duty to mitigate damages)	The consumer is not entitled to a remedy to the extent that he has contributed to the lack of conformity or its effects	No specific rule
TIME LIMITS FOR NON-CONFORMITY			
Notification period	Can be contractually agreed; minimum two months from discovery of non-conformity[221]	No notification period	No notification period
Guarantee period	Two years as from delivery, but possible to hold the seller liable for latent defects after that on the basis of general sales law	Two years (without possible deviation for latent defects after the two-year period)	No restricted guarantee period[222] (without prejudice to the national prescription rules)
Suspension of guarantee period	Suspension for the duration of repair or replacement[223]	No explicit provision	N/A
Second-hand goods	Parties may agree on a shorter guarantee period with a minimum of one year[224]	No deviation	N/A
PRIMARY REMEDIES FOR NON-CONFORMITY			
Choice between repair and replacement	Consumer's choice, unless: – impossible (including unlawful?) – disproportionate	Consumer's choice, unless: – impossible – disproportionate – unlawful	N/A

(continued)

221 Included by the Belgian legislator, as allowed under Article 5(2) CSD.
222 This does not derogate from Belgian general sales law.
223 Not provided in CSD.
224 Included by the Belgian legislator, as allowed under Article 7(1) CSD.

Table 2 *continued*

	1649*bis* ff. Belgian CC (consumer sales)	**ODSD**	**DCD**
Method and conditions	Within a reasonable time and without significant inconvenience to the consumer Free of charge	Within a reasonable time and without significant inconvenience to the consumer Free of charge	Within a reasonable time and without significant inconvenience to the consumer Free of charge
Installed goods	No explicit rule, but according to CJEU case law, seller obliged to remove the non-conforming goods and to install the replacement goods	Seller obliged to remove the non-conforming goods and to install the replacement goods	N/A
Obligation to pay for use prior to replacement?	No explicit rule, but no obligation to pay for prior use according to CJEU case law	No	N/A
Withholding payment as remedy for purchaser	No explicit specific rule in sales law (but available as a general contract law rule)	Explicit rule: yes, until the goods are brought into conformity	No explicit rule
SECONDARY REMEDIES FOR NON-CONFORMITY: WHEN CAN THEY BE INVOKED?			
Situations	– Consumer is entitled to neither repair nor replacement – Primary remedy not completed within a reasonable time – Primary remedy not completed without significant inconvenience to consumer	– Impossible – Unlawful – Primary remedy not completed within a reasonable time – Primary remedy would cause significant inconvenience to consumer – Seller will not bring goods into conformity within a reasonable time	– Impossible – Unlawful – Disproportionate – Primary remedy not completed within a reasonable time – Primary remedy would cause significant inconvenience to consumer – Supplier will not bring goods into conformity within a reasonable time
PRICE REDUCTION			
Amount	Appropriate	Proportionate to the decrease in the value of the goods	Proportionate to the decrease in the value of the digital content
TERMINATION			
How?	No explicit provision; in principle, judicial termination	By notice	By notice

(continued)

Table 2 *continued*

	1649*bis* ff. Belgian CC (consumer sales)	**ODSD**	**DCD**
Termination for what non-conformity?	No right to terminate where the lack of conformity is minor	Right to terminate even where the lack of conformity is minor	Right to terminate if the lack of conformity impairs functionality, interoperability and other main performance features
Rules on restitution in case of termination?	No explicit rule	Yes	Yes
Pay for use prior to termination?	Yes	No	No
Rules on partial termination?	No explicit rule	Yes, if only some of the delivered goods are non-conforming	Yes, if digital content is supplied over time and was non-conforming for only a part of that period
Rules on the effect of termination on accessory goods/digital content	No explicit rule	Consumer may also terminate the contract in relation to goods accessory to the non-conforming goods	No explicit rule
Rules on termination of linked or ancillary contracts	No explicit rule	No explicit rule	No explicit rule
DAMAGES			
Additional damages?	Yes, but no detailed rules in consumer sales law	No explicit provision	Limited right to damages: the supplier is liable for economic damage to the digital environment caused by lack of conformity (or failure to deliver)

3.3.2. *Conclusions and Recommendations*

The new proposals increase consumer protection with respect to various areas compared to current Belgian law.

- Under the ODSD, the consumer may also terminate a contract for the distance sale of goods if the lack of conformity is only minor.
- Under both proposals, the consumer may unilaterally terminate the contract by giving notice.

- Under both proposals, the consumer does not have to notify a lack of conformity within a particular maximum time limit agreed between the parties.
- Under the ODSD, the guarantee period for second-hand goods cannot be shorter than two years.
- The ODSD expressly allows the consumer to withhold payment until the goods are brought into conformity with the contract.
- Both proposals clarify certain rules and codify existing case law (e.g. no choice between repair and replacement if one of the options is unlawful, repair and replacement of installed goods, standard of calculating the price reduction, payment for use, partial termination and restitution).
- The DCD finally introduces (mandatory) rules tailored to digital content contracts, albeit limited to consumer contracts.

Even though many provisions will result in a high level of consumer protection, this observation cannot be extended to all of the proposed rules. Certain rules would cause a reduction in consumer protection.

First of all, it would no longer be possible for the consumer to hold the seller liable for latent defects in goods after the lapse of a two-year period, unless the parties agreed to a longer contractual guarantee period. This will be important especially with respect to durable goods. This not only decreases the level of consumer protection, but also seems to contradict the idea of durable consumption which the Commission values highly on the strength of the references to it in the ODSD. It must be considered whether the two-year guarantee period should not be extended under certain circumstances, especially for goods which may be expected to be durable (such as a washing machine, a laptop, a TV, etc.).

Secondly, the provision on damages in the DCD is written in such a way that it might be interpreted as a limitation of the supplier's liability for damage to the consumer's digital environment, excluding all other losses the consumer might suffer. Not only does such a rule offer too low a level of consumer protection, it might also establish an unjustifiable distinction between the digital content industry and other businesses. It is strongly recommended that the DCD is amended in order to clarify that losses other than the loss covered by Article 14 DCD should be governed by national law and are not excluded by the DCD from compensation.

Thirdly, some rules stand out in terms of vagueness and ambiguity. This will further erode legal certainty and does not benefit consumer protection and confidence. One example of this vagueness is the effect of termination of a digital content contract on data collected by the supplier. It is not clear how far the supplier's obligation to return the data and to refrain from making further use of it extends.

Certain topics are also insufficiently dealt with in the proposals. The main gaps are a clear set of rules for 'smart' goods as well as for linked contracts and accessory digital content.

4. MODIFICATION OF DIGITAL CONTENT AND LONG-TERM CONTRACTS FOR THE SUPPLY OF DIGITAL CONTENT

4.1. GENERAL

Article 13 DCD deals with termination as a remedy for the lack of conformity of the digital content with the contract (and, according to Article 11, for failure to supply the digital content). This was discussed above.[225] There are two more provisions dealing with termination, but this time not as a remedy for non-conformity with the contract.

Article 15 DCD gives the consumer the right to terminate in certain situations where the supplier has modified the digital content. Article 16 DCD envisages termination of long-term contracts regardless of any non-conformity, failure to supply or modification by the supplier.

Articles 15 and 16 DCD deal with contracts whereby the digital content is supplied over time (and not in a single one-off transfer). This encompasses some of the most common digital content, such as cloud storage services (e.g. Dropbox), music and film streaming services (e.g. iTunes and Netflix), social media networks (e.g. Facebook), mobile apps (e.g. Candy Crush), anti-virus software (e.g. Avast!) and many more.

It should be pointed out that the current proposal is not completely clear in its wording on the relationship between Article 13 DCD on the one hand and Articles 15–16 DCD on the other hand. Based on mere sight of the provisions of Article 13 DCD, which is simply captioned 'Termination', they could also be applicable if a consumer terminates for reasons other than non-conformity, including termination in the case of modification of digital content and long-term contracts.[226] However, it can be derived from the entirety of the proposal that Article 13 DCD is intended to apply to termination in case of non-conformity and failure to deliver:

- Article 13(5)–(6) DCD (dealing with partial termination) expressly refers to non-conformity.
- Article 15 DCD expressly renders Article 13(2)(c) DCD applicable. This reference suggests that the provisions of Article 13 DCD are only applicable to the extent that Article 15 DCD refers to it in the case of modification of digital content.
- Articles 15 and 16 DCD copy certain provisions of Article 13 DCD, but not all of them. The provisions would not have been copied if Article 13 DCD was applicable in all situations, and this method suggests that Articles 15–16

225 Above, Section 3.2.4.3.

226 Fauvarque-Cosson, n 162 above, 11.

DCD deviate from Article 13 DCD where the provisions are not copied or referred to.

- Article 11 renders the remedy of termination applicable when the supplier has failed to supply the digital content in accordance with Article 5 DCD. Article 13 is in between Article 12 and Article 14 which are remedies for the lack of conformity (and, as to Article 14, for failure to supply the digital content).

It is nevertheless expedient from a law-drafting perspective to clarify this before the final vote in order to avoid all ambiguity.

4.2. MODIFICATION OF DIGITAL CONTENT

4.2.1. General

The rules of Articles 15 and 16 DCD deviate from the distinction in general contract law established in many legal systems between contracts for a determinate duration and those concluded for an indeterminate period of time. The former are binding until the lapse of the agreed term, while the latter can be terminated unilaterally at any time by giving notice as long as they are terminated in good faith, with a reasonable period of notice.

4.2.2. Supplier's Right to Modify the Digital Content Combined with Consumer's Right to Terminate

The supplier has the right to modify the digital content supplied over a period of time. This may not come as a surprise, because it is very common for suppliers to update their digital content for technical or other reasons. Such modifications are indispensable in the fast-moving digital industry, and often the supplier will improve certain features of the digital content for the benefit of the consumer.[227]

However, the supplier may also modify the digital content in a way which negatively affects the consumer's access to or use of the digital content. Think, for example, of the situation where an update makes the software incompatible with the (outdated) operating system of the consumer's computer. Such modifications which have a negative impact on the consumer should be subject to certain conditions. These are set out in Article 15 DCD.

More precisely, the DCD stipulates that such adverse modifications are subject to certain conditions if they relate to the functionality, interoperability or

[227] Commission Staff Working Document Impact Assessment, SWD(2015) 274, Brussels, 9 December 2015, 47.

other main performance features of the digital content, such as its accessibility, continuity and security.[228]

Moreover, a supplier may only implement such 'adverse' modifications to the main features of the digital content if the contract so stipulates.

In addition, the consumer must be notified reasonably far in advance of the modification by means of an explicit notice on a durable medium. Within no less than 30 days from receipt of this notice, the consumer must be allowed to terminate the contract free of any charges.[229] It is notable (but we have no criticism of this) that no formalities have been provided for in the proposal such as a duty to inform the consumer of this right whenever notice of the modification is given.

Modifications that have no impact on the main performance features of the digital content are not subject to these conditions. This might result in debates whereby a consumer claims that a modification relates to a main performance feature while the supplier claims that it just relates to a minor feature. The question arises how to assess whether a modification impacts on a main performance feature. Should this be determined from an objective point of view or from the point of view of the individual consumer? A modification which has little importance for most consumers may be of crucial importance for an individual consumer. For example, imagine that an online movie streaming service decides to stop providing Swedish subtitles to consumers in Belgium. This will not be of much importance to most Belgian consumers. But this modification is of importance for a Swede living in Belgium who only understands Swedish.

Given the enumeration 'functionality, interoperability and other main performance features of the digital content such as its accessibility, continuity and security', it seems that functionality and operability are main performance features and that therefore any modification of functionality or interoperability implies the right of the consumer to terminate the contract under Article 15 DCD. The same is true for accessibility, continuity and security. From a law-drafting perspective, it is not clear why functionality and interoperability are not mentioned on the same level as accessibility, continuity and security.

Unlike Articles 13 and 16 DCD, Article 15 DCD does not stipulate how the consumer is to exercise this right to terminate the contract. It may be useful to provide that termination may occur, for example, by notice given by any means, in order to avoid contractual clauses which make the method of termination too formalistic.

This right to modify the digital content needs to be read together with article VI.83 of the Belgian Code of Economic Law,[230] which provides a list of

---

228 Article 15(1) DCD.

229 Article 15(1)(a)–(c) DCD.

230 And with the general clause on the unfair control of contract terms, see Explanatory Memorandum DCD, 3.

unlawful terms in contracts between consumers and businesses. These include contractual terms enabling a business to unilaterally modify the characteristics of the product to be provided if those characteristics are essential for the consumer or for the intended use, insofar as this use was known to the business and accepted by it or insofar as this use was reasonably foreseeable.[231]

4.2.3. *Effects of Termination*

Upon termination, the supplier must provide the consumer with the technical means to retrieve all content provided.[232]

Where relevant, the supplier is obliged to reimburse that part of the price paid corresponding to the period of time after the modification of the digital content.[233] Since the consumer had access to the digital content which worked as it should before the modification, it is normal that he should have to pay for the time before the modification.

If the consumer provided a counter-performance other than money in exchange for the digital content, the supplier must refrain from using it. The supplier must also refrain from using any other data collected in relation to the supply of digital content, including any content provided by the consumer.[234] It is notable that Article 15 DCD obliges the supplier to refrain from all further use of the collected content and data, even though it was collected before the modification of the contract. This is particularly awkward when compared to the scenario in Article 13(4)–(5) DCD of partial termination for lack of conformity or failure to supply. As we discussed above,[235] if digital content is supplied over a period of time, the consumer can only terminate the contract for non-conformity in relation to the period when the digital content was not in conformity with the contract. In that situation, restitution is also limited. The supplier need (i) only reimburse part of the price corresponding to the period of time when the digital content was not in conformity with the contract, and (ii) only refrain from use of collected data and content in regard to the period during which the digital content was not in conformity with the contract.[236] Article 15(2) DCD limits the reimbursement of the price as well, but it does not make such a qualification with respect to the obligation to refrain from use of the collected data and content. It seems that the supplier must refrain from using all the data and content collected since the start of the contractual relationship if the consumer terminates the

231 Article VI.83, 4° Code of Economic Law.
232 Article 15(1)(d) DCD. In accordance with Article 13(2)(c) DCD, above, Section 3.2.4.3.
233 Article 15(2)(a) DCD.
234 Article 15(2)(b) DCD.
235 Above, Section 3.2.4.3.
236 Article 13(5)–(6) DCD.

contract due to modification of the digital content. We will further discuss the policy reasons in favour of and against such an obligation below.[237]

It is striking that certain effects of termination for non-conformity are not copied in the provision concerning termination in case of modification of the digital content. There seems to be no good reason for these distinctions. Article 13(2)(d) DCD expressly states that, upon termination, the consumer must refrain from making further use of the digital content and the supplier may prevent any further use of the digital content. These rules should apply in all situations of termination (unless otherwise agreed), but by not including these explicit rules in Article 15 DCD, the Commission could create the impression that these effects are not applicable when terminating the contract on the basis of Article 15 DCD.

4.2.4. Consumer's Right to Essential Updates?

Above,[238] we discussed the situation where the supplier modifies the digital content in a way that negatively affects the consumer's access to or use of the digital content. However, refusal by the supplier to modify the digital content may also be to the detriment of the consumer. Specifically, regular updates of the digital content may be essential in order for it to maintain its functionalities.

Take the example of anti-virus software. When a consumer installs anti-virus software, the device on which it is installed should be protected against viruses and malware known at that point in time. However, new viruses and malware are constantly arising. Therefore, it is critical to regularly update the anti-virus software in order to stay protected against such new threats. Anti-virus software that is a few years old and has never been updated will provide insufficient protection.

Article 6(1)(d) DCD states that, in order to be in conformity with the contract, the digital content must be updated as stipulated by the contract. However, this provision only provides a right to updates if such is provided for in the contract. The DCD does not provide an explicit right for the consumer to receive essential updates when this has not been agreed in the contract.[239] In certain cases, Article 6(3) DCD might offer a solution. Under this provision, where the contract stipulates that the digital content will be supplied over a period of time, the digital content must be in conformity throughout that period. Digital content supplied over a period of time that is not updated might cease to be in conformity with the contract, thus allowing the supplier to be held liable.

---

237 Below, Section 4.3.3.

238 Above, Section 4.2.2.

239 H. Beale, n 19 above, 27.

4.3. RIGHT TO TERMINATE LONG-TERM CONTRACTS

4.3.1. General

Article 16 DCD grants the consumer the right to terminate long-term contracts on certain conditions. The rationale for this provision is that consumers should be able to switch between suppliers without being locked in by legal, technical or practical obstacles. This should benefit competition in the digital single market.[240] This right to terminate long-term contracts could also be useful when a consumer decides to change his hardware and his new hardware no longer supports the digital content he has contracted for.

4.3.2. Requirements to Exercise the Right to Terminate

Under existing Belgian law, there are no specific provisions dealing with the right to terminate long-term contracts regarding digital content. According to general contract law, contracts concluded for an indeterminate period can be terminated at any time by either party without giving reasons (for convenience),[241] albeit in good faith[242] and therefore, in principle, with a term of notice.[243] In principle, a contract concluded for a fixed period of time (e.g. three years) cannot be terminated unilaterally without a breach of contract (unless otherwise agreed). Contracts for performing defined work can be unilaterally terminated by the employer, but he has to compensate for all damage, including lost profit (according to the default rule of article 1794 CC). Belgian consumer law further stipulates that, after tacit renewal of a contract for the supply of services (or a contract that has both goods and services as its object) concluded for a fixed time, a consumer may terminate the contract at any time, taking into account the contractual term of notice, which cannot in any event exceed two months.[244]

Under the DCD, consumers have a right to terminate long-term contracts for the supply of digital content. Long-term contracts have a broad meaning under the DCD. They are contracts concluded for an indeterminate period or contracts where the initial contract duration or any combination of renewal periods exceeds 12 months. While consumer contracts concluded for longer contractual periods are not unlawful as such, consumers have the right to terminate

240 Recital 46 DCD.

241 Court of Cassation 9 March 1973, *Arr.Cass.* 1973, 671, *Pas.* 1973, 640; Court of Cassation 22 November 1973, *Arr.Cass.* 1974, 327,*Pas.* 1974, 312; F. Vermander, *De opzegging van overeenkomsten*, Antwerp, Intersentia, 2014, 461–98.

242 Article 1134, third paragraph CC.

243 See, for example, Court of Cassation 20 November 2009, AR C.080507.F, http://jure.juridat.just.fgov.be/pdfapp/download_blob?idpdf=F-20091120-1.

244 Articles VI.91 and XIV.58 of the Belgian Code of Economic Law.

these long-term contracts after the lapse of the first 12-month period.[245] The requirement for a lapse of time of 12 months is justified by the interests of the supplier, for whom it is important to protect existing investments and the trust in concluded contracts.[246]

There are no strict formal requirements for consumers in order to exercise this termination right. The consumer simply has to give notice to the supplier by any means. The termination already becomes effective 14 days after receipt of the notice.[247]

It is remarkable that contracts for an indeterminate duration are also envisaged, because this gives the impression that the consumer in that situation is now bound for a minimum period of 12 months. If that is indeed the intention of the drafters, the question arises whether the supplier is also bound, in a contract for an indeterminate duration, to a minimum period of 12 months, or whether it is still free, within that period, to terminate the contract at will, albeit in good faith.

4.3.3. *Effects of Termination*

Where the digital content was supplied in exchange for the payment of a price, the consumer is obliged to pay part of the price corresponding to the period before the effective termination.[248] This is different from non-conformity because, in the hypothesis of Article 16 DCD, the consumer normally had access to well-functioning digital content.

Where relevant, the consumer must also delete usable copies, render the digital content unintelligible, and refrain from using it.[249] The supplier has the right to prevent the consumer from making any further use of the digital content, e.g. by making it inaccessible to the consumer or by disabling the consumer's user account.[250] We have already discussed above the fact that such provision can easily remain a dead letter in practice.[251]

The supplier, for his part, is obliged to take all measures which could be expected in order to refrain from using the counter-performance or any other data and content provided by the consumer.[252]

In addition, the supplier must provide the technical means to allow the consumer to retrieve the content and data provided by the consumer. The

245 Article 16(1) DCD.
246 Recital 46 DCD.
247 Article 16(2) DCD.
248 Article 16(3) DCD.
249 Article 16(4)(c) DCD.
250 Article 16(5) DCD.
251 Above, Section 3.2.4.3.
252 Article 16(4)(a) DCD.

consumer has the right to retrieve all content without significant inconvenience, in reasonable time and in a commonly used data format.[253] This provision offers a solution for an important practical obstacle to switching suppliers. Switching to another provider often requires moving personal and other data from the former provider to the new provider. This requires data portability. For example, a user of a cloud storage service may want to switch to another supplier, but is hindered from doing so because he has no easy way to transfer all his content, stored with the current provider, to the new provider.[254] The DCD intends to eliminate such practical obstacles.

It is not always clear why the effects of termination as a remedy for non-conformity in Article 13 DCD differ in some respects from the effects of termination of long-term contracts in Article 16 DCD.

First, both provisions oblige the supplier to refrain from continuing to use the counter-performance where the contract has been terminated. However, only Article 13(2)(b) DCD provides an exception to this for content which has been generated jointly by the consumer and others who continue to make use of the content. It is not clear why this exception has not been expressly provided for in the case of termination of long-term contracts.[255]

Secondly, while both termination provisions oblige the supplier to enable the consumer to retrieve the content provided by the consumer, Article 13(2)(b) DCD expressly provides that the consumer is entitled to do so free of charge, but Article 16(4)(b) DCD has no such provision. This seems to imply that a supplier can charge a fee to the consumer for the retrieval of the content if the consumer terminates a long-term contract on the basis of Article 16 DCD.

Some of the wording used to describe the effects of termination in Article 13 and in Article 16 is different, even though the intended effect seems to be the same.[256] Both provisions should use the same wording wherever possible in order to avoid confusion and diverging interpretations where these are not intended.

---

253 Article 16(4)(b) DCD.

254 For more about data portability upon switching to another cloud computing provider, see: I. Overing, 'Discussion paper on switching – data portability upon switching', *Expert Group on Cloud Computing Contracts*, 29 January 2014, http://ec.europa.eu/justice/contract/files/expert_groups/discussion_paper_topic_4_switching_en.pdf (consultation 23 April 2016).

255 B. Fauvarque-Cosson, n 162 above, 15.

256 For instance, Article 13(2)(e) DCD states: 'where digital content was not supplied on a durable medium, the consumer shall refrain from using the digital content or making it available to third parties, in particular by deleting the digital content or rendering it otherwise unintelligible.' Article 16(4)(c) DCD seems to be the mirror image of this provision in the case of termination of long-term contracts, although it stipulates this in different wording: 'where applicable, the consumer shall delete any usable copy of the digital content, render it unintelligible or otherwise refrain from using it including by making it available to a third party.'

It could also be argued that the 'restitution' effect is less evident in the case of termination of a long-term contract than in the case of termination for non-conformity. The restitution effect here refers to the obligation of the supplier to refrain from using the data and content provided by the consumer. In the event of termination for non-conformity, this form of 'restitution' makes sense. But in this case there is no breach of contract committed by the supplier. The consumer, having used the digital content freely for some time in exchange for data, chooses to terminate the contract for reasons other than breach of contract by the supplier. The supplier must nevertheless restore the non-monetary price that the consumer 'paid' for using the service in the past.

On the one hand, it could be argued that such restitution does not fit in the situation where the contract is terminated without any breach of contract on the part of the supplier.[257]

- In the case of partial termination due to non-conformity,[258] the supplier also does not have to refrain from using the provided counter-performance in relation to the period during which the digital content was in conformity with the contract.
- The DCD seems to miss the point that the data and content provided constitute a real price paid by the consumer for accessing the service. If money was paid, the supplier would not have to pay it back after the contract was terminated (except in the event of a breach of contract by the supplier). The consumer paid with personal data rather than with money; why is restitution of the 'price paid' required when terminating without any breach of contract? It is even quite possible that the supplier has not yet made use of the consumer's data at all – because it is still developing its database, for example.
- Such a provision may hinder the industry when it comes to offering 'gratuitous' digital content in return for data. The 'gratuitous' digital content is of benefit to consumers.

On the other hand, there are also reasonable arguments in favour of the supplier's obligation to refrain from making further use of the consumer's data once the long-term contract is terminated.

- Data cannot be compared to money, in particular when this involves personal data and therefore affects the individual's fundamental right to privacy. This

[257] The same is true for termination in the case of modification of digital content, but to a lesser extent because the supplier modified the digital content which adversely affected the consumer. Thus, in contrast to termination of a long-term contract, the termination results from an act of the supplier to the detriment of the consumer. This justifies the prohibition on the supplier making further use of the data more than in the case of termination of long-term contracts.

[258] Article 13(5) DCD.

justifies the restitution of personal data if the data subject ends the contractual relationship with the supplier.

- Consumers do not reasonably expect that suppliers of digital content would continue to store and use their (personal) data after the consumer has ended the contractual relationship.
- One might say that there is no real transfer of data to the supplier; the consumer only gives the supplier the right to (temporary) use of the data, which ends when the contractual relationship ends.
- This is more consistent with the General Data Protection Regulation, which gives the data subject the right to erasure of personal data when he withdraws his consent and where this consent was the ground for processing the data.[259]

4.4. OVERVIEW OF THE RIGHT TO TERMINATE IN THE DIFFERENT PROVISIONS

Table 3. Right to terminate under the DCD

	Termination for non-conformity (Article 13 DCD)	**Termination in case of modification of the digital content (Article 15 DCD)**	**Termination of long-term contracts (Article 16 DCD)**
Formal requirements for exercising the right to terminate	Notice by any means	No explicit provision	Notice by any means
Supplier must reimburse the price	Yes (but in the case of partial termination, only the part of the price corresponding to the period when the digital content was not in conformity)	Yes, but only the part of the price corresponding to the period after the modification	No
Supplier must refrain from using the counter-performance	Yes (but in the case of partial termination, only the part of the data corresponding to the period when the digital content was not in conformity)	Yes	Yes
Supplier must provide the consumer with the technical means to retrieve the content and data	Yes	Yes	Yes

(continued)

[259] Article 17 GDPR.

Table 3 *continued*

	Termination for non-conformity (Article 13 DCD)	**Termination in case of modification of the digital content (Article 15 DCD)**	**Termination of long-term contracts (Article 16 DCD)**
Consumer must refrain from using the digital content	Yes	No explicit provision	Yes
Supplier may prevent the consumer's further use	Yes	No explicit provision	Yes
Pay for use prior to termination	No	Yes (prior to modification)	Yes

5. CONCLUSION

The Commission's objective with the ODSD and the DCD is twofold: providing a high level of consumer protection and increasing legal certainty. This, in turn, should boost e-commerce. After having analysed the ODSD and DCD provisions on remedies and termination, it is highly doubtful whether these objectives will be accomplished with the current proposals.

First, even though the new set of rules introduces additional consumer protection with respect to certain topics, there are also areas where consumer protection would decrease compared to current Belgian law. An important example is the strict limitation of the guarantee period in the ODSD to two years, without the possibility of holding the seller liable for latent defects after the expiry of this two-year period, despite the fact that sustainable products are expected to function properly for a longer period of time. Another important issue is the risk that the current provision on damages in the DCD might be interpreted as a limitation of the supplier's liability, excluding the possibility for consumers to hold the supplier liable for types of damage other than damage to their digital environment.

It is also hard to accept that no maximum notification period is provided for in the proposed directives. The goal is to protect consumers against non-conformities, not to incentivise stale claims.

In the digital world we live in, the question also arises whether the ODSD and DCD should be merged into one single instrument. Consumer goods are increasingly embedded with digital content (so-called 'smart goods'). Despite the blurring borders between tangible goods and digital content, the legislative framework, regrettably, is still based upon that distinction.

Moreover, it is highly debatable whether legal certainty is served by the proposed set of rules. The new proposals would contribute to the further fragmentation of the existing consumer acquis by providing a set of rules specifically designed for distance sales contracts. The distinction between distance contracts and face-to-face contracts leads to an unnecessary complexity of the consumer acquis. For the most part, there is no sufficient reason for subjecting the two types of contracts to a different set of rules. When implementing the Directives, it might not be a bad idea for the Belgian legislature to amend the general consumer sales law in order to bring the rules for face-to-face sales in line with the new rules for distance sales. This suggestion may also be the solution that some are hoping for in silence because of the lower degree of consumer protection in some respects, even if the recitals give the impression that omni-channel businesses will rather apply 'the respective higher standards to all of their sales'.[260]

In addition, a number of the rules proposed are ambiguous. For example, the effects of termination of a contract for the supply for digital content are anything but clear. Certain rules should definitely be tweaked and fine-tuned in order to clarify their scope and effect.

Finally, the Commission claims that these sets of uniform rules will result in fewer disparities and trade barriers across the European Union. Businesses would no longer need to take into account the different mandatory consumer rules in the EU Member States when doing business cross-border. The Commission's claim should be put into question in the light of the limited scope of the proposals. As the proposals themselves indicate, only certain areas (the so-called 'key contractual rights') are harmonised. All other issues remain to be governed by the diverging national laws, such as the obligations of the consumer towards the supplier and the supplier's remedies, the classification of the contracts,[261] the legality of the contract,[262] the formation and validity of the contracts, the effects of the contracts,[263] (at least to some extent) the damages remedy, limitation periods, rights of redress, even commercial guarantees,[264] mixed contracts,[265] and

> the detailed conditions for the exercise of rights, such as the right to damages to the extent not covered by the Directive, or rules which provide for the consequences of termination of the contract which apply in addition to restitution rules regulated by this Directive.[266]

---

260 Explanatory Memorandum ODSD, 12.
261 See Explanatory Memorandum DCD, 6.
262 Explanatory Memorandum DCD, 15.
263 Explanatory Memorandum DCD, 12.
264 Recital 14 ODSD.
265 Recital 12 ODSD.
266 Explanatory Memorandum DCD, 15.

It seems that the problem of the diverging rules among the Member States is far from being solved by the new proposals. It is hard to believe that the two proposals tackle 'in a consistent manner contract law-related obstacles for the supply of digital content [and goods] while preventing legal fragmentation', while knowing that we will now possibly have separate legal regimes for general sales law, international sales law (CISG), consumer face-to-face sales, consumer distance sales, and consumer digital content supply contracts, which all have to be combined to some (differing) extent with general contract law and sometimes with general sales, services or rental law. In conclusion, while legislative action in the field of online and digital contracts should be welcomed, there is still much work to be done on both proposals in order to avoid the new Directives running counter to the goals that were set.

COMMERCIAL GUARANTEES IN THE PROPOSAL FOR A DIRECTIVE ON CERTAIN ASPECTS CONCERNING CONTRACTS FOR THE ONLINE AND OTHER DISTANCE SALES OF GOODS

Evelyne Terryn and Sanne Vandemaele

1. INTRODUCTION

A commercial guarantee – in the sense of a voluntary service that may be offered by a seller, a producer or a third party in addition to the legal guarantee – can definitely have benefits for consumers. Such guarantees are commonly offered – an ECC-net survey found that 60 per cent of online offers referred to commercial guarantees – and an important percentage of consumers do buy commercial guarantees (often in the form of 'extended warranties').[1]

There are definitely potential benefits: the rights the consumer has under the legal guarantee can be extended; repair at the home of the consumer may be offered as well as a courtesy replacement product during examination or repair; the reversal of the burden of proof may be extended; the hierarchy of remedies may be waived, etc.

There are, however, also potential disadvantages. Costs may be involved to obtain a commercial guarantee and the benefits of such guarantee may vary considerably; long lists of exclusions may be involved; geographical limitations may be imposed etc. Another recurring problem is that the information provided may be limited to the commercial warranty and the consumer may be misled about his legal rights.[2]

As such commercial guarantees are voluntary, the regulatory framework specifically with regard to commercial guarantees is thus far limited. This, however, does not mean that there are no tools to combat misleading or unfair practices and terms. Horizontal instruments like the Unfair Commercial Practices Directive[3] and the Unfair Contract Terms Directive[4] have proved useful in this regard.

This chapter focuses on the Proposal for a directive on certain aspects concerning contracts for the online and other distance sales of goods (ODSD Proposal)[5] and the improvements it may bring in comparison to the existing legal framework.

We will therefore set out the current legislative framework and its evolution (Section 2). We will then briefly discuss the *Apple case* as this case is a clear illustration of the problems with commercial guarantees and the drawbacks

---

1 In an ECC Survey in 2014, 56% of the respondents said they had bought a commercial guarantee: http://www.europe-consommateurs.eu/fileadmin/user_upload/eu-consommateurs/PDFs/PDF_EN/REPORT-_GUARANTEE/Garanties_2014_FINAL.pdf.

2 See also, Ch. von Bar, E. Clive, H. Schulte-Nölke, H. Beale, J. Herre, J. Huet, P. Schlechtriem, M.E. Storme, S. Swann, P. Varul, A. Veneziano and F. Zoll (eds.), *Principles, definitions and model rules of European private law: Draft Common Frame of Reference (DCFR)*, 2009, 1418: http://ec.europa.eu/justice/contract/files/european-private-law_en.pdf.

3 Directive 2005/29/EC of the European Parliament and of the Council of 11 May 2005 concerning unfair business-to-consumer commercial practices in the internal market and amending Council Directive 84/450/EEC, Directives 97/7/EC, 98/27/EC and 2002/65/EC of the European Parliament and of the Council and Regulation (EC) No 2006/2004 of the European Parliament and of the Council, *OJ* 11 June 2005, L 149/22 (hereafter 'UCPD' or 'Unfair Commercial Practices Directive').

4 Directive 93/13/EEC of the Council of 5 April 1993 on unfair terms in consumer contracts, *OJ* 21 April 1993, L 95/29 (hereafter 'UCTD' or 'Unfair Contract Terms Directive').

5 European Commission, Proposal for a Directive of the European Parliament and of the Council on certain aspects concerning contracts for the online and other distance sales of goods, COM(2015) 635 final, Brussels, 9 December 2015.

and the limitations of the current legal framework (Section 3). We will finally analyse the proposed Article 15 ODSD Proposal, which regulates commercial guarantees (Section 4).

2. EVOLUTION OF THE EUROPEAN LEGISLATION ON COMMERCIAL GUARANTEES

2.1. INTRODUCTION: A LENGTHY PROCESS

The European legislator had discussed (commercial) guarantees for a long time before the first European instrument was adopted. The first time (commercial) guarantees were on the agenda was in 1975.[6] After the matter was judged too important to be regulated in the annex of the UCTD,[7] the Green Paper on Guarantees of 1993 comprehensively discussed the legislative options for (commercial) guarantees.[8] The Green Paper analysed the existing framework for (commercial) guarantees, pointed out the problems market participants experienced and provided possible solutions without taking a stance on the most appropriate solution.[9] Although the Green Paper was rather ambitious, in the years that followed the enthusiasm dampened.[10] In 1999, the Directive on certain aspects of the sale of consumer goods and associated guarantees (CSD) was adopted,[11] with only limited substantive rules on commercial guarantees.

6 Council Resolution of 14 April 1975 on a preliminary programme of the European Economic Community for a consumer protection and information policy, *OJ* 25 April 1975, L 92/1; Y. Ninane and O. Gilard, *La garantie des biens de consommation*, Waterloo, Kluwer, 2010, 22; J. Stuyck, 'Historiek en toepassingsgebied van de richtlijn consumentenkoop en van de omzettingswet' in S. Stijns and J. Stuyck (eds.), *Het nieuwe kooprecht. De wet van 1 september 2004 betreffende de bescherming van de consumenten bij verkoop van consumptiegoederen*, Antwerp, Intersentia, 2005, 5.

7 European Commission, Proposal for a Council Directive on unfair terms in consumer contracts, COM(90) 322 final, *OJ* 28 September 1990, C 243/2; Opinion of the Economic and Social Committee on the proposal for a Council Directive on unfair terms in consumer contracts, Brussels, *OJ* 17 June 1991, C 159/36.

8 European Commission, Green Paper on guarantees for consumer goods and after-sales services, COM(93) 509 final, Brussels, 15 November 1993.

9 European Commission, Green Paper on guarantees for consumer goods and after-sales services, COM(93) 509 final, Brussels, 15 November 1993, 167–69.

10 Opinion of the Economic and Social Committee on the Green Paper on guarantees for consumer goods and after-sales services, Brussels, *OJ* 22 October 1994, C 295/16; European Commission, Proposal for a European Parliament and Council Directive on the sale of consumer goods and associated guarantees, COM(95) 520 final, *OJ* 16 October 1996, C 307/8.

11 Directive 1999/44/EC of the European Parliament and of the Council of 25 May 1999 on certain aspects of the sale of consumer goods and associated guarantees, *OJ* 7 July 1999, L 171.

In 2011, the Consumer Rights Directive (CRD) added a new definition of commercial guarantees and limited additional information requirements.[12] That same year, a Proposal for a far more ambitious Regulation on a Common European Sales Law was published, that was, however, never adopted.[13] The relevant provisions on commercial guarantees as well as the scope of application of the mentioned instruments are briefly discussed below.

2.2. DIRECTIVE ON SALE OF CONSUMER GOODS AND ASSOCIATED GUARANTEES

The Consumer Sales Directive only regulates certain aspects of the sale of consumer goods and focuses on the legal guarantee of conformity with the contract by the seller,[14] with a limited number of provisions concerning commercial guarantees. It is a minimum harmonisation directive.[15]

The CSD applies to contracts for sale of consumer goods between the consumer and the (final) seller. A consumer is 'any natural person who, in the contracts covered by this Directive, is acting for purposes which are not related to his trade, business or profession',[16] while a seller is 'any natural or legal person who, under a contract, sells consumer goods in the course of his trade, business or profession'.[17] Only sales contracts concerning tangible movable items fall within the scope of application.[18] In principle the Directive also applies to

---

12 Directive 2011/83/EU of the European Parliament and of the Council of 25 October 2011 on consumer rights, amending Council Directive 93/13/EEC and Directive 1999/44/EC of the European Parliament and of the Council and repealing Council Directive 85/577/EEC and Directive 97/7/EC, *OJ* 22 November 2011, L 304.

13 COM(2011) 635 final, 2011/0284 (COD), Proposal for a Regulation on a Common European Sales Law (hereafter 'CESL').

14 Recital 6 CSD.

15 Art. 114 TFEU, recitals 1–5 and Art. 1(1) CSD. A. Luna Serrano, 'Article 1: Scope and definitions' in M.C. Bianca and S. Grundmann (eds.), *EU Sales Directive – Commentary*, Antwerp, Intersentia, 2002, (91) 93–94; M. Scotton, 'Directive 99/44/EC on Certain Aspects of the Sale of Consumer Goods and Associated Guarantees', *ERPL* 2001, (297) 299; D. Staudenmayer, 'Die EG-Richtlinie über den Verbrauchsgüterkauf', *NJW* 1999, (2393) 2393.

16 Art. 1(2)(a) CSD; H.-W. Micklitz and N. Reich, 'Sale of Consumer Goods' in N. Reich, H.-W. Micklitz, P. Rott and K. Tonner (eds.), *European Consumer Law*, Antwerp, Intersentia, 2014, (165) 172.

17 Art. 1(2)(c) CSD; H.-W. Micklitz and N. Reich, 'Sale of Consumer Goods' in N. Reich, H.-W. Micklitz, P. Rott and K. Tonner (eds.), *European Consumer Law*, Antwerp, Intersentia, 2014, (165) 173.

18 Art. 1(2)(b) CSD; M. Tenreiro and S. Gomez, 'La directive 1999/44/CE sur certains aspects de la vente et des garanties des biens de consommation', *REDC* 2000, (5) 11. Excluded from the scope of application are: goods sold by way of execution or otherwise by authority of law, water and gas where they are not put up for sale in a limited volume or set quantity and electricity.

second-hand goods, but the Member States can exclude these goods if sold at a public auction where consumers have the opportunity of attending the sale in person.[19] The Directive does not clearly define a sales contract, but clarifies that not only pure sales contracts but also contracts for the supply of consumer goods to be manufactured or produced are considered.[20]

Under the CSD a commercial guarantee is:

> any undertaking by a seller or producer to the consumer, given without extra charge, to reimburse the price paid or to replace, repair or handle consumer goods in any way if they do not meet the specifications set out in the guarantee statement or in the relevant advertising.[21]

The commercial guarantee is a voluntary undertaking, but it does create certain obligations.[22] Each commercial guarantee is legally binding on the offeror. The CSD does not, however, determine the legal nature of this obligation.[23] The offeror is bound by the conditions laid down in the guarantee statement and the associated advertising. One of the main goals of the CSD concerning commercial guarantees is protecting the consumer against misleading practices.[24] In order to attain this goal, Article 6(2) CSD stipulates that the guarantee must contain some essential particulars. First of all, the guarantee shall state that the consumer has legal rights under the applicable national legislation governing the sale of consumer goods, and make clear that those rights are not affected by the guarantee. Furthermore, the contents of the guarantee and the essential particulars necessary for making claims under the guarantee should be stated in plain, intelligible language.[25] Examples of these essential particulars are the

---

19 Art. 1(3) CSD; H.-W. Micklitz and N. Reich, 'Sale of Consumer Goods' in N. Reich, H.-W. Micklitz, P. Rott and K. Tonner (eds.), *European Consumer Law*, Antwerp, Intersentia, 2014, (165) 170.

20 Art. 1(4) CSD; M. Tenreiro and S. Gomez, 'La directive 1999/44/CE sur certains aspects de la vente et des garanties des biens de consommation', *REDC* 2000, (5) 13.

21 Art. 2(2)(e) CSD.

22 Ph. Malinvaud, 'Article 6: Guarantees' in M.C. Bianca and S. Grundmann (eds.), *EU Sales Directive - Commentary*, Antwerp, Intersentia, 2002, (219) 223.

23 In the explanatory memorandum of the Proposal for a directive on the sale of consumer goods and associated guarantees the Commission pointed out that the proposal itself does not imply any legal qualification in respect of the guarantee (contract, unilateral promise, etc.), which could also vary depending on the person of the guarantor and national legal traditions. European Commission, Proposal for a European Parliament and Council Directive on the sale of consumer goods and associated guarantees, COM(95) 520 final, Brussels, 18 June 1996, 15.

24 Recital 21 CSD; H.-W. Micklitz and N. Reich, 'Sale of Consumer Goods' in N. Reich, H.-W. Micklitz, P. Rott and K. Tonner (eds.), *European Consumer Law*, Antwerp, Intersentia, 2014, (165) 188.

25 Compare with Art. 5 UCTD: 'In the case of contracts where all or certain terms offered to the consumer are in writing, these terms must always be drafted in plain, intelligible language.

duration and territorial scope of the guarantee as well as the name and address of the guarantor. This enumeration is obviously not limitative, but only indicates a minimum.[26] Finally, the offeror shall make the guarantee available in writing or through another durable medium if the consumer requests it.[27] These transparency rules enable the consumer on the one hand to be informed before the purchase and on the other hand to have the necessary information to take action under the guarantee[28] (below, Section 4.1). The CSD does not provide for sanctions in case of non-compliance of the transparency rules. Article 6(5) only states that if the guarantee infringes these requirements, this does not affect the validity of the commercial guarantee and, in consequence, the consumer can still rely on it and can require that it will be honoured.[29]

The notion of 'commercial guarantee' under the CSD is on the one hand rather large, but on the other hand also restrictive.[30] It is large because it applies to the final seller, the producer, the importer or any other person purporting to be a producer by placing his name, trade mark or other distinctive sign on the consumer goods.[31] The range of obligations that can be undertaken by the offeror is also broad: this can be the reimbursement of the price paid, the replacement or repair of the goods or any other possible way to handle the non-conformity.

It is restrictive because guarantees with an extra charge seem to fall outside the scope of application, even though the choice of the adjective 'extra' in the definition illustrates the awareness that a commercial guarantee is never really for free, since the charge is included in the purchase price.[32]

Where there is doubt about the meaning of a term, the interpretation most favourable to the consumer shall prevail. This rule on interpretation shall not apply in the context of the procedures laid down in Article 7 (2).'

26 Art. 6(2) CSD. We can derive the non-exhaustive nature of the enumeration from the use of the term 'notably'. Ph. Malinvaud, 'Article 6: Guarantees' in M.C. Bianca and S. Grundmann (eds.), *EU Sales Directive – Commentary*, Antwerp, Intersentia, 2002, (219) 229.

27 Art. 6(3) CSD; Ph. Malinvaud, 'Article 6: Guarantees' in M.C. Bianca and S. Grundmann (eds.), *EU Sales Directive – Commentary*, Antwerp, Intersentia, 2002, (219) 225; M. Tenreiro and S. Gomez, 'La directive 1999/44/CE sur certains aspects de la vente et des garanties des biens de consommation', *REDC* 2000, (5) 32.

28 Ph. Malinvaud, 'Article 6: Guarantees' in M.C. Bianca and S. Grundmann (eds.), *EU Sales Directive – Commentary*, Antwerp, Intersentia, 2002, (219) 229.

29 Art. 6(5) CSD.

30 A. Luna Serrano, 'Article 1: Scope and definitions' in M.C. Bianca and S. Grundmann (eds.), *EU Sales Directive – Commentary*, Antwerp, Intersentia, 2002, (91) 100.

31 *Cf.* Art. 1(2)(d) CSD.

32 See also below nn 41 and 96. F. Faust, '§443 Garantie' in H.G. Bamberger and H. Roth (eds.), *Beck'scher Online-Kommentar BGB*, Munich, Beck, 2014, para. 23; Ph. Malinvaud, 'Article 6: Guarantees' in M.C. Bianca and S. Grundmann (eds.), *EU Sales Directive – Commentary*, Antwerp, Intersentia, 2002, (219) 223.

2.3. DIRECTIVE ON CONSUMER RIGHTS

In 2011, some limited additional provisions concerning commercial guarantees were adopted in the CRD. Contrary to the proposal for the CRD,[33] the text as adopted does not regulate (legal or commercial) guarantees in an extensive way. The relevant provisions are limited to a definition of commercial guarantee, and some additional information requirements. The CRD does not provide new substantive rules on commercial guarantees. The CRD sets out a level of maximum harmonisation, unless otherwise provided for in the Directive.[34] The level of harmonisation only binds the Member States, so traders can always offer consumers contractual arrangements which go beyond the protection provided for.[35]

The CRD has a very broad scope of application as it applies – in principle – to 'any contract between a trader and a consumer'.[36] It is a *lex generalis* so specific regulation has priority.[37] Contrary to the CSD, electricity is not excluded as a consumer good if it is put up for sale in a limited volume or a set quantity.[38]

33 European Commission, Proposal for a Directive of the European Parliament and of the Council on consumer rights, COM(2008) 614 final, Brussels, 8 October 2008; A. Van Oevelen, 'Het voorstel voor een richtlijn consumentenrechten: voorstellen tot wijziging van de consumentenkoop inzake de garantie – en de meldingstermijn, de sancties bij niet-conformiteit en de handelsgaranties', *DCCR* 2009, 204–29. This proposal was the result of a revision of the European Consumer Acquis that started in 2004. Communication from the Commission to the European Parliament and the Council of 11 October 2003, European Contract Law and the revision of the acquis: the way forward, COM(2004) 651 final, *OJ* 20 January 2005, C 14/6. This has led to a Green Paper on this revision in 2007: European Commission, Green Paper on the Review of the Consumer Acquis, COM(2006) 744 final, *OJ* 15 March 2007, C 61/1. C. Twigg-Flesner, 'The impact of the Consumer Rights Directive (2011/83/EU) on Consumer Sales Contracts', *R.A.E.* 2012, (563) 563.

34 Art. 4 CRD; E. Cruysmans, C. Delforge, G. de Pierpont, C. Donnet, Y. Ninane, M.-P. Noël, Ph. Stroobant and J. van Zuylen, 'La directive 2011/83/UE du 25 octobre 2011 relative aux droits des consommateurs', *TBBR* 2013, (174) 180.

35 Art. 3(6) CRD.

36 Art. 3(1) CRD. Consumer is 'any natural person who, in contracts covered by this Directive, is acting for purposes which are outside his trade, business, craft or profession' (Art. 2(1) CRD) and a trader is 'any natural person or any legal person, irrespective of whether privately or publicly owned, who is acting, including through any other person acting in his name or on his behalf, for purposes relating to his trade, business, craft or profession in relation to contracts covered by this Directive' (Art. 2(2) CRD).

The Directive shall also apply to contracts for the supply of water, gas, electricity or district heating, including by public providers, to the extent that these commodities are provided on a contractual basis. However, Art. 3(3) provides a list of 13 types of contracts excluded from the Directive; J. Goddaer, 'De Richtlijn Consumentenrechten – Gevolgen voor de WMPC en de Wet Elektronische Handel', *DCCR* 2012, (7) 23.

37 Art. 3(2) CRD.

38 Art. 2(3) CRD; J. Goddaer, 'De Richtlijn Consumentenrechten – Gevolgen voor de WMPC en de Wet Elektronische Handel', *DCCR* 2012, (7) 12.

The CRD also contains a definition of 'sales contract', once more contrary to the CSD. A sales contract means

> any contract under which the trader transfers or undertakes to transfer the ownership of goods to the consumer and the consumer pays or undertakes to pay the price thereof, including any contract having as its object both goods and services.[39]

In the CRD, commercial guarantee is defined as

> any undertaking by the trader or a producer (the guarantor) to the consumer, in addition to his legal obligation relating to the guarantee of conformity, to reimburse the price paid or to replace, repair or service goods in any way if they do not meet the specifications or any other requirements not related to conformity set out in the guarantee statement or in the relevant advertising available at the time of, or before the conclusion of the contract.[40]

There are several differences in comparison with the definition in the CSD. First, the new definition does not mention that a guarantee must be 'given without extra charge'. This omission results in a larger scope of application: both commercial guarantees free of charge and for payment are covered. By consequence, the offeror cannot ask for a (minor) consideration with the intention to rule out the applicable requirements.[41] Secondly, Article 2(14) stipulates expressly that the undertaking must be 'in addition to his legal obligation relating to the guarantee of conformity'. This is only a confirmation of what was already commonly accepted and also resulted from the CSD, namely the impossibility of the offeror infringing the consumers' legal rights because of their imperative nature. The third difference concerns the situations that can be covered by the guarantee. Next to the specifications set out in the guarantee statement or in the relevant advertising which were also covered under the CSD, also 'any other requirement not related to conformity' can now be covered. Until now a commercial guarantee was considered to be connected to the conformity of the goods. Traditionally, a guarantee covers a certain quality of the goods during a certain period.[42] This connection with conformity is essential in Belgium, for

---

39 Art. 2(5) CRD.

40 Art. 2(14) CRD.

41 S. Grundmann, 'Introduction' in M.C. Bianca and S. Grundmann (eds.), *EU Sales Directive – Commentary*, Antwerp, Intersentia, 2002, (15) 33; D. Staudenmayer, 'Die EG-Richtlinie über den Verbrauchsgüterkauf', *NJW* 1999, (2393) 2394. See also concerning the DCFR: Ch. Twigg-Flesner, 'Consumer Goods Guarantees in the DCFR', *ERPL* 2009, (641) 643.

42 *Cf.* Art. IV.A-6:101(2)(a) DCFR: 'apart from misuse, mistreatment or accident ...' and Art. IV.A-6:104(b) DCFR: the conformity requirement has been chosen as the default rule. See, Ch. von Bar, E. Clive, H. Schulte-Nölke, H. Beale, J. Herre, J. Huet, P. Schlechtriem, M.E. Storme, S. Swann, P. Varul, A. Veneziano and F. Zoll (eds.), *Principles, definitions and model rules of European private law: Draft Common Frame of Reference (DCFR)*, 2009,

example, to make the distinction from an insurance. Under Belgian insurance law,[43] the performed activity, namely offering insurances, is decisive for the applicability of the mandatory provisions on insurance contracts. The FSMA – the Financial Services and Markets Authority – recently issued an opinion concerning the essential elements of insurance with a focus on the distinction between commercial guarantees and insurances.[44] The distinguishing criterion according to the FSMA is the independent nature of the insurance. The FSMA argues that a commercial guarantee against payment is additional to a 'non-uncertain main performance' (typically a sales contract) and tends to compensate for and/or repair defects of which the cause is inherent to the main performance or the subject of this performance (defect in the material or due to the production).[45] So, the commercial guarantee does not have the same independent nature as an insurance. The new definition of commercial guarantee seems to include defects of which the cause is not inherent to the main performance or the subject of this performance, so the question will be whether such commercial guarantees should now be qualified as insurances with the application of the mandatory rules on insurances as a consequence.

The CRD, furthermore, only mentions the commercial guarantee in the list of information that must be provided to the consumer. The CRD is basically divided in three parts: the provisions concerning consumer information for contracts other than distance or off-premises contracts (chapter II), the provisions on consumer information and right of withdrawal for distance and off-premises contracts (chapter III) and finally the provisions concerning other consumer rights (chapter IV). Commercial guarantees figure in chapters II and III. Both for distance and off-premises contracts and for other than distance or off-premises contracts, the trader has to inform the consumer about the existence and the conditions of after-sales services and commercial guarantees, where applicable, before the consumer is bound by a contract or any corresponding offer.[46] He has to do this in a clear and comprehensible manner. For contracts

1441–43, http://ec.europa.eu/justice/contract/files/european-private-law_en.pdf for a discussion of the situation in different Member States and which makes clear that in almost all cases there is a (close) connection with the notion of conformity. See also, Commission des Clause Abusives, *Avis nr. 33 sur les clauses relatives à la garantie commerciale en cas de vente de biens de consommation*, Brussels, 27 February 2013, 12, http://economie.fgov.be/fr/binaries/CCA33d%C3%A9f_tcm326-223757.pdf.

43 Act of 4 April 2014 concerning insurance, *Belgian Official Gazette* 30 April 2014.

44 Position de la FSMA en ce qui concerne les éléments essentiels du contrat d'assurance, FSMA_2015_13, 26 August 2015.

45 Position de la FSMA en ce qui concerne les éléments essentiels du contrat d'assurance, FSMA_2015_13, 26 August 2015, 4–5. See also: Wetsontwerp op de landverzekeringsovereenkomst – Memorie van toelichting, *Parl.St.* Kamer 1990–91, nr. 1586/001, 9; B. Toussaint and J.-M. Binon, 'Assurances – Législation – Position de la FSMA en ce qui concerne les éléments essentiels du contrat d'assurance, FSMA_2015_13 du 26 août 2015', *TBH* 2015, (933) 934.

46 Arts. 5(1)(e) and 6(1)(m) CRD.

other than distance or off-premises contracts, the trader must not provide this information if it is already apparent from the context.[47] The CRD repeats the obligation to point out the existence of the legal guarantee to the consumer. Finally, it is remarkable that only for distance and off-premises contracts has the trader the obligation to inform the consumer about the existence and the conditions of after-sale customer assistance.[48] It is not clear why the trader only has this obligation for these contracts. A possible explanation for the difference is that Article 5 on other than distance and off-premises contracts is minimum harmonisation,[49] while Article 6 is a full harmonisation provision.[50]

2.4. PROPOSAL FOR A COMMON EUROPEAN SALES LAW

Even though the proposal for regulation for a Common European Sales Law (CESL) was withdrawn by the European Commission,[51] the Commission clearly does not want to abandon all efforts. The ODSD Proposal is considered to be the substitute of the CESL.[52] The scope of application of the new proposal is much narrower, but it is not ruled out that these harmonised rules can be expanded in the future. In other words, there is still some hope for a Common European Sales Law, but not for now.[53]

---

47 Art. 5(1) CRD.

48 Art. 6(1)(m) CRD.

49 Art. 5(4) CRD; E. Cruysmans, C. Delforge, G. de Pierpont, C. Donnet, Y. Ninane, M.-P. Noël, Ph. Stroobant and J. van Zuylen, 'La directive 2011/83/UE du 25 octobre 2011 relative aux droits des consommateurs', *TBBR* 2013, (174) 192; M.B.M. Loos and J.A. Luzak, 'De nieuwe Richtlijn Consumentenrechten', *TvC* 2011, (184) 186.

50 E. Terryn, 'Richtlijn 2011/83/EU betreffende consumentenrechten – Nieuwe regels op komst voor de directe verkoop', *RW* 2012–13, (922) 927.

51 Communication from the Commission to the European Parliament, the Council, the European Economic and Social Committee and the Committee of the Regions, Commission Work Programme 2015 – A New Start, COM(2014) 910 final, Strasbourg, 16 December 2014, annex 2, para. 60.

52 European Commission, Proposal for a Regulation of the European Parliament and of the Council on a Common European Sales Law, COM(2011) 635 final, Brussels, 11 November 2011.

53 In the Explanatory Memorandum of the ODSD Proposal the Commission says: 'At the same time, harmonising the rules on distance sales may bear the risk to have rules on the distance sales which are different from the rules on the face-to-face sales. Given the increasing importance of the omni-channel distribution model (i.e. selling at the same time via multiple channels such as directly in a shop, online or otherwise at a distance), the Commission will take steps to avoid such a result and ensure that consumers and traders will indeed be able to rely on a coherent legal framework which is simple to apply everywhere in the EU.' European Commission, Proposal for a Directive of the European Parliament and of the Council on certain aspects concerning contracts for the online and other distance sales of goods, COM(2015) 635 final, Brussels, 9 December 2015, 3. E.H. Hondius, 'Gemeenschappelijk Europees kooprecht van de baan: tijdelijk of definitief?', *TCR* 2015, (195) 195–96.

As regards content, the CESL Proposal is practically identical to the – limited provisions of – the Consumer Rights Directive, so that this will not be discussed in further detail. The scope of application of the instrument is nevertheless worth a moment's thought. The CESL would have been applicable to cross-border transactions, with the possibility for the Member States to expand the scope of its application to national transactions.[54] The CESL could be used for sales contracts, contracts for the supply of digital content and related service contracts.[55] The contracting parties have to opt in, and must thus make a positive choice for the applicability of the CESL.[56] If the contract concerns a trader and a consumer, the agreement on the use of the Common European Sales Law will be valid only if the consumer's consent is given by an explicit statement which is separate from the statement indicating the agreement to conclude a contract.[57] However, the scope of application is not limited to B2C contracts. The contracting parties could not only choose to apply the CESL if the seller is a trader, but also if both parties are traders and at least one of those parties is a small or medium-sized enterprise (SME).[58] This was therefore the first European proposal in which the European legislator set out rules on (legal and commercial) guarantees that could be applicable in other than B2C relations.

---

54 Arts. 4 and 13(a) RegCESL (P); M. Piers and C. Vanleenhove, 'Gemeenschappelijk Europees Kooprecht. Een nieuw instrument van uniform toepasselijk recht', *NJW* 2012, (2) 5; Ch. Wendehorst, 'Regulation – Arts. 1–16 RegCESL (P)' in R. Schulze (ed.), *Common European Sales Law (CESL): commentary*, Baden-Baden, Nomos, 2012, (9) 35; S. Whittaker, 'The optional instrument of European Contract Law and freedom of contract', *ERCL* 2011, (371) 385.

55 Art. 5 RegCESL (P); R. Feltkamp and F. Vanbossele, 'Remedies under the optional common European sales law – A good alternative for Belgian sales law?' in I. Claeys and R. Feltkamp (eds), *The draft Common European Sales Law: towards an alternative sales law?*, Antwerp, Intersentia, 2013, (185) 192; Ch. Wendehorst, 'Regulation – Arts. 1–16 RegCESL (P)' in R. Schulze (ed.), *Common European Sales Law (CESL): commentary*, Baden-Baden, Nomos, 2012, (9) 43–48.

56 Art. 3 RegCESL (P); A. De Boeck, 'Overzicht van en beschouwingen bij de precontractuele informatieplichten in het nieuwe gemeenschappelijk Europees kooprecht (GEKR)', *MvV* 2012, (221) 221; M. Hesselink, 'How to opt into the Common European Sales Law? Brief comments on the Commission's Proposal for a regulation', *ERPL* 2012, (195) 207; Ch. Wendehorst, 'Regulation – Arts. 1–16 RegCESL (P)' in R. Schulze (ed.), *Common European Sales Law (CESL): commentary*, Baden-Baden, Nomos, 2012, (9) 30.

57 Art. 8(3) RegCESL (P); M. Hesselink, 'How to opt into the Common European Sales Law? Brief comments on the Commission's Proposal for a regulation', *ERPL* 2012, (195) 207; Ch. Wendehorst, 'Regulation – Arts. 1–16 RegCESL (P)' in R. Schulze (ed.), *Common European Sales Law (CESL): commentary*, Baden-Baden, Nomos, 2012, (9) 60.

58 Art. 7(2) RegCESL (P) prescribes: 'For the purposes of this Regulation, an SME is a trader which (a) employs fewer than 250 persons; and (b) has an annual turnover not exceeding EUR 50 million or an annual balance sheet total not exceeding EUR 43 million, or, for an SME which has its habitual residence in a Member State whose currency is not the euro or in a third country, the equivalent amounts in the currency of that Member State or third country.' M. Piers and C. Vanleenhove, 'Gemeenschappelijk Europees Kooprecht. Een nieuw instrument van uniform toepasselijk recht', *NJW* 2012, (2) 5; Ch. Wendehorst, 'Regulation – Arts. 1–16 RegCESL (P)' in R. Schulze (ed.), *Common European Sales Law (CESL): commentary*, Baden-Baden, Nomos, 2012, (9) 54.

3. COMMERCIAL GUARANTEES IN THE CURRENT REGULATORY FRAMEWORK – THE *APPLE CASE*

3.1. INTRODUCTION AND RELEVANT PROVISIONS OF THE UCPD AND UCTD

The previous section thus makes clear that the specific provisions regulating commercial guarantees are limited at the moment. In addition to these specific provisions, there are, however, other (horizontal) consumer law instruments that allow the address – to a certain extent – of some of the problems with commercial guarantees, more specifically the Unfair Contract Terms Directive and the Unfair Commercial Practices Directive.

In particular, the following provisions of the UCPD can potentially be relied on:[59]

- Article 6 UCPD on misleading commercial practices; more specifically Article 6(1)(g) that prohibits misleading practices concerning the consumer's rights, including the consumer's rights under the CSD;
- Article 7 UCPD on misleading omissions, that can be invoked if material information is omitted or provided in an unclear or unintelligible way (Article 7(1) and (2) UCPD);
- Paragraph 10 of Annex I UCPD that prohibits – as a misleading commercial practice in all circumstances – presenting existing legal rights of the consumer as a distinctive feature of the trader's offer.

As for the UCTD, specifically Article 5 is relevant, which imposes a transparency requirement and requires terms to be drafted in plain, intelligible language. The Directive does not provide for an explicit sanction in case clauses are not transparent, but the CJEU has in the meantime made clear that transparency plays an important role in determining whether a clause creates a significant imbalance and is therefore unfair.[60] In a number of Member States, this sanction is expressly provided for in the legislation.[61]

---

59 See the final report of the CoJEF (Consumer Justice Enforcement Forum) Project, May 2013, http://www.cojef-project.eu/IMG/pdf/Conclusions_document_cases__FINAL_8_May.pdf, p. 12 *et seq.*

60 See CJEU 26 April 2012, *Nemzeti v Invitel*, ECLI:EU:C:2012:242: curia.europa.eu/juris/documents.jsf?num=C-472/10 and CJEU 21 March 2013, *RWE Vertrieb AG v Verbraucherzentrale Nordrhein-Westfalen eV*, ECLI:EU:C:2013:180: curia.europa.eu/juris/documents.jsf?num=C-92/11.

61 For Germany, see in §307 Abs. 1, Satz 1 u. 2 BGB: '(1) Bestimmungen in Allgemeinen Geschäftsbedingungen sind unwirksam, wenn sie den Vertragspartner des Verwenders

The famous – or rather infamous – *Apple case* illustrates the possibilities and the limitations of the current regulatory framework.

3.2. FACTS AND OUTCOME OF THE CASE

The *Apple case* concerned the unfair practices of the US-based company Apple in relation to the guarantee on its hardware products. It was more specifically, the one-year 'manufacturer's warranty' that was considered to mislead consumers about the rights under the EU-wide minimum two-year legal guarantee.[62]

The trigger for a pan-European action against Apple by several consumer organisations was a decision by the Italian Competition Authority (Autorità Garante della Concorrenza e del Mercato, ICA). The ICA made a priority of the legal guarantee regime and carried out 34 infringement proceedings against major retail chains.[63] The most important case was the *Apple case*, in which the ICA imposed fines of a total amount of EUR 900,000.

The case was initiated subsequent to a complaint by Altroconsumo.[64] The Italian consumer organisation performed investigations (such as recording the behaviour of shop assistants in Apple stores) and held that Apple pursued a commercial strategy aiming at misleading consumers on their legal guarantee rights in order to promote and sell the Apple Care Protection Plan, their commercial guarantee.[65] Apple provided a one-year (free) manufacturer's warranty. After one year, the services offered could be prolonged (against payment) through the 'Apple Care Protection Plan'. This was marketed as a useful extension of the one-year manufacturer's warranty, but consumers were thus paying for rights they already enjoyed under their two-year legal guarantee without being informed of this.

---

entgegen den Geboten von Treu und Glauben unangemessen benachteiligen. Eine unangemessene Benachteiligung kann sich auch daraus ergeben, dass die Bestimmung nicht klar und verständlich ist.'; for Belgium, see Art. VI.82 Code of Economic Law: 'the clarity and intelligibility of a term in the sense of article VI.37 §1 Code of Economic Law is taken into account in the assessment of the fairness of a term.'

62 See for an overview, J. Berti and P. Occhiuzzi, 'The Apple case: a successful enforcement action', *Revista Italiana di Antitrust*, 2013, 75–78; see also CoJEF I and CoJEF II Reports, CoJEF (Consumer Justice Enforcement Forum), http://www.cojef-project.eu.

63 J. Berti and P. Occhiuzzi, 'The Apple case: a successful enforcement action', *Revista Italiana di Antitrust*, 2013, 75–78.

64 See Consiglio di Stato, decision of 17 November 2015 no. 0523/2015, available at: https://www.giustizia-amministrativa.it/cdsintra/cdsintra/AmministrazionePortale/DocumentViewer/index.html?ddocname=CUQXZN4L2NU4USFL7NB2H6DZ6M&q=.

65 See the final report of the CoJEF (Consumer Justice Enforcement Forum) Project, May 2013, http://www.cojef-project.eu/IMG/pdf/Conclusions_document_cases__FINAL_8_May.pdf, p. 12 *et seq.*

The ICA both fined Apple for not respecting the two-year legal guarantee and for misleading practices concerning its commercial warranty.[66] The information provided to consumers about the one-year limited free 'manufacturer's warranty', was found to mislead consumers about their benefits from the two-year legal guarantee. Prominently advertising the one-year free manufacturer's warranty in order to promote a payable extension of this commercial guarantee in the form of the Apple Care Protection Plan was also held to mislead consumers, in particular on the basis of Article 6(1)(g) of the UCPD. This decision was confirmed by the highest Italian court.

Altroconsumo subsequently informed the CoJEF network of the case,[67] and it appeared that Apple's practices were not limited to Italy. The proceedings in Italy furthermore did not lead to automatic changes in all European countries. Eleven consumer associations then joined in an action under the co-ordination of BEUC.[68,69] The organisations either demanded the company to cease the unfair practices or called on their national competent authority to investigate the practices.

The cease and desist letters led to a partial modification of Apple's web-pages. That was, however, not considered sufficient by most consumer organisations to stop the misleading practices.[70] This led to court actions by certain consumer organisations[71] and certain public enforcement authorities.[72] European Commissioner Reding also supported the co-ordinated action by the consumer organisations and sent a letter to all EU Ministers with competence for

---

66 Decision of 21 December 2011, PS7256, *Autorità Garante della Concorrenza e del Mercato, COMET-APPLE-Prodotti in garanzia*, summary in J. Berti and P. Occhiuzzi, 'The Apple case: a successful enforcement action', *Revista Italiana di Antitrust*, 2013, 76. The decision was appealed before the Regional Administrative Court of Lazio (Il Tribunale Amministrativo Regionale per il Lazio), that confirmed the ICA's decision. Apple subsequently appealed the decision of Regional Administrative Court of Lazio before the Council of the State (Consiglio di Stato – the highest administrative court), that also confirmed the judgment under appeal and the fine (decision of 17 November 2015 no. 0523/2015, available at https://www.giustizia-amministrativa.it/cdsintra/cdsintra/AmministrazionePortale/DocumentViewer/index.html?ddocname=CUQXZN4L2NU4USFL7NB2H6DZ6M&q=).

67 The network of consumer organisations coordinated by BEUC and supported by the European Commission that allows the exchange of best practices and the training of consumer organisations to build enforcement strategies, see http://www.cojef-project.eu.

68 Final report of the CoJEF I Project, May 2013, http://www.cojef-project.eu/IMG/pdf/Conclusions_document_cases__FINAL_8_May.pdf, p. 12 *et seq.*

69 BEUC is the European Consumer Organisation – the umbrella organisation that represents national consumer organisations at European level.

70 Final report of the CoJEF I Project, May 2013, http://www.cojef-project.eu/IMG/pdf/Conclusions_document_cases__FINAL_8_May.pdf, p. 12 *et seq.*

71 Actions for injunctions were introduced by Test-Achats/Test-Aankoop, Belgium; DECO, Portugal; Vzbv, Germany and ULC, Luxembourg.

72 In Denmark and Slovenia.

consumer affairs to draw attention to a more stringent and consistent enforcement action at EU level.[73]

The actions for injunctions eventually led to settlements in several countries, including Belgium and Luxembourg and to clearer information and a 'warranty notice' on the website, as well as on the homepage. The notice described the legal guarantee and was easily accessible and visible to consumers. That link, however, disappeared on the Luxembourg website, as well as on several other national websites and the information was only available after several clicks or, for certain specific products, in a promotion concerning the commercial guarantee (against payment). After further correspondence with the Union Luxembourgeoise des Consommateurs, Apple reintroduced the link in some of the countries that had started proceedings.[74]

In Germany, the case was not settled but further pursued in court. Apple had changed the clauses concerned, but it refused to sign the cease and desist declaration that the applicant Vzbv asked for, so that the court action was continued. Vzbv challenged several clauses of the manufacturer's guarantee and of Apple's Care Protection Plan. In 2015, the Berlin Kammergericht (Court of Appeal) decided that all challenged clauses in the manufacturer's guarantee and the Apple Care Protection Plan were invalid.[75] It confirmed the earlier decision of the district court (Landgericht) of Berlin of November 2014.[76] There are several important elements for commercial guarantees in these decisions.

First of all, in so far that any doubt could have existed, it was confirmed that commercial guarantees are also subject to the judicial control on unfair contract terms, even if the content of such contracts goes unregulated[77] and even if the manufacturer is not obliged to provide a free warranty.[78]

Secondly, these decisions illustrate the importance of the transparency requirement in the UCTD. This requirement applies to all contractual clauses

---

[73] Letters sent in September 2012 and March 2013, see http://europa.eu/rapid/press-release_SPEECH-13-237_en.htm and http://www.europarl.europa.eu/sides/getAllAnswers.do?reference=E-2013-003053&language=PT.

[74] Inter alia in Luxembourg, see CoJEF II Final Report June 2016, http://www.beuc.eu/publications/beuc-x-2016-051_cojef_ii-enforcement_of_consumer_rights.pdf.

[75] See Kammergericht Berlin, 3 August 2015, 23 U 15/15 and Kammergericht Berlin, 11 September 2015, 23 U 15/15, available at: http://www.vzbv.de/urteil/apple-garantiebedingungen-waren-unzulaessig.

[76] Landgericht Berlin, 28 November 2014, 15 O 601/12 (CoJEF database). See also on this decision, M. Namyslowska, 'Der Biss in den (sauren) Apfel oder die europäische Durchsetzung von Verbraucherrechten auf dem Prüfstand', *VuR* 2015, 403–07.

[77] Landgericht Berlin, 28 November 2014, 15 O 601/12; Kammergericht Berlin, 3 August 2015, 23 U 15/15, and also: Bundesgerichtshof, 6 July 2011 – VIII ZR 293/10, *NJW* 2011, 3510, Rn. 11.

[78] Kammergericht Berlin, 3 August 2015, 23 U 15/15.

in consumer contracts, even to those clauses that determine the main subject-matter of the contract or the price and remuneration.[79]

The Landgericht and the Kammergericht found the challenged clauses of the manufacturer's guarantee and the Apple Care Protection Plan to be contrary to the transparency requirement.[80] This requirement implies an obligation to describe the rights and duties of contracting partners as clearly and precisely as possible.[81] In combination with the requirement of Article 6(2) CSD,[82] this implies that a guarantee must be drafted in a straightforward and understandable way and that the reference to the legal rights of the consumer must make clear that his rights are not restricted by the guarantee. According to the Kammergericht, this requires an unambiguous and clear distinction to be made between the rights that stem from the manufacturer's guarantee and the legal rights regarding non-conformity. This is only possible if it is made clear that the legal rights (repair, replacement, price reduction, termination, damages) are unaffected and that the rights stemming from the manufacturer's guarantee are additional rights.[83]

The manufacturer's guarantee did not comply with these requirements. Even if in certain clauses a distinction was made between the rights against the seller and the manufacturer's guarantee, this information was blurred by several other clauses. It was, for example, mentioned that the consumer 'may have further reaching rights, differing from country to country and that Apple does not exclude these rights'. This was then inter alia contradicted by a clause determining that the manufacturer's guarantee, in so far as legally allowed, excluded all other guarantees and rights. According to the Kammergericht, the clauses gave the impression of a restriction of the legal rights of the consumer.[84] Further lack of clarity followed from the limitation of the guarantee to products used 'in conformity with the Apple guidelines on normal use', guidelines that were not part of the general terms and conditions, so that the notion of 'normal use' remained unclear.[85] The lack of transparency also stemmed from the structure of the general terms and conditions: a set of clauses with 'universal' application, followed by modification per country to bring the clauses into conformity with national law. The consumer then has to combine two sets of clauses, without

---

79 Landgericht Berlin, 28 November 2014, 15 O 601/12; Kammergericht Berlin, 3 August 2015, 23 U 15/15; see also art. 4(2) UCTD.

80 Art. 5 UCTD, implemented in §307 Abs. 1, Satz 1 u. 2 BGB ('Transparenzgebot').

81 Kammergericht Berlin, 3 August 2015, 23 U 15/15.

82 That requires the guarantee to state that the consumer has legal rights under applicable national legislation governing the sale of consumer goods and to make clear that those rights are not affected by the guarantee, transposed in §477 Abs. 1 Satz 1, 2 nr. 1 BGB.

83 Kammergericht Berlin, 3 August 2015, 23 U 15/15.

84 Kammergericht Berlin, 3 August 2015, 23 U 15/15.

85 Kammergericht Berlin, 3 August 2015, 23 U 15/15; Landgericht Berlin, 28 November 2014, 15 O 601/12.

even being clear in what circumstances the national modifications apply. Such an approach was considered incomprehensible.[86] This is, of course, not specific to commercial guarantees, but we mention it nevertheless as it is a current practice of several international companies.

Several clauses of the Apple Care Protection Plan also infringed the transparency requirement. One of the clauses did mention that the rights stemming from the Plan existed in addition to the legal consumer rights, but with the confusing addition that the Plan only left 'mandatory' provisions unaffected. The Court of Appeal held that this was incomprehensible to the average consumer who does not know the law.[87] The exact scope of the guarantee and its effects on the legal rights of the consumer therefore remained unclear.

3.3. EVALUATION OF THE APPLE CASE

The *Apple case* in any event makes clear that the UCPD and the UCTD (in combination with Article 6(2) CSD) allow the combatting of misleading practices and terms with regard to commercial guarantees. The case, however, also demonstrates the weaknesses of the current regulatory framework. Although the open norms of both the UCPD and the UCTD (in combination with Article 6(2) CSD) allow the prohibition of misleading practices and clauses that are not transparent; they provide little guidance on what information should be given to comply with the law and to be transparent. The absence of positive obligations that describe what information the consumer needs leads to uncertainty for traders but also makes it difficult for enforcers.

The notice used by Apple (in some countries and for some time) with a clear comparison between their legal rights and the (benefits of) commercial guarantee – on all pages where the (commercial) guarantee was mentioned was welcomed by the consumer organisations as best practice. The open norms of the current legislation, however, make it difficult to impose such comparison.

On a more general level – that is, however, not the core subject of this paper – the *Apple case* also illustrates the problems with national enforcement in a globalised context.[88] Companies operate internationally and the same practices often occur in different countries. The enforcement tools are, however,

86 Landgericht Berlin, 28 November 2014, 15 O 601/12. See also on the possible misleading effect of the combination of different guarantee clauses: S. Vandemaele, 'Garantieclausules' in G.-L. Ballon, H. De Decker, V. Sagaert, E. Terryn, B. Tilleman and A.-L. Verbeke (eds.), *Koop – gemeen recht*, Antwerp, Intersentia, 2016, (327) 375–77.

87 Kammergericht Berlin, 3 August 2015, 23 U 15/15.

88 See, for more examples, the Consumer Justice Enforcement Forum Report – CoJEF II Final Report May 2016, http://www.beuc.eu/publications/beuc-x-2016-051_cojef_ii-enforcement_of_consumer_rights.pdf.

national. The *Apple case* illustrates that a condemnation in one country does not necessarily lead to an adaptation of the illegal practice in all countries, but that it may stay limited to those countries in which enforcement steps are taken, either by public or private enforcers.

4. COMMERCIAL GUARANTEES IN THE ODSD PROPOSAL

4.1. OVERVIEW OF THE MAIN NOVELTIES

With the ODSD Proposal, the Commission now drops the plan for an (optional) comprehensive European sales regime for now and focuses on specific and fully harmonised rules.[89] The restricted scope of application of the new proposal can be regretted all the more because the European Commission once again stresses in the explanatory memorandum that the level of harmonisation of the CSD, namely minimum harmonisation, has as a consequence that there are still important differences between the national consumer sales laws.[90] For a detailed discussion of the scope of application of the proposal we refer to the chapter by Jansen and Stijns. We will only briefly discuss some elements. The proposal relates to online and other distance B2C sales of goods and, more particularly, regulates conformity[91] and the remedies for the consumer in case of lack of conformity and the modalities of these remedies.[92] The ODSD Proposal does not apply to any durable medium incorporating digital content where the durable medium has been used exclusively as a carrier for the supply of the digital content to the consumer.[93] Such durable media continue to be governed by the CSD, of which the scope of application would be adapted so that online and other distance sales contracts fall exclusively under the proposed directive.[94] As mentioned before, the proposal imposes maximum harmonisation, except for some areas that are not regulated by the directive, namely limitation periods for exercising the consumer's rights, commercial guarantees and the right of redress of the

89 Art. 3 ODSD Proposal and Explanatory Memorandum ODSD Proposal, 2.

90 Explanatory Memorandum ODSD Proposal, 3 and 7.

91 Concerning the discussion if the ODSD Proposal covers conformity with the contract or conformity of the goods, see S. Jansen and S. Stijns in this volume, Section 3.4.

92 Art. (1)1 ODSD Proposal. A distance sales contract is: 'any sales contract concluded under an organised distance scheme without the simultaneous physical presence of the seller and the consumer, with the exclusive use of one or more means of distance communication, including via internet, up to and including the time at which the contract is concluded' (Art. 2(e) ODSD).

93 Art. (1)3 ODSD Proposal.

94 Art. 19 ODSD Proposal.

seller.[95] The definition of commercial guarantees is identical to the definition in the CRD. This definition is substantially broader than the definition in the CSD as was discussed in detail above (above, Section 2.3). The implications of the wider definition in the CRD remained limited, as the CRD did not have any substantive rules on commercial guarantees. The ODSD does regulate commercial guarantees in a similar, but more far-reaching way to the CSD. This has as a consequence that for distance sales contracts, both commercial guarantees offered for free and against payment have to comply with the regulatory provisions; whereas for offline sales contracts, only commercial guarantees 'without extra charge'[96] are covered. It is clear that there is no justification for such a distinction between distance and other sales contracts.

Contrary to the CRD, the proposal contains also some specific rules on commercial guarantees. Article 15 ODSD Proposal is clearly inspired by Article 6 CSD, but with some substantial differences.

First, Article 15 clarifies the significance of the binding nature of the guarantee: it is binding in accordance with the conditions contained in pre-contractual information (irrespective of the form), advertising and in the guarantee statement.[97] The CSD already mentioned the guarantee statement and advertising;[98] the ODSD adds pre-contractual information to the list. Furthermore, the relation between the guarantee statement and the pre-contractual information and advertising is determined. If the conditions differ, the most advantageous conditions will prevail.[99] The latter change was meant to improve legal certainty and to avoid consumers being misled.[100]

In addition, Article 15(2) sharpens the information duties for the offeror. The offeror not only has to point out the existence and imperative nature of the legal guarantee, but he also has two new information duties. First, he has to provide 'a clear statement of the legal rights of the consumer'. This already goes beyond the requirements of the CSD, that merely requires him to state 'that the consumer has legal rights under applicable national legislation governing the sale of consumer goods and make clear that those rights are not affected

95 Recital 14, Arts. 14, 15(4) and 16 ODSD Proposal.

96 We want to stress that we make an abstraction of the discussion on the interpretation of 'without extra charge'. Tackling this discussion would lead us too far and is of limited importance for this chapter since the new definition doesn't repeat this wording.

97 Art. 15(1) ODSD Proposal.

98 Art. 6(1) CSD.

99 Compare with the German 'Rosinentheorie' according to which the consumer can combine the most beneficial elements of the advertising and the guarantee statement. See M. Eisenhut, *Die kaufrechtliche Garantie*, Frankfurt am Main, Peter Lang, 2005, 125; F. Faust, '§443 Garantie' in H.G. Bamberger and H. Roth (eds.), *Beck'scher Online-Kommentar BGB*, Munich, C.H. Beck, 2014, para. 24.

100 Recital 34 ODSD Proposal.

by the guarantee'.[101] A clear statement of the legal rights of the consumer is furthermore not equivalent to a reproduction of the relevant legal provisions. Simply reproducing the articles of law concerning the legal guarantee can indeed be too much information for the consumer.[102] Secondly, he has to indicate which terms of the commercial guarantee go beyond the legal rights of the consumer.[103] These two elements should enable consumers to evaluate and compare commercial guarantees.[104] Especially when the consumer has to pay for the commercial guarantee, he should be in a position to better assess the benefits of the instrument he is paying for. The requirement that these rights should be mentioned in a clear statement combined with highlighting of the merits of the commercial guarantee is potentially a huge step forward in informing consumers. These requirements may also discourage the guarantor from providing guarantees with no additional protection or even less protection than under the legal guarantee.

This information duty imposed is, however, not easy to comply with. It could therefore be helpful to both guarantors and consumers to provide a standard information form that could serve as a source of inspiration and could be easily adapted to the specific circumstances. This would not be a novelty, the Commission Guidance on the Consumer Rights Directive also provides for a model for the display of consumer information on digital online products.[105] Such a model can help to provide information in a uniform and comparable way. It can also help traders to comply with the information requirements.[106] The use of the model could be voluntary and could provide just one possible way to comply with the information duties. The duty to indicate the terms that go beyond the legal guarantee is furthermore an interesting argument in the debate about the positive nature of the guarantee. Some authors argue that the requirement that the commercial guarantee must be undertaken in addition to the legal obligations means that the commercial guarantee should grant the consumer at every point more rights than the legal guarantee if it is offered by the

---

101 Art. 6(2) CSD.

102 O. Ben-Shahar and C.E. Schneider, 'The failure of mandated disclosure', *U.Penn.L.Rev.* 2011, (647) 687.

103 *Cf.* Art. IV.A-6:103(1)(b) DCFR; Ch. Twigg-Flesner, 'Consumer Goods Guarantees in the DCFR', *ERPL* 2009, (641) 645–46.

104 This provision clearly was inspired by Art. IV.A-6:103(1)(b) DCFR; Ch. Twigg-Flesner, 'Consumer Goods Guarantees in the DCFR', *ERPL* 2009, (641) 645–46. Twigg-Flesner correctly mentions that a commercial guarantee provided by a manufacturer is as such beneficial for consumers because the manufacturer has no legal obligations towards the consumer. He also argues that this can become quite an onerous obligation on the guarantor if the 'advantage' effectively has to be something that adds substantively to consumers' legal rights.

105 See Annex I DG Justice Guidance Document concerning Directive 2011/83/EU: http://ec.europa.eu/justice/consumer-marketing/files/crd_guidance_en.pdf; Annex I – Model for the Display of Consumer Information about Online Digital Products.

106 DG Justice Guidance Document concerning Directive 2011/83/EU, p. 69.

seller.[107] This information duty can be an argument to indicate the opposite. In our view, every undertaking alongside the legal obligations is taken in addition and is advantageous for the consumer as long as he is well informed about his legal rights.[108]

Another improvement in the proposal is the obligation to make the guarantee statement available on a durable medium.[109] Under the CSD, this was only required upon request by the consumer.[110] However, the overall opinion was that this was an unfortunate expression. There is no doubt that Article 6 CSD should be interpreted in the sense that the guarantor has the duty to provide the commercial guarantee on a durable medium once the goods have been purchased, independent of any request of the consumer. Besides, paragraph 3 has to be interpreted in the sense that the consumer must have the possibility to consult the guarantee freely *before* the purchase.[111] To this end, he can ask to obtain the guarantee in writing or in another durable medium. In any case, it is to be welcomed that the ODSD Proposal does not repeat the unfortunate expression of the CSD and now clearly states that the commercial guarantee must in any event be made available on a durable medium.

Article 6(4) CSD gave the Member States the option to provide that the guarantee be drafted in one or more languages which they shall determine from among the official languages of the Community. Different Member States used this possibility, e.g. Cyprus, Denmark, Estonia, Greece, Italy, Luxembourg, the UK, Belgium, etc.[112] The ODSD does not expressly refer to this possibility, but

---

107 I. Samoy, 'Garantie op transparantie? De conventionele garantie in het Wetsontwerp tot omzetting van de Richtlijn Consumentenkoop', *TBH* 2003, (383) 389; P.-J. Van de Walle and T. Polet, 'De consumentenkoopwet: een nieuwjaarsgeschenk voor de consument?', *CJ* 2005, (1) 11.

108 S. Vandemaele, 'Garantieclausules' in G.-L. Ballon, H. De Decker, V. Sagaert, E. Terryn, B. Tilleman and A.-L. Verbeke (eds.), *Koop – gemeen recht*, Antwerp, Intersentia, 2016, (327) 375. See also concerning the DCFR: Ch. Twigg-Flesner, 'Consumer Goods Guarantees in the DCFR', *ERPL* 2009, (641) 643.

109 Article 15(2) ODSD.

110 Article 6(3) CSD.

111 *Cf.* also Art. 5(2) European Commission, Proposal for a European Parliament and Council Directive on the sale of consumer goods and associated guarantees, *OJ* 16 October 1996, C 307/8: 'The guarantee must feature in a written document which must be freely available for consultation before purchase'. I. Demuynck, 'De nieuwe garantieregeling voor consumptiegoederen' in K. Bernauw, P. Colle, M. Dambre and I. Demuynck (eds.), *Liber amicorum Yvette Merchiers*, Bruges, die Keure, 2001, (867) 896; Y. Ninane and O. Gilard, *La garantie des biens de consommation*, Waterloo, Kluwer, 2010, 77; I. Samoy, 'Garantie op transparantie? De conventionele garantie in het Wetsontwerp tot omzetting van de Richtlijn Consumentenkoop', *TBH* 2003, (383) 387; M. Tenreiro and S. Gomez, 'La directive 1999/44/CE sur certains aspects de la vente et des garanties des biens de consommation', *REDC* 2000, (5) 32–33.

112 Communication from the Commission to the Council and the European Parliament on the implementation of Directive 1999/44/EC of the European Parliament and of the Council of 25 May 1999 on certain aspects of the sale of consumer goods and associated guarantees including analysis of the case for introducing direct producers' liability, COM(2007) 210

since Article 15 is a minimum harmonisation provision, the Member States will be able to maintain the concerned provisions.[113]

As was also required by the CSD, the guarantee statement has to include some essential particulars. The enumeration of these particulars, however, contains some new elements such as the transferability, the existence of any charges which the consumer might incur in order to benefit from the commercial guarantee and the name and address of the person (if different from the guarantor) against whom any claim is to be made and the procedure by which the claim is to be made. As mentioned for the CSD (above, Section 2.2), this enumeration is not limitative, but adding these elements to the list eliminates any possible discussion about the necessity of these particulars.

It is not the first time the European Commission has proposed further reaching obligations concerning the transferability of commercial guarantees. The proposal of the CRD also mentioned this.[114] According to Article 29 CRD Proposal, the guarantee statement shall set out, where applicable, that the commercial guarantee cannot be transferred to a subsequent buyer.[115] In addition, the CRD Proposal presumed to be unfair any contract term which has the object or effect of restricting the consumer's right to re-sell the goods by limiting the transferability of any commercial guarantee provided by the trader. A term excluding transferability is therefore only valid if the trader can prove that the term is fair in accordance with Article 32 CRD Proposal.[116]

The ODSD Proposal does not address the problem of transferability of the guarantee itself, nor of the validity of clauses limiting or prohibiting transferability. This issue was also not regulated by the CSD and is addressed very differently in the Member States. Most often, specific legislation is absent. In some Member States, the accepted solution is that the guarantee is transferable to the subsequent owner.[117] This is mostly a default rule that parties can

final, Brussels, 24 April 2007, 9. See also: European Consumer Centres Network, *Commercial warranties – Are they worth the money?*, 2015, 55, http://www.eccbelgium.be/20150320/commercial-warranties-are-they-worth-the-money-Attach_s83561.pdf.

113 See the chapter by G. Straetmans and S. Meys in this volume.

114 European Commission, Proposal for a Directive of the European Parliament and of the Council on consumer rights, COM(2008) 614 final, Brussels, 8 October 2008.

115 *Cf.* also Art. IV.A-6:102(2) DCFR: 'in favour of every owner of the goods within the duration of the guarantee'. The default rule is that the guarantee is freely transferable. Ch. Twigg-Flesner, 'Consumer Goods Guarantees in the DCFR', *ERPL* 2009, (641) 644.

116 Article 35 CRD Proposal. The trader would have to demonstrate that the term is not contrary to the requirement of good faith and does not cause a significant imbalance in the parties' rights and obligations arising under the contract, to the detriment of the consumer.

117 E.g. Belgian, French and Dutch law. Also in Scots, English and Finnish law, although under specific conditions. See Ch. von Bar, E. Clive, H. Schulte-Nölke, H. Beale, J. Herre, J. Huet, P. Schlechtriem, M.E. Storme, S. Swann, P. Varul, A. Veneziano and F. Zoll (eds.), *Principles, definitions and model rules of European private law: Draft Common Frame of Reference (DCFR)*, 2009, 1430–31, http://ec.europa.eu/justice/contract/files/european-private-law_en.pdf.

deviate from.[118] This seems also to be the case under Belgian law,[119] but the Commission des Clauses Abusives has expressed a different opinion.[120] The Commission is of the opinion that every consumer who acquires the goods can invoke the guarantee based on the binding nature of the guarantee and that contract terms excluding transferability can entail an unlawful restriction of the consumer's rights.[121] The Commission des Clauses Abusives does not explain this opinion in more detail. It is indeed important that consumers are well informed about the exclusion of transferability and of the fact that this only counts for the commercial guarantee, that this does not affect the transferability of the legal guarantee in any way.[122] However, provided that these requirements are fulfilled, it seems difficult under current Belgian law, to consider clauses excluding transferability as such invalid.[123]

The information duty concerning transferability in the ODSD Proposal is in any event to be welcomed. The further reaching solution in the CRD Proposal (with a presumption of unfairness of clauses limiting transferability) was, however, more consumer friendly and also in line with reality. A (commercial) guarantee is more closely connected to the goods that are sold than to the buyer. This is all the more so because in the current B2C relations with standardised contracts and mass production, the seller (guarantor) most often does not know his buyer. As a consequence, the capacity of the buyer cannot influence the commercial guarantee, and the position of the guarantor is – as a rule – not

118 An exception is Czech case law according to which the rights stemming from liability for defects do not pass to subsequent owners. See Ch. von Bar, E. Clive, H. Schulte-Nölke, H. Beale, J. Herre, J. Huet, P. Schlechtriem, M.E. Storme, S. Swann, P. Varul, A. Veneziano and F. Zoll (eds.), *Principles, definitions and model rules of European private law: Draft Common Frame of Reference (DCFR)*, 2009, 1431, http://ec.europa.eu/justice/contract/files/european-private-law_en.pdf.

119 Art. 1615 CC; S. Vandemaele, 'Garantieclausules' in G.-L. Ballon, H. De Decker, V. Sagaert, E. Terryn, B. Tilleman and A.-L. Verbeke (eds.), *Koop – gemeen recht*, Antwerp, Intersentia, 2016, (327) 370.

120 Commission des Clause Abusives, *Avis nr. 33 sur les clauses relatives à la garantie commerciale en cas de vente de biens de consommation*, Brussels, 27 February 2013, 13, http://economie.fgov.be/fr/binaries/CCA33d%C3%A9f_tcm326-223757.pdf. See on this opinion: S. Vandemaele, 'Actualiteit: Commissie voor Onrechtmatige Bedingen: Advies inzake bedingen met betrekking tot de commerciële garantie bij de verkoop van consumptiegoederen', *DCCR* 2013, 93–100.

121 Article 1649*septies*, §1 CC.

122 S. Vandemaele, 'Garantieclausules' in G.-L. Ballon, H. De Decker, V. Sagaert, E. Terryn, B. Tilleman and A.-L. Verbeke (eds.), *Koop – gemeen recht*, Antwerp, Intersentia, 2016, (327) 370–71.

123 The validity of (standard) terms excluding transferability was also accepted in Germany (Ch. von Bar, E. Clive, H. Schulte-Nölke, H. Beale, J. Herre, J. Huet, P. Schlechtriem, M.E. Storme, S. Swann, P. Varul, A. Veneziano and F. Zoll (eds.), *Principles, definitions and model rules of European private law: Draft Common Frame of Reference (DCFR)*, 2009, 1431, http://ec.europa.eu/justice/contract/files/european-private-law_en.pdf).

aggravated if the goods and the guarantee are transferred to the subsequent buyer.[124] A presumption that (standard) clauses excluding transferability are unfair therefore seems appropriate. The guarantor can prove the contrary in the – unlikely – event that the buyer's profile was relevant for the guarantor.

The information on the charges which the consumer might incur in order to benefit from the commercial guarantee is also an interesting innovation. The legal guarantee entitles the consumer to have the goods brought into conformity by the seller, free of charge.[125] This is not imposed for commercial guarantees. In principle, the guarantor freely determines the conditions of the guarantee, with respect of the legal rights of the consumer. Charges can therefore only be imposed for repair or replacement if the defect is not covered by the legal guarantee.

One such charge concerns the costs of making a cost estimate, these are the costs that have to be incurred in order to assess whether the defect falls within the guarantee. Contract terms which charge the consumer in any event (even if the defect is covered by the legal guarantee) can be considered unfair and contrary to the aforementioned free character of repair and replacement under the legal guarantee.[126] Under a commercial guarantee the guarantor is free to charge for such costs. In most cases, the consumer will not be charged if the goods do not fall under the commercial guarantee, but he still wants them to be repaired. In that case, the guarantor compensates the consumer for the costs of making a cost estimate with the repair costs. It is in any event to be welcomed that the guarantor now expressly has to inform the consumer about these and other charges concerning the commercial guarantee.

Like Article 6(5) CSD, Article 15(3) ODSD Proposal prescribes that non-compliance with the information duties shall not affect the binding nature of the commercial guarantee for the guarantor. The civil sanction that the commercial guarantee would not be binding on the consumer – as laid down in Article 6 UCTD – will, in general, not be beneficial for the consumer. However, the consumer may not always want the guarantee to be binding – especially if he paid

---

124 M. Hostens, 'De rechtstreekse aanspraak van de consument: Een nieuw pijnpunt in ons dualistisch kooprecht?' (noot onder Luik 5 november 2009), *DCCR* 2010, (87) 90; Ch. Twigg-Flesner, 'Consumer Goods Guarantees in the DCFR', *ERPL* 2009, (641) 644; A. Van Oevelen, 'Het voorstel voor een richtlijn consumentenrechten: voorstellen tot wijziging van de consumentenkoop inzake de garantie- en de meldingstermijn, de sancties bij niet-conformiteit en de handelsgaranties', *DCCR* 2009, (204) 225.

125 Art. 9 ODSD Proposal; see the chapter by I. Claeys in this volume. See also CJEU 17 April 2008, Case C-404/06, EU:C:2008:231, *Quelle AG v Bundesverbraucherzentralen und Verbraucherverbände* and CJEU 16 June 2011, Joined Cases C-65/09 and C-87/09, EU:C:2011:396, *Gebruder Weber GmbH v Wittmer* and *Putz v Medianess Electronics GmbH.*

126 See in this sense Commission des Clause Abusives, *Avis nr. 33 sur les clauses relatives à la garantie commerciale en cas de vente de biens de consommation*, Brussels, 27 February 2013, 26, http://economie.fgov.be/fr/binaries/CCA33d%C3%A9f_tcm326-223757.pdf.

for a commercial guarantee that has no or only limited benefits compared to the legal guarantee. The UCTD then provides some possibilities for protection: if the commercial guarantee contains unfair terms, it will no longer be binding if it is not capable of continuing in existence without the unfair terms. The UCPD and its implementing legislation may also be useful. As is clear from the *Apple case*, the consumer may have been induced to pay for such commercial guarantee further to a misleading practice, prohibited by the UCPD. The UCPD itself, however, does not regulate the consequences for the validity of a contract thus entered into, but a number of Member States do provide for a civil law sanction (such as the nullity of the contract) that may be useful for consumers.[127]

According to the ODSD Proposal, Member States shall furthermore 'ensure that adequate and effective means exist to ensure compliance with this Directive.'[128] Although the CSD contained no such provision, such obligation already followed from the general principles of effectiveness and equivalence as consistently interpreted by the CJEU.[129] The explicit reference in Article 17 ODSD Proposal to such obligation is in line with other consumer protection directives.[130]

---

127 Under Belgian law, Art. VI.38 Code of Economic Law allows the consumer to request reimbursement (and to keep the goods or the service) if a contract was concluded as a consequence of an unfair commercial practice; under Dutch law an act of 2014 added a third paragraph to Art. 6:193j of the Civil Code stating that a contract is voidable if concluded as a consequence of an unfair commercial practice. Unlike the Belgian remedy, the application of this remedy causes not only the reimbursement of the paid sums to the consumer, but also the return of the delivered goods or services; in the UK an amendment of 2014 introduced a 'Part 4A Consumer's right to redress' in the Consumer Protection Regulations 2008. In the first place there is the right to unwind the contract (Reg. 27E CP(A)Rs 2014) which can be claimed by the consumer within a relevant period of 90 days in case of a misleading action to be qualified as 'a significant factor' in the consumer's decision to enter into the contract or make the payment. The right to unwind contains the right for the consumer to receive the reimbursement of the paid sums and the obligation to return the delivered products. Secondly, the consumer has a right to discount (Reg. 27I CP(A)Rs 2014). It is, however, only possible to claim this right if the consumer did not exercise his right to unwind the contract before. The scope of the above-mentioned remedies is restricted and is subjected to several conditions.

128 Art. 17 ODSD.

129 See e.g. recently CJEU 6 October 2015, Case C-61/14, *Orizzonte Salut.e – Studio Infermieristico Associato*, ECLI:EU:C:2015:655, 'The Court has consistently held that, in the absence of EU rules governing the matter, it is for each Member State, in accordance with the principle of the procedural autonomy of the Member States, to lay down the detailed rules of administrative and judicial procedures governing actions for safeguarding rights which individuals derive from EU law. Those detailed procedural rules must, however, be no less favourable than those governing similar domestic actions (principle of equivalence) and must not render practically impossible or excessively difficult the exercise of rights conferred by EU law (principle of effectiveness) (judgments in *Club Hotel Loutraki and Others*, C-145/08 and C-149/08, EU:C:2010:247, paragraph 74, and *eVigilo*, C-538/13, EU:C:2015:166, paragraph 39).'

130 *Cf.* Art. 7 UCTD; similarly also Art. 13 UCPD.

Such a provision has, however, not proved sufficient to ensure efficient enforcement of consumer law, especially in case of pan-European infringements.[131] The tools available to private and public enforcers continue to differ widely; co-operation in case of cross-border infringements in the framework of the CPC (Consumer Protection Cooperation) network does not function optimally.[132] Much more is therefore to be expected of the far reaching recent proposal to review the CPC regulation.[133] The minimum enforcement powers of the national consumer authorities would be substantially increased,[134] and in addition, instruments to address widespread infringements are further developed. These include not only coordinated actions, but also common actions against widespread infringements with an EU dimension and concerted investigations of consumer markets. A further reaching role for the European Commission in the enforcement of consumer law is also proposed. The *Apple case* has certainly made clear that this review is to be welcomed.

A well-known difficulty with (commercial) guarantees concerns the influence on the duration of the commercial guarantee of the time necessary to negotiate with the guarantor or to repair or replace the goods.[135] The DCFR remedied this problem by prolonging the guarantee period for a period equal to the period

131 See the mentioned *Apple case*, where enforcement was mainly based on the UCTD and the UCPD, see also the CoJEF II Report for more examples.

132 Regulation (EC) No. 2006/2004 of the European Parliament and of the Council of 27 October 2004 on cooperation between national authorities responsible for the enforcement of consumer protection laws, *OJ*, 9 December 2004, L 364, and see inter alia External Evaluation of the Consumer Protection Regulation, Final Report by the Consumer Policy Evaluation Consortium, 17 December 2012 ('Evaluation'), http://ec.europa.eu/consumers/enforcement/docs/cpc_regulation_inception_report_revised290212_en.pdf, and Report from the Commission to the European Parliament and the Council on the application of Regulation (EC) 2006/2004, COM(2012) 0100 final, 12 March 2012, and the 2014 Commission Report on the functioning of the CPC Regulation, COM(2014) 439 final, http://ec.europa.eu/consumers/enforcement/crossborder_enforcement_cooperation/docs/140701_commission_report_cpc_reg_en.pdf.

133 Proposal for a Regulation on cooperation between national authorities responsible for the enforcement of consumer protection laws, COM(2016) 283 final, 25 May 2016, 2016/0148 (COD), http://ec.europa.eu/consumers/consumer_rights/unfair-trade/docs/cpc-revision-proposal_en.pdf.

134 To also include the power to make test purchases and carry out mystery shopping, power to adopt interim measures, block websites and the power to impose penalties and to safeguard consumer compensation in a cross-border context; COM(2016) 283 final, p. 13.

135 This problem is not limited to commercial guarantees, but also applies to legal guarantees and was acknowledged by the European legislator. Following recital 18 of the CSD, 12 Member States decided that during repair or replacement the two-year duration of the legal guarantee is suspended and resumes as soon as the consumer receives the repaired or replacement item (Belgium, Bulgaria, Cyprus, Ireland, Italy, Latvia, Lithuania, Luxembourg, Malta, the Netherlands, Norway and Romania). See: European Consumer Centres Network, *Commercial warranties – Are they worth the money?*, 2015, 37–38 (for legal guarantees) and 63 (for commercial guarantees), http://www.eccbelgium.be/20150320/commercial-warranties-are-they-worth-the-money-Attach_s83561.pdf.

during which the guarantee holder could not use the goods due to the defect or failure.[136] Commercial guarantees are not fully harmonised under the ODSD Proposal, so Member States can still meet this difficulty.[137] However, it could be considered to adapt Article 15 ODSD Proposal and insert a provision that prescribes the consequences of this situation. One possibility is to prescribe that the guarantee period is suspended during the period necessary to negotiate or to repair or replace the goods.[138] Another possibility is to prescribe that the guarantee period starts to run anew from the time of repair or replacement.[139] Given the voluntary nature of the commercial guarantee and the freedom of contract, this is, however, rather (too) far-reaching so that the first possibility is recommended, at the very least as a default rule.

The discussion on the possible extension of consumer protection rules to (some) B2B relations is ongoing and is of course much broader than commercial guarantees.[140] One such rule that does seem fit to be applied in B2B relations, at least when the buyer is an SME, is Article 15 (except for paragraph 2(a)) ODSD Proposal. Commercial guarantees are still voluntary undertakings. The trader can choose freely to grant a commercial guarantee. The information duties of Article 15 (except for paragraph 2(a)) can be considered as a very minimum and thus necessary, especially if the contracting party is an SME. The biggest obstacle in this discussion is probably not deciding if SMEs deserve the same

---

136 Art. IV.A-6:108 DCFR; Ch. Twigg-Flesner, 'Consumer Goods Guarantees in the DCFR', *ERPL* 2009, (641) 650. Twigg-Flesner questions the practicability of this provision.

137 Under French law, Art. L211-16 (L217-16 as from 1 July 2016 – *cf.* Ordonnance no 2016-301, 14 March 2016) Code de la consommation provides for a prolongation of the guarantee period for the period necessary for repair or replacement if this period exceeds seven days. Similar regulations (without requiring a minimum period of immobilisation) could be found under Estonian, Czech, Hungarian, Slovenian and Swedish law. See Ch. von Bar, E. Clive, H. Schulte-Nölke, H. Beale, J. Herre, J. Huet, P. Schlechtriem, M.E. Storme, S. Swann, P. Varul, A. Veneziano and F. Zoll (eds.), *Principles, definitions and model rules of European private law: Draft Common Frame of Reference (DCFR)*, 2009, 1452–53, http://ec.europa.eu/justice/contract/files/european-private-law_en.pdf.

138 *Cf.* Art. IV.A-6:108 DCFR; Ch. Twigg-Flesner, 'Consumer Goods Guarantees in the DCFR', *ERPL* 2009, (641) 650. Compare with the French regulation: Art. L211-16 Code de la consommation. Here the prolongation only happens if the time necessary to bring the goods into conformity lasts longer than seven days.

139 This is the case for the legal guarantee under Austrian, Croatian, Estonian, Greek and Icelandic law. Also in Poland, Portugal and Slovakia a new guarantee period starts in the case of a replacement. See: European Consumer Centres Network, *Commercial warranties – Are they worth the money?*, 2015, 38, http://www.eccbelgium.be/20150320/commercial-warranties-are-they-worth-the-money-Attach_s83561.pdf.

140 See on this issue: H. Beale, *Scope of application and general approach of the new rules for contracts in the digital environment – in-depth analysis*, 28, http://www.epgencms.europarl.europa.eu/cmsdata/upload/4a1651c4-0db0-4142-9580-89b47010ae9f/pe_536.493_print.pdf; and CCBE position concerning contract rules for online purchases of goods and digital content, COM(2015) 634 and 635, 18 March 2016, http://www.ccbe.eu/fileadmin/user_upload/NTCdocument/20160318_EN_CCBE_pos1_1458897955.pdf.

protection, but to delimit the notion of 'small and medium-sized enterprise'. The legal uncertainty about the interpretation of this notion was mentioned as one of the biggest concerns for the parties to the contract in the CESL Proposal.[141] This delimitation problem could be avoided if the rules were applicable to all traders, but reaching an understanding about such expansion of the protective rules has already proved to be very difficult.[142]

4.2. IMPLICATIONS FOR COMMERCIAL GUARANTEES OF CHANGES TO THE LEGAL GUARANTEE

With regard to the legal guarantee, the ODSD Proposal mainly repeats the provisions of the CSD, completed with the case-law of the Court of Justice concerning consumer sales (for a detailed discussion, see Jansen and Stijns in this volume, Section 3.1). In addition, the ODSD Proposal also contains some new elements that can heavily influence commercial guarantees. It is important to stress that the interpretation of the legal guarantee also determines the interpretation of commercial guarantees. If we take the Belgian situation as an example, the common sales law (in principle) only provides the remedies price reduction and termination if goods are defective.[143] Especially before the implementation of the provisions on consumer sales, commercial guarantees granted the buyers a right to repair or replace the defective goods.[144] After the implementation of the CSD, one of the main arguments to provide a commercial guarantee in consumer contracts was the reversal of the burden of proof during the full period of the guarantee.[145] Article 5(3) CSD introduced a presumption of the existence of the lack of conformity at the time of delivery if it becomes apparent within six months of delivery. As a consequence, a commercial guarantee of one or two years expanded the presumption. Article 8(3) ODSD Proposal now expands the presumption to two years for the legal guarantee. This reduces the added value of the commercial guarantee which does not last longer than two years. It is possible that this could result in a shift to commercial

---

141 Ch. Wendehorst, 'Regulation – Arts. 1–16 RegCESL (P)' in R. Schulze (ed.), *Common European Sales Law (CESL): commentary*, Baden-Baden, Nomos, 2012, (9) 57.

142 *Cf.* Public consultation on contract rules for online purchases of digital content and tangible goods – summary of results, 3, http://ec.europa.eu/justice/newsroom/contract/opinion/150609_en.htm. For example considering it not appropriate to extend the scope of the Unfair Commercial Practices Directive to B2B relations: European Parliament, Report on the implementation of the Unair Commercial Practices Directive 2005/29/EC, A7-0474/2013, 19 December 2013.

143 Art. 1644 Code Civil.

144 S. Stijns, 'De richtlijn consumentenkoop en het Belgische recht' in J. Smits (ed.), *De richtlijn consumentenkoop in perspectief*, The Hague, Boom Juridische Uitgevers, 2003, (41) 66.

145 *Cf.* Art. IV.A-6:107 DCFR.

guarantees that will mainly be provided for a certain period after this two years. Practice already shows this tendency today as guarantors want to be sure that their commercial guarantee goes beyond the legal guarantee.

Another possible influence can result from the right for the consumer to terminate the contract even for minor defects.[146] Commercial guarantees often tend to relax the modalities of the remedies. For example, there can be no hierarchy between the different remedies in the commercial guarantee, so the consumer can choose freely.[147] Also not requiring any seriousness of the defect is a possible benefit that can be granted in the commercial guarantee.[148] The absence of any seriousness requirement for the legal guarantee can once more affect the content of commercial guarantees.

These amendments of the legal guarantee are without any doubt beneficial for the consumer. It is, however, very important that the consumer is aware of his legal rights, especially in view of the growing fragmentation. The new information duty for the guarantor will therefore be all the more important.

Finally, the increasing fragmentation that would result from the ODSD Directive seems detrimental rather than beneficial, also for sellers. A possible reaction of a trader can be to adapt his terms and conditions for 'ordinary' sales contracts – at least at some points that are not too burdensome – to the required level of protection for online sales. To this end, he could grant a commercial guarantee for 'ordinary' sales contracts that incorporates the same rights that follow from his legal obligations under the ODSD Proposal. This would be beneficial for consumers, who would have additional rights and who would profit from a simpler system. The question is whether it should depend on the sole will of the seller to simplify things in his own interest to avoid confusing and misleading consumers. It is clear that the fragmentation caused by this proposal does not serve the goal of a high level of consumer protection that is set forward in the European Union (Article 114(3) TFEU).[149]

---

146 Arts. 9 and 13 ODSD Proposal; H. Beale, *Scope of application and general approach of the new rules for contracts in the digital environment – in-depth analysis*, 16, http://www.epgencms.europarl.europa.eu/cmsdata/upload/4a1651c4-0db0-4142-9580-89b47010ae9f/pe_536.493_print.pdf.

147 It is important to note that some countries haven't implemented the hierarchy of the CSD (e.g. Greece, Lithuania, Portugal). This would now be contrary to the maximum harmonisation level of the ODSD Proposal and should be adapted for the contracts that fall under this scope of application.

148 An example of such guarantee clause is a clause that guarantees the perfect functioning of a machine during a certain period and grants the consumer the right to choose freely between the remedies of repair, replacement or termination.

149 In the same sense: CCBE position concerning contract rules for online purchases of goods and digital content, COM(2015) 634 and 635, 18 March 2016, http://www.ccbe.eu/fileadmin/user_upload/NTCdocument/20160318_EN_CCBE_pos1_1458897955.pdf.

5. CONCLUSION

If we compare Article 15 ODSD Proposal with the abandoned CESL Proposal and the existing rules on commercial guarantees in the CSD and CRD, we can only welcome the proposal. The current regulation does not sufficiently ensure transparency of commercial guarantees. The additional information requirements imposed by the ODSD are therefore definitely an improvement. By contrast, we do not see any justification to limit the proposed changes to online and other distances sales of goods. The proposal with its current scope of application will only lead to further fragmentation and will not reduce the complexity of the legal framework, although this is precisely one of its aims.

ANNEX: COMPARISON OF THE CSD AND THE ODSD

CSD	ODSD
Article 1(e) 'guarantee': shall mean any undertaking by a seller or producer to the consumer, given without extra charge, to reimburse the price paid or to replace, repair or handle consumer goods in any way if they do not meet the specifications set out in the guarantee statement or in the relevant advertising	Article 2(g) 'commercial guarantee' means any undertaking by the seller or a producer (the guarantor) to the consumer, in addition to his legal obligation relating to the guarantee of conformity, to reimburse the price paid or to replace, repair or service goods in any way if they do not meet the specifications or any other requirements not related to conformity set out in the guarantee statement or in the relevant advertising available at the time of, or before the conclusion of the contract;
Article 6 Guarantees 1. A guarantee shall be legally binding on the offerer under the conditions laid down in the guarantee statement and the associated advertising. 2. The guarantee shall: – state that the consumer has legal rights under applicable national legislation governing the sale of consumer goods and make clear that those rights are not affected by the guarantee, – set out in plain intelligible language the contents of the guarantee and the essential particulars necessary for making claims under the guarantee, notably the duration and territorial scope of the guarantee as well as the name and address of the guarantor.	Article 15 Commercial guarantees 1. Any commercial guarantee shall be binding on the guarantor under the conditions laid down in: (a) pre-contractual information provided by the seller, including any pre-contractual statement which forms an integral part of the contract; (b) advertising available at the time of or before the conclusion of the contract; and (c) the guarantee statement. If the guarantee statement is less advantageous to the consumer than the conditions laid down in pre-contractual information provided by the seller or advertising, the commercial guarantee shall be binding under the conditions laid down in the pre-contractual information or advertising relating to the commercial guarantee.

CSD	ODSD
3. On request by the consumer, the guarantee shall be made available in writing or feature in another durable medium available and accessible to him. 4. Within its own territory, the Member State in which the consumer goods are marketed may, in accordance with the rules of the Treaty, provide that the guarantee be drafted in one or more languages which it shall determine from among the official languages of the Community. 5. Should a guarantee infringe the requirements of paragraphs 2, 3 or 4, the validity of this guarantee shall in no way be affected, and the consumer can still rely on the guarantee and require that it be honoured.	2. The guarantee statement shall be made available on a durable medium and drafted in plain, intelligible language. It shall include the following: (a) a clear statement of the legal rights of the consumer as provided for in this Directive and a clear statement that those rights are not affected by the commercial guarantee; and (b) the terms of the commercial guarantee that go beyond the legal rights of the consumer, information about the duration, transferability, territorial scope and existence of any charges which the consumer might incur in order to benefit from the commercial guarantee, the name and address of the guarantor and, if different from the guarantor, the person against whom any claim is to be made and the procedure by which the claim is to be made. 3. Non-compliance with paragraph 2 shall not affect the binding nature of the commercial guarantee for the guarantor. 4. The Member States may lay down additional rules on commercial guarantees insofar as those rules do not reduce the protection set out in this Article.

RIGHT OF REDRESS

Bert Keirsbilck*

1. INTRODUCTION

On 9 December 2015, the Commission adopted the so-called Digital Contract Proposals. Both the Digital Content Directive (DCD) Proposal[1] and the Online

* Special thanks to Miss Eveline Vanthorre for providing me with relevant legal materials.

[1] Proposal for a Directive of the European Parliament and of the Council on certain aspects concerning contracts for the supply of digital content, 9 December 2015, COM(2015) 634 final.

and Distance Sales of Goods (ODSG) Proposal[2] contain an article that provides the seller/supplier with a right of redress in case of an act or omission by previous parties in the chain of transactions which triggered the seller/supplier's liability for the legal guarantee towards the consumer. Both provisions state that the modalities for exercising this right are to be regulated by the national laws of the Member States. Both Article 17 DCD Proposal and Article 16 ODSG Proposal are clearly inspired by Article 4 of the Consumer Sales Directive 1999/44/EC (CSD), which provides that the seller who is held liable towards a consumer for a lack of conformity shall be entitled to pursue remedies against previous sellers in the contractual chain or against the producer (redress along the contractual chain).

In this chapter, we will first give an overview of the genesis of Article 4 CSD and the original plans to introduce direct producer's liability. This will prove relevant in understanding the basic approach of Article 17 DCD Proposal and Article 16 ODSG Proposal (redress along the contractual chain). Subsequently, we will give a quick overview of the implementation of Article 4 CSD in Belgium with a view to the forthcoming implementation of Article 17 DCD Proposal and Article 16 ODSG Proposal. After that, we will analyse the case for introducing direct producers' liability at the EU level. Finally, we will draw some conclusions.

2. GENESIS OF ARTICLE 4 CSD

As mentioned, Article 17 DCD Proposal and Article 16 ODSG are clearly inspired by Article 4 CSD. Before discussing the basic approach of Article 17 DCD Proposal and Article 16 ODSG Proposal, it might therefore be relevant to recall the genesis of Article 4 CSD and to explain that ultimately no direct producer's liability for the legal guarantee was established at the EU level.[3]

2.1. GREEN PAPER ON GUARANTEES FOR CONSUMER GOODS AND AFTER-SALES SERVICES

On 15 November 1993, the Commission presented its *Green Paper on guarantees for consumer goods and after-sales services*.[4] As regards the subject-matter of the

---

2 Proposal for a Directive of the European Parliament and of the Council on certain aspects concerning contracts for the online and other distance sales of goods, 9 December 2015, COM(2015) 635 final.

3 See also M. Bridge, 'Article 4: Right of redress' in M.C. Bianca and S. Grundmann (eds.), *EU Sales Directive, Commentary*, Antwerp, Intersentia, 2002, 180–82.

4 Green Paper on guarantees for consumer goods and after sales services, 15 November 1993, COM(1993) 509 final.

legal guarantee scheme, the Commission proposed the notion of failure to meet 'the consumer's legitimate expectations'.

As regards the persons liable for the legal guarantee, the Commission proposed joint, though not necessarily identical, liability on the part of the seller and the producer.[5]

The Commission started from the observation that, in modern consumer societies, based on systems of mass production and distribution, consumer confidence concerns the product as such, and is bound up more with the consumers' faith in the producer than in the seller: competition between similar products is also more between brands than between retailers (who mainly compete on the basis of price and after-sales service).

The Commission argued that it would be illogical if, when a product's defect results from its production, the retailer, who has no influence on the production process and who in many cases may not even have packed the product, would be the only person to whom the consumer can turn.[6]

Moreover, the Commission was of the opinion that it would be counter-intuitive that the producer were held liable, under the Product Liability Directive 85/374, when the defective product caused injury to individuals or (in certain cases) to other goods, but that he would be able to disclaim liability when, quite simply, the product failed to work or when a defect resulting from its production caused damage to the product itself.[7]

According to the Commission, granting the consumer a direct action against the producer on the legal guarantee would also enhance the consumer's prospects of recovery, given the greater resources that producers have than retailers.[8] As regards cross-border sales, the Commission argued that extending the liability under the legal guarantee to the producer would give the consumer a genuine opportunity to invoke the guarantee, since normally it is a lot easier for him to address a representative or a branch of the producer in his own country than to address a foreign seller.[9]

In addition, the Commission argued that to allow the consumer directly to address the producer would truncate the legal process and would 'simply bring the law more into line with reality', because the relation between the consumer and the seller (to whom the defective product is returned) normally falls back on the producer anyhow (when the seller sends the defective product back to the producer).[10]

---

5 Ibid, 87.
6 Ibid, 86–87.
7 Ibid, 87.
8 Ibid, 87.
9 Ibid, 87.
10 Ibid, 87.

Finally, the Commission observed that certain legal systems (including France and Belgium) had already moved towards making the producer directly liable for the legal guarantee vis-à-vis the consumer.[11]

Yet, the Commission recognised that the joint liability of the final seller and the producer under the legal guarantee should not be identical.

As regards the assessment of the defect, the Commission stated that the proposed notion of 'the consumer's legitimate expectations' could be used against the producer only in relation to the features for which he is liable. The seller's declarations concerning the product's quality and the content of the contract could not normally be taken into account in assessing the existence of a product defect vis-à-vis the producer. On the other hand, advertising by the producer would be a decisive feature.

As regards the consumer's remedies against the producer, the Commission was of the opinion that these should not include either termination of the contract or price reduction; the consumer would only be entitled to require the producer either to replace or to repair the product or to reimburse the consumer in full or in part only in the event that such a replacement or repair was not or could not be realised.[12]

The Commission also suggested an alternative, 'quasi-subsidiary' solution, whereby the buyer could go against the manufacturer only if it was impossible or unduly onerous to sue the seller. In addition to the case of cross-border purchases, this would include both the seller's insolvency and his withdrawal from the market. This quasi-subsidiary solution could be implemented without a radical change in existing national rules.[13]

2.2. CSD PROPOSALS AND CSD AS FINALLY ADOPTED

In contrast to the *Green Paper*, the Original[14] and Amended CSD Proposal,[15] and the CSD as finally adopted, lay down the principle that the goods must be in conformity with the contract, covering a whole range of situations, i.e. not just the criterion of 'the consumer's legitimate expectations'.

---

11 Ibid, 87.

12 Ibid, 87–88.

13 Ibid, 88. See also H. Cousy, 'Het regres van de eindverkoper en andere aansprake lijkheidsvorderingen' in S. Stijns and J. Stuyck (eds.), *Het nieuwe kooprecht. De wet van 1 september 2004 betreffende de bescherming van de consumenten bij verkoop van consumptiegoederen*, Antwerp, Intersentia, 2005, 129, 131.

14 Proposal for a European Parliament and Council Directive on the sale of consumer goods and associated guarantees, 18 June 1996, COM(1995) 520 final.

15 Amended Proposal for a European Parliament and Council Directive on the sale of consumer goods and associated guarantees, 31 March 1998, COM(1998) 217 final.

Interestingly, one of the conformity criteria in Article 2 CSD (and also in Article 4 ODSG Proposal and in Article 6 DCD Proposal) is whether the quality and performance of the product are fine, given the nature of the product and taking into account the public statements made about them (e.g. advertising), not only by the seller, but also by the producer or his representative, unless the seller shows that: he was not, and could not reasonably have been, aware of the statement in question; by the time of conclusion of the contract the statement had been corrected; or the decision to buy the product could not have been influenced by the statement. Consequently, the seller is liable for both his own advertising statements and for those made by the producer.[16]

In contrast to the *Green Paper*, the CSD, in its various drafts, allows the consumer recourse only against the final seller, who in the event of being held liable on the legal guarantee, is granted a 'right of redress' against prior sellers in the distribution chain.[17] Article 4 CSD as finally adopted does not give the final seller a direct action in respect of the legal guarantee against a remote seller:

Article 3(5) Original CSD Proposal	**Article 3(7) Amended CSD Proposal**	**Article 4 CSD Right of redress**
'Where the final seller is liable to the consumer because of a lack of conformity resulting from an act of commission or omission by the producer, a previous seller in the same chain of contracts or any other intermediary, the final seller shall be entitled to pursue remedies against *the responsible person*, under the conditions laid down by national law.'	'Where the final seller is liable to the consumer because of a lack of conformity resulting from an act of commission or omission by the producer, a previous seller in the same chain of contracts or any other intermediary, the final seller shall be entitled to pursue remedies against *the persons liable*, under the conditions laid down by national law.'	'Where the final seller is liable to the consumer because of a lack of conformity resulting from an act or omission by the producer, a previous seller in the same chain of contracts or any other intermediary, the final seller shall be entitled to pursue remedies against *the person or persons liable in the contractual chain. The person or persons liable against whom the final seller may pursue remedies, together with the relevant actions* and conditions of exercise, shall be determined by national law.'

The Amended Proposal only differed from the Original Proposal in that 'the responsible person' became 'the persons liable'. Bridge notes that there were two points of significance in this change. The first constituted the substitution of 'liable' for 'responsible'. Given that, at this stage, (only) the conditions concerning the seller's recovery were to be determined by national law, the question was whether Article 4 itself prescribed liability on the part of prior sellers and whether, in this regard, the change of wording from 'responsible' to 'liable' was

16 M. Ebers, A. Janssen and O. Meyer, 'Comparative report' in M. Ebers, A. Janssen and O. Meyer (eds.), *European perspectives on producers' liability: direct producers' liability for non-conformity and the sellers' right of redress*, Munich, Sellier, 2009, 3, 37, noting that such rule was previously unknown in many Member States.

17 M. Bridge, n 3 above, 180–81.

significant. Secondly, the transformation of the final seller's target into the plural 'persons' pointed to more than one person in the distribution chain and not just to the immediately prior seller.[18]

Bridge further explains that the differences between the Amended Proposal and the CSD as finally adopted are, first, that the final seller's recourse is now expressly confined to immediate or remote sellers in the distribution chain. Article 4 CSD therefore does not admit tort actions against wrongdoers outside the distribution chain, though it says nothing about the nature of the action, tortious or contractual, that the final seller may bring against parties who are in the distribution chain. By adding the words 'in the contractual chain', Article 4 also deprives the words 'or any other intermediary' of significance. The second difference in the final version of Article 4 is that it now remits to the national law not only the 'conditions' but also the 'actions' of the final seller's exercise of his right of redress.[19]

In the Explanatory Memorandum to the Original CSD Proposal, the Commission argued that national provisions governing sales between professionals are normally less strict than those governing sales between a professional and a consumer. Thus, sellers may often include in these contracts clauses disclaiming their liability for the legal guarantee (see also further below). According to the Commission, this situation could create an injustice in that the entire liability for defects ultimately resulting from an action or omission on the part of another party could fall upon the final sellers. This is notably the case as regards manufacturing defects (due to problems in the production process), defects caused by improper handling on the part of an intermediary in the contractual chain or indeed any lack of conformity resulting from the public statements made by the producer or his representative.[20]

Therefore, it was deemed necessary to include a provision granting the final seller the right to pursue remedies against the person liable in the contractual chain 'so that he can recover the costs caused by defects which can be imputed to that person'.[21] The basic intention was the protection of SMEs. In a certain way, it was the consequence of the introduction in the first place by the CSD of the liability of the final seller; the seller should not be left with the liability where he is not the cause of the lack of non-conformity.[22]

---

18 Ibid, 181.

19 Ibid, 181.

20 See also M. Ebers, A. Janssen and O. Meyer, n 16 above, 38.

21 Proposal for a European Parliament and Council Directive on the sale of consumer goods and associated guarantees, 18 June 1996, COM(1995) 520 final, 14. See also H. Cousy, n 13 above, 132: 'wordt in artikel 4 in een soort indirecte bescherming van de financiële belangen van de consument nagestreefd door te voorzien in een verhaalsmogelijkheid van de eindverkoper tegen zijn voormannen in de distributieketen'.

22 D. Staudenmayer, 'The Directive on the Sale of Consumer Goods and Associated Guarantees – a Milestone in the European Consumer and Private Law', *ERPL* 2000, 547, 559.

It should be noted that the Commission did not really explain why direct producer's liability for the legal guarantee was eventually no longer deemed feasible and desirable (see also further below).

3. RIGHT OF REDRESS UNDER ARTICLE 4 CSD, ARTICLE 17 DCD PROPOSAL AND ARTICLE 16 ODSG PROPOSAL

3.1. REDRESS ALONG THE CONTRACTUAL CHAIN

Just like Article 4 CSD, Article 17 DCD Proposal and Article 16 ODSG Proposal start from the position of relativity of contract. Their basic approach to the problem of defects is to have the final consumer claim against the final seller/supplier, which, in turn, will claim over against its seller/supplier and so on, until liability is pinned upon the seller/supplier responsible for the defect (e.g. the producer).[23] This is also clearly explained in Recital 9 CSD, Recital 47 DCD Proposal and Recital 35 ODSG Proposal.

Recital 9 CSD	Recital 47 DCD Proposal	Recital 35 ODSG Proposal
'(9) Whereas the seller should be directly liable to the consumer for the conformity of the goods with the contract; whereas this is the traditional solution enshrined in the legal orders of the Member States; whereas nevertheless the seller should be free, as provided for by national law, to pursue remedies against the producer, a previous seller in the same chain of contracts or any other intermediary, unless he has renounced that entitlement; …; whereas the rules governing against whom and how the seller may pursue such remedies are to be determined by national law;'	'(47) The lack of conformity with the contract of the final digital content as supplied to the consumer is often due to one of the transactions in a chain, from the original designer to the final supplier. While the final supplier should be liable towards the consumer in case of lack of conformity with the contract between these two parties, it is important to ensure that the supplier has appropriate rights vis-a-vis different members of the chain of transactions in order to be able to cover his liability towards the consumer. However, it should be for the applicable national law to identify the members of the chains of transactions against which the final supplier can turn and the modalities and conditions of such actions.'	'(35) Considering that the seller is liable towards the consumer for any lack of conformity of the goods resulting from an act or omission of the seller or a third party it is justified that the seller should be able to pursue remedies against the responsible person earlier in the chain of transactions … The details for exercising that right, in particular against whom and how such remedies are to be pursued, should be provided by the Member States.'

23 M. Bridge, n 3 above, 184–85.

Article 4 CSD Right of redress	Article 17 DCD Proposal Right of redress	Article 16 ODSG Proposal Right of redress
'Where the final seller is liable to the consumer because of a lack of conformity resulting from an act or omission by the producer, a previous seller in the same chain of contracts or any other intermediary, the final seller shall be entitled to pursue remedies against the person or persons liable in the contractual chain. The person or persons liable against whom the final seller may pursue remedies, together with the relevant actions and conditions of exercise, shall be determined by national law.'	'Where the supplier is liable to the consumer because of any failure to supply the digital content or a lack of conformity with the contract resulting from an act or an omission by a person in earlier links of the chain of transactions, the supplier shall be entitled to pursue remedies against the person or persons liable in the chain of transactions. The person against whom the supplier may pursue remedies and the relevant actions and conditions of exercise, shall be determined by national law.'	'Where the supplier is liable to the consumer because of lack of conformity with the contract resulting from an act or an omission by a person in earlier links of the chain of transactions, the supplier shall be entitled to pursue remedies against the person or persons liable in the chain of transactions. The person against whom the supplier may pursue remedies and the relevant actions and conditions of exercise, shall be determined by national law.'

Article 4 CSD, Article 17 DCD Proposal and Article 16 ODSG Proposal attempt to lay down an EU principle of liability, which, within narrow limits, can be filled in by national laws. These provisions state that the final seller/supplier 'shall' be entitled to pursue 'remedies' against 'the person or persons liable in the contractual chain / chain of transactions', with the exception that 'the actions and relevant conditions of exercise' are determined by national law. As the titles of these provisions recognise, the final seller/supplier is granted a 'right of redress'.[24]

As regards the second sentence of Article 4 CSD, Article 17 DSD Proposal and Article 16 ODSG Proposal, the words 'persons or persons liable' suggest that national law will comply with these provisions if the final seller/supplier has a right of redress against some person in the distribution chain, even if that person is not the immediately prior seller/supplier. Moreover, the words 'relevant actions' suggest that the label to be attached to the final seller's/supplier's cause of action (tort or contract), should be a matter for the national law.[25] The national law also governs the 'conditions of exercise' of that claim for redress.[26]

3.2. FACTORS THAT MAY INTERRUPT THE REMISSION OF LIABILITY BACK UP THE DISTRIBUTION CHAIN

It is well known, however, that distribution chains are innately difficult to handle when it comes to the remission of liability back up the chain to the

24 Ibid, 195–96; H. Cousy, n 13 above, 133.

25 M. Bridge, n 3 above, 196–97.

26 Ibid, 197.

point of production. In the following paragraphs, I will briefly touch upon four well-known factors that tend to interrupt the remission of liability to the source of non-conforming goods or digital content. The presence of such factors may undermine the noble goal of Article 4 CSD, Article 17 DCD Proposal and Article 16 ODSG Proposal, i.e. to allow the final seller/supplier to recover the costs caused by defects which can be imputed to the person(s) liable in the chain of transactions (e.g. the producer of the goods or the original designer of the digital content).[27]

First of all, it cannot be assumed, simply because there is a successful claim in respect of non-conforming products at the end of the chain (by the final consumer against his immediate seller/supplier), that all previous buyers will have a similar claim for the supply of non-conforming products against their sellers/suppliers.[28] Although the final seller/supplier can seek redress along the contractual chain, his claim for redress is often governed by specific rules on commercial sales which in most Member States are more restrictive than the provisions of consumer sales (both as regards the definition of non-conformity and available remedies).[29] This factor might arrest the process of indemnification, with liability coming to rest in the middle of the distribution chain.[30]

The final seller's/supplier's claim to be indemnified may also be blocked by the insolvency of his upstream contracting party. The final seller/supplier will have no choice but to prove in the insolvent liquidation or bankruptcy of its seller/supplier and recover the usual meagre dividend. It will make no difference that the insolvent seller/supplier could, in turn, have passed liability back up the chain to a previous seller/supplier and have recovered in full. Nor does the final seller in such circumstances have the ability to 'jump' one of the links in the chain so as to bring a contract action directly against a remote seller.[31]

A third factor that can impede indemnification by a previous seller/supplier in the chain is the presence of an exclusion or limitation of liability clause in the contract between two sequential sellers. The result may, therefore, be that the loss associated with defective goods/digital content comes to rest somewhere in the chain and not with the party responsible for the defect.[32]

Recital 9 CSD and Recital 35 ODSG Proposal state that the Directive does not affect the principle of freedom of contract between the seller, the producer,

---

27 Ibid, 186.
28 Ibid, 186–87.
29 M. Ebers, A. Janssen and O. Meyer, n 16 above, 38 and 48–50.
30 M. Bridge, n 3 above, 186–87.
31 Ibid, 189–90; M. Ebers, A. Janssen and O. Meyer, n 16 above, 38.
32 M. Bridge, n 3 above, 192.

a previous seller or any other intermediary; this is not explicitly stated in Recital 47 DCD Proposal:

Recital 9 CSD	Recital 47 DCD Proposal	Recital 35 ODSG Proposal
'(9) … whereas this Directive does not affect the principle of freedom of contract between the seller, the producer, a previous seller or any other intermediary;'	'(47)	'(35) … However, this Directive should not affect the principle of freedom of contract between the seller and other parties in the chain of transactions.'

In general terms, Article 4 CSD and Article 17 DCD Proposal seem not to be aimed at eliminating obstacles to the 'right of redress' which are caused by party agreement.[33] It is unclear whether the omission of reference to the freedom of contract in Recital 47 DCD Proposal is deliberate and/or of any relevance in understanding Article 16 ODSG Proposal.

A fourth factor than can impede the flow of indemnity back to the source of the defect in the goods, is the presence of limitation periods. This creates the risk that the final seller/supplier, eventually confronting a claim from the consumer, will find itself already out of time against its supplier.[34]

3.3. NEED OF ECJ INTERPRETATION OF THE 'RIGHT OF REDRESS'

Until now, the Court of Justice has not told us anything of interest about Article 4 CSD, except for the fact that this provision seeks to protect the seller's financial interests. According to the Court, the fact that the Directive makes the seller liable to the consumer for any lack of conformity which exists at the time the goods are delivered, is thus compensated for by the fact that the seller can, in accordance with the applicable rules of national legislation, pursue remedies against the producer, a previous seller in the same chain of contracts or any other intermediary.[35]

It would be particularly interesting to get to know the Court's view on whether Article 4 CSD requires the Member States to remove any, or all, of the above-mentioned obstacles faced by the final seller when seeking redress. Does Article 4 CSD establish minimum requirements in order to allow the final seller to exercise his rights effectively against the person liable in the contractual chain? For example, should the obstacles to the 'right of redress' which are caused by party agreement be eliminated or not?[36]

---

33 Ibid, 199; M. Ebers, A. Janssen and O. Meyer, n 16 above, 38; H. Cousy, n 13 above, 133.

34 M. Bridge, n 3 above, 190–91.

35 ECJ *Gebruder Weber GmbH v Jürgen Wittmer* and *Ingrid Putz v Medianess Electronics GmbH*, Joined Cases C-65/09 and C-87/09, ECLI:EU:C:2011:396. para 58.

36 M. Ebers, A. Janssen and O. Meyer, n 16 above, 40; H. Cousy, n 13 above, 134.

4. IMPLEMENTATION OF ARTICLE 4 CSD IN BELGIUM – ARTICLE 17 DCD PROPOSAL AND ARTICLE 16 ODSG PROPOSAL

Article 4 CSD does not compel the Member States to introduce a direct claim for the final seller against the responsible link in the contractual chain. As a result, in the majority of the Member States, it is only possible to pass back liability via the contractual chain, in line with the approach of Article 4 CSD. Ergo, a final seller who is liable to a consumer for non-conformity can seek redress against his immediate seller (not against the producer or any other prior seller), and redress is further realised through a series of actions along the contractual chain until liability arrives at the party responsible for the non-conformity.[37]

Belgium has also adopted the traditional model of redress along the contractual chain. However, the final seller is granted an additional direct claim (doctrine of qualitative rights and Article 1649*sexies* of the Belgian Civil Code). The final seller can therefore claim not only against his immediate prior seller, but also against all previous sellers further up the chain. Under Belgian law, the consumer can seek redress against the final seller (under the rules implementing the CSD) as well as against all prior sellers (under the doctrine of qualitative rights).

4.1. 'ENHANCED' RIGHT OF REDRESS OF THE FINAL SELLER AGAINST ALL PRIOR SELLERS

Based on the doctrine of qualitative rights, Belgian law grants the final seller a direct right of redress against all prior sellers in the contractual chain, including the initial seller (e.g. the producer).[38] However, the chain of liability

---

37 M. Ebers, A. Janssen and O. Meyer, n 16 above, 37 and 47.

38 In its landmark judgment of 5 December 1980, the Belgian Court of Cassation ruled that the obligation to deliver the sold goods extends to the accessories and to all that is necessary for the durable use of the goods. The right of redress that the first buyer (e.g. the wholesaler, or retailer) is entitled to against the initial seller (e.g. the producer) is to be considered as such an accessory of the goods sold by the first buyer to the second buyer (e.g. the retailer or consumer). Consequently, the second buyer has a direct right of redress against the initial seller without having to address the first buyer. See Court of Cassation 5 December 1980, *Arr. Cass.* 1980–81, 382, as explained in S. Rutten, G. Straetmans and D. Wuyts, 'Rights of Redress and Direct Producer's Liability in Consumer Sales in Belgium: a Critical Appraisal' in M. Ebers, A. Janssen and O. Meyer (eds.), *European perspectives on producers' liability: direct producers' liability for non-conformity and the sellers' right of redress*, Munich, Sellier, 2009, 195, 200. See also S. Stijns and I. Samoy, 'Le nouveau droit de la vente: la transposition en droit belge de la Directive européenne sur la vente des biens de consummation', *Tijdschrift voor Belgisch burgerlijk recht* 2003, vol 17(1), 29; H. Cousy, n 13 above, 137.

is broken as soon as an exoneration clause is stipulated by the intermediate parties.[39]

Article 1649*sexies* of the Belgian Civil Code provides for an 'enhanced' right of redress of the final seller that is liable towards the consumer because of lack of conformity resulting from an action or omission of a remote seller:

Article 1649*sexies* of the Belgian Civil Code
'Where the seller is liable towards the consumer because of a lack of conformity, he shall be entitled to pursue remedies against the producer or any other contractual intermediary in the transfer of ownership of the consumer goods based on their contractual liability with regard to the goods, without any clause limiting or excluding liability being invoked against him.'

In addition to the existing right of redress of the final seller against all prior sellers in the contractual chain (based on the doctrine of qualitative rights), the Belgian legislator enhanced this right with a rule of non-opposability of exoneration clauses in the contractual chain. In doing so, the Belgian legislator went beyond the requirements of the CSD.

It should be noted that if the final seller has replaced or repaired the non-conforming goods, as required under the CSD, he can only seek a price reduction or termination of the contract with his own seller or claim damages in case of knowledge of the defect by the seller; under the applicable general regime of sale of goods, he cannot claim repair or replacement. Moreover, it should be noted that, under that very regime, the final seller who is confronted with a hidden defect, must lodge his claim within a 'short period of time'; yet, this period starts to run only as from the date of the lodging of the consumer's claim against the final seller.[40]

The only really new rule set out in Article 1649*sexies* is the non-opposability of exoneration clauses limiting the contractual liability of persons liable in the contractual chain.[41] However, this rule has limited added value, in light of the well-established case law on the presumption of the knowledge of producers and specialised sellers of hidden defects; hence, the relevance of non-opposability of exoneration clauses set out in Article 1649*sexies* mainly pertains to the situation where the final seller bought the good from a professional but not specialised seller.[42]

39 S. Rutten, G. Straetmans and D. Wuyts, n 38 above, 200.

40 H. Cousy, n 13 above, 139–40 and 142; S. Rutten, G. Straetmans and D. Wuyts, n 38 above, 201; M. Hostens, 'De rechtstreekse aanspraak van de consument: Een nieuw pijnpunt in ons dualistisch kooprecht?', *DCCR* 2010, vol 87, 94.

41 H. Cousy, n 13 above, 141–42; S. Rutten, G. Straetmans and D. Wuyts, n 38 above, 201.

42 H. Cousy, n 13 above, 141–42.

4.2. RIGHT OF REDRESS OF THE CONSUMER AGAINST THE FINAL SELLER AND AGAINST ALL PRIOR SELLERS

Under the doctrine of qualitative rights, the consumer has a right of redress against the producer and other persons in the contractual chain.[43] Based on that doctrine, clauses limiting or excluding liability are not opposable to the consumer.[44] Since the consumer's right is based on the general regime of sale of goods, he cannot claim repair or replacement and he must bring his claim before court within a short period of time.[45]

4.3. WHICH IMPLEMENTATION OF ARTICLE 17 DCD PROPOSAL AND ARTICLE 16 ODSG PROPOSAL?

At this point of time, it is unclear how the rights of redress set out in Article 17 DCD Proposal and Article 16 ODSG Proposal, if ever adopted, will be implemented and whether Article 1649*sexies* of the Belgian Civil Code will and should serve as a source of inspiration. There will be room for debate, notwithstanding the full harmonisation character of Article 17 DCD Proposal and Article 16 ODSG Proposal. In any event, the doctrine of qualitative rights continues to apply, meaning that the final seller/supplier and the final consumer can claim not only against their immediate prior sellers, but also against all prior sellers in the chain of transactions.

5. THE CASE FOR EU DIRECT PRODUCERS' LIABILITY

It has been explained above that eventually no direct producer's liability for the legal guarantee was established at the EU level. However, Recital 23 CSD provides that legislation and case law in this area in the various Member States show that there is growing concern to ensure a high level of consumer protection and that, in the light of this trend and the experience in implementing this Directive, 'it may be necessary to envisage more far-reaching harmonisation, notably by providing for the producer's direct liability for defects for which he is responsible'. In addition, Article 12 CSD provides that the Report on the implementation of the CSD 'shall examine, inter alia, the case for introducing the producers' direct liability and, if appropriate, shall be accompanied by proposals.'

---

43 Ibid, 142–43; S. Rutten, G. Straetmans and D. Wuyts, n 38 above, 202 and 207.

44 S. Stijns and I. Samoy, n 38 above, 29. Compare H. Cousy, n 13 above, 142–43; S. Rutten, G. Straetmans and D. Wuyts, n 38 above, 202 and 207.

45 S. Stijns and I. Samoy, n 38 above, 29; S. Rutten, G. Straetmans and D. Wuyts, n 38 above, 202 and 207.

In April 2007, the Commission adopted its *Report on the implementation of the CSD including analysis of the case for introducing direct producers' liability.*[46] The Commission stated that the existence of diverging regimes of direct producers' liability was a 'potential problem for the internal market'. However, the Commission was unable, at that stage, to draw final conclusions on the need to provide for an EU right of redress by the final buyer against the producer. There was 'not enough evidence to determine whether the lack of EU rules on direct producers' liability has a negative effect on consumer confidence in the internal market'. For these reasons, the Commission decided not to submit any proposal and announced to explore the issue further in the context of the *Green Paper on the review of the consumer acquis.*

One of the questions in the *Green Paper on the review of the consumer acquis*, which the Commission had adopted in February 2007, was whether EU-wide direct producers' liability should be introduced so that consumers would be able to request certain remedies directly from the manufacturer (and possibly from the importer) throughout the EU.

The Commission noted that a number of Member States had introduced various forms of direct liability of producers, and that these forms differ(ed) considerably as to the conditions and modalities. The Commission was of the opinion that EU-wide rules on producers' direct liability would eliminate possible internal market barriers and would favour especially consumers buying cross-border.[47]

In October 2008, the Commission adopted its Proposal for a Directive on consumer rights (CRD Proposal), that contained modernised and fully harmonised rules on the legal guarantee in consumer sales.[48] Yet, it did not contain a provision granting a 'right of redress' to the final seller. Neither did it establish direct producer's liability.

Eventually, however, the regulation of the legal guarantee in consumer sales (and unfair terms in consumer contracts) were evacuated from the 'CRD file'. It is well known that the Consumer Rights Directive 2011/83/EU (CRD)[49] as finally

---

46 Communication from the Commission to the Council and the European Parliament on the implementation of Directive 1999/44/EC of the European Parliament and of the Council of 25 May 1999 on certain aspects of the sale of consumer goods and associated guarantees including analysis of the case for introducing direct producers' liability, 24 April 2007, COM(2007) 210 final.

47 Green Paper on the review of the consumer acquis presented by the European Commission, 8 February 2007, COM(2006) 744 final.

48 Proposal for a Directive of the European Parliament and of the Council on consumer rights, 8 October 2008, COM(2008) 614 final.

49 The Consumer Rights Directive lays down the pre-contractual information requirements and the consumer's right to withdraw from distance and off-premises contracts (contracts concluded outside business premises). It also regulates the consequences of non-delivery of goods, limits any additional costs imposed on the consumer for the use of specific means of payment and prohibits the use of default settings ('pre-ticked boxes') for charging additional payments.

adopted mainly pertains to off-premises and distance contracts (information requirements and withdrawal rights); this most recent instrument of 'general' or 'horizontal' EU consumer legislation, that is based on full harmonisation, does not deal with consumer sales (or unfair terms).

It is equally well-known that the review of the consumer acquis (that resulted in the CRD and in the review of a number of sector-specific directives) was a spin-off project of the broader project to make EU contract law more coherent; this broader project was launched in 2001 and imploded in 2015 with the withdrawal of the Proposal for a Regulation establishing a Common European Sales Law (CESL).[50]

In this context, it can also be noted that the CESL Proposal, which contained modernised rules on the legal guarantee in consumer sales of goods and digital content, did not contain a provision granting a right of redress to the final seller/supplier.[51]

6. CONCLUSION

The full harmonisation DCD and ODSG Proposals, if ever adopted, will have a considerable impact on national private laws. Article 17 DCD Proposal and Article 16 ODSG Proposal provide the seller/supplier with a right of redress in case of an act or omission by previous parties in the chain of transactions which triggered the seller/supplier's liability under the legal guarantee towards the consumer. These provisions are clearly inspired by Article 4 CSD; the option of direct producer's liability was disregarded. It remains to be seen how the debate on the right of redress, which involves a balancing of consumer and business economic interests, will evolve in the forthcoming months.

50 Commission Proposal for a Regulation establishing a Common European Sales Law, 11 October 2011, COM(2011) 635 final.

51 See M. Ilmer and J.C.M. Dastis, 'Redress in Europe and the Trap under the CESL', *ERCL* 2013, 109–42.

PART III

PROPOSAL FOR A REGULATION ON CROSS-BORDER PORTABILITY OF ONLINE CONTENT SERVICES IN THE INTERNAL MARKET

'CONTENT-WHEREVER-YOU-GO'

Towards Cross-Border Portability of Online Digital Content*

Eva LIEVENS

1. INTRODUCTION

Almost half of European Internet users access content, such as music, movies, video and games, online.[1] Consumers can either purchase or rent such content[2] or

* Please note that this chapter takes into account developments until 1 March 2017.

1 Eurostat, 'Community survey on ICT usage on households and by individuals', 2014: as mentioned in European Commission, Proposal for a Regulation of the European Parliament and of the Council on ensuring the cross-portability of online content services in the internal market, COM(2015) 627 final, 9 December 2015, http://eur-lex.europa.eu/legal-content/EN/TXT/?qid=1462785103065&uri=CELEX:52015PC0627, 2 (hereinafter: POSCR).

2 Such *transactional* services allow users to either download the content to their device and/or to have unlimited access to the content from a 'digital locker', i.e. an online storage service

subscribe to services to have access to a provider's content catalogue.[3] According to a 2015 Eurobarometer survey, two in ten Internet users pay a subscription to access online digital content.[4] Having bought such content, however, does not necessarily mean that consumers can also access the content that they have acquired the right to use in all EU Member States.[5] A Belgian consumer who has a Telenet subscription, for instance, will not be able to use the Yelo TV app when travelling to another Member State. Yet, 33 per cent of those European Internet users who do not currently have a paid subscription (for audiovisual content, music, e-books or video games) state that if they took out such a service in the future it would be important for them to be able to access it when in another Member State.[6] In order to remove the barriers that hamper access and use of such online content services across borders,[7] the European Commission issued a proposal for a Regulation on ensuring the cross-border portability of online content services in the internal market (POCSR) on 9 December 2015.

2. BACKGROUND

In its Digital Single Market Strategy for Europe, published in May 2015, the European Commission introduced the three pillars on which the Digital Single Market should be built: (1) better access for consumers and businesses to online goods and services across Europe, (2) creating the right conditions for digital networks and services to flourish, and (3) maximising the growth potential of the European Digital Economy.[8] Under the first pillar, better access to digital

---

for digital content, or through streaming (purchase) or to access the content for a specified period of time (rental). With regard to the instance where the content is downloaded to the user's device, portability is not an issue. It may be an issue, however, with regard to the other modes of access. *Cf.* European Commission, Commission Staff Working Document Impact Assessment accompanying the document Proposal for a Regulation of the European Parliament and of the Council to ensure the cross-border portability of online content services in the internal market, SWD(2015) 270 final, 9 December 2015, 7 (hereinafter: POSCR Impact Assessment).

3 These types of services are *subscription* services, which may either be obtained in return for the payment of a fee, or may be free of charge, for instance when the service is funded by means of advertising. *Cf.* POSCR Impact Assessment, 7.

4 Eurobarometer, Survey 411: Cross-border access to online content, 2015, http://ec.europa.eu/COMMFrontOffice/PublicOpinion/index.cfm/Survey/getSurveyDetail/instruments/FLASH/surveyKy/2059.

5 POSCR, recital 3.

6 Eurobarometer, Survey 411: Cross-border access to online content, 2015, http://ec.europa.eu/COMMFrontOffice/PublicOpinion/index.cfm/Survey/getSurveyDetail/instruments/FLASH/surveyKy/2059.

7 POSCR, recital 1.

8 European Commission, Communication from the Commission 'A Digital Single Market Strategy for Europe', COM(2015) 192 final, 6 May 2015, http://eur-lex.europa.eu/legal-content/EN/TXT/PDF/?uri=CELEX:52015DC0192&from=EN.

content and a modern, more European copyright framework was put forward as one of the priorities. It is within this priority that the portability of legally acquired content was indicated as one of the areas in which a legislative proposal would be drafted.[9] However, prior to the adoption of the Digital Single Market Strategy, the issue of content portability had already been addressed in the Commission's 2012 Communication on Content in the Digital Single Market and in the Public Consultation on the Review of the EU Copyright Rules.[10] The 2012 Communication shaped a structured stakeholder dialogue, called 'Licences for Europe', with the aim of delivering practical industry- or market-led solutions for certain issues, portability of services being one of them. This resulted in the publication of the 'Ten pledges to bring more content online' in 2013.[11] In that context, representatives from the audiovisual sector confirmed their willingness to continue to work towards the further development of cross-border portability. However, in its impact assessment accompanying the POCSR, the Commission argued that no tangible progress had been made by the sector, and that hence a legislative initiative was necessary.[12]

3. RATIONALE AND OBJECTIVE

In its Communication 'Towards a modern, more European copyright framework', which accompanied the POSCR, the Commission stated that 'when it comes to copyright-protected content crossing borders, the digital single market is not yet a reality', one reason being that 'content is not "portable"'.[13] Yet, content is increasingly consumed by means of portable devices, such as tablets and smart phones. These portable devices, the proliferation of which

---

9 This was confirmed in the 'Mission letter' from President Juncker to Commissioner Oettinger, in which the former emphasised the importance for citizens of 'access to services, music, movies and sports events on their electronic devices wherever they are in Europe and regardless of borders': *cf.* J.-C. Juncker, Mission letter to Günther Oettinger Commissioner for Digital Economy and Society, 1 November 2014, http://ec.europa.eu/commission/sites/cwt/files/commissioner_mission_letters/oettinger_en.pdf.

10 European Commission, Communication from the Commission 'On content in the Digital Single Market', COM(2012) 789 final, 18 December 2012, https://ec.europa.eu/transparency/regdoc/rep/1/2012/EN/1-2012-789-EN-F1-1.pdf; European Commission, Report on the responses to the Public Consultation on the Review of the EU Copyright Rules, July 2014, http://ec.europa.eu/internal_market/consultations/2013/copyright-rules/docs/contributions/consultation-report_en.pdf.

11 http://ec.europa.eu/internal_market/copyright/docs/licences-for-europe/131113_ten-pledges_en.pdf.

12 POSCR Impact Assessment, 14, fn 79, and 18.

13 European Commission, Communication 'Towards a modern, more European copyright framework', COM(2015) 626 final, 9 December 2015, 3–4.

is undeniable,[14] facilitate the use of online content services regardless of the location of the user.[15]

There are various reasons why users cannot access their (legally acquired) digital content when they are outside of the borders of the Member State in which they reside. First, online service providers sometimes decide to offer their services only in certain markets.[16] Regulatory requirements, technological constraints, lack of demand or the position of competitors may be motives for such commercial practices.[17] Second, in order to be able to provide content to users, service providers need to have acquired the relevant rights for the relevant countries, and, hence, the authorisation of the right-holders (such as authors, performers, producers or broadcasting organisations) or sports organisers.[18] Yet, the rights for the transmission of content that is protected by copyright, or related rights, such as audiovisual works, and the transmissions of broadcasting organisations (e.g. of sports events[19]), are often licensed on a country-by-country and/or on an exclusive basis.[20] Country-by-country licensing ensures that rights-holders can tailor the remuneration to the specific market, depending on, for instance, the economic climate, the standard of living or the interest of users in the content.[21] Moreover, exclusivity within specific territories allows rights-holders to obtain higher remuneration[22] or pre-sale financing for the production of content,[23] and enables broadcasting organisations and service providers to

---

14 According to the iMinds Digimeter survey, for instance, in 2015, 58.3% of Flemish citizens had access to a tablet in their household, and 68.5% had access to a smart phone: B. Vanhaelewyn *et al.*, *Digimeter: Measuring digital media trends in Flanders*, 2015, https://www.iminds.be/en/gain-insights/digimeter/2015.

15 POCSR, recital 2.

16 POCSR, recital 4.

17 POSCR Impact Assessment, 16.

18 POCSR, recitals 8 and 9. Please note that from this point onwards the notion of 'right-holders' is used in a broadly interpreted manner, including 'holders of copyright and related rights or those holding any other rights relevant for the access to and use of content on online content services'.

19 Although sporting events as such are not protected by copyright, transmissions of sport events do often include copyright protected elements, such as music, opening or closing video sequences and graphics; *cf.* POSCR, recital 5.

20 POCSR, recitals 4, 5 and 10.

21 D. Visser and P. Kreijger, 'Online diensten over de grens', *Nederlands Tijdschrift voor Europees Recht* 2016, no. 2, 61.

22 T. Madiega, 'European Parliamentary Research Service Briefing EU legislation in progress: Cross-border portability of online content services', February 2016, https://epthinktank.eu/2016/02/20/cross-border-portability-of-online-content-services-eu-legislation-in-progress/, 4.

23 I. Schooneknaep and K. Donders, 'SMIT Policy Brief: The "Digital Single Market": Waar leidt de Europese Commissie ons naartoe en willen we dat wel?', 4 May 2016, https://gallery.mailchimp.com/9d2e727554b9a31ef98885aba/files/POLICY_BRIEF4.pdf; POSCR Impact Assessment, 13–14. Also: F. Cabrera Blázquez, M. Cappello, C. Grece and S. Valais, 'Territoriality and its impact on the financing of audiovisual works', *IRIS Plus* 2015-2, 26: in this context, according to Cabrera Blázquez et al., '[r]ight-holders, some providers of

ask for higher advertising fees and increase their subscription fees.[24] Sports broadcasting rights, especially for premium sports content, are also often sold on an exclusive territorial basis.[25] In order to guarantee exclusivity, licence contracts often include clauses that require that users are prevented from accessing the content outside of the territory for which the rights have been acquired (for instance, by blocking access from IP addresses outside of that territory, through so-called 'geo-blocking').[26] Such restrictions are also reflected in the contracts between online service providers and their customers.[27] The terms of use of Netflix, for instance, contain the following clause:

> 4.3. You may view a movie or TV show through the Netflix service primarily within the country in which you have established your account and only in geographic locations where we offer our service and have licensed such movie or TV show. The content that may be available to watch will vary by geographic location and will change from time to time. The number of devices on which you may simultaneously watch depends on your chosen subscription plan and is specified on the 'Your Account' page.

The objective of the POCSR, according to recital 12 and Article 1, is to adjust the legal framework in order to guarantee that the licensing of rights no longer presents barriers to cross-border portability of online content services.[28] As such, subscribers to online content should be enabled to access and use those services when temporarily present in another Member State.[29]

4. IMPACT ASSESSMENT

The Impact Assessment which accompanies the POSCR emphasises that cross-border portability is a self-standing issue which requires a specific solution and cannot be addressed as part of other initiatives within the Digital Single Market Strategy.[30] The timing is considered appropriate, taking into account the elimination of mobile roaming charges by 2017.[31] As mobile phone users will

audiovisual services, film producers and broadcasters also emphasise the role territoriality plays in maintaining cultural and linguistic diversity in Europe and in guaranteeing a high level of quality in the films on offer to consumers and end-users'.

24 T. Madiega, 'European Parliamentary Research Service Briefing EU legislation in progress: Cross-border portability of online content services', February 2016, https://epthinktank.eu/2016/02/20/cross-border-portability-of-online-content-services-eu-legislation-in-progress/, 4.

25 POCSR Impact Assessment, 6.

26 POSCR, recital 10.

27 POSCR, recital 10.

28 POSCR, recital 12.

29 Article 1 POSCR.

30 POSCR Impact Assessment, 3.

31 POSCR Impact Assessment, 3.

pay the same fees when travelling across the EU, consumer demand for portable services is likely to increase.[32]

Figure 1. Problem tree

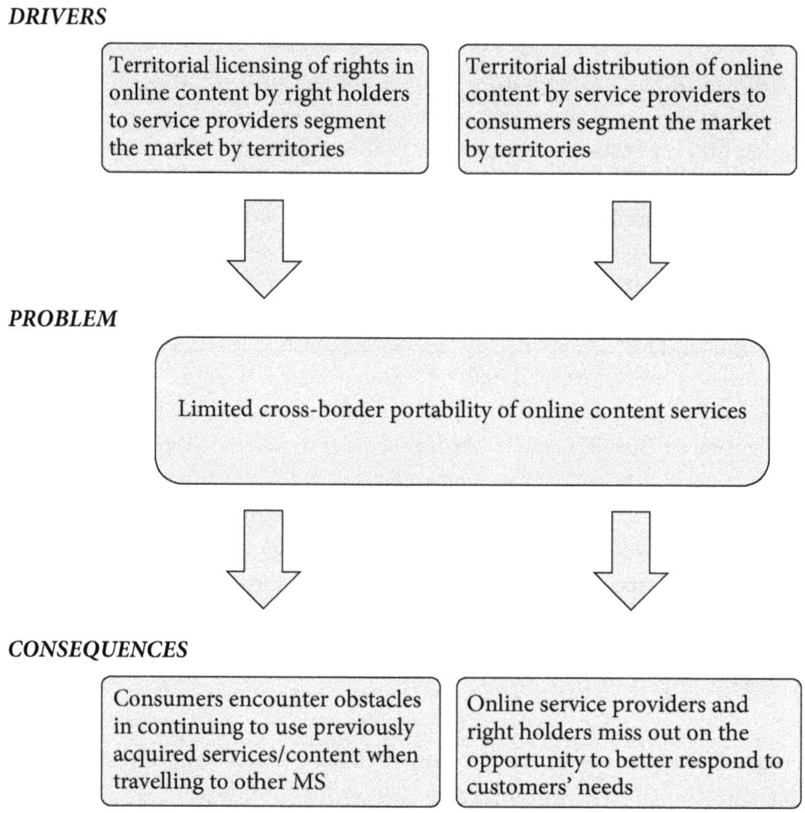

Source: POSCR Impact Assessment, 7.

The Impact Assessment considered three policy options, aside from the baseline (i.e. no intervention): (1) *guidance*, i.e. encouraging right-holders to grant rights allowing for cross-border portability when issuing licences, and encouraging online content service providers to enable cross-portability across the EU, (2) legislation *facilitating* cross-border portability, and (3) legislation *ensuring* cross-border portability.[33] Having considered all three options, the third option is proposed as the preferred option, being the most effective in meeting the

32 POSCR Impact Assessment, 18.

33 POSCR Impact Assessment, 23–44. Other options such as 'the introduction of a rule localising all copyright-relevant acts occurring online combined with a further harmonisation of copyright law or by a full harmonisation of EU copyright law and a single European copyright title' were discarded in the Impact Assessment as disproportionate for the current objectives. POSCR Impact Assessment, 23.

objective. Three considerations led to this decision: first, as mentioned above, the lack of tangible progress in the context of the 'Licences for Europe' stakeholder dialogue; secondly, the appraisal that the difficulties with regard to reviewing licensing contracts and defining uniform conditions for portability would be too significant for an industry-led approach to succeed; and thirdly, the fact that the second option would entail a slow and heterogeneous evolution, if contracts could still override or limit the facilitation mechanism in place and if service providers could still choose not to offer cross-border portability to users.

5. LEGAL BASIS AND CHOICE OF INSTRUMENT

The legal basis for the POSCR is Article 114 of the Treaty on the Functioning of the European Union (TFEU), which states that the EU has the power to adopt measures, including a regulation, that have as their purpose the establishment and the functioning of the internal market.[34] According to the Impact Assessment, eliminating current barriers to the portability of content when being temporarily present in another Member State could facilitate and encourage the free movement of services in the internal market.[35] Online content services which would be affected by EU action rely on content which is protected by copyright, an area which has been harmonised by the EU,[36] or which contains elements to which other rules that have been the subject of EU harmonisation apply (e.g. the Audiovisual Media Services Directive,[37] containing rules on television transmission of sporting events). Hence, due to the harmonisation, Member States are not in a position to ensure cross-portability themselves.[38] The added value of EU action with regard to portability lies in its inherent cross-border nature, as well as the fact that reviewing existing contracts in order to

34 POSCR Impact Assessment, 19. Other EU policies with which consistency should be ensured according to the proposal are related to 'cultural aspects' (Article 167 TFEU) and 'consumer protection' (Article 169 TFEU).

35 POSCR Impact Assessment, 19.

36 The relevant Directives in this field are: Directive 96/9/EC of the European Parliament and of the Council of 11 March 1996 on the legal protection of databases, *OJ* L 077, 27.3.1996, 20–28; Directive 2001/29/EC of the European Parliament and of the Council of 22 May 2001 on the harmonisation of certain aspects of copyright and related rights in the information society, *OJ* L 167, 22.6.2001, 10–19; Directive 2006/115/EC of the European Parliament and of the Council of 12 December 2006 on rental right and lending right and on certain rights related to copyright in the field of intellectual property, *OJ* L 376, 27.12.2006, 28–35; and Directive 2009/24/EC of the European Parliament and of the Council of 23 April 2009 on the legal protection of computer programs, *OJ* L 111, 5.5.2009, 16–22.

37 Directive 2010/13/EU of the European Parliament and of the Council of 10 March 2010 on the coordination of certain provisions laid down by law, regulation or administrative action in Member States concerning the provision of audiovisual media services, *OJ* L 95, 15.4.2010, 1–24 (hereinafter: AVMS Directive).

38 POSCR, recital 29.

enable cross-border portability would not only take a long time, but would also result in fragmentation and diverse solutions.[39] Finally, according to the Impact Assessment, EU action that leads to the harmonisation of conditions would enhance legal certainty for online service providers.[40]

The choice of a regulation has been considered 'remarkable', as it is the first time that this type of instrument is being opted for in the field of copyright law, instead of a directive.[41] A regulation is directly applicable in all Member States.[42] According to the proposal this is necessary in order to ensure 'a uniform application of the cross-border portability rules across Member States and their entering into force at the same time with regard to all online content services'.[43] It is argued that only a regulation guarantees the degree of legal certainty which is necessary in order to enable consumers to fully enjoy cross-border portability across the EU.[44]

6. KEY ELEMENTS, DEFINITIONS AND SCOPE OF APPLICATION OF THE POSCR

The POSCR is built on three key elements. First, Article 3 imposes an *obligation* on the provider of an online content service to enable a subscriber who is temporarily present in a Member State to access and use the online content service. Secondly, Article 4 establishes a *legal fiction* which implies that the provision of an online content service to, as well as the access to and the use of this service by a subscriber, shall be deemed to occur solely in the Member State of residence. Thirdly, Article 5 renders unenforceable any *contractual provision* contrary to this obligation.

Before analysing these key elements and the scope of application in greater detail, it is necessary to explore the definitions that are at the centre of the POSCR. Article 2 provides the following definitions:

(a) 'Subscriber' means any consumer who, on the basis of a contract for the provision of an online content service with a provider, may access and use such service in the Member State of residence

39 POSCR Impact Assessment, 20–21.

40 POSCR Impact Assessment, 21.

41 D. Visser and P. Kreijger, 'Online diensten over de grens,' *Nederlands Tijdschrift voor Europees Recht* 2016, no. 2, 63; G. Mazziotti and F. Simonelli, 'Regulation on "cross-border portability" of online content services: Roaming for Netflix or the end of copyright territoriality?', CEPS Commentary, 15 February 2016, https://www.ceps.eu/publications/regulation-%E2%80%98cross-border-portability%E2%80%99-online-content-services-roaming-netflix-or-end.

42 Also: Article 8 POSCR: 'This regulation shall be binding in its entirety and directly applicable in all Member States'.

43 POSCR, recital 28.

44 POSCR, recital 28.

(b) 'Consumer' means any natural person who, in contracts covered by this Regulation is acting for purposes which are outside his or her trade, business, craft or profession
(c) 'Member State of residence' means the Member State where the subscriber is habitually residing
(d) 'Temporarily present' means a presence of a subscriber in a Member State other than the Member State of residence
(e) 'Online content service' means a service as defined by Articles 56 and 57 of the [TFEU] that a service provider is lawfully providing online in the Member State of residence on a portable basis and which is an audiovisual media service within the meaning of Directive 2010/13/EU or a service the main feature of which is the provision of access to and use of works, other protected subject matter or transmissions of broadcasting organisations, whether in a linear or an on-demand manner,
which is provided to a subscriber on agreed terms either:
(1) against payment of money; or
(2) without payment of money provided that the subscriber's Member State of residence is verified by the provider;
(f) 'Portable' means subscribers can effectively access and use the online content service in the Member State of residence without being limited to a specific location.

The way in which key notions such as 'online content services' are defined has an important impact on the scope of application of the POSCR. A first limitation relates to the fact that cross-portability must be offered to consumers who have a 'contract' with a provider which allows them to legitimately access and use online content in their Member State of residence. This entails that instances where there is no such contract are excluded from the scope of the Regulation. Agreeing with terms and conditions of a service will in all probability constitute such a contract,[45] whereas the acceptance of http cookies or a registration to receive alerts will not be regarded as causing a contractual relationship.[46] Secondly, the Regulation applies to services which either fall under the definition of 'audiovisual media services',[47] as stipulated in the AVMS Directive, or services

45 D. Visser and P. Kreijger, 'Online diensten over de grens', *Nederlands Tijdschrift voor Europees Recht* 2016, no. 2, 63. *Cf.* also the definition of 'online content service' in POSCR Article 2 (e): 'which is provided to a subscriber on agreed terms'.

46 POSCR, recital 13 and POSCR Impact Assessment, 8.

47 Article 1(1)(a)(i) of the AVMS Directive defines an 'audiovisual media service' as 'a service as defined by Articles 56 and 57 of the Treaty on the Functioning of the European Union which is under the editorial responsibility of a media service provider and the principal purpose of which is the provision of programmes, in order to inform, entertain or educate, to the general public by electronic communications networks within the meaning of point (a) of Article 2 of Directive 2002/21/EC. Such an audiovisual media service is either a television broadcast as defined in point (e) of this paragraph or an on-demand audiovisual media service as defined in point (g) of this paragraph'.

the *main feature* of which is the provision of access to and use of works, other protected subject-matter or transmissions of broadcasting organisations. This implies that if a service uses works, other subject-matter or transmissions of broadcasting organisations merely in an ancillary manner, for instance when graphical elements or music are used as background, the Regulation will not apply.[48] Thirdly, only online content services which are either provided *against payment* of money, or *without payment* of money if the subscriber's Member State of *residence is verified* by the provider, fall within the scope. Recital 16 clarifies that suppliers of services which are provided against payment are in a position to verify the Member State of residence of their subscribers. Payment may either be made directly to the provider of the online content service, or to another party, for instance when a consumer buys a package which consists of a telecommunications service and an online content service operated by another provider.[49] If no payment is made, the Regulation is applicable only to services for which providers verify the Member State of residence of their subscribers. Requiring service providers that do not check the location of users to comply with the obligations of the Regulation would involve significant changes to their business practice, and would entail disproportionate costs.[50] Recital 17 refers to 'reasonable indicators' that can be relied on to verify the Member State in which a subscriber resides, including information regarding the payment of a licence fee for other services in the Member State of residence, the existence of a contract for Internet or telephone connection, IP address or other means of authentication.[51]

Finally, only online content services that are provided to the subscriber on a *portable* basis (so on a laptop, tablet or smart phone) in the Member State of residence fall within the scope of the Regulation. This element has been added to ensure that service providers that do not offer this functionality to their subscribers in their home country (for instance, when certain content can only be watched on the device connected to a digital recorder and not on a tablet) would not be obliged to offer this in cross-border situations.[52]

7. OBLIGATION TO ENABLE CROSS-BORDER PORTABILITY OF ONLINE CONTENT SERVICES

According to Article 3 POSCR, online content service providers must enable subscribers who are temporarily present in a Member State to access and use the

48 POSCR, recital 14.
49 POSCR, recital 16.
50 POSCR, recital 17.
51 POSCR, recital 17.
52 POSCR, recital 15.

online content service. Recital 18 emphasises that this obligation is mandatory, and, hence, that parties may not exclude it, derogate from it or vary its effect. As such, subscribers must, in that Member State, have access to the same content on the same range and number of devices, for the same number of users and with the same range of functionalities.[53] However, the online content service provider is not required to deliver a service of the same quality as in the Member State of residence, unless the service provider has explicitly committed to do this.[54] This provision has been included in the POSCR in order to not to inflict substantial costs on providers.[55] The quality of the access may for instance be influenced by the quality of the Internet connection that is used by the consumer in the Member State of temporary residence. Hence, according to Article 3(2), if the quality of access is lower the provider will not be held liable.[56] In any case, the service provider must inform the subscriber of the quality of delivery of the online content service provided in the Member State of temporary residence.

An essential element of Article 3 is the fact that cross-border portability must be provided to subscribers that are 'temporarily' present in another Member State. Article 2(d) defines this as 'a presence of a subscriber in a Member State other than the Member State of residence'. This rather limited definition, which does not contain an indication of the period of time that 'temporary' could refer to, has raised questions. Where would someone who works in one Member State during the week and resides in another Member State during the weekend be considered to 'habitually reside'[57] and be 'temporarily present'? What about students who are living in another Member State for a number of months in the framework of an Erasmus exchange programme?[58] The absence of a time period in the definition has been both defended and questioned by commentators and stakeholders. On the one hand, right-holders, for instance, ask for clear criteria, and a specification of the maximum length of stay in order to prevent 'abuses and cross-border access through the back door'.[59] Commentators have also argued that monitoring of IP addresses (in order to check the location of the consumer) requires a definition of the maximum duration of a temporary presence abroad

53 POSCR, recital 18.

54 Article 3(2) POSCR.

55 POSCR, recital 19.

56 POSCR, recital 19.

57 *Cf.* Article 2(c), which defines the 'Member State of residence' as 'the Member State where the subscriber is habitually residing'.

58 P. Malaquias, 'The Proposal for a Regulation on cross-border portability of online content', 26 February 2016, https://www.law.kuleuven.be/citip/blog/the-proposal-for-a-regulation-on-cross-border-portability-of-online-content/.

59 Society of Audiovisual Authors, 'EC Proposal for a Regulation on cross-border portability of online content services in the internal market SAA comments', March 2016, http://www.saa-authors.eu/dbfiles/mfile/8800/8805/SAA_position_paper_cross_border_portability_regulation_21.3.2016.pdf.

and the criteria that would be used to establish that duration (e.g. number of days abroad per year, number of days spent in a certain country or number of consecutive days abroad).[60] On the other hand, consumer organisations have voiced their support for the absence of time limits, as consumers may have different reasons to travel abroad (work, tourism, study) and setting a maximum number of days or a fixed time period would not be appropriate. BEUC even asked to include an explicit prohibition in the text of the POSCR to impose such a time limit.[61] Commissioner Ansip also rejected a proposal from some Member States to limit the number of days as this, in his view, would entail more costs.[62]

8. LOCALISATION OF THE PROVISION, ACCESS TO AND USE OF ONLINE CONTENT SERVICES

In order to enable online content service providers to provide access to content for which they may not have acquired the relevant rights in the Member State of temporary residence, a legal fiction[63] is established in Article 4 of the POCSR. This legal fiction determines that the provision of, as well as access to and use of, an online content service *shall be deemed to occur solely in the Member State of residence* for the purpose of the relevant Directives with regard to copyright and related rights[64] and the AVMD Directive. Consequently, right-holders in the Member State of temporary presence will not be able to argue that there is a breach of copyright (or other relevant rights) and prohibit providers from the Member State of residence from granting temporary access to their subscribers, as no relevant acts (such as reproduction, or communication to the public) will 'occur' in the Member State of temporary presence.[65] According to recital 21,

60 G. Mazziotti and F. Simonelli, 'Regulation on "cross-border portability" of online content services: Roaming for Netflix or the end of copyright territoriality?', CEPS Commentary, 15 February 2016, https://www.ceps.eu/publications/regulation-%E2%80%98cross-border-portability%E2%80%99-online-content-services-roaming-netflix-or-end.

61 BEUC, 'Proposal for a Regulation on cross-border portability of online content: BEUC position', 2016, http://www.beuc.eu/publications/beuc-x-2016-022_are_proposal_for_a_regulation_on_ensuring_cross-border_portability_of_content_services.pdf.

62 *Euractiv*, 'Ansip fires back against member states' push to limit digital content portability', 15 April 2016, http://www.euractiv.com/section/digital/news/ansip-fires-back-against-member-states-push-to-limit-digital-content-portability/.

63 G. Mazziotti and F. Simonelli, 'Regulation on "cross-border portability" of online content services: Roaming for Netflix or the end of copyright territoriality?', CEPS Commentary, 15 February 2016, https://www.ceps.eu/publications/regulation-%E2%80%98cross-border-portability%E2%80%99-online-content-services-roaming-netflix-or-end.

64 I.e. Directive 96/9/EC, Directive 2001/29/EC, Directive 2006/115/EC, Directive 2009/24, see n 36 above.

65 D. Visser and P. Kreijger, 'Online diensten over de grens', *Nederlands Tijdschrift voor Europees Recht* 2016, no. 2, 64.

the providers will be deemed to carry out such acts on the basis of the respective authorisations from the right-holders concerned in the Member State of residence. As such, according to Visser and Kreijger, the legal fiction does not impinge upon the principle of territoriality, as it does not preclude right-holders from licensing content on a territorial basis and, hence, offering subscriptions to consumers on the basis of their residence.[66] However, Mazziotti and Simonelli argue that the legal fiction *does* restrict the effect of the territoriality principle, as the territorial scope of licences is expanded.[67]

9. CONTRACTS

A final key element of the POSCR relates to the contracts between right-holders and service providers, on the one hand, and contracts between service providers and subscribers, on the other hand. According to Article 5(1) any contractual provision in such contracts which are contrary to Article 3 (obligation to ensure cross-portability) and Article 4 (localisation in the Member State of residence) are unenforceable. Recital 22 emphasises that service providers should not be liable for infringement of any contractual provisions contrary to the obligation to enable their subscribers to access their content in the Member States of their temporary residence. However, right-holders may require that the service provider uses effective means to verify that the online content service is provided in conformity with the conditions provided for in Article 3.[68] Article 5(2) states that those means must be reasonable and not go beyond what is necessary in order to achieve their purpose. Recital 23 lists a number of possible measures that providers could be asked to undertake, such as sampling of IP addresses, providing transparent information to individuals about methods used for verification and its purposes, as well as adopting appropriate security measures. The required proportionality of the measures could entail that the Member State where the user resides is identified, rather than determining the precise location of the subscriber, and that authentication, instead of identification, may be sufficient.[69] Overall, Article 5 leaves much leeway for concrete implementation. This raises concerns for right-holders (see below) and causes uncertainty for online content service providers. Should they, for instance, verify the location

---

66 D. Visser and P. Kreijger, 'Online diensten over de grens', *Nederlands Tijdschrift voor Europees Recht* 2016, no. 2, 64.

67 G. Mazziotti and F. Simonelli, 'Regulation on "cross-border portability" of online content services: Roaming for Netflix or the end of copyright territoriality?', CEPS Commentary, 15 February 2016, https://www.ceps.eu/publications/regulation-%E2%80%98cross-border-portability%E2%80%99-online-content-services-roaming-netflix-or-end.

68 Article 5(2) POSCR.

69 POSCR, recital 23.

at regular intervals in order to ascertain whether the subscriber is still in the Member State of temporary presence, or back home again, in his or her Member State of residence?[70] From the Questions and Answers Fact Sheet that was published by the European Commission at the time of the announcement of the POSCR, it seemed that this could be a measure that right holders could expect a service provider to take.[71]

Given that licensing contracts are often concluded for long periods,[72] the Commission considered it necessary to enable the retroactive application of the Regulation to existing contracts and rights acquired before its entry into force. This is laid down in Article 7 of the POSCR, in order to ensure that EU consumers will benefit from the cross-portability rules on 'an equal basis in time and without undue delay' (also if they have a long-term or open-ended subscription),[73] and that service providers can operate in a level playing-field and can offer portability for their entire content catalogue.[74] Existing contracts will thus not have to be renegotiated.

10. PROTECTION OF PERSONAL DATA AND OTHER RIGHTS

Article 6 asserts, rather obviously, that when personal data are processed for the purposes of the regulation, for instance in the context of the verification referred to by Article 5(2), this should be done in compliance with the EU legislative framework with regard to data protection, more specifically Directives 95/46/EC[75] and 2002/58/EC.[76,77]

---

70 D. Visser and P. Kreijger, 'Online diensten over de grens', *Nederlands Tijdschrift voor Europees Recht* 2016, no. 2, 66.

71 European Commission, Fact Sheet: Making EU copyright rules fit for the digitale age: Questions & Answers, 9 December 2015, http://europa.eu/rapid/press-release_MEMO-15-6262_en.htm.

72 POSCR, recital 26.

73 BEUC, 'Proposal for a Regulation on cross-border portability of online content: BEUC position', 2016, http://www.beuc.eu/publications/beuc-x-2016-022_are_proposal_for_a_regulation_on_ensuring_cross-border_portability_of_content_services.pdf.

74 PSCOR, recital 26.

75 Directive 95/46/EC of the European Parliament and of the Council of 24 October 1995 on the protection of individuals with regard to the processing of personal data and on the free movement of such data, *OJ* L 281, 23.11.1995, 31–50.

76 Directive 2002/58/EC of the European Parliament and of the Council of 12 July 2002 concerning the processing of personal data and the protection of privacy in the electronic communications sector (Directive on privacy and electronic communications), *OJ* L 201, 31.07.2002, 37.

77 Note that Directive 95/46/EC will be replaced by the Regulation on the protection of natural persons with regard to the processing of personal data and on the free movement of such data, and repealing Directive 95/46/EC (General Data Protection Regulation) in the course of 2018.

Recital 24 confirms that the regulation should be interpreted and applied in accordance with the rights to respect for private and family life and to protection of personal data, freedom of expression and freedom to conduct a business, as laid down in the Charter of Fundamental Rights of the EU.

11. APPLICATION

Article 8 POSCR indicates that the Regulation will apply from six months following its publication. This six-month period should allow right-holders and service providers to make the necessary arrangements to adjust to the new cross-portability rules.[78]

12. ASSESSMENT OF THE PROPOSAL

The POSCR has been argued to be a relatively 'light' proposal.[79] Although it is true that the proposal does not depart from the principle of territoriality,[80] which remains very important in the domain of copyright and related rights and especially in the audiovisual and sports content sector, the text does contain a certain number of elements which raise questions and concerns for right-holders, online content service providers and consumers.

Right-holders fear that the lack of precise definitions and the vagueness of certain concepts,[81] such as 'temporary presence', could lead to potential abuses or circumvention of the rules.[82] The Society of Audiovisual Authors (SAA) argues that in order to prevent such circumvention, the country of residence

78 POSCR, recital 27.

79 D. Visser and P. Kreijger, 'Online diensten over de grens', *Nederlands Tijdschrift voor Europees Recht* 2016, no. 2, 66.

80 In its 2016 Resolution, the European Parliament welcomed the POSCR and stressed that 'there is no contradiction between the principle of territoriality and measures to remove barriers to portability of content': European Parliament, Resolution Towards a Digital Single Market Act, 2015/2147(INI), 19 January 2016, http://www.europarl.europa.eu/sides/getDoc.do?pubRef=-//EP//TEXT+TA+P8-TA-2016-0009+0+DOC+XML+V0//EN.

81 T. Madiega, 'European Parliamentary Research Service Briefing EU legislation in progress: Cross-border portability of online content services', February 2016, https://epthinktank.eu/2016/02/20/cross-border-portability-of-online-content-services-eu-legislation-in-progress/, 9; Vlaams Parlement, Schriftelijke vraag nr. 106 van Lionel Bajart aan Sven Gatz: Vlaams Minister van Cultuur, Media, Jeugd en Brussel, 15 January 2016, http://docs.vlaamsparlement.be/pfile?id=1158288.

82 For instance: a consumer succeeds in pretending that he is a resident of Member State A, in which an online content service provider offers a substantially cheaper subscription than in Member State B, and then benefits, through the application of the cross-portability rules, from access to the content in Member State B where he is actually spending most of his time.

must be verified.[83] In the POSCR, in Article 5(2), the burden of negotiating whether effective means for verification should be used by content providers is put on the right-holders. The SAA argues that instead, an obligation to verify the country of residence of a subscriber should be imposed on online content service providers.[84] In addition, the lack of specification with regard to the methods and the information that may be used for verification raises questions. Are the indicators that are mentioned in recital 17 the only ones that could be used or could other information be considered, such as banking details?[85] Mazziotti and Simonelli argue that depending on which indicators are used, consumers that own a second home in another Member State or even just a bank account (for instance, expats) would be able to surreptitiously benefit from the cross-border portability rules.[86] Will providers choose the methods themselves, and if so, will this not lead to a lack of uniformity and, consequently, differing treatment of consumers?[87] Moreover, will such methods also ensure that subscriptions are not shared across borders (e.g. by limiting the number and location of simultaneous connections)?[88] In essence, right-holders are concerned that a loose interpretation of the regulation would lead to the potential 'erosion' of the territoriality principle, which could then lead to a lower remuneration for

---

83 Society of Audiovisual Authors, 'EC Proposal for a Regulation on cross-border portability of online content services in the internal market SAA comments', March 2016, http://www.saa-authors.eu/dbfiles/mfile/8800/8805/SAA_position_paper_cross_border_portability_regulation_21.3.2016.pdf. Also: G. Mazziotti and F. Simonelli, 'Regulation on "cross-border portability" of online content services: Roaming for Netflix or the end of copyright territoriality?', CEPS Commentary, 15 February 2016, https://www.ceps.eu/publications/regulation-%E2%80%98cross-border-portability%E2%80%99-online-content-services-roaming-netflix-or-end.

84 Society of Audiovisual Authors, 'EC Proposal for a Regulation on cross-border portability of online content services in the internal market SAA comments', March 2016, http://www.saa-authors.eu/dbfiles/mfile/8800/8805/SAA_position_paper_cross_border_portability_regulation_21.3.2016.pdf: the SAA proposes to add a fourth paragraph to Article 3 which states 'the provider shall make use of effective means in order to verify the Member State of residence of a subscriber and its temporary presence in another Member State when accessing the service'.

85 The Impact Assessment seems to confirm that this is the case: POSCR Impact Assessment, 40.

86 G. Mazziotti and F. Simonelli, 'Regulation on "cross-border portability" of online content services: Roaming for Netflix or the end of copyright territoriality?', CEPS Commentary, 15 February 2016, https://www.ceps.eu/publications/regulation-%E2%80%98cross-border-portability%E2%80%99-online-content-services-roaming-netflix-or-end.

87 Society of Audiovisual Authors, 'EC Proposal for a Regulation on cross-border portability of online content services in the internal market SAA comments', March 2016, http://www.saa-authors.eu/dbfiles/mfile/8800/8805/SAA_position_paper_cross_border_portability_regulation_21.3.2016.pdf.

88 T. Madiega, 'European Parliamentary Research Service Briefing EU legislation in progress: Cross-border portability of online content services', February 2016, https://epthinktank.eu/2016/02/20/cross-border-portability-of-online-content-services-eu-legislation-in-progress/, 9.

the licensing of their rights.[89] However, Visser and Kreijger contend that it remains possible to factor in the number of users and tailor the remuneration to that number of users at the moment of licensing, as the regulation only limits the exercise of their rights in relation to consumers who already have a subscription allowing them legitimately to access the content in their Member State of residence.[90]

Online content service providers would benefit from a loose interpretation of the notion of 'temporary presence', not only to attract more subscribers,[91] but also because recurrent monitoring of the location of users could require more effort and costs. The Impact Assessment includes a detailed analysis of the costs that providers (who either offer their service against payment, or for free provided that they verify the consumers' Member State of residence (see above)) will (possibly) incur. The main costs for online service providers are related to the verification measures. If geo-blocking is already used, the cross-portability rules will necessitate a re-configuration from a geo-blocking approach to a temporary access approach. According to the Commission, this will only result in marginal administrative costs. Furthermore, the Impact Assessment states that the vast majority of affected service providers already have authentication systems (such as checking IP addresses against national registries, or using credit card information or geolocation of devices) in place.[92] The Commission did not succeed in obtaining information in order to quantify the costs of implementation for providers who would need to install such measures, but argues that IP address authentication entails a 'relatively low marginal cost'.[93] However, given the concerns of right-holders related to potential abuses or circumvention of the rules, it does not seem far-fetched that right-holders will (on the basis of Article 5(2) POSCR) demand more accurate and costly methods of authentication.[94] However, according to the Impact Assessment, costs 'are not expected to be significant and could be absorbed in the routine software maintenance costs of service providers'.[95] Additional (potential) costs for

89 G. Mazziotti and F. Simonelli, 'Regulation on "cross-border portability" of online content services: Roaming for Netflix or the end of copyright territoriality?', CEPS Commentary, 15 February 2016, https://www.ceps.eu/publications/regulation-%E2%80%98cross-border-portability%E2%80%99-online-content-services-roaming-netflix-or-end.

90 D. Visser and P. Kreijger, 'Online diensten over de grens', *Nederlands Tijdschrift voor Europees Recht* 2016, no. 2, 65.

91 G. Mazziotti and F. Simonelli, 'Regulation on "cross-border portability" of online content services: Roaming for Netflix or the end of copyright territoriality?', CEPS Commentary, 15 February 2016, https://www.ceps.eu/publications/regulation-%E2%80%98cross-border-portability%E2%80%99-online-content-services-roaming-netflix-or-end.

92 POSCR Impact Assessment, 40.

93 POSCR Impact Assessment, 40.

94 POSCR Impact Assessment, 40.

95 POSCR Impact Assessment, 41.

providers could relate to reviewing the terms of use of their services, as well as costs related to network infrastructure, if they would opt to offer the same quality of delivery to users that are temporarily present in another Member State, for instance for reputational reasons.[96] In any case, for small online content service providers (and especially those who offer their services for 'free') the (potential) costs will have a more significant impact than for large players.

Consumers are the main beneficiaries of the regulation,[97] and especially those who spend significant time in other Member States would prefer a flexible interpretation of 'temporary presence'. Consumer organisations stress that the methods that are used to verify the residence of subscribers should not be too privacy-invasive, or too burdensome for those subscribers.[98] Constant tracking of consumers' activities, for instance, is considered disproportionate. This was also addressed in the Impact Assessment, in which it was stated that the verification of the temporary presence in another Member State does not require the permanent control of location, only an 'occasional check' as to in which Member State the consumer is present.[99] In any case, more clarity on the measures which could or should be used would also be beneficial for consumers. Another relevant question for consumers is whether the regulation will lead to higher prices for online digital content, because right-holders would ask for a higher remuneration for their rights or because online content service providers would set higher subscription fees to compensate for their investment in the verification measures. According to the Commission's Impact Assessment, increases in licence fees would be marginal, as portability could not be seen as an additional or optional functionality and hence, a competitive advantage, due to the fact that it is the result of an obligation.[100] This, however, will largely depend on the bargaining position of right-holders. Especially negotiating with large (globally operating) online content service providers may be tough. Whether online content service providers will transfer the costs to consumers will likely depend on the extent of the investment in effective means that will be required by right-holders (see above). Slight increases in subscription fees are thus within the bounds of possibility.

---

96 POSCR Impact Assessment, 42.

97 P. Malaquias, 'The Proposal for a Regulation on cross-border portability of online content', 26 February 2016, https://www.law.kuleuven.be/citip/blog/the-proposal-for-a-regulation-on-cross-border-portability-of-online-content/.

98 BEUC, 'Proposal for a Regulation on cross-border portability of online content: BEUC position', 2016, http://www.beuc.eu/publications/beuc-x-2016-022_are_proposal_for_a_regulation_on_ensuring_cross-border_portability_of_content_services.pdf. Also: BEUC, 'Portability of content in the European Union: Consumer recommendations for the trilogue negotiations', 3 February 2017, http://www.beuc.eu/publications/beuc-x-2017-009_dmafsi_portability_-_beuc_demands_for_trilogue_negotiations.pdf.

99 POSCR Impact Assessment, 36, fn 121.

100 POSCR Impact Assessment, 37–38.

13. RECENT DEVELOPMENTS

In April 2016, a Dutch Council Presidency compromise proposal was made public.[101] This version of the text was drafted for discussions within the Working Party on Intellectual Property of the EU Council. It contains substantial changes to the original POSCR as proposed by the Commission. The recitals contain a number of clarifications, such as the fact that the payment of a mandatory fee (e.g. a broadcasting licence fee) should not be regarded as a payment of money for receiving an online content service.[102] In addition, given the concerns regarding the notion of 'temporary presence' (above), it could be expected that amendments would be made to the definitions. Yet, the new proposal does not modify the definition of 'temporarily present'. Instead, the notion of the 'Member State of residence' is slightly adapted and now reads 'the Member State, established on the basis of Article 3B, where the subscriber has his or her actual and stable residence to which he or she returns regularly'.[103]

One of the most noteworthy changes to the original POSCR relates to the fact that providers of online content services which are provided *without payment* of money are now given the *option* to be included in the scope of the Regulation, because they 'normally do not verify the Member State of residence of their subscribers' and hence their inclusion would 'involve disproportionate costs'.[104] If they do opt to be included they should comply with the provisions of the Regulation in the same way as providers who offer services against payment, and inform subscribers thereof.[105] Due to this change of approach, the definition of 'online content service' (Article 2(e)) no longer refers to this element of 'a service being offered against or without payment to a subscriber'.[106]

A second significant change is that a new article 3B now contains an *obligation* for online content service providers to use effective means in order to verify the Member State of residence, unless otherwise expressly agreed with right-holders. This shifts the burden from those right-holders, who under

101 Council of the European Union, Proposal for a Regulation on ensuring the cross-border portability of online content services in the Internal Market – Presidency Compromise Proposal, 7891/16, 13 April 2016, http://data.consilium.europa.eu/doc/document/ST-7891-2016-INIT/en/pdf (hereinafter: POSCR Presidency Compromise Proposal).

102 POSCR Presidency Compromise Proposal, recital 16.

103 Article 2(c) POSCR Presidency Compromise Proposal.

104 POSCR Presidency Compromise Proposal, recital 17.

105 Article 3A and recital 17 POSCR Presidency Compromise Proposal.

106 The new version of this definition is limited to a 'service as defined by Articles 56 and 57 of the Treaty on the Functioning of the European Union that a service provider is lawfully providing to a subscriber in the latter's Member State of residence on agreed terms, online and on a portable basis and which is: (i) an audiovisual media service within the meaning of Directive 2010/13/EU, or (ii) a service the main feature of which is the provision of access to and use of works, other protected subject matter or transmissions of broadcasting organisations, whether in a linear or an on-demand manner'.

Article 5(2) POSCR were expected to take the initiative to require the use of effective means, to the providers. In order to guarantee legal certainty,[107] Article 3B(2) also includes a list of verification means that service providers should rely on to establish the Member State of residence:

(a) an identity card or any other valid document confirming subscriber's Member State of residence;
(b) the billing address or the postal address of the subscriber;
(c) bank details such as bank account, local credit or debit card of the subscriber;
(d) the place of installation of a set top box or a similar device used for supply of services to the subscriber;
(e) the subscriber being a party to a contract for internet or telephone connection in the Member State;
(f) the subscriber paying a licence fee for other services provided in the Member State, such as public service broadcasting;
(g) sampling or periodic checking of Internet Protocol (IP) address to identify the Member State where the subscriber accesses and uses the online content service or identifying that Member State by other means of geolocation;
(h) a declaration by the subscriber on their Member State of residence;
(i) registration on electoral rolls, if publicly available;
(j) the payment of local/poll taxes, if publicly available.[108]

The lack of such a list was indeed an often heard concern since the publication of the POSCR. However, Article 3B(3) still leaves the possibility for providers and right-holders to agree on other means, not included in the list, but which are in accordance with Article 3B(1). Furthermore, Article 3B(4) stipulates that providers are entitled to request the necessary information from the subscriber. If the subscriber does not offer this information, resulting in the impossibility of verifying his or her location, the provider will not be required to provide the subscriber who is temporarily present in another Member State with access to and use of the content, for as long as the subscriber's Member State of residence cannot be verified. Given the addition of Article 3B, the Presidency Compromise Proposal replaces the former Article 5(2) with a new paragraph which specifies that the Regulation will apply irrespective of the law applicable to contracts between providers and right-holders and contracts between providers and subscribers.[109]

---

107 POSCR Presidency Compromise Proposal, recital 23.

108 According to Article 3B(1a) '[u]nless the Member State of residence can be sufficiently established on the basis of a single verification means, the provider of an online content service shall rely on a combination of means'.

109 Recital 22 POSCR Presidency Compromise Proposal clarifies that providers and right-holders should not be allowed to circumvent the application of the Regulation by choosing the law of a non-member country as the law applicable to contracts between them or to contracts between providers and subscribers.

On 13 May 2016, a broad agreement was reached on this Presidency compromise proposal.[110] At that time, two outstanding issues remained: the notion of temporary presence and the verification waiver by right-holders.

On 7 February 2017, an overall compromise package was agreed upon in the trilogue.[111] The text builds on the POSCR Presidency Compromise Proposal, keeping the fundamental principles proposed therein (obligation in case of services against payment, option in case of services without payment, obligation to verify Member State of residence and list of means of verification) intact. Noteworthy changes are related to the definitions of 'Member State of residence' ('the Member State, determined on the basis of Article 3a, where the subscriber had his or her actual and stable residence', Article 2(c)) and 'temporarily present in a Member State' ('the presence of a subscriber in a Member State other than his or her Member State of residence for a limited period of time', Article 2(d)), the integration of stronger data protection safeguards (Article 6) and the nine-month time frame for applicability (Article 8). Certain articles contain clarifications (for instance, that no additional charges should be imposed on subscribers, Article 3(1a); or that the Member State of residence should be verified at the conclusion and the renewal of a contract and can be repeated in case of reasonable doubts, Article 3A(1) and (2)). Article 3A(4) confirms the possibility of a verification waiver by right-holders. Article 7(2) contains an obligation to verify the Member State of residence of subscribers who concluded contracts for the provision of online content services before the date of application of the Regulation.

The next step in the adoption process is a formal approval of the final text by the Council of the EU and the European Parliament.

14. CONCLUSION

At first sight, the POSCR seems to yield advantages for all parties involved. Consumers will have uninterrupted access to their content when travelling to other Member States. Right-holders will (possibly) benefit from the fact that increased legitimate access to content will decrease the use of technical means, such as virtual private networks (VPNs), to bypass current territorial

110 Council of the European Union, Proposal for a Regulation on ensuring the cross-border portability of online content services in the Internal Market – General approach, 8939/16, 18 May 2016, http://data.consilium.europa.eu/doc/document/ST-8939-2016-INIT/en/pdf.

111 Council of the European Union, Proposal for a Regulation on ensuring the cross-border portability of online content services in the Internal Market – Analysis of the final compromise text with a view to agreement, 6091/17, 13 February 2017, http://data.consilium.europa.eu/doc/document/ST-6091-2017-INIT/en/pdf.

restrictions,[112] while still being able to enter into territorial, exclusive licensing agreements. Online content service providers will be able to offer a better service to their subscribers, (possibly) attracting new subscribers who value the functionality of cross-border portability, without incurring significant additional costs. However, as always, the devil will be in the implementation. Right-holders, for instance, are still concerned about possible abuses, because the list of verification means contain means that do not guarantee residency on their own, and because of the market power of large providers of services who may pressure right-holders into waiving the verification.[113] In order for the interests of all stakeholders to be taken to heart in achieving the Digital Single Market Strategy, with particular attention to the promotion of diversity and creativity and support for European players, large and small, the assessment of the application of the Regulation in the light of legal, technological and economic developments, as foreseen in Article 7A of the final text, will be crucial.

---

112 G. Petteri, 'The plan for a digital Single Market in Europe and reforming EU copyright rules to develop a market-oriented approach to reduce infringement on the internet', *European Intellectual Property Review* 2016, 38(1), 55; T. Madiega, 'European Parliamentary Research Service Briefing EU legislation in progress: Cross-border portability of online content services', February 2016, https://epthinktank.eu/2016/02/20/cross-border-portability-of-online-content-services-eu-legislation-in-progress/, 5.

113 Society of Audiovisual Authors, Portability Regulation – Audiovisual authors regret holes in final agreement, 20 February 2017, http://www.saa-authors.eu/en/news/339-portability-regulation---audiovisual-authors-regret-holes-in-final-agreement.

PART IV

CONCLUSION

THE NEW PROPOSALS FOR DIRECTIVES CONCERNING DIGITAL CONTENT AND ONLINE/DISTANCE SALES

What Impact on Consumer Protection?

Gert Straetmans and Shana Meys

1. INTRODUCTION

For the last decade European consumer law has been characterised by an increasing number of full, total or maximum harmonisation measures. The proposals for directives which are the subject of this chapter also introduce fully harmonised standards.

The preference for fully harmonised (minimal) standards of consumer protection fits well into the confidence-building policy of the European legislature, especially in fields which were formerly subject to minimum harmonisation. It also complements the Court of Justice's efforts to interpret existing (minimum) harmonisation directives concerning consumer contracts so as to reduce national divergences.[1]

This creeping evolution towards minimal uniform standards became already apparent in a number of consumer contract directives, which contained conflict of laws rules limiting the choice for and application of the law of a third country provided the contract has a close link/connection with the territory of one or more Member States.[2] The underlying reasons are well known: assuring consumers are confident in the legal environment in other Member States so that they will shop there, and furthermore encouraging under-confident businessmen to overcome their reluctance to risk doing business in other states if the legal regimes are not identical.[3] This legislative technique pays off best in those areas in which freedom of contract alone is incapable of guaranteeing informed decisions.[4]

---

1 See on this point, G. Howells, 'The Rise of European Consumer Law – Whither National Consumer Law?', *Sydney Law Review*, 2006, vol. 28, 73–77. See also G. Straetmans, 'The consumer concept in EC law' in J. Meeusen, M. Pertegás and G. Straetmans (eds.), *Enforcement of international contracts in the European Union*, Antwerp-Oxford-New York, Intersentia, 2004, 295–322.

2 E.g. Article 6(2) of Directive 93/13. Some authors called the introduction of such unilateral private international law rules in directives 'einer ubertriebenen Neigung zur Sicherung der EG-Standards' [an exaggerated tendency to secure EU standards], see A. Junker, 'Vom Citoyen zum Consommateur', *IPRax.*, 1998, para. 2, 74. See also Article 9 of the Time-share Directive (if the immovable property concerned is situated within the territory of a Member State), Article 12(2) of the Directive on the protection of consumers in respect of distance contracts, Article 7(2) of the sale of consumer goods and associated guarantees Directive, and on their relation with Article 5 of the Rome Convention, see G. Fischer, 'Das Kollisionsrecht der Verbraucherverträge jenseits von Art. 5 EVÜ' in U. Hübner and W. Ebke (eds.), *Festschrift für Bernhard Grossfeld zum 65.Geburtstag*, Heidelberg, Verlag Recht und Wirtschaft, 1999, 280 ff. See also Article 12, §2 of Directive 2002/65 concerning the distance marketing of consumer financial products, and about this provision, G. Straetmans, 'Richtlijn 2002/65 betreffende de verkoop op afstand van financiële diensten aan consumenten', *D.C.C.R.* 2003, nr. 59, 24–28. Whether these provisions should be regarded as internationally mandatory rules or merely as specific purpose mandatory rules of substantive law which call for an application alongside the applicable conflicts provisions, is further discussed in M. Fallon and S. Francq, 'Towards internationally mandatory directives for consumer contracts' in J. Basedow (ed.), *Private law in the international arena – Liber amicorum Kurt Siehr*, The Hague, T.M.C. Asser Press, 2000, 158. In the Ingmar-case, the Court even applied mandatory provisions of Directive 86/653 which were not endowed with a conflict of law dimension to an agency contract which had a relevant link with the Community, *alongside the validly chosen law of a third country*. This was of importance in the consumer contract field as well, especially for the directives concerning doorstep selling, package travel and consumer credit. See on this point the critical comments by W.-H. Roth, 'Comments on Ingmar', *C.M.L.Rev.*, 2002, 374–83.

3 See G. Howells, 'The Rise of European Consumer Law – Whither National Consumer Law?', *Sydney Law Review*, 2006, vol. 28, 67 and 71. See also N. Reich, 'Protection of Consumer's Economic Interests by EC Contract Law', *Sydney Law Review*, 2006, vol. 28, 39.

4 In favour of total harmonisation, J. Drexl, 'Continuing Contract Law Harmonisation under the White Paper of 1985 – Partly with Modifications' in S. Grundman and J. Stuyck (eds.), *SECOLA Conference*, Leuven, 2001, 15. See also J. Basedow, 'A Common Contract Law for the Common Market', *C.M.L.Rev.*, 1996, vol. 33, 1169, who also argued that even a general 'European contract law would serve the purposes of the internal market well and thereby

In the same vein and in contrast with the minimum harmonisation character of the Consumer Sales Directive, the new proposals for directives concerning the supply of digital content and online and other distance sales of goods aim at the adoption of sets of uniform minimal standards.[5] The proposals must be seen as a further step towards the creation of an internal market for digital content and services.[6] Together with the proposal for a regulation on ensuring the cross-border portability of online content services in the internal market, the proposals for directives form one set of new rules.

According to the European Commission, the incoherence between the Member States leads to uncertainty both by businessman and consumers as to the applicable legal framework. Due to the complexity of this legal framework, businesses face additional costs when examining and adapting their contracts to specific mandatory rules, which make them reluctant to offer their goods and services across the internal market. Conversely, consumers lack certainty about their key contractual rights and thus miss opportunities. The purpose of the proposals is to foster cross-border trade by eliminating its barriers. Both traders and consumers should have a stable contract law environment, which will reduce the costs and increase the consumer trust. Therefore the Commission considers a shift from a minimum level of protection to fully harmonised rules necessary.[7]

A thorough evaluation of the proposals' impact on the existing level of consumer protection necessitates a brief account of the underlying objectives of both proposals for directives.[8] Section 2 of this chapter will therefore briefly focus on the objectives of the two proposals for directives. In Section 3 the level

fall into the competence of the Community because: it would create uniform conditions for marketing in Europe, would avoid the risk of choosing or being submitted to an unknown legal order, and would save transaction costs for parties contracting across borders'.

5 This is a set of totally harmonised rules which offers the confident consumer adequate protection, no matter where goods are purchased within the Community. To put it another way: a maximum standard of protection for all internal market consumers. Given the total harmonisation approach, uniform European rules will supersede conflicting national law, whereas unilateral scope rules in the field of consumer contract law secure a minimum set of harmonised rules which supersedes conflicting third country laws.

6 See also the Digital Single Market Strategy, adopted by the European Commission in 2015; http://ec.europa.eu/priorities/digital-single-market.

7 See Article 4 of the Proposal for a directive of the European Parliament and of the Council on certain aspects concerning contracts for the supply of digital content, COM(2015) 634 and Article 3 of the Proposal for a directive of the European Parliament and of the Council on certain aspects concerning contracts for the online and other distance sales of goods, COM(2015) 635: 'Member states shall not maintain or introduce provisions diverging from those laid down in this Directive including more or less stringent provisions to ensure a different level of consumer protection'. Full harmonisation 'precludes member states, within its scope of application, from providing any further formal or substantive requirements', see Recital 9 Proposal for a directive of the European Parliament and of the Council on certain aspects concerning contracts for the supply of digital content, COM(2015) 634.

8 An analysis of the proposal for a Regulation on cross-border portability of online content services and its impact on consumer protection will be the subject of another chapter in this volume. See particularly the chapter by E. Lievens.

of consumer protection of the constitutive aspects of the proposed directives will be assessed in the light of the existing Belgian legislation. Subsequently the precise scope of both proposals (Section 3.1), the new rules on conformity of the goods (Section 3.2), the rules on remedies (Section 3.3), the new provisions concerning time limits (Section 3.4) and commercial guarantees (Section 3.5), the right of redress (Section 3.6) and the right to terminate long-term contracts (Section 3.7) will be dealt with. In Section 4 the focus shifts to the European perspective. This section will take the Belgian law based analyses as a starting point for the assessment, from a European perspective, of the level of consumer protection. The analysis will be complemented with comparisons of the proposals for directives with the proposal for a Regulation on a Common European Sales Law and with some aspects of neighbouring national legal orders. A concluding Section 6 will bring all relevant findings together.

2. KEY OBJECTIVES OF THE PROPOSALS FOR DIRECTIVES

The two proposals for directives concerning the supply of digital content and online sales of goods will have a major impact on the existing Directive 1999/44/EC on certain aspects of the sale of consumer goods and associated guarantees (the Consumer Sales Directive or CSD),[9] which will be partly replaced by the new rules. As mentioned above the CSD introduced a system based on minimum harmonisation that allows Member States to adopt or retain legislation which provides a higher level of consumer protection.[10] In consequence thereof Member States made use of their discretion and went beyond the harmonised standards, introducing rules that ensure a higher level of consumer protection. As a result consumer contract law in the Member States remained to a significant extent divergent even with regard to key issues such as the absence or existence of a hierarchy of remedies, the period of the legal guarantee, the period of the reversal of the burden of proof and the notification of the defect to the seller.[11]

The finding that national legislation concerning online and other distance sales of goods is to a great extent fragmented lies at the core of the new legislative initiatives. Indeed, the findings that divergent rules create obstacles to trade and to the objective to achieve a genuine digital market strengthened the Commission

---

9 Directive 1999/44/EC of 25 May 1999 on certain aspects of the sale of consumer goods and associated guarantees, *OJ* L 171/12 (hereafter: Consumer Sales Directive).

10 Article 8 Consumer Sales Directive.

11 Recital 5 Proposal for a directive of the European Parliament and of the Council on certain aspects concerning contracts for the online and other distance sales of goods, COM(2015) 635. For an overview, see: C. Twigg-Flesner, 'Consumer Sales Directive (99/44)' in H. Schulte-Nölke, C. Twigg-Flesner and M. Ebers (eds.), *EC Consumer Law Compendium. The Consumer Acquis and its transposition in the Member States*, Munich, Sellier, 2008, 407–51.

in its belief that a high level of consumer protection and full harmonisation of certain key aspects concerning contracts for the sale of goods is the only way forward.[12] Hence, the proposals introduce fully harmonised rules on conformity requirements, on remedies available to consumers for lack of conformity of the goods with the contract and on the modalities for their exercise.[13]

Furthermore, the proposal concerning contracts for the supply of digital content aims to fill in a lacuna. Although the Consumer Rights Directive harmonised certain rules for the supply of digital content, they were mainly restricted to pre-contractual information requirements and the right of withdrawal. To date a clear overall contractual framework for digital content is missing and the differences in national legislation resulting therefrom are creating new obstacles to trade which the new proposal seeks to remove.[14] According to the European Commission there is a pressing need to legislate at EU level to fill this current legal gap in the *consumer acquis* as consumers also will benefit from fully harmonised rights for digital content at a high level of protection.[15] As a result, the new proposal on digital content includes rules on some key aspects like the conformity of the digital content, the remedies available to consumers in cases of lack of conformity of digital content with the contract, etc.

More generally the European Commission is convinced that these sets of fully harmonised rules will at least maintain, and in a number of cases significantly improve, the level of protection that consumers enjoy under the existing Consumer Sales Directive.[16]

This prognosis of the European Commission will be assessed hereafter from both a Belgian and a European perspective. In this analysis the fully harmonised rules of the Consumer Rights Directive[17] on pre-contractual information requirements, the right of withdrawal, delivery conditions and the passing of risk[18] will only be taken into account where they are relevant. The European

12 Recital 2 Proposal for a directive of the European Parliament and of the Council on certain aspects concerning contracts for the online and other distance sales of goods, COM(2015) 635.

13 Recital 11 Proposal for a directive of the European Parliament and of the Council on certain aspects concerning contracts for the online and other distance sales of goods, COM(2015) 635.

14 Recital 3 Proposal for a directive of the European Parliament and of the Council on certain aspects concerning contracts for the supply of digital content, COM(2015) 634.

15 Recital 2 Proposal for a directive of the European Parliament and of the Council on certain aspects concerning contracts for the supply of digital content, COM(2015) 634.

16 Proposal for a directive of the European Parliament and of the Council on certain aspects concerning contracts for the online and other distance sales of goods, COM(2015) 635, 6. See also Recital 2 Proposal for a directive of the European Parliament and of the Council on certain aspects concerning contracts for the supply of digital content, COM(2015) 634.

17 Proposal for a directive on consumer rights of the Commission, 8 October 2008, COM(2008) 614.

18 See C. Twigg-Flesner, 'The Impact of the Consumer Rights Directive (2011/83/EU) on Consumer Sales Contracts', *RAE* 2012, (563) 566; K. Tonner, 'The Consumer Rights

analysis will take account of the relevant rules of the proposal for a Regulation on a Common European Sales Law,[19] since that proposal inspired to a great extent the current proposals for directives after it had been withdrawn by the European Commission at the end of 2014.

3. ANALYSIS FROM A BELGIAN PERSPECTIVE

The Consumer Sales Directive has been implemented in 2004 by the Belgian Consumer Sales Act: 'Wet van 1 september 2004 betreffende de bescherming van de consumenten bij verkoop van consumptiegoederen',[20] which also inserted a new section on consumer sales (Articles 1649*bis*–1649*octies*) into the Belgian Civil Code (CC). Together with the new Article 1604 CC that requires the seller to deliver the goods in conformity with the contract, the new Articles 1649*bis*–1649*octies* CC constitute a literal transposition of the CSD.

Before examining the substantive provisions of the proposed directives, first their scope of application will be compared with that of the existing Belgian legislation to set out relevant differences.

3.1. SCOPE OF APPLICATION

3.1.1. Contracts for the Sale of Consumer Goods

The Consumer Sales Act applies to contracts for the sale of consumer goods by a seller to a consumer. Goods are defined in Article 1649*bis* CC as 'any tangible

---

Directive and its impact on internet and other distance consumer contracts' in N. Reich, H. Micklitz, P. Rott and K. Tonner (eds.), *European Consumer Law*, Cambridge, Intersentia, 2014, (393) 409.

19 Proposal for a Regulation of the European Parliament and of the Council on a Common European Sales Law, COM(2011) 635. See: I. Claeys and R. Feltkamp (eds.), *The Draft Common European Sales Law: Towards an Alternative Sales Law? A Belgian Perspective*, Antwerp, Intersentia, 2013. See also M.B.M. Loos, 'Herziening van het Europese consumentenrecht', *NTER* 2008, 29–39 and 74–83; G. Howells and R. Schulze, 'Overview of the Proposed Consumer Rights Directive' in G. Howells and R. Schulze (eds.), *Modernising and Harmonising Consumer Contract Law*, Munich, Sellier, 2009, 3–25 and more specific for consumer sales: C. Twigg-Flesner, 'Fit for Purpose? The Proposals on Sales' in G. Howells and R. Schulze (eds.), *Modernising and Harmonising Consumer Contract Law*, Munich, Sellier, 2009, 147–76; A. Verhoeven, 'Consument en interne markt – Beschouwingen bij het voorstel van Richtlijn betreffende consumentenrechten' in J. Meeusen, G. Straetmans and A.-M. Van den Bossche (eds.), *Het EG-consumentenacquis: nu en straks*, Antwerp, Intersentia, 2009, 39–54; M. Loos, 'Consumer Sales Law in the Proposal for a Consumer Rights Directive', *ERPL* 2010, 15–55; K. Tonner, 'The Consumer Rights Directive and its impact on internet and other distance consumer contracts' in N. Reich, H. Micklitz, P. Rott and K. Tonner (eds.), *European Consumer Law*, Cambridge, Intersentia, 2014, (393) 396.

20 Belgian Official Gazette 21 September 2004 (hereafter: Consumer Sales Act).

movable item, with the exception of goods sold by way of execution or otherwise by authority of law; water and gas where they are not put up for sale in a limited volume or set quantity, and electricity'. The definition has been adopted verbatim from the CSD (cf. Article 1(2)(b)).

Nevertheless the Act covers also certain contracts of services. According to Article 1649*bis*, §3 CC, contracts for the supply of consumer goods which have to be manufactured or produced qualify as consumer sale contracts even when the consumer supplied the materials.[21] Furthermore, the Consumer Sales Act applies to mixed agreements which combine the supply of goods with the duty to provide a service. Article 1649*ter*, §4 CC provides that any lack of conformity resulting from an incorrect installation of the consumer goods shall be deemed to be equivalent to a lack of conformity of the goods if the installation forms a part of the contract of sale of the goods and the goods were installed by the seller or under his responsibility.[22]

Like the CSD, the proposal for a directive on electronic and other distance sales of goods defines 'goods' in conformity with the current acquis, notably as 'any tangible movable items with the exception of (a) items sold by way of execution or otherwise by authority of law; (b) water, gas and electricity unless they are put up for sale in a limited volume or a set quantity'.[23] Thus the scope of both the proposal for a directive and the CSD remains confined to tangible goods sold in a business-to-consumer (B2C) context.

Also the concept of 'consumer' is defined by reference to the standard definition in consumer directives, namely 'every natural person who is acting for purposes which are outside that person's trade, business, craft or profession'.[24] Whereas the Consumer Rights Directive in its preamble explicitly hinted at a broader personal scope including mixed contracts and legal persons to some

---

21 P. Brulez, 'Het privaatrechtelijk onderscheid tussen goederen en diensten' in B. Tilleman and A. Verbeke (eds.), *Knelpunten Verkoop roerende goederen*, Antwerp, Intersentia, 2009, (1) 17, para. 29; B. Tilleman, *Overeenkomsten, Deel 2. Bijzondere overeenkomsten, A. Verkoop, Deel 2. Gevolgen van de koop* in *Beginselen van Belgisch Privaatrecht*, Mechelen, Kluwer, 2012, 580, para. 705; R. Steennot, 'Commentaar bij art. 1649*bis* BW' in *Comm.Bijz. Ov.*, 2015, 12, para. 13.

22 S. Stijns, 'De consumentenkoop: actuele knelpunten' in B. Tilleman and A. Verbeke (eds.), *Knelpunten Verkoop roerende goederen*, Antwerp, Intersentia, 2009, (21) 28, para. 11; B. Tilleman, *Overeenkomsten, Deel 2. Bijzondere overeenkomsten, A. Verkoop, Deel 2. Gevolgen van de koop* in *Beginselen van Belgisch Privaatrecht*, Mechelen, Kluwer, 2012, 579, para. 705; R. Steennot, 'Commentaar bij art. 1649*bis* BW' in *Comm.Bijz.Ov.*, 2015, 12, para. 13.

23 Article 2(d) Proposal for a directive of the European Parliament and of the Council on certain aspects concerning contracts for the online and other distance sales of goods, COM(2015) 635.

24 See Article 2(4) Proposal for a directive of the European Parliament and of the Council on certain aspects concerning contracts for the supply of digital content, COM(2015) 634 and see Article 2(b) Proposal for a directive of the European Parliament and of the Council on certain aspects concerning contracts for the online and other distance sales of goods, COM(2015) 635.

extent and the proposal for a Regulation on a Common European Sales Law even included small and medium-sized enterprises in its personal scope as weaker parties,[25] the new proposals for directives contain no references to that end. As regards the definition of consumer the detailed explanation of Article 2 of the Proposal for a directive on electronic and other distance sales contracts spells out that this definition must be applied and interpreted in a manner consistent with the acquis.[26] This seems to indicate that the Community legislature in the end falls back on the ECJ's interpretation of the consumer concept in *Gruber*,[27] where it held that consumer contracts include contracts that a natural person concludes for purposes that are exclusively outside his business as well as contracts that are in part outside and in part within his trade or profession, provided the trade or professional purpose is so limited as to be negligible in the overall context of the supply.[28]

As regards contracts that include elements of both sale of goods and provision of services, the proposal for a directive on electronic and other distance sales of goods applies only to the part relating to the sale of goods, in line with the approach taken by the Consumer Rights Directive (2011/83/EU).[29]

3.1.2. Contracts for the Supply of Digital Content

It was pointed out above that the scope of application is restricted to tangible goods. In contrast to some other Member States the Belgian legislator did not broaden the scope of application to intangible goods. This raises problems of classification in the case of contracts for the supply of digital content, since digital content is generally considered an intangible good.

Digital content can be delivered either on a tangible medium such as a CD, DVD, USB stick, etc. or through electronic means. A movie incorporated in a

25 In this regard the detailed explanation of Article 3 of the Proposal for a directive on the supply of digital content indicates that 'contract law related problems in B2B relations, especially in relation to specific needs of SMEs, has been recognised in the Digital Single Market Strategy and will be analysed in the context of other actions announced in the Strategy'. See Proposal for a directive of the European Parliament and of the Council on certain aspects concerning contracts for the supply of digital content, COM(2015) 634, p. 11.

26 For other definitions like, for instance, the definition of 'distance sales' the detailed explanation insists on an application and interpretation in accordance with either the Consumer Rights Directive or the proposal for a Regulation on CESL, depending on which of the two instruments the definition originates from. See Proposal for a directive of the European Parliament and of the Council on certain aspects concerning contracts for the online and other distance sales of goods, COM(2015) 635, p. 14.

27 ECJ Case C-464/01, *Gruber v Bay Wa AG*, ECLI:EU:C:2005:32.

28 ECJ Case C-464/01, *Gruber v Bay Wa AG*, ECLI:EU:C:2005:32, para. 54.

29 Recital 12 Proposal for a directive of the European Parliament and of the Council on certain aspects concerning contracts for the online and other distance sales of goods, COM(2015) 635.

DVD would then be tangible, whereas the same movie downloaded through the Internet would be intangible.[30] Furthermore, the classification of digital content as either goods or a service is quite a challenge too. While the distinction between goods and services often can be made intuitively, for instance a movie distributed via a CD versus a film made available through the Internet, the classification of the acquisition of an Internet game with a monthly subscription poses more problems in practice.

It indeed proves very difficult to determine what types of digital content are sufficiently tangible from the perspective of the Consumer Sales Directive to fall within the definition of 'goods'.[31] In the Consumer Rights Directive the European legislator defined 'digital content' as data which are produced and supplied in digital form,[32] but left open the question whether digital content is considered goods or a service. The Community legislature, well aware of the divergent classifications in the Member States, deliberately avoided any classification of digital content. In doing so both forms of digital content delivery, tangible or not, would fall under the scope of that Directive. It follows that every contract for the supply of digital content falls within the scope of the Consumer Rights Directive, whether it is supplied on a tangible medium such as a CD or a DVD or not, and that contracts for digital content which are not supplied on a tangible medium are, for the purpose of the Consumer Rights Directive, classified neither as sales contracts nor as service contracts.[33]

To date the extent to which the Belgian Consumer Sales Act applies to contracts for the supply of digital content is unclear. The point of departure in Belgian doctrine is that the medium in which the digital content is embodied essentially determines the tangible or intangible nature of the content and consequently whether the Consumer Sales Act applies. Digital content which is supplied on a durable medium like DVDs or CDs, etc. is seen as a tangible good and therefore falls within the scope of the Act, whereas digital content

---

30 See also N. Helberger, L. Guibault, M. Loos, C. Mak, L. Pessers and B. van der Sloot, *Digital Consumers and the Law. Towards a Cohesive European Framework*, Alphen Aan den Rijn, Kluwer, 2013, 21.

31 See on this point also N. Helberger, L. Guibault, M. Loos, C. Mak, L. Pessers and B. van der Sloot, *Digital Consumers and the Law. Towards a Cohesive European Framework*, Alphen aan den Rijn, Kluwer, 2013, 22.

32 Article 2(11) of the Directive 2011/83/EU of the European Parliament and of the Council of 25 October 2011 on consumer rights, amending Council Directive 93/13/EEC and Directive 1999/44/EC of the European Parliament and of the Council and repealing Council Directive 85/577/EEC and Directive 97/7/EC of the European Parliament and of the Council, *OJ* L 304, 22 November 2011, 64–88.

33 Recital 19 of Directive 2011/83/EU of the European Parliament and of the Council of 25 October 2011 on consumer rights, amending Council Directive 93/13/EEC and Directive 1999/44/EC of the European Parliament and of the Council and repealing Council Directive 85/577/EEC and Directive 97/7/EC of the European Parliament and of the Council, *OJ* L 304, 22 November 2011, 64–88.

distributed in an intangible form does not.[34] For the purpose of the Consumer Sales Act, Belgian legal doctrine further distinguishes the mode of supply and the specific type of digital content. Particularly in cases where digital content is supplied through a sale or a licence, the specific mode of supply will be of importance. If the digital content is supplied through a licensing contract, the Consumer Sales Act will not apply, even when the licence as such is sold, because software supplied that way will be considered intangible goods.[35]

The proposal for a directive on the supply of digital content now introduces a broader notion of digital content as compared to the Consumer Rights Directive. It covers not only data produced and supplied in digital form but also services which allow the creation, processing or storage of data and which allow sharing of and any other interaction with data.[36]

Furthermore the proposal introduces a new criterion of delimitation with the CSD. The proposal for a directive on digital content will only apply to those services whose *main subject-matter* is providing digital content. Services which are personally performed and where the digital means are only used for access or delivery purposes are excluded.[37] It follows that the proposal applies to a whole range of modes of supply of digital content, regardless which medium is used for the transmission of the digital content, such as a durable medium, downloading by consumers on their devices, web-streaming, allowing access to digital content storage capabilities or access to the use of social media used for its transmission.[38]

---

[34] C. Cauffman, 'De nieuwe wet op de consumentenkoop', *TPR* 2005, (787) 799, para. 24; A. Van Oevelen, 'De Wet Consumentenkoop' in *CBR Jaarboek 2005–06*, Antwerp, Maklu, 2006, (117) 124, para. 9; P. Brulez, 'Het privaatrechtelijk onderscheid tussen goederen en diensten' in B. Tilleman and A. Verbeke (eds.), *Knelpunten Verkoop roerende goederen*, Antwerp, Intersentia, 2009, (1) 18, para. 32; S. Stijns, 'De consumentenkoop: actuele knelpunten' in B. Tilleman and A. Verbeke (eds.), *Knelpunten Verkoop roerende goederen*, Antwerp, Intersentia, 2009, (21) 32, para. 18; B. Tilleman, *Overeenkomsten, Deel 2. Bijzondere overeenkomsten, A. Verkoop, Deel 2. Gevolgen van de koop* in *Beginselen van Belgisch Privaatrecht*, Mechelen, Kluwer, 2012, 581, para. 710; R. Steennot, 'Commentaar bij art. 1649bis BW' in *Comm.Bijz.Ov.*, 2015, 10, para. 10.

[35] C. Cauffman, 'De nieuwe wet op de consumentenkoop', *TPR* 2005, (787) 799, para. 24; P. Brulez, 'Het privaatrechtelijk onderscheid tussen goederen en diensten' in B. Tilleman and A. Verbeke (eds.), *Knelpunten Verkoop roerende goederen*, Antwerp, Intersentia, 2009, (1) 19, para. 32; S. Stijns, 'De consumentenkoop: actuele knelpunten' in B. Tilleman and A. Verbeke (eds.), *Knelpunten Verkoop roerende goederen*, Antwerp, Intersentia, 2009, (21) 33, para. 18; B. Tilleman, *Overeenkomsten, Deel 2. Bijzondere overeenkomsten, A. Verkoop, Deel 2. Gevolgen van de koop* in *Beginselen van Belgisch Privaatrecht*, Mechelen, Kluwer, 2012, 582, para. 710; R. Steennot, 'Commentaar bij art. 1649*bis* BW' in *Comm.Bijz.Ov.*, 2015, 10, para. 10.

[36] Article 2(1) and recital 11 Proposal for a directive of the European Parliament and of the Council on certain aspects concerning contracts for the supply of digital content, COM(2015) 634.

[37] Recital 19 Proposal for a directive of the European Parliament and of the Council on certain aspects concerning contracts for the supply of digital content, COM(2015) 634.

[38] Recital 11 Proposal for a directive of the European Parliament and of the Council on certain aspects concerning contracts for the supply of digital content, COM(2015) 634.

Yet, when the digital content is incorporated in a durable medium, the directive will[39] only apply where the durable medium has been used *exclusively as carrier* of digital content.[40] This means that the proposal for a directive applies to goods such as DVDs and CDs, incorporating digital content in such a way that the goods function only as a carrier of the digital content independently of whether it is sold at a distance or in face-to-face situations.[41] Consequently, the proposal for a directive will not apply to digital content which is embedded in goods in such a way that it operates as an integral part of the goods and its functions are subordinate to the main functionalities of the goods.[42]

In sum, the supply of digital content turns out to fall partly within the scope of the Consumer Sales Directive and consequently the Belgian Consumer Sales Act and partly outside their scope. Even though the purpose is to avoid overlap and to better reflect the scope of the CSD in relation to the new proposals,[43] the new criterion of delineation raises multiple questions (see below Section 3.1.4).[44] Wording such as 'where a durable medium is *used exclusively* as a carrier of digital content' (emphasis added), which is the connecting factor for the application of the new digital content directive, and 'digital content embedded in goods in such a way that its functions are *subordinate to the main functionalities* of the goods' (emphasis added), as the connecting factor for the application of the CSD and hence the new proposal for a directive on electronic and other distance sales of goods, require further clarification.

3.1.3. Contracts for the Online and Other Distance Sales of Goods

The proposal for a directive on certain aspects concerning contracts for the online and other distance sales of goods will apply to *distance sales contracts*

39 In exception to Articles 5 and 11 of the Proposal concerning the supply and the remedy for this failure.

40 Article 3(3) Proposal for a directive of the European Parliament and of the Council on certain aspects concerning contracts for the supply of digital content, COM(2015) 634.

41 Recital 12 Proposal for a directive of the European Parliament and of the Council on certain aspects concerning contracts for the supply of digital content, COM(2015) 634. See also Recital 13 Proposal for a directive of the European Parliament and of the Council on certain aspects concerning contracts for the online and other distance sales of goods, COM(2015) 635.

42 Recital 11 Proposal for a directive of the European Parliament and of the Council on certain aspects concerning contracts for the supply of digital content, COM(2015) 634.

43 Recital 50 Proposal for a directive of the European Parliament and of the Council on certain aspects concerning contracts for the supply of digital content, COM(2015) 634.

44 The proposal for a directive on digital content further adjusts the definition of 'consumer goods' correspondingly. See Article 20(1) Proposal for a directive of the European Parliament and of the Council on certain aspects concerning contracts for the supply of digital content, COM(2015) 634.

concluded between the seller and the consumer.[45] The scope of the Consumer Sales Directive comprises *sales contracts* concluded between the seller and the consumer, regardless of whether they are distance sales contracts or not. Article 19 of the new proposal amends the CSD and limits its scope to contracts for the sale of consumer goods and associated guarantees, *which are not distance sales contracts*. The definition of distance sales is taken verbatim from the Consumer Rights Directive.[46]

3.1.4. *Intermediary Conclusion*

Both the proposal on electronic and distance sales contracts and the proposal on the supply of digital content carve out relevant parts from the scope of the Consumer Sales Directive. At first glance overlap between the existing CSD and the new proposals is thereby avoided via the introduction of a new criterion of delineation and corresponding amendments of the CSD. Thus, the CSD will no longer apply to any durable medium incorporating digital content, like DVDs and CDs, where the durable medium has been used exclusively as a carrier for the supply of the digital content to the consumer. A corresponding exception is included in the proposal on electronic and other distance sales contracts for goods so that the proposal on contracts for the supply of digital content will exclusively cover those contracts. In contrast, the supply of digital content which is embedded in goods in such a way that it operates as an integral part of the goods and its functions are subordinate to the main functionalities of the goods remains within the ambit of the CSD and the new proposal on electronic and other distance sales.

However, the new proposals give no further clarification on how these new criteria should be applied in practice. It was pointed out above that this will certainly give rise to new delineation issues in practice. Also the approach of the Digital Content Directive towards mixed contracts raises questions. Where a contract includes elements in addition to the supply of digital content, the new directive would only apply to the obligations and remedies of the parties as supplier and consumer of the digital content.[47] It follows that the only part of

---

45 Article 1(1) Proposal for a directive of the European Parliament and of the Council on certain aspects concerning contracts for the online and other distance sales of goods, COM(2015) 635.

46 See Article 2(e) Proposal for a directive of the European Parliament and of the Council on certain aspects concerning contracts for the online and other distance sales of goods, COM(2015) 635. See also Recital 15 Proposal for a directive of the European Parliament and of the Council on certain aspects concerning contracts for the online and other distance sales of goods, COM(2015) 635 which spells out that, where referring to the same concepts, the rules of the new directive should be applied and interpreted in a manner consistent with the rules of the CSD and CRD.

47 See Article 3(6) Proposal for a directive of the European Parliament and of the Council on certain aspects concerning contracts for the supply of digital content, COM(2015) 634.

mixed contracts governed by the new proposal will be the part relating to the digital content.

Hence, it remains to be seen how this interrelates with the delimitation criterion according to which the digital content proposal only applies to any tangible medium incorporating digital content if the durable medium has been used exclusively as a carrier of digital content,[48] and with the criterion that excludes the proposal's application to digital content embedded in goods in such a way that its functions are subordinate to the main functionalities of the goods. Consequently digital content that is embedded in goods where its functions are subordinate to the main functionalities of those goods will be integrally governed by the CSD or the new proposal on electronic or other distance sales when the goods are supplied within the framework of a distance contract, whereas digital content where its functions equate or consist in the main functionalities of the goods, necessitate a more targeted classification. In the latter case the classification must be split up into a digital content part, governed by the digital content directive, and the other parts, governed by the other regimes. This will certainly give rise to forms of unequal treatment, as a different regime will apply to contracts where consumers buy, for instance, operating software separately for their PC and contracts where consumers make use of embedded operating software.[49]

3.2. SUBSTANTIVE RULES ON CONFORMITY WITH THE CONTRACT

The two proposals hold the supplier liable for any lack of conformity with the contract.[50] In contrast with the proposal on electronic and other distance sales contracts, the proposal on digital content also allocates liability to the supplier for any failure to supply the digital content.[51] Under current Belgian legislation, delays in delivery or the supply at the wrong place or at the wrong time are not deemed to be equivalent to a lack of conformity with the contract and hence do not fall within the scope of the Consumer Sales Act. However, any failure to supply the goods concerned will be classified as a lack of conformity as well as any failure to supply the accessories.[52]

---

48 See Article 3(6) Proposal for a directive of the European Parliament and of the Council on certain aspects concerning contracts for the supply of digital content, COM(2015) 634.

49 See for further illustrations of this point and possible solutions, the chapter by R. STEENNOT and S. GEIREGAT in this volume.

50 Article 10 Proposal for a directive of the European Parliament and of the Council on certain aspects concerning contracts for the supply of digital content, COM(2015) 634; Article 8(1) Proposal for a directive of the European Parliament and of the Council on certain aspects concerning contracts for the online and other distance sales of goods, COM(2015) 635.

51 Articles 5 and 10 Proposal for a directive of the European Parliament and of the Council on certain aspects concerning contracts for the supply of digital content, COM(2015) 634.

52 S. JANSEN, *Prijsvermindering*, Antwerp, Intersentia, 2015, 307–08, paras. 346–47.

3.2.1. *Conformity Criteria*

The new proposals restate that the seller must deliver goods to the consumer that are in conformity with the contract of sale. Consumer goods are considered to be in conformity with the contract of sale when they primarily meet the conditions which were promised in the contract, and secondly comply with a list of conditions on the conformity. These are the so called subjective and objective conformity criteria. Whereas the Consumer Sales Directive mentions those criteria in one provision, the proposals now make a clear distinction between both types of criteria with evident repercussions for the level of consumer protection.

3.2.1.1. Subjective Criteria

The two proposals contain subjective conformity criteria which the goods have to meet in order to conform with the contract. According to the proposal on electronic and distance sales contracts, the goods have to be of the quantity, quality and description required by the contract, which includes that where the seller shows an example or a model to the consumer, the goods will be of the same quality of and correspond to the description of this sample or model. The provision restates the requirements of quality and correspondence to the description, but now considers them as aspects of the duty to comply with the conditions set out in the agreement between the parties. The second criterion replicates the condition of a particular purpose.[53] The third condition introduces a new criterion, namely that the goods must possess the qualities and performance capabilities indicated in any pre-contractual statement which forms an integral part of the contract.

The proposal on electronic and distance sales contracts contains the possibility to exclude, derogate from or vary the effects of the objective criteria listed in Articles 5 and 6.[54] This is explained as follows in the preamble:

> While freedom of contract with regard to the criteria of conformity with the contract should be ensured, in order to avoid circumvention of the liability for lack of conformity and ensure a high level of consumer protection, any derogation from the mandatory rules on criteria of conformity and incorrect installation, which is detrimental to

---

53 Article 4(1)(b) Proposal for a directive of the European Parliament and of the Council on certain aspects concerning contracts for the online and other distance sales of goods, COM(2015) 635; Article 6(1)(b) Proposal for a directive of the European Parliament and of the Council on certain aspects concerning contracts for the supply of digital content, COM(2015) 634.

54 Article 4(3) Proposal for a directive of the European Parliament and of the Council on certain aspects concerning contracts for the online and other distance sales of goods, COM(2015) 635.

> the interests of the consumer, shall be valid only if the consumer has been expressly informed and has expressly consented to it when concluding the contract.[55]

The proposal on digital content does not as such contain a similar provision, yet the fact that the enumeration of the objective criteria is preceded by the words 'to the extent that the contract does not stipulate'[56] amounts to the same effect, as it points to the same possibility for the contracting parties to deviate from the criteria.

Although a detailed analysis of the conformity criteria goes far beyond the scope of this chapter, it must be observed that the CSD remained silent about this possibility for the parties. On closer analysis it even becomes clear that the new system differs from the approach taken in the CSD, as most of the conformity criteria listed in the CSD were objective criteria. It seems now that the subjective conformity criteria prevail in the new proposals.

This critique must be somewhat nuanced in the Belgian context. According to Belgian legal doctrine it results from the principle of freedom of contract that the contracting parties have the freedom to clarify the conformity of the sold goods by deviating from the list of conformity criteria listed in Article 1649*ter*, §1 CC. An agreement excluding or derogating from this provision is, even under the regime of the CSD, valid if, at the time of the conclusion of the contract, the consumer knew of the specific condition of the goods and expressly accepted this specific condition when concluding the contract.[57]

There is, however, another difference to be noted between the two proposals. Whereas the distance sales contracts proposal stipulates that in order to conform with the contract, the goods *must also* meet the objective requirements of Articles 5, 6 and 7, notwithstanding the possibility for parties to deviate therefrom at the time of the conclusion of the contract, the proposal on the supply of digital content only requires that *to the extent that the contract does not stipulate*, where relevant, *in a clear and comprehensive manner*, the requirements for the digital content, this digital content must meet additional objective criteria set out in the proposal.

---

55 See Recital 22 Proposal for a directive of the European Parliament and of the Council on certain aspects concerning contracts for the online and other distance sales of goods, COM(2015) 635.

56 Article 6(2) Proposal for a directive of the European Parliament and of the Council on certain aspects concerning contracts for the supply of digital content, COM(2015) 634.

57 A. Van Oevelen, 'Het nieuwe begrip conformiteit' in S. Stijns and J. Stuyck (eds.), *Het nieuwe kooprecht*, Antwerp, Intersentia, 2005, (29) 36, para. 10; C. Cauffman, 'De nieuwe wet op de consumentenkoop', *TPR* 2005, (787) 813, para. 46; A. Van Oevelen, 'De Wet Consumentenkoop' in *CBR Jaarboek 2005–06*, Antwerp, Maklu, 2006, (117) 128, para. 15; A. Lenaerts, 'Het nieuwe begrip conformiteit in het Belgisch en het Duits kooprecht', *TBBR* 2006, (81) 87–88, para. 15; B. Tilleman, *Overeenkomsten, Deel 2. Bijzondere overeenkomsten, A. Verkoop, Deel 2. Gevolgen van de koop* in *Beginselen van Belgisch Privaatrecht*, Mechelen, Kluwer, 2012, 592, para. 720; R. Steennot, 'Commentaar bij art. 1649*ter* BW' in *Comm.Bijz. Ov.*, 2015, 13, para. 15.

It means in the latter case that only in absence of specifications on conformity in the contract should recourse be had to the additional objective criteria. The justification for this subordination of the objective criteria to what has been stipulated in the contract lies in the promotion of 'innovation in the Digital Single Market' and in the goal to 'cater for technological developments reflected in the fast changing characteristics of digital content'.[58] Leaving aside whether these could be convincing arguments for subjecting the objective criteria to the subjective criteria stipulated in the contract, it remains to be seen whether the average consumer will be in a sufficiently strong bargaining position to influence the contract on these points.

Admittedly, the freedom to contract is instantly mitigated by the fact that the conformity specifications in the contract only prevail where they are stipulated in a clear and comprehensive manner. Taking the ECJ's case law regarding unfair contract terms and more particularly its analysis of a similar requirement for the core provisions of a contract to escape the application of the Unfair Contract Terms Directive as the logical starting point for the assessment of their unfair character, the requirement that contractual criteria are drafted in a clear and comprehensive manner not only means that the terms are grammatically understandable to the average consumer, but more importantly also the criteria must allow the consumer to evaluate the personal economic consequences resulting therefrom.[59] Although an application by analogy of the ECJ's case law would obviously contribute to the improvement of the position of consumers, it clearly does not entirely solve the bargaining position problem of average consumers when stipulating the contractual terms with suppliers of digital content.

3.2.1.2. Objective Criteria

Turning back to the objective criteria, both proposals restate in general wording that the goods shall be fit for the purpose for which goods of the same description would ordinarily or normally be used. Whereas the proposal on digital content mentions the 'normal' use,[60] the proposal on distance sales contracts now refers to 'ordinarily' instead of 'normally',[61] but this seems only a linguistic change.

---

58 See Recital 24 Proposal for a directive of the European Parliament and of the Council on certain aspects concerning contracts for the supply of digital content, COM(2015) 634.

59 See in particular ECJ Case C-26/13, *Árpád Kásler and Hajnalka Káslerné Rábai v OTP Jelzálogbank Zrt*, EU:C:2014:282; see also ECJ Case C-92/11, *RWE Vertrieb AG v Verbraucherzentrale Nordrhein-Westfalen eV*, EU:C:2013:180.

60 Article 6(2) Proposal for a directive of the European Parliament and of the Council on certain aspects concerning contracts for the supply of digital content, COM(2015) 634.

61 Article 5(a) Proposal for a directive of the European Parliament and of the Council on certain aspects concerning contracts for the online and other distance sales of goods, COM(2015) 635.

Article 5(c) of the proposal on electronic and distance sales contracts replicates the criteria of the possession of qualities and of performance capabilities which are normal in goods of the same type and which the consumer may expect given the nature of the goods and taking into account any public statement. The latter factor is also replicated in the proposal on digital content contracts (Article 6(2)(c)). Whereas Belgian law refers to any public statement made by the seller, the producer or his representative in Article 1649*ter*, §2 CC, the new proposals include any public statement made by or on behalf of the seller or other persons in earlier links of the chain of transactions, including public statements made by the producer. In the same vein, the new proposals contain the same exceptions according to which the seller shall not be bound by public statements.[62]

In order to conform with the contract, goods that need to be installed must also meet additional conformity requirements. In this respect both proposals spell out the requirement that those goods have to be installed properly. Digital content is not 'installed' as such but integrated into the consumer's digital environment. Any lack of conformity resulting from an incorrect installation or integration is therefore to be regarded as a lack of conformity of the goods/digital content itself if the reason for the incorrect installation is within the sphere of the seller.[63] This principle is in line with Belgian law, which states that the seller is liable for a defect caused by incorrect installation if the installation forms part of the contract of sale of the goods and the goods were installed by the seller or under his responsibility (see Article 1649*ter*, §4 CC). This will apply equally if the product, intended to be installed by the consumer, is installed by the consumer and the incorrect installation is due to a shortcoming in the installation instructions. However, it must be observed in this regard that contrary to the CSD, the proposals for directives no longer require that the installation or integration requirement forms part of the contract of sale or supply itself.[64] This clearly enhances the level of consumer protection as it will rule out from the outset any discussion about whether the installation/integration service was included in the sale/supply contract.

62 Article 6(2)(c) Proposal for a directive of the European Parliament and of the Council on certain aspects concerning contracts for the supply of digital content, COM(2015) 634; Article 5(c) Proposal for a directive of the European Parliament and of the Council on certain aspects concerning contracts for the online and other distance sales of goods, COM(2015) 635.

63 Article 6 Proposal for a directive of the European Parliament and of the Council on certain aspects concerning contracts for the online and other distance sales of goods, COM(2015) 635; Article 7 Proposal for a directive of the European Parliament and of the Council on certain aspects concerning contracts for the supply of digital content, COM(2015) 634.

64 Compare Article 6(a) Proposal for a directive of the European Parliament and of the Council on certain aspects concerning contracts for the online and other distance sales of goods, COM(2015) 635 with Article 7(a) Proposal for a directive of the European Parliament and of the Council on certain aspects concerning contracts for the supply of digital content, COM(2015) 634.

3.2.1.3. The Rights of Third Parties

The proposals both contain a new rule concerning the rights of third parties.[65] According to the European Commission, conformity should not only cover material defects, but also legal defects. Third party rights and other legal defects might effectively bar the consumer from enjoying the goods of digital content in accordance with the contract when the right-holder rightfully compels the consumer to stop infringing those rights. Therefore the seller should ensure that the goods are free from any right of a third party, which precludes the consumer from enjoying the goods in accordance with the contract.[66] Furthermore, in the European legislature's view, legal defects are particularly important for digital content, which by its nature, is subject to intellectual property rights.[67]

Although this rule is novel in comparison to the Consumer Sales Directive, Belgian common sales law already provided for such protection (see Articles 1626–1640 CC). These provisions impose the obligation on the seller to warrant that the buyer will have the undisturbed possession of the goods by ensuring that the buyer's rights will not be infringed upon either by himself or by third parties. In contrast with the proposals, which consider any breach of this provision as a lack of conformity with the contract, the Belgian guarantee is viewed as a distinct obligation of the seller which entitles the buyer who meets certain requirements to specific remedies provided by law.[68]

3.2.2. Relevant Time for Establishing Conformity with the Contract

Under the regime of the Consumer Sales Directive the seller is liable to the consumer for any lack of conformity which exists at the time the goods are delivered. Article 1604 CC defines delivery as the transfer of the sold goods into the control and the possession of the seller. The proposal on electronic and distance sales contracts replaces the moment of delivery with the time of the passing of the risk. In doing so this proposal is brought into line with the Consumer Rights Directive, which introduced identical rules on passing of risk. The passing of the risk refers to the moment in time when the risk of damage to,

65 Article 7 Proposal for a directive of the European Parliament and of the Council on certain aspects concerning contracts for the online and other distance sales of goods, COM(2015) 635; Article 8 Proposal for a directive of the European Parliament and of the Council on certain aspects concerning contracts for the supply of digital content, COM(2015) 634.

66 Recital 21 Proposal for a directive of the European Parliament and of the Council on certain aspects concerning contracts for the online and other distance sales of goods, COM(2015) 635.

67 Recital 31 Proposal for a directive of the European Parliament and of the Council on certain aspects concerning contracts for the supply of digital content, COM(2015) 634.

68 According to the Explanatory Memorandum, Bill 31 March 2004, *Parl.St.* Kamer 2003–04, no. 982/001, 6, this regime applies to consumer sales.

or deterioration or destruction of, the goods is transferred from the seller to the buyer. This is the moment where the consumer or a third party designated by the consumer obtains the physical possession of the goods. Only in cases where the carrier was commissioned by the consumer has the risk already passed upon delivery to the carrier. This means that a consumer is protected during a transport arranged or carried out by the seller, even where the consumer has chosen a particular method of delivery from a range of options offered by the seller. As was pointed out above, these rules stem from the Consumer Rights Directive and were transposed into Belgian law in Article VI.44 of the Belgian Code of Economic Law.[69]

Article 8 of the proposal on electronic and other distance sales contracts further adds that in cases where the goods need to be installed, the relevant time for establishing conformity is when the installation is completed or in cases where the consumer installs the goods, after a reasonable time for the installation, but in any case not later than 30 days from the moment of passing of risk.

3.2.3. *Obligation to Notify*

Whereas the Consumer Sales Directive allows the Member States to provide a duty to notify the trader of a lack of conformity within two months of the discovery of the defect,[70] the new proposals preclude this possibility.[71] Under Belgian law there is no duty to notify of a lack of conformity within a specific period after its discovery, but in accordance with the CSD the Consumer Sales Act allows parties to specify a notification period (which, however, cannot be less than two months), and to stipulate the consequences in the case that the agreed notification period has not been complied with.[72] In the absence of a specific notification obligation imposed by law on the consumer, only the seller will benefit from the possibility to stipulate such an obligation in the contract.[73]

---

69 See more in detail, G. Straetmans and J. Laffineur, 'La directive 2011/83 relative aux droits des consommateurs: les modifications de la réglementation concernant les ventes aux consommateurs et les autres droits des consommateurs', *European Journal of Consumer Law*, 2014, vol. 13:3–4, 475–98.

70 Article 5(2) Consumer Sales Directive.

71 Recital 25 Proposal for a directive of the European Parliament and of the Council on certain aspects concerning contracts for the online and other distance sales of goods, COM(2015) 635. The proposal on digital content remains, however, silent about any obligation to notify.

72 Article 1649*quater*, §2 CC.

73 C. Cauffman and A. Verbeke, 'Een jaar Wet Consumentenkoop' in B. Tilleman and A. Verbeke (eds.), *Themis Bijzondere Overeenkomsten*, Bruges, die Keure, 2005, (27) 41, para. 53; A. Van Oevelen, 'De Wet Consumentenkoop' in *CBR Jaarboek 2005–06*, Antwerp, Maklu, 2006, (117) 139 para. 27; B. Tilleman, *Overeenkomsten, Deel 2. Bijzondere overeenkomsten, A. Verkoop, Deel 2. Gevolgen van de koop* in *Beginselen van Belgisch Privaatrecht*, Mechelen, Kluwer, 2012, 607, para. 741.

However, if the proposals are enacted, the full harmonisation of the rules introduced therein will prevent parties from stipulating notification obligations in the contract. This must be viewed as an important modification in favour of the consumer.

3.2.4. Burden of Proof

Article 1649*quater*, §4 CC contains a presumption in favour of the consumer according to which, unless proved otherwise, any lack of conformity which becomes apparent within six months after delivery of the goods shall be presumed to have existed at the time of delivery. Article 8(3) of the proposal on electronic and other distance contracts confirms this so-called 'reversed burden of proof', but extends the supplier's burden of proof for the absence of lack of conformity to a period of two years. It follows that the consumer within the first two years after the delivery of the goods only has to establish that there is a non-conformity and consequently is relieved from the additional burden of proving that the lack of conformity existed at the time of delivery. Hence, during these two years the burden of proof shifts to the seller who will have to prove that there is no lack of conformity. This extension of the presumption to two years is unmistakably a considerable improvement of the consumers' rights.

An even better distribution of the burden of proof is incorporated in Article 9 of the proposal on digital content contracts. If the consumer raises a lack of conformity, it will be up to the supplier to prove that the supplied digital content *is* in conformity with the contract. Only in cases where the supplier shows that the lack of conformity is due to the non-compatible digital environment of the consumer, and that the consumer was informed of the interoperability and other technical requirements of the digital content before the conclusion of the contract, will the burden of proof shift again to the consumer.

In comparison with the rules on burden of proof in the proposal on electronic and other distance sales contracts, this provision is much more in favour of the consumer, as it straightforwardly shifts the burden of proof for lack of conformity to the supplier of digital content. The reason for this at first glance revolutionary rule lies in the specific nature of digital content, which is highly complex. Due to the supplier's better knowledge, he is in a far better position than the consumer to assess whether the lack of conformity with the contract is due to the incompatibility of the consumer's digital environment with the technical and interoperability requirements of the digital content supplied by him.[74] From a purely theoretical and consumer perspective, this solution is to be welcomed. However, it remains to be seen what the exact economic impact will

---

[74] Recital 32 Proposal for a directive of the European Parliament and of the Council on certain aspects concerning contracts for the supply of digital content, COM(2015) 634.

be of this rather drastic shift of the burden of proof without any specific time bar. All in all it cannot be excluded that this new provision might entail costs which, in the end once again, will be transferred by traders to the consumers.

3.3. REMEDIES

The new proposals for directives largely confirm the system of remedies introduced by the CSD. The four remedies, i.e. the repair, replacement, price reduction and termination of the contract, are maintained, as well as their 'two-stage' hierarchy. It implies that the consumer first is entitled to have the goods repaired or replaced free of charge within a reasonable time and without any significant inconvenience. As regards digital content the proposal simply states that the consumer is entitled to have the digital content brought into conformity with the contract, without further specifications. In a second, subsidiary step the consumer can have recourse to a price reduction or the termination of the contract where the lack of conformity is not or cannot be remedied through repair or replacement. Yet, the conditions for exercising the remedies are now drawn up in more detail.

3.3.1. First Stage Remedies: Repair and Replacement

3.3.1.1. Repair or Replacement Free of Charge

The consumer is entitled, as he currently is under the Belgian Consumer Sales Act,[75] to repair or replacement, free of charge. The expression 'free of charge' is defined in Article 3(4) of the CSD as referring to 'the necessary costs incurred to bring the goods into conformity, particularly the cost of postage, labour and materials'. It follows from the use by the Community legislature of the adverb 'particularly' that this list is illustrative and not exhaustive.[76] This remedy from the CSD is confirmed in both proposals.[77]

---

75 Compare with Article 1649*quinquies*, §§1–2 CC: free of charge means that the costs necessarily incurred in order to bring the goods into conformity, particularly the cost of postage, labour and materials, are borne by the seller.

76 ECJ, 17 April 2008, Case C-204/06, *Quelle*, *D.C.C.R.* 2008, 75, note M. Dupont; C. Schneider and F. Amtenbrink, 'Quelle: the possibility for the seller, to ask for a compensation for the use of goods in replacement of products not in conformity with the contract', *REDC* 2007–08, 301–09.

77 Article 12(1) Proposal for a directive of the European Parliament and of the Council on certain aspects concerning contracts for the supply of digital content, COM(2015) 634; Article 9(1) Proposal for a directive of the European Parliament and of the Council on certain aspects concerning contracts for the online and other distance sales of goods, COM(2015) 635.

Furthermore, the proposal on electronic and other distance sales contracts now consolidates the *Weber and Putz* judgment[78] of the Court of Justice and specifies in its Article 10 concerning the replacement of the goods that the seller shall take back the replaced goods at his own expense, which includes the costs of the removal of the non-conforming goods and the installation of the replacement goods. The seller may take back the defective goods and install the new ones himself or commission a third party to do that at the seller's expense. However, the provision does not contain a similar limitation[79] as it does not allow limitation of the consumer's right to reimbursement of the cost of removing the defective goods and of installing the replacement goods to an amount proportionate to the value the goods would have if there were no lack of conformity and proportionate to the significance of the lack of conformity. Prior to the *Weber and Putz* judgment of the Court of Justice, Belgian legal doctrine already considered that the seller had to bear the costs of installation.[80]

Paragraph 3 of Article 10 states that the consumer shall not be obliged to pay for any use made of the replaced goods in the period prior to the replacement. This paragraph confirms the judgment of the Court of Justice in *Quelle*,[81] where the Court held that Article 3 of the Consumer Sales Directive is to be interpreted as precluding national legislation under which a seller who has sold consumer goods which are not in conformity may require the consumer to pay compensation for the use of those defective goods until their replacement with new goods.

---

78 See ECJ, 16 June 2011, Joined Cases C-65/09 and C-87/09, *Gebruder Weber GmbH v Wittmer and Putz v Medianess Electronics GmbH*, ECLI:EU:C:2011:396: 'where consumer goods not in conformity with the contract which were installed in good faith by the consumer in a manner consistent with their nature and purpose, before the defect became apparent, are restored to conformity by way of replacement, the seller is obliged either himself to remove the goods from where they were installed and to install the replacement goods there or else to bear the cost of that removal and installation of the replacement goods. That obligation on the seller exists regardless of whether he was obliged under the contract of sale to install the consumer goods originally purchased. (para. 62).

79 See ECJ, 16 June 2011, Joined Cases C-65/09 and C-87/09, *Gebruder Weber and Putz*, ECLI:EU:C:2011:396, para. 74: the CSD 'does not preclude the consumer's right to reimbursement of the cost of removing the defective goods and installing the replacement goods from being limited, where necessary, to an amount proportionate to the value the goods would have if there were no lack of conformity and proportionate to the significance of the lack of conformity. Such limitation leaves intact the consumer's right to seek replacement of goods not in conformity'.

80 S. Stijns, 'De remedies van de koper bij niet-conformiteit' in S. Stijns and J. Stuyck (eds.), *Het nieuwe kooprecht*, Antwerp, Intersentia, 2005, (53) 61, para. 20; A. Van Oevelen, 'De Wet Consumentenkoop' in *CBR Jaarboek 2005–06*, Antwerp, Maklu, 2006, (117) 142–43, no. 30; S. Stijns, 'De consumentenkoop: actuele knelpunten' in B. Tilleman and A. Verbeke (eds.), *Knelpunten Verkoop roerende goederen*, Antwerp, Intersentia, 2009, (21) 58, para. 53; B. Tilleman, *Overeenkomsten, Deel 2. Bijzondere overeenkomsten, A. Verkoop, Deel 2. Gevolgen van de koop* in *Beginselen van Belgisch Privaatrecht*, Mechelen, Kluwer, 2012, 625, para. 759.

81 ECJ, 17 April 2008, Case C-204/06, *Quelle*, *D.C.C.R.* 2008, 75, note M. Dupont.

Current Article 1649*quinquies*, §1 CC, second paragraph, is less straightforward in that it takes account of the aggravation of damage resulting from the consumer's use after the lack of conformity is established. This rule originates from the principle that a creditor should not be entitled to recover damages for a loss which could have been avoided if he had taken reasonable steps to do so.[82] According to the provision, which is of general application in Belgian consumer sales law, the consumer cannot be liable for mere use of the goods concerned if that use did not aggravate the damage.[83]

3.3.1.2. Right of Option of the Consumer

Both the Consumer Sales Directive and the Belgian Consumer Sales Act leave the consumer the choice of remedy. Recital 10 expresses the optional right for a consumer to choose between repair and replacement, while Article 1649*quinquies*, §1 CC enumerates the remedies which the consumer can invoke.[84] The new proposal on electronic and other distance sales contracts maintains the consumer's discretion to choose between repair and replacement. The right of the consumer to choose is, however, conditional upon the feasibility, the lawfulness and the proportionality of the remedy. For instance a situation of non-conformity only needs to be remedied by repair or replacement where repair or replacement is neither impossible nor unreasonable.

Whether and when a remedy is considered 'disproportionate' is to be assessed according to the existing objective criteria. A remedy will be deemed disproportionate if it imposes costs on the seller which, in comparison with the *alternative* remedy, are unreasonable. For instance, it might be disproportionate to request the replacement of goods because of a minor scratch where this replacement would create significant costs while, at the same time, the scratch could easily be repaired.[85]

In the *Weber and Putz* judgment the Court of Justice clarifies that the term 'disproportionate' (regarding replacement) is exclusively related to the other remedy (repair), thus limiting the balancing exercise to cases of relative lack of

---

82 C. Cauffman, 'De nieuwe wet op de consumentenkoop', *TPR* 2005, (787) 833, para. 84; S. Stijns, 'De consumentenkoop: actuele knelpunten' in B. Tilleman and A. Verbeke (eds.), *Knelpunten Verkoop roerende goederen*, Antwerp, Intersentia, 2009, (21) 52, para. 44; R. Steennot, 'Commentaar bij art. 1649*quinquies* BW' in *Comm.Bijz.Ov.*, 2015, 25, para. 29.

83 S. Stijns, 'De remedies van de koper bij niet-conformiteit' in S. Stijns and J. Stuyck (eds.), *Het nieuwe kooprecht*, Antwerp, Intersentia, 2005, (53) 57, para. 11.

84 S. Stijns, 'De remedies van de koper bij niet-conformiteit' in S. Stijns and J. Stuyck (eds.), *Het nieuwe kooprecht*, Antwerp, Intersentia, 2005, (53) 58, para. 14; S. Stijns, 'De consumentenkoop: actuele knelpunten' in B. Tilleman and A. Verbeke (eds.), *Knelpunten Verkoop roerende goederen*, Antwerp, Intersentia, 2009, (21) 60, para. 57.

85 Recital 27 Proposal for a directive of the European Parliament and of the Council on certain aspects concerning contracts for the online and other distance sales of goods, COM(2015) 635.

proportionality, the reason being that the other remedies of price reduction or termination of the contract have other objectives than securing the performance of the contractual obligations and ensuring that goods in conformity are supplied. The consequence of the legislator's preference for repair or replacement is that if only one of the two remedies is possible the seller may not refuse the only remedy which allows the goods to be brought into conformity with the contract. As already mentioned, the disproportionate cost of replacement would only allow the seller to reduce them to an amount proportionate to the value the goods would have if there were no lack of conformity and proportionate to the significance of the lack of conformity.[86]

The proposal provides for a new criterion, namely in cases where repair or replacement is unlawful, but fails to indicate how this notion must be interpreted. It is our view that the new wording does not extend the scope of impossibility. If a performance is 'unlawful', it must also be regarded as judicially impossible.[87]

3.3.2. Second Stage Remedies: Price Reduction and Termination

The 'second level' remedy available to the consumer is the right to an appropriate reduction of the price or to termination of the contract. Only if the consumer is entitled to neither repair nor replacement, or if the seller has not completed the first level remedy within a reasonable time, or if the seller has not completed the first level remedy without significant inconvenience to the consumer, may the consumer require an appropriate reduction of the price or have the contract terminated without having to satisfy further requirements.[88]

3.3.2.1. Price Reduction

Although Article 3(2) of the Consumer Sales Directive and its Belgian counterpart, Article 1649*quinquies* CC, provide for the remedy of price reduction, they do not further elaborate on the practical application of this remedy. The remedy of price reduction was, prior to the CSD, not established in Belgian law as a general remedy for non-conformity. The Consumer Sales

---

86 See ECJ, 16 June 2011, Joined Cases C-65/09 and C-87/09, *Gebruder Weber and Putz*, *C.M.L.Rev.* 2012, 793, note A. Johnston and H. Unberath, *D.C.C.R.* 2013, 49, note Y. Ninane. See for an exception to this rule, above Section 3.3.1, the Proposal for a directive for the supply of digital content.

87 *Cf.* A. Van Oevelen, 'Het voorstel voor een richtlijn consumentenrecht: voorstellen tot wijziging van de consumentenkoop inzake de garantie- en de meldingstermijn, de sancties bij niet-conformiteit en de handelsgarantie', *D.C.C.R.* 2009, (204) 217.

88 Article 12(3) Proposal for a directive of the European Parliament and of the Council on certain aspects concerning contracts for the supply of digital content, COM(2015) 634; Article 9(3) Proposal for a directive of the European Parliament and of the Council on certain aspects concerning contracts for the online and other distance sales of goods, COM(2015) 635.

Act refers only to a price reduction that is adequate, i.e. proportional to the depreciation generated by the defect of the market value of the goods. In this respect, Belgian scholars often refer to the so-called 'proportionate reduction', according to which the price is to be reduced by the same ratio as the value of the delivered goods compared to the value they would have had if they had been delivered in conformity with the contract.[89] This method of calculation is now also expressed in the two new proposals.[90]

However it must be submitted that also on this point the proposals for directives remain rather vague. In contrast with Belgian law,[91] there is, for example, no guideline on whether any use the consumer may have had since the delivery of the goods concerned must be taken into account when refunding. Moreover, there is no indication by whom the price reduction is to be determined. Will the price reduction be determined by the court, by the consent of the parties on the reduced price or by a third party? The proposals remain silent on this issue, which may hamper the enforceability of this provision in the national legal orders.[92] In the Belgian context, some legal scholars argue that the remedy of price reduction can be invoked unilaterally, but even then the intervention of a judge will be in any case necessary if there is a dispute between the parties concerning the amount of the price reduction.[93]

3.3.2.2. Termination of the Contract

Both the proposals restate the remedy of termination of the contract but additionally provide, in contrast with the Consumer Sales Directive, detailed rules with regard to the modalities and the consequences of exercising the right to termination.

---

89 A. Van Oevelen, 'De Wet Consumentenkoop' in *CBR Jaarboek 2005–06*, Antwerp, Maklu, 2006, (117) 145, para. 33; S. Jansen, 'Price reduction as a remedy in European contract law' in A.L.M. Keirse and M.B.M. Loos (eds.), *Alternative Ways to Ius Commune*, Antwerp, Intersentia, 2012, (169) 184.

90 Article 12 Proposal for a directive of the European Parliament and of the Council on certain aspects concerning contracts for the online and other distance sales of goods, COM(2015) 635; Article 12(4) Proposal for a directive of the European Parliament and of the Council on certain aspects concerning contracts for the supply of digital content, COM(2015) 634.

91 Article 1649*quinquies*, §3 CC; B. Tilleman, *Overeenkomsten, Deel 2. Bijzondere overeenkomsten, A. Verkoop, Deel 2. Gevolgen van de koop* in *Beginselen van Belgisch Privaatrecht*, Mechelen, Kluwer, 2012, 629, para. 765.

92 See also with respect to the CESL, R. Feltkamp and F. Vanbosselе, 'Remedies under the optional Common European Sales Law' in I. Claeys and R. Feltkamp (eds.), *The Draft Common European Sales Law: Towards an Alternative Sales Law? A Belgian Perspective*, Antwerp, Intersentia, 2013, (185) 239, para. 50.

93 S. Jansen, 'Price reduction as a remedy in European contract law' in A.L.M. Keirse and M.B.M. Loos (eds.), *Alternative Ways to Ius Commune*, Antwerp, Intersentia, 2012, (169) 178; S. Jansen, *Prijsvermindering*, Antwerp, Intersentia, 2015, 340, para. 382.

First of all, the proposal on digital content and the proposal on electronic and other distance sales contracts indicate that the consumer must exercise the right to terminate the contract by notice to the seller given by any means.[94]

This novelty will bring about a major change for Belgian consumers. Under current Belgian law the contracting parties can only terminate the contract by intervention of the court. Only in exceptional circumstances are parties allowed to invoke termination extra-judicially or unilaterally, namely in the case of an express termination clause,[95] or in extraordinary circumstances whereby judicial review would be redundant, for instance in the case of emergency, bad faith of the seller or a loss of confidence between parties.[96] But even then the remedy of termination without court intervention is seen as a very exceptional situation.[97] In that respect, the new proposals for directives significantly deviate from Belgian law in a more favourable way for consumers, who will get the right to terminate the contract unilaterally and extra-judicially.

In Belgian common sales law the buyer is entitled to claim the termination of the contract as long as the non-performance is sufficiently serious.[98] This is in line with the CSD, which denies the consumer the right to have the contract terminated if the lack of conformity is minor.[99] In those circumstances the consumer can only have recourse to a price reduction.[100] The proposal on electronic and other distance sales contracts now grants the consumer the possibility to terminate the

94 Article 13 Proposal for a directive of the European Parliament and of the Council on certain aspects concerning contracts for the supply of digital content, COM(2015) 634; Article 13 Proposal for a directive of the European Parliament and of the Council on certain aspects concerning contracts for the online and other distance sales of goods, COM(2015) 635.

95 Such a clause will rarely be stipulated in the contract.

96 S. Stijns, 'De remedies van de koper bij niet-conformiteit' in S. Stijns and J. Stuyck (eds.), *Het nieuwe kooprecht*, Antwerp, Intersentia, 2005, (53) 75, para. 52; B. Tilleman, *Overeenkomsten, Deel 2. Bijzondere overeenkomsten, A. Verkoop, Deel 2. Gevolgen van de koop* in *Beginselen van Belgisch Privaatrecht*, Mechelen, Kluwer, 2012, 628, para. 764; W. Van Gerven and A. Van Oevelen, *Verbintenissenrecht*, Leuven, Acco, 2015, 197–98; R. Steennot, 'Commentaar bij art. 1649*quinquies* BW' in *Comm.Bijz.Ov.*, 2015, 19, para. 24.

97 Although the Belgian Supreme Court (the Court of Cassation) expressed its views on extrajudicially termination of the contract in three judgments, it did so in rather ambiguous terms which are nowadays subject of speculation, see Cass. 2 May 2002, C.99.0277.N, *RW* 2002–03, 501, comments by A. Van Oevelen, *TBBR* 2003, 337; Cass. 2 May 2002, C.01.0185.N, *RCJB* 2004, 293, comments by P. Wéry, *TBBR* 2003, 339; Cass. 16 February 2009, *RW* 2011–12, 1843, comments by J. Baeck.

98 A. Van Oevelen, 'De Wet Consumentenkoop' in *CBR Jaarboek 2005–06*, Antwerp, Maklu, 2006, (117) 142–45, no. 32; B. Tilleman, *Overeenkomsten, Deel 2. Bijzondere overeenkomsten, A. Verkoop, Deel 2. Gevolgen van de koop* in *Beginselen van Belgisch Privaatrecht*, Mechelen, Kluwer, 2012, 626, para. 761.

99 Article 3(6) Consumer Sales Directive.

100 C. Cauffman, 'De nieuwe wet op de consumentenkoop', *TPR* 2005, (787) 831, para. 79; A. Van Oevelen, 'De Wet Consumentenkoop' in *CBR Jaarboek 2005–06*, Antwerp, Maklu, 2006, (117) 142–45, no. 33; S. Jansen, *Prijsvermindering*, Antwerp, Intersentia, 2015, 323, para. 361.

contract even when the lack of conformity is minor.[101] In striking contrast, the proposal on digital content allows the consumer to terminate the contract only if the lack of conformity pertains to the main performance features of the digital content. This is the case when the lack of conformity with the contract impairs functionality, interoperability or other main performance features such as the accessibility of the digital content, the continuity and its security where required in the contract.[102] There is no specific justification given in the proposals for this difference in treatment.

As regards the proposal on electronic and other distance sales contracts an interesting parallel is to be drawn with the *Duarte Hueros* case of the ECJ.[103] In that case Spanish procedural rules did not allow the national court hearing the dispute to grant of its own motion an appropriate reduction in the price of goods which were the subject of a contract of sale in the case where a consumer who was entitled to such a reduction brought proceedings which were limited to seeking only termination of that contract and such termination could not be granted because the lack of conformity in those goods was minor, even though that consumer was not entitled to refine his initial application or to bring a fresh action to that end. Despite the fact that the ECJ seemed to introduce in its judgment the right of the consumer to a remedy, the case mainly focused on procedural issues like the principle of procedural autonomy of the Member States, and the principles of equivalence and effectiveness imposed by European law. Even though the ECJ concluded that the Spanish procedural system did

> not appear to comply with the principle of effectiveness, in so far as, in proceedings brought by consumers in cases where the goods delivered are not in conformity with the contract of sale, it makes the enforcement of the protection which Directive 1999/44 seeks to provide to those consumers excessively difficult, if not impossible,[104]

it could not offer a sufficient justification for the policy change towards lack of conformity which is minor. The CESL, which will be the subject of a brief analysis in Section 4.1 below, probably offers a better explanation, as it abolished the hierarchy of remedies introduced by the CSD and provided for limitations of remedies only in respect of digital content not supplied in exchange for a price,[105] even though its Article 114(2) also stated that termination of the contract in a B2C context was only available when the lack of conformity was 'not insignificant'.[106]

---

101 Recital 29 Proposal for a directive of the European Parliament and of the Council on certain aspects concerning contracts for the online and other distance sales of goods, COM(2015) 635.

102 See Article 12(5) Proposal for a directive of the European Parliament and of the Council on certain aspects concerning contracts for the supply of digital content, COM(2015) 634.

103 See ECJ Case C-32/12, *Duarte-Hueros v Autociba*, ECLI:EU:C:2013:637.

104 See ECJ Case C-32/12, *Duarte-Hueros v Autociba*, ECLI:EU:C:2013:637, para. 41.

105 See Article 107 of the Regulation on a Common European Sales Law, COM(2011) 635 final.

106 See Article 114(2) of the Regulation on a Common European Sales Law, COM(2011) 635 final.

If the consumer terminates the contract due to the lack of conformity, the new proposals for directives prescribe the main effects and modalities of the right of termination, in particular the obligation for the parties to return what they have received. Generally, restitution after termination is executed along the following principles: each party is obliged to return what he has received from the other party. Preference is given to restitution in kind of the received performance, but when the received performance cannot be returned in kind, the party has to pay its monetary value. It follows that in the case of termination the seller will be obliged to refund the price received from the consumer and the consumer has the obligation to return the goods.[107]

The detailed rules on how to exercise the right to terminate must be welcomed. In addition to those rules in the proposal on electronic and other distance sales contracts, the proposal on digital content contains precise provisions that require the seller to take all the measures necessary in order to enable the consumer to comply with his obligation of restitution. These measures, such as for instance to disable the user account of the consumer or to provide technical means to retrieve all content provided by the consumer, can be regarded as restitution in kind.

The monetary value which the consumer must pay if the goods cannot be returned will be established according to the value the goods would have had at the date when the return was to be made, if they had been kept by the consumer without destruction or loss until that date, unless the destruction or loss has been caused by a lack of conformity of the goods with the contract.[108] In so stating, the proposals determine at what time the monetary value must be determined. This fills an existing lacuna in Belgian law where this issue remains, to date, unsettled.[109] However, it is noteworthy that the proposal on digital content, unlike the proposal on electronic and other distance sales contracts, does not impose any obligation to pay the monetary value of the digital content which is supplied on a durable medium, if this cannot be returned. Moreover, in stating that destruction or loss are not taken into account for determining the monetary value, this provision is in line with the prevailing view in Belgian doctrine that a party is not liable to pay any compensation in the case of accidental destruction or loss of the goods received.[110]

---

107 Article 13 Proposal for a directive of the European Parliament and of the Council on certain aspects concerning contracts for the supply of digital content, COM(2015) 634; Article 13(3) Proposal for a directive of the European Parliament and of the Council on certain aspects concerning contracts for the online and other distance sales of goods, COM(2015) 635.

108 Article 13(3)(c) Proposal for a directive of the European Parliament and of the Council on certain aspects concerning contracts for the online and other distance sales of goods, COM(2015) 635.

109 J. Baeck, *Restitutie na vernietiging of ontbinding van overeenkomsten*, Antwerp, Intersentia, 2012, 139, para. 204, who defends the value of the goods at the moment of the receipt.

110 J. Baeck, *Restitutie na vernietiging of ontbinding van overeenkomsten*, Antwerp, Intersentia, 2012, 71, para. 107.

Yet, the proposal on electronic and other distance sales contracts imposes on the consumer under certain strict conditions an obligation to pay for the diminution of the value of the goods. As a consequence the consumer will be obliged to pay for any decrease in the value of the goods albeit only to the extent that the decrease in value exceeds depreciation through regular use, regardless of the underlying cause. This payment for use 'in excess', however, may never exceed the price paid for the goods.[111] In contrast, the proposal on digital content expresses that the consumer shall not be liable for any use made of the digital content in the period prior to the termination of the contract.[112] Bearing in mind the full harmonisation of the proposal it seems that Member States will no longer be allowed to adopt deviating rules. Consequently there is no longer room for the Member States to stipulate rules which require the consumer to pay for any use made of the sold goods in the period prior to the termination of the contract in the case of digital content supplies.

Finally, both the proposal on digital content and the proposal on electronic and other distance sales contracts impose the costs of restitution on the seller. This must be welcomed as a rule which is clearly in favour of the consumer. It also deviates from existing Belgian law, according to which each party has to bear its own costs of restitution.[113]

3.3.3. Compensation for Damage

Both proposals contain rules concerning compensation for damage but deal with the issue in a rather different way. The discrepancy lies in the extent to which domestic laws are designed to deal with the matter.

Thus, the proposal on electronic and other distance sales contracts expressly indicates that it leaves provisions on the consumer's rights to receive compensation for the losses caused by a lack of conformity entirely to national laws.[114] This outcome corresponds to the current situation under the Consumer Sales Directive where the possibility to claim compensation was simply mentioned without any further specification. Damages can consequently be

---

111 Article 13(3)(d) Proposal for a directive of the European Parliament and of the Council on certain aspects concerning contracts for the online and other distance sales of goods, COM(2015) 635; J. Baeck, *Restitutie na vernietiging of ontbinding van overeenkomsten*, Antwerp, Intersentia, 2012, 139, para. 204.

112 Article 13(4) Proposal for a directive of the European Parliament and of the Council on certain aspects concerning contracts for the supply of digital content, COM(2015) 634. See also: J. Baeck, *Restitutie na vernietiging of ontbinding van overeenkomsten*, Antwerp, Intersentia, 2012, 146, para. 216.

113 J. Baeck, *Restitutie na vernietiging of ontbinding van overeenkomsten*, Antwerp, Intersentia, 2012, 262, para. 411.

114 Proposal for a directive of the European Parliament and of the Council on certain aspects concerning contracts for the online and other distance sales of goods, COM(2015) 635, p. 3.

claimed by consumers for as long as Member States foresee so.[115] Conversely, there is no obligation imposed by European law on Member States to introduce any such right to damages.

Quite in contrast the proposal on digital content expressly mentions that the consumer is entitled to compensation for damage caused to the consumer's digital environment by a lack of conformity with the contract or a failure to supply the digital content.[116] It further defines 'damage' as a sum of money to which consumers may be entitled as compensation for economic damage to their digital environment.[117]

This results in a somewhat conflicting situation where in cases of distance sales contracts the recognition of the consumer's right to damages depends completely upon the Member States whereas the proposal on digital content imposes an obligation on the Member States to provide for a right to damages for compensation of economic loss only. In the latter case the European legislature was of the opinion that this right had to be regulated at Union level, since it is considered as an essential element in order to increase consumers' trust in digital content.[118] Yet, the obligation to provide a pan-European right to damages is restricted solely to damage for economic loss, which could raise the question, in light of the full harmonisation character, whether Member States would then be prevented from maintaining or introducing additional rules for other types of damages?

The Community legislature seemed to be aware of the divergent interpretations that often come across with full harmonisation measures and took some efforts to clarify the proposals' scope in the introductory recitals. In the case of full harmonisation these clarifications are most welcome.

Introductory recital 10 of the proposal for a directive concerning contracts for the supply of digital content states that

> Member States should also remain free to provide rules for the detailed conditions for the exercise of rights, *such as* the right to damages to the extent not covered by the Directive, or rules which provide for the consequences of termination of the contract which apply in addition to restitution rules regulated by this Directive (emphasis added).

---

115 S. Whittaker, 'Unfair Contract Terms and Consumer Guarantees: the Proposal for a Directive on Consumer Rights and the Significance of Full Harmonisation', *ERCL* 2009, (223) 247; S. Jansen, 'Price reduction as a remedy in European contract law' in A.L.M. Keirse and M.B.M. Loos (eds.), *Alternative Ways to Ius Commune*, Antwerp, Intersentia, 2012, (169) 186.

116 Article 14 Proposal for a directive of the European Parliament and of the Council on certain aspects concerning contracts for the supply of digital content, COM(2015) 634.

117 Article 2(5) Proposal for a directive of the European Parliament and of the Council on certain aspects concerning contracts for the supply of digital content, COM(2015) 634.

118 Recital 44 Proposal for a directive of the European Parliament and of the Council on certain aspects concerning contracts for the supply of digital content, COM(2015) 634.

It offers Member States the opportunity to maintain existing rights to damages for consumers but obliges them to introduce a specific right to compensation for economic loss.

This is to be welcomed and signals a new era when compared to, for instance, the Product Liability Directive,[119] which according to most legal scholars excludes compensation for economic loss. This Directive regulates the liability for death or personal injury and damage to or destruction of property intended for private use or consumption and mainly used as such by the injured party. The ECJ has stated that these heads of damage are exhaustive and the only heads of damage possible under the Directive.[120] Insofar as consequences of death or personal injury are concerned, compensation for non-material damage is left to be governed solely by national law. Financial loss consequential on personal injury or on material damage to or loss of property falls within the scope of the Directive insofar as it is recoverable. Yet, by putting non-material damage on the same footing as the two other headings of damages (personal injury and damage to property) the ECJ's judgment in *Veedfald* can be read as if Article 9(2) includes, inter alia, pure economic loss.[121] However, the structure of both Article 9 and recital 9 of the Directive's preamble clearly indicate that pure economic loss which is not a consequence of physical deterioration of property is outside the scope of the Directive.[122]

Notwithstanding the essential nature in terms of consumers' trust of the right to damages for economic loss, and acknowledging the positive effect of this evolution, it must be observed that the rules on how to exercise the rights thereof are completely left to national law.[123]

One may wonder, in the light of the above, whether the proposed directives will be capable of attaining the proclaimed goals, even though fully harmonised rules are proposed. By leaving it to the Member States how this right to damages must be exercised in practice, the proposals rather seem to facilitate fragmentation instead of removing it. In that respect it may be deplored that there apparently existed insufficient political will to adopt the well-developed set of rules on this point in the CESL.[124]

The overall outcome of both proposals on this issue is, also when seen from a purely Belgian perspective, unsatisfactory. The proposals will certainly not end

---

119 See Directive 1985/374/EEC on Liability for Defective Products, *OJ* 1985 L 210/29.

120 ECJ Case C-203/99, *Veedfald v Arhus Amtskommune* [2001] ECR I-3569, para. 32.

121 *Cf.* J.-S. Borghetti, in E. Terryn, G. Straetmans and V. Colaert (eds.), *Landmark Cases of EU Consumer Law: Essays in honour of Jules Stuyck*, Antwerp-Cambridge, Intersentia, 2013, 321: 'the drafters' intention most likely was to keep some kinds of damage, such as pure economic loss, outside the Directive. Veedfald has brought them into it.'

122 See on this point S. Whittaker, *Liability for Products. English Law, French Law and European Harmonization*, Oxford, Oxford University Press, 2005, 506–07.

123 Recital 44 Proposal for a directive of the European Parliament and of the Council on certain aspects concerning contracts for the supply of digital content, COM(2015) 634.

124 See also below, Section 4.

current discussions among Belgian legal scholars about what rules govern the remedy of compensation. Current Article 1649*quinquies*, §1 CC gives an overview of the four remedies available to the consumer in case of non-conformity and also confirms the possibility of a complementary compensation, albeit without specifying the regime of this compensation. This gap led to uncertainty about whether Belgian common law further governed this compensation and more specifically whether the general law of obligations (Articles 1149–1151 CC) or the provisions of the common sales law (Articles 1645–1646 CC) had to apply.

On the one hand some Belgian legal scholars proposed Article 1645 CC of the common sales law as the legal basis for these complementary damages. It would allow the consumer to claim an indemnification if he suffers damage due to the non-performance of the contract. In the case of latent defects, the consumer is entitled to compensation for any damage suffered if the seller was aware of the defect. According to the well-established case law of the Belgian Supreme Court the professional seller is deemed to have knowledge of the defect unless he proves that it was entirely impossible for him to detect the defect.[125]

On the other hand, in respect of Article 1649*quater*, §5 CC the common sales law does not apply during the two-year period of the Consumer Sales Act. It follows therefrom that the application of the specific rules on latent defects are excluded during that two-year period. This exclusion brought the majority of the Belgian legal scholars to advance Article 1149 ff CC as the legal bases for the right to damages. According to those provisions all losses due to the defective performance of the seller have to be compensated for, insofar as the existence of the damage was foreseeable when the contract was concluded.[126]

3.3.4. *Right to Withhold Performance*

Article 9(4) of the proposal on electronic and other distance sales contracts provides that the consumer shall be entitled to withhold the payment of

---

125 S. Stijns, 'De remedies van de koper bij niet-conformiteit' in S. Stijns and J. Stuyck (eds.), *Het nieuwe kooprecht*, Antwerp, Intersentia, 2005, (53) 73, para. 50; S. Stijns, 'De consumentenkoop: actuele knelpunten' in B. Tilleman and A. Verbeke (eds.), *Knelpunten Verkoop roerende goederen*, Antwerp, Intersentia, 2009, (21) 65, para. 65; B. Tilleman, *Overeenkomsten, Deel 2. Bijzondere overeenkomsten, A. Verkoop, Deel 2. Gevolgen van de koop* in *Beginselen van Belgisch Privaatrecht*, Mechelen, Kluwer, 2012, 630, para. 767.

126 L. Peeters, 'De nieuwe wetgeving voor Consumentenkoop … (eindelijk) in het B.W.', *RW* 2004–05, (441) 450, para. 27; C. Cauffman and A. Verbeke, 'Een jaar Wet Consumentenkoop' in B. Tilleman and A. Verbeke (eds.), *Themis Bijzondere Overeenkomsten*, Bruges, die Keure, 2005, (27) 46, para. 72; A. Van Oevelen, 'De Wet Consumentenkoop' in *CBR Jaarboek 2005–06*, Antwerp, Maklu, 2006, (117) 142–46, para. 34; C. Cauffman, 'Vijf jaar Wet Consumentenkoop. Overzicht van rechtspraak' in K. Wauters (ed.), *Feestbundel Monard-D'hulst 20 jaar: diversiteit in eenheid*, Ghent, Larcier, 2010, (155) 174, para. 32; R. Steennot, 'Commentaar bij art. 1649*quinquies* BW' in *Comm.Bijz.Ov.*, 2015, 21, para. 25.

any outstanding part of the price, until the seller has brought the goods into conformity with the contract. The provision introduces the remedy of suspension into European legislation, also known as the right to withhold performance or the *exceptio non adimpleti contractus*.

The current Consumer Sales Directive does not contain any rule concerning the right to withhold performance and neither does the Belgian Consumer Sales Act. In this respect, the explanatory memorandum to the Belgian Act points out that this remedy is regulated by general national contract law, which is in accordance with the minimum harmonisation principle of the Consumer Sales Directive.[127]

Although it has been argued in Belgian legal doctrine that this remedy is not available in the event of latent defect, the remedy of suspension in Belgian law is seen as a temporary means of defence that is applied as a general matter to reciprocal contracts.[128] The remedy allows a party to withhold his performance without prior court intervention and for as long as the other party fails to perform his own obligations.[129] Although it must be admitted that there is no general provision on the right to withhold performance in the Civil Code, the Court of Cassation pointed out that the right to withhold performance is to be regarded as a general principle of law, originating from the interdependence of reciprocal obligations.[130]

However, the remedy of suspension may only be invoked provided the following conditions are fulfilled. First, the party invoking the remedy must be the creditor of a debt that is certain and claimable before the party's own performance becomes due. The party can only withhold his own performance if he is able to prove that the other party has not performed what was agreed.

---

127 Explanatory Memorandum, Bill 31 March 2004, *Parl.St.* Kamer 2003–2004, no. 0982/1, 11; C. Cauffman and A. Verbeke, 'Een jaar Wet Consumentenkoop' in B. Tilleman and A. Verbeke (eds.), *Themis Bijzondere Overeenkomsten*, Bruges, die Keure, 2005, (27) 47, para. 74; B. Tilleman, *Overeenkomsten, Deel 2. Bijzondere overeenkomsten, A. Verkoop, Deel 2. Gevolgen van de koop* in *Beginselen van Belgisch Privaatrecht*, Mechelen, Kluwer, 2012, 612, para. 748.

128 C. Cauffman, 'De wet op de consumentenkoop', *TPR* 2005, (787) 833, para. 83; B. Tilleman, *Overeenkomsten, Deel 2. Bijzondere overeenkomsten, A. Verkoop, Deel 2. Gevolgen van de koop* in *Beginselen van Belgisch Privaatrecht*, Mechelen, Kluwer, 2012, 349, para. 432 and references there.

129 E. Swaenepoel, 'Bedingen over de exceptie van niet-uitvoering' in S. Stijns and K. Vanderschot (eds.), *Contractuele clausules rond de (niet-)uitvoering en de beëindiging van contracten*, Antwerp, Intersentia, 2006, (133) 134, para. 3; W. Van Gerven and A. Van Oevelen, *Verbintenissenrecht*, Leuven, Acco, 2015, 210.

130 Cass. 25 March 2005, *JLMB* 2005, 1039, note P. Henry; Cass. 21 November 2003, *Pas.* 2003, 1864 and *TBBR* 2006, 39, note P. Wéry; Cass. 22 April 2002, *Pas.* 2002, 970; Cass. 15 June 2000, *Arr.Cass.* 2000, 1112 and *Pas.* 2000, 1094; Cass. 2 November 1995, *Arr.Cass.* 1995, 946 and *Pas.* 1995, 977; Cass. 26 May 1989, *Arr.Cass.* 1988–89, 1131 and *Pas.* 1989, 1020; Cass. 6 March 1986, *Arr.Cass.* 1985–86, 935, *Pas.* 1986, 849 and *RCJB* 1990, 559, note J. Herbots; Cass. 15 June 1981, *Arr.Cass.* 1980–81, 1190 and *Pas.* 1981, 1179.

Furthermore, suspension must be invoked in good faith. This means that the party invoking the suspension should not have *caused* the non-performance of the other party. Good faith also involves that withholding performance must be reasonable and thus proportional as compared to the non-performance of the other party. Moreover, the non-performance should be serious enough to justify the withholding of the performance. Finally, the party invoking the remedy should have notified the non-performance.[131] The remedy may be invoked without prior court intervention, but a court may evidently *a posteriori* verify its application.

This general rule of suspension has no mandatory nature. It follows that contracting parties have the freedom to exclude or derogate from the principle. However, in relation to a consumer the contracting parties have to take account of the unfair terms provisions. More particularly the Code of Economic Law prohibits the seller from denying the plea of suspension to the consumer in the case of his non-performance (Article VI.83, 9°) and from excluding or restricting the rights of the consumer in an inappropriate way in the case of non-performance (Article VI.83, 30°). Both unfair terms are listed in a so-called black list of unfair contract terms which the Belgian legislature has adopted in transposition of the Unfair Contract Terms Directive.

In the light of the foregoing, the provision in the proposal for a directive on electronic and other distance sales contracts remains rather vague, merely stating in general that the consumer is entitled to withhold payment until the seller has brought the goods into conformity with the contract. This raises the question whether the additional conditions imposed by Belgian law will continue to apply? It was already mentioned above that this must be assessed in the light of the scope of the full harmonisation brought about at Community level by the proposal. In this respect introductory recital 14 to the proposal may be recalled, which states that Member States apart from the areas not regulated by the proposal should also be free

> to provide more detailed conditions in relation to aspects regulated in this Directive to the extent those are not fully harmonised by this Directive: this concerns limitation periods for exercising the consumers' rights, commercial guarantees and the right of redress of the seller.[132]

131 E. Swaenepoel, 'Bedingen over de exceptie van niet-uitvoering' in S. Stijns and K. Vanderschot (eds.), *Contractuele clausules rond de (niet-)uitvoering en de beëindiging van contracten*, Antwerp, Intersentia, 2006, (133) 137–40, paras. 10–13; W. Van Gerven and A. Van Oevelen, *Verbintenissenrecht*, Leuven, Acco, 2015, 211–12.

132 Recital 14 Proposal for a directive of the European Parliament and of the Council on certain aspects concerning contracts for the online and other distance sales of goods, COM(2015) 635.

The closed list of issues mentioned in the preamble that remain within the sovereignty of Member States seems to exclude further national specification of the right to withhold performance. In the absence of more detailed rules in the proposal itself about how to exercise this new right, this outcome seems to be undesirable, so that the regulation of the modalities to exercise the rights thereof remains within the competence of the Member States. It follows that those modalities fall outside the extent of the full harmonisation of the proposal.

3.3.5. *The Consumer's Contribution to the Lack of Conformity*

According to Article 9(5) of the proposal of electronic and other distance sales contracts, the consumer shall not be entitled to a remedy to the extent that the consumer has contributed to the lack of conformity with the contract or its effects. This is in line with Belgian law, which in circumstances where the victim has committed a fault which was a cause of his loss, splits liability between the creditor and the victim so that the latter will have to bear a part of the loss himself.

The Belgian Consumer Sales Act contains also a particular provision according to which there is no lack of conformity with the contract in the case that the consumer was aware, or could not reasonably be unaware, of the lack of conformity, or when the lack of conformity has its origin in materials supplied by the consumer.[133] This provision was based on Article 2(3) of the Consumer Sales Directive, but is no longer included in the new proposals.[134] The aforementioned Article 9(5) reflects to a certain extent the same idea, and consequently could be seen as an illustration of how the consumer might contribute to the lack of conformity, notably in supplying defective materials.

3.4. TIME LIMITS

3.4.1. *Guarantee Period*

The Consumer Sales Directive as well as Belgian law hold the seller liable where the lack of conformity becomes apparent within two years from the delivery of the goods.[135] This two-year period is, however, not deemed to be in favour of the consumer. First, a similar period does not apply in common sales law and secondly, this period is not adapted to each consumer good, since durable

133 Article 1649*ter*, §3 CC.

134 It follows that a consumer who is aware of the non-conformity at the time of the conclusion of the sale and nevertheless concludes the sale would still be entitled to have recourse to the remedies for lack of conformity.

135 Article 1649*quater*, §1 CC.

products, such as vehicles and electronic household equipment, are sold with the expectation that they will last for more than two years.[136]

As a consequence, the Belgian legislator specified in Article 1649*quater*, §5 CC that once the two-year period has expired, the warranty of latent defects of the common sales law must revive. This provision raised no problems in respect of the Consumer Sales Directive because of the minimum harmonisation brought about by this directive. Member States were free to provide a higher level of protection for the consumers.

In the same vein the proposal on electronic and other distance sales contracts maintains the time limit of two years for the availability of the remedies. Thus, the consumer remains entitled to a remedy for the lack of conformity with the contract of the goods where the lack of conformity becomes apparent within two years as from the relevant time for establishing conformity. As already mentioned, the relevant time for the start of this two-year period of liability is no longer the moment of delivery but the time at which the risk passes on to the consumer.

It follows that the period of time during which the burden of proof is reversed in favour of the consumer coincides with the period during which the seller is held liable for any lack of conformity.[137] There is, however, a major difference. The full harmonisation of the proposal turns the existing minimum period of two years into a maximum period during which the consumer is entitled to a remedy for a lack of conformity. This full harmonisation consequently prevents Member States from maintaining or introducing other provisions, including more or less stringent provisions to ensure a higher level of consumer protection. The question then arises whether Article 1649*quater*, §5 CC can be maintained? It needs no further illustration that the uniform two-year period introduced by the proposal would be undermined if the consumer would be entitled to invoke the common sales law provisions including those relating to latent defects after expiry of that two-year period.[138] It consequently follows that

---

136 C. Cauffman and A. Verbeke, 'Een jaar Wet Consumentenkoop' in B. Tilleman and A. Verbeke (eds.), *Themis Bijzondere Overeenkomsten*, Bruges, die Keure, 2005, (27) 39, para. 45; S. Stijns, 'De consumentenkoop: actuele knelpunten' in B. Tilleman and A. Verbeke (eds.), *Knelpunten Verkoop roerende goederen*, Antwerp, Intersentia, 2009, (21) 46, para. 35; B. Tilleman, *Overeenkomsten, Deel 2. Bijzondere overeenkomsten, A. Verkoop, Deel 2. Gevolgen van de koop* in *Beginselen van Belgisch Privaatrecht*, Mechelen, Kluwer, 2012, 604, para. 737.

137 Recitals 32 and 33 Proposal for a directive of the European Parliament and of the Council on certain aspects concerning contracts for the online and other distance sales of goods, COM(2015) 635.

138 See A. Van Oevelen, 'Het voorstel voor een richtlijn consumentenrecht: voorstellen tot wijziging van de consumentenkoop inzake de garantie- en de meldingstermijn, de sancties bij niet-conformiteit en de handelsgarantie', *D.C.C.R.* 2009, (204) 210.

the full harmonisation of the new proposal will have the effect in Belgium that revival of the extended liability for hidden defects will no longer be allowed.[139]

Quite in contrast, the proposal on digital content contracts provides for a solution that is much more in favour of consumers. Instead of introducing a fixed period within which the supplier is held liable for any lack of conformity which exists at the time of the supply of the digital content, no specific period is introduced. Consequently, Member States must, due to the full harmonisation of that proposal, refrain from maintaining or introducing any such period.[140]

3.4.2. *Prescription Period*

Article 1649*quater*, §3 CC introduces a prescription period of one year within which the consumer is entitled to exercise his rights. It further states that this prescription period will not expire before the guarantee period of two years has lapsed. The two new proposals for directives point out that the Member States remain free to provide prescription rules in order to ensure legal certainty in relation to claims based on the lack of conformity.[141] Even in the presence of full harmonisation Member States will thus be free to maintain existing rules or adapt them.

3.4.3. *Suspension or Interruption*

The Consumer Sales Directive granted the option for Member States to provide for a suspension or an interruption of the period during which any lack of conformity must become apparent and of the limitation period, where the seller attempts to repair or replace the non-conforming goods, or is in negotiations with the consumer over a settlement.[142] The Belgian legislator made use of this option and sets out in Article 1649*quater*, §1 CC that the two-year period for the availability of the remedies will be suspended during the repair or replacement or in case of negotiations in view of an amicable settlement. The time already

139 See also on this point, M. Loos, 'Consumer Sales Law in the Proposal for a Consumer Rights Directive', *ERPL* 2010, (15) 28.

140 Recital 43 Proposal for a directive of the European Parliament and of the Council on certain aspects concerning contracts for the supply of digital content, COM(2015) 634.
According to Article 19 of the Proposal on digital content, the contracting parties are only allowed to derogate from the national measures transposing the Directive to the detriment of the consumer after the lack of conformity with the contract is brought to the supplier's attention by the consumer.

141 Recital 43 Proposal for a directive of the European Parliament and of the Council on certain aspects concerning contracts for the supply of digital content, COM(2015) 634; Recital 14 Proposal for a directive of the European Parliament and of the Council on certain aspects concerning contracts for the online and other distance sales of goods, COM(2015) 635.

142 Recital 18 Consumer Sales Directive.

lapsed is not cleared, but rather the prescription ceases to run. It must be noticed that for the prescription period itself no suspension or interruption is provided.

The new proposal for a directive for electronic and other distance sales contracts does not contain any similar recital concerning the possibility of suspension or interruption of the guarantee period. This raises the fundamental question whether the Belgian legislator can maintain Article 1649*quater*, §1 CC? In respect of the full harmonisation such a provision would impair the two-year period since suspension of this period will certainly lead to an extension of the guarantee period. Hence the provision must probably be removed. This will obviously be very disadvantageous for the consumer.

3.4.4. *Reduced Liability Period for Second-Hand Goods*

Article 1649*quater*, §1 CC converts a regulatory option under the Consumer Sales Directive into a firm rule, by permitting the parties to the consumer sales contract to agree on a shorter liability period of at least one year in the case of second-hand goods.

In contrast, the proposals for directives do not contain any provisions concerning second-hand goods. The lack of a particular regime for second-hand goods can be interpreted in two different ways. Either they provide for no particular regime for second-hand goods because second-hand goods now fall within the general scope of the proposals and thus are to be dealt with under the 'common' regime, or in remaining silent about second-hand goods the proposals seem to indicate that the Member States remain free to provide their own deviating rules.

Bearing in mind the approach of the European legislator in the Consumer Sales Directive, the first interpretation seems to prevail. In respect of the Consumer Sales Directive second-hand goods were treated under the general regime of conformity and deemed to fall within the definition of 'consumer goods'. This analysis is supported by Article 1(3), which allows Member States to exclude from the definition of 'consumer goods' second-hand goods sold at public auctions where consumers have the opportunity of attending the sale in person. Furthermore, the fact that Member States were free to provide for a shorter period of liability for second-hand goods strengthens the analysis that second-hand goods are covered by the common regime.[143] Also the case law of the ECJ occasionally dealt with second-hand goods under the common regime.[144] This brings us to the conclusion that the absence of any reference to second-hand goods in the new proposals for directives has no other meaning

---

143 Article 7(1) Consumer Sales Directive.

144 See for instance ECJ, 4 June 2015, Case C-497/13, *Froukje Faber v Autobedrijf Hazet Ochten BV*, ECLI:EU:C:2015:357.

than that second-hand goods simply fall within their scope without any further exception needed.

3.5. COMMERCIAL GUARANTEES

The proposal on electronic and other distance sales contracts restates to a great extent the provisions concerning commercial guarantees from the Consumer Sales Directive. Any commercial guarantee shall be binding on the guarantor under the conditions laid down in the guarantee statement, and the advertising available at the time of or before the conclusion of the contract. The new rules further specify that pre-contractual information provided by the seller which forms an integral part of the contract, is also binding.[145] Moreover, in order to improve legal certainty and to avoid consumers being misled, the proposal provides that where commercial guarantee conditions contained in advertisements or pre-contractual information are more favourable to the consumer than those included in the guarantee statement the more advantageous conditions should prevail.[146]

An important improvement is that the proposal now requires that the guarantee statement is to be made available to the consumer on a durable medium, even without the consumer's prior request.[147] In Belgian law availability on a durable medium was hitherto only required upon the consumer's request.[148] Yet, Article 1649*septies*, §3 CC, second paragraph requires that all the information referred to in Article 1649*septies*, §2 CC must be mentioned in the sales contract when the sales contract is in writing. The precise purpose of this requirement remained unclear. Some legal scholars pointed to the possible benefit for consumers and the requirement of ensuring that the consumer knows the precise content of the guarantee statement before concluding the contract.[149]

---

145 Article 15(1) Proposal for a directive of the European Parliament and of the Council on certain aspects concerning contracts for the online and other distance sales of goods, COM(2015) 635.

146 Recital 34 Proposal for a directive of the European Parliament and of the Council on certain aspects concerning contracts for the online and other distance sales of goods, COM(2015) 635.

147 Article 15(2) Proposal for a directive of the European Parliament and of the Council on certain aspects concerning contracts for the online and other distance sales of goods, COM(2015) 635.

148 Article 1649*septies*, §3, first sentence CC.

149 I. Samoy, 'Commerciële garanties en het dwingend karakter van de nieuwe regels' in S. Stijns and J. Stuyck (eds.), *Het nieuwe kooprecht*, Antwerp, Intersentia, 2005, (103) 117, para. 32; C. Cauffman, 'De nieuwe wet op de consumentenkoop', *TPR* 2005, (787) 843, para. 102; A. Van Oevelen, 'De Wet Consumentenkoop' in *CBR Jaarboek 2005–06*, Antwerp, Maklu, 2006, (117) 153, para. 41; R. Steennot, 'Commentaar bij art. 1649*septies* BW' in *Comm.Bijz. Ov.*, 2015, 12, para. 15.

In light of the new requirement to make the guarantee statement available (in writing) on a durable medium, this discussion will become redundant.

Finally, Article 15(4) states that the Member States may lay down additional rules on commercial guarantees insofar as those rules do not reduce the protection set out in this Article.[150] It follows that the provision concerning the required language, which can be found in Article VI.8 Code of Economic Law and which was based on the option left for the Member States to determine the languages in which the guarantee has to be drafted,[151] can be maintained.

3.6. THE RIGHT OF REDRESS

Like the Consumer Sales Directive the new proposals grant the final seller a right of redress against the person liable in the contractual chain. Belgian law entitles the final seller to pursue remedies against the producer, a previous seller in the same chain of contract or any other intermediary for an act or omission resulting in the lack of conformity.[152] The purpose is to prevent the final seller's liability for damage which was actually caused by the misconduct of a third party. Furthermore Article 1649*sexies* CC provides that terms restricting or excluding the liability towards the seller who is liable to a consumer for a lack of conformity resulting from an act or omission by a previous seller in the contractual chain, are ineffective in relation to the consumer.

This specific rule is not included in the new proposals which, however, also state that the modalities and conditions of exercise of the right of redress remain to be regulated by the national laws of the Member States.[153] It is obvious that the Belgian CC, which renders all terms restricting or excluding liability ineffective, goes beyond the proposals. Nevertheless Article 1649*sexies* CC must be seen as a provision that regulates the modalities and conditions of exercise of the right of redress and can be maintained in that capacity as an exception to the full harmonisation.

3.7. THE RIGHT TO TERMINATE LONG-TERM CONTRACTS

The proposal on digital content entitles the consumer to terminate the contract that altogether lasts for a period longer than 12 months, irrespective of whether

150 Recital 14 Proposal for a directive of the European Parliament and of the Council on certain aspects concerning contracts for the online and other distance sales of goods, COM(2015) 635.

151 Article 6(4) Consumer Sales Directive.

152 Article 1649*sexies* CC.

153 Article 17 Proposal for a directive of the European Parliament and of the Council on certain aspects concerning contracts for the supply of digital content, COM(2015) 634.

the contract is of indeterminate duration or is extended automatically or following a subsequent agreement by the parties, after the expiration of the first 12-month period.[154]

In contrast to distance sales contracts, contracts concerning the supply of digital content are mostly continuing performance contracts that can be divided into contracts with an agreed term and contracts with unlimited time. Under Belgian law contracts of unlimited duration can be terminated at all times by either party, as opposed to contracts with an agreed duration.[155] The latter contracts will be terminated when the agreed duration expires, unless the contracting parties have expressed the possibility to terminate otherwise in their contract.

The new provision in the proposal for digital content can be seen as a contract term in the latter sense which clarifies the notice period and the means of cancellation. But, contrary to the existing legislation in Belgium, the possibility to terminate the contract after 12 months is also extended to contracts of indeterminate duration. This is a deviation from Belgian law which is arguably disadvantageous for consumers.

4. SCOPE OF APPLICATION OF THE PROPOSALS: ANALYSIS FROM A EUROPEAN PERSPECTIVE

4.1. COMMON EUROPEAN SALES LAW

In line with the current proposals for directives, the purpose of the proposal for a regulation on a common European sales law was to improve the conditions for the establishment and the functioning of the internal market.

However, in striking contrast with the current proposals, this beneficial outcome for the internal market was to be attained by making available *a uniform set of contract law rules* as set out in Annex I: 'the Common European Sales Law' of the proposal (emphasis added).[156] These rules could then be used for cross-border transactions for the sale of goods, for the supply of digital content and for related services where the parties to a contract agree to do so.[157]

It would enable traders to rely on a common set of rules and use the same contract terms for all their cross-border transactions thereby reducing

---

154 Article 16 Proposal for a directive of the European Parliament and of the Council on certain aspects concerning contracts for the supply of digital content, COM(2015) 634.

155 F. Vermander, *De opzegging van overeenkomsten*, Antwerp, Intersentia, 2014, 461, para. 559.

156 See Article 1(1) of the Regulation on a Common European Sales Law, COM(2011) 635 final.

157 For a critical analysis, see among others M. Loos, 'The regulation of digital content B2C contracts in CESL' in K. Purnhagen and P. Rott (eds.), *Varieties of European Economic Law and Regulation*, Heidelberg, Springer, 2014, 611 ff.

unnecessary costs while providing a high degree of legal certainty and in relation to contracts between traders and consumers, it would provide for a comprehensive set of consumer protection rules to ensure a high level of consumer protection, to enhance consumer confidence in the internal market and encourage consumers to shop across borders.

4.1.1. *Scope of Application*

Although the proposed common European sales law (CESL) was optional[158] in nature and confined to cross-border contracts,[159] it was to be used for sales contracts without exception, including contracts for the supply of digital content (whether or not supplied on a tangible medium) which can be stored, processed or accessed, and re-used by the user, irrespective of whether the digital content is supplied in exchange for the payment of a price, and also related service contracts, irrespective of whether a separate price was agreed for the related service.

The hampering effect of the optional nature on the application of the CESL in daily practice had to be nuanced to a certain extent because once parties have validly agreed to use the CESL, only the CESL would govern the matters addressed in its rules.[160] Furthermore, the cross-border nature of the CESL could be extended as Member States were allowed to make the CESL available for intra-state contracts and even contracts where all the parties are traders.[161] The last option derogates from Article 7 of the proposed regulation which required that where all the parties to a contract are traders at least one of those parties had to be a small or medium-sized enterprise.

In comparison with the scope of the proposals for directives, the CESL avoided as much as possible fragmentation. The CESL, for example, made no distinction between face-to-face and distance sales contracts. Also the new criterion for the delineation between contracts for the supply of digital content regarded as sale of goods contracts and digital content contracts brought under a *sui generis* regime was absent in that proposal for a regulation.[162] Under the regime of CESL only mixed-purpose contracts (other than sale of goods, supply of digital content and related services) and contracts linked to a consumer credit agreement were excluded from its scope.

The CESL also took the freedom of contract as the point of departure, but the parties' freedom, apart from being subject to any applicable mandatory rules, to

---

158 See Article 3 of the Regulation on a Common European Sales Law, COM(2011) 635 final.

159 See the definition of cross-border contracts in Article 4 of the Regulation on a Common European Sales Law, COM(2011) 635 final.

160 See Article 11 of the Regulation on a Common European Sales Law, COM(2011) 635 final.

161 See Article 13 of the Regulation on a Common European Sales Law, COM(2011) 635 final.

162 It has been pointed out above that the criterion whether the durable medium has been used exclusively as carrier of digital content will create delimitation problems in practice.

exclude the application of any of the provisions of CESL or derogate from or vary their effects is confirmed only if not otherwise stated in those provisions. Most of its essential provisions could not be derogated from.

Having, then, a closer look at the precise rules which were proposed in the CESL, their comprehensiveness is immediately striking. The CESL comprises detailed rules on pre-contractual information B2C and B2B, including remedies for breach of information duties and additional information and confirmation requirements for off-premises sales, distance sales contracts and contracts concluded by electronic means, and also rules on the offer and on the conclusion of a contract. Most of the pre-contractual information requirements and the provisions concerning the right to withdraw from distance and off-premises contracts stem from the Consumer Rights Directive and the Directive on Electronic Commerce.

Further, CESL contained rules on the burden of proof, the time of conclusion of the contract, and rules on unfair contract terms (B2B and B2C – the latter taken from the Unfair Contract Terms Directive), provisions on the modes of giving notice, rules concerning termination of the contract and how to exercise this right, as well as detailed rules on remedies. Detailed rules on the seller's obligations including delivery and detailed rules concerning the buyer's remedies further complemented the aforementioned provisions.

Although some of the principles from the CESL are taken into the proposals for directives such as the criteria for conformity, incorrect installation, third party rights or claims, the relevant time for establishing conformity and the abolition of the obligation to notify, other rules, for instance the detailed rules on the buyer's remedies as well as the rules on damages and interests, are missing.

A comprehensive analysis of the new proposals in the light of the withdrawn CESL goes far beyond the scope of this chapter. Therefore, the analysis hereafter will focus on the most noteworthy differences.

4.1.2. Overview of Major Differences

The proposals for directives adhere to the 'two-stage' hierarchy among the remedies which was introduced by the CSD. A consumer should first request repair or replacement (the first-stage remedies) before invoking a price reduction or the termination of the contract, and is entitled only to a price reduction or the termination of the contract where the lack of conformity is not or cannot be remedied through repair or replacement.

In striking contrast, the CESL did not contain such a hierarchy of remedies. It spelled out on this point that: 'In the case of non-performance of an obligation by the seller, the buyer *may do any of the following*'.[163] Thus, the consumer

[163] Article 106(1) of the Regulation on a Common European Sales Law, COM(2011) 635 final.

would have been entirely free to choose the remedy he wanted. He could claim performance or immediately revert to termination.[164] Nevertheless, the CESL expressly provided that accumulation of remedies could be allowed only to the extent that such accumulation is not incompatible, but this only limited the consumer's choice to a logical extent.[165] It meant for example that requesting performance in kind and termination of the sales contract at the same time would not be possible.

Some other remarkable deviations can be noticed in relation to some remedies. More particularly the right to withhold performance, the right to terminate the contract and the right to claim damages present significant changes. Whereas the proposals for directives only mention the possibility for the consumer to withhold the payment of any outstanding part of the price until the seller has brought the goods into conformity with the contract, Article 113 CESL allowed a buyer to withhold performance not only when he has to perform at the same time or after the seller's performance, but even when the buyer has to perform before the seller but reasonably believes that there will be non-performance by the seller when his performance becomes due. Needless to add, Article 113 CESL provides for a much more extended right to withhold performance than the new proposals for directives.

Conversely, as regards the remedy of termination of the contract, the proposal on electronic and other distance sales contracts grants the consumer the possibility to terminate the contract even when the lack of conformity is minor,[166] whereas the CESL only enabled the consumer to terminate the contract where there is a non-performance because the goods do not conform to the contract, when the lack of conformity is not insignificant.[167]

It further is remarkable that the European Commission did not insert the detailed rules on damages of the CESL into the new proposals for directives. In the proposal on electronic and other distance sales contracts the recognition of the right to damages is completely left over to the Member States, whereas the proposal on digital content admittedly imposes the obligation on the Member States to provide for a right to damages for compensation of economic loss but remains silent about any other right to damages. It was pointed out above that the restriction to economic loss in the latter proposal leaves the Member States

164 See, however, Article 111(2) of the Regulation on a Common European Sales Law, COM(2011) 635 final: 'If the consumer has required the remedying of the lack of conformity by repair or replacement ... the consumer may resort to other remedies only if the trader has not completed repair or replacement within a reasonable time, not exceeding 30 days. However the consumer may withhold performance during that time'.

165 Article 106(6) of the Regulation on a Common European Sales Law, COM(2011) 635 final.

166 Recital 29 Proposal for a directive of the European Parliament and of the Council on certain aspects concerning contracts for the online and other distance sales of goods, COM(2015) 635.

167 Article 114(2) of the Regulation on a Common European Sales Law, COM(2011) 635 final.

free to introduce or maintain rules for other types of damages despite the full harmonisation character of the proposal. When compared to the CESL 'loss' was defined much more broadly as encompassing 'economic loss and non-economic loss in the form of pain and suffering, excluding other forms of non-economic loss such as impairment of the quality of life and loss of enjoyment'.[168]

In contrast with the current CSD and the proposal on electronic and other distance sales contracts, according to which the seller is liable where the lack of conformity becomes apparent within two years as from the delivery of the goods, the proposal on digital content, likewise the CESL, does not impose a specific guarantee period. It follows that in the latter case the availability of the remedies is not limited to a period wherein the lack of conformity should become apparent.

This brief analysis demonstrates that where the new proposals for directives deviate from the CESL regime, such as for instance with regard to time limits and remedies, they often do so in a less favourable way for consumers. Even though the optional nature[169] of the CESL must be taken into account when comparing the two regimes it may be submitted that the legislature missed an excellent opportunity with the launch of the new proposals for directives to introduce a more comprehensive CESL-like regime as regards time limits and damages.

4.2. THE REGIME OF LATENT DEFECTS IN NEIGHBOURING NATIONAL LEGAL ORDERS

It seems interesting to compare the impact of the proposals for directives, giving their intrusive effect on the Belgian regime for latent defects,[170] with some neighbouring national legal orders and in particular with their national sales laws.

From the outset two general remarks have to be made. First, the monist approach of the European legislator in the new proposals for directives endorsing the full harmonisation principle will prevent Member States from maintaining a dualist system in their national consumer sales law. Second, the rather limited scope of application of the proposals for directives could lead to fragmentation of the national common sales law. These two aspects will now be analysed briefly.

---

168 Article 2(c) of the Regulation on a Common European Sales Law, COM(2011) 635 final.

169 Article 8(2) of the Regulation on a Common European Sales Law, COM(2011) 635 final. In requiring the agreement of the contracting parties about the application of CESL and in B2C contracts the explicit choice for the application of CESL in a separate statement, it remained to be seen whether CESL in practice would be experiencing such a boom.

170 See above.

4.2.1. Dualist Systems in National Consumer Sales Law No Longer Allowed

By integrating the duty to deliver goods that are in conformity with the contract and the duty to deliver goods free of latent defects into one broadly defined obligation to deliver goods that are in conformity with the sales contract, the European legislator opts for a monist system.

It must be observed in that respect that not all of the Member States of the EU adhere to a monist system. For instance Belgian and French sales law impose two separate obligations on the seller, namely the duty to deliver the goods sold and the duty to guarantee (Article 1603 CC). The duty to guarantee is composed of two components, the duty to guarantee the undisturbed possession of the goods sold and the duty to guarantee the absence of latent defects (Article 1625 CC). The duty to deliver the sold goods comprises the duty to deliver goods that are in conformity with the provisions of the contract (Article 1604 CC). It follows that the duty to deliver does not encompass the duty to deliver goods without latent defects which is, as mentioned above, a component of the seller's duty to guarantee. This system which distinguishes between a duty to deliver and a duty to guarantee the absence of latent defects, is called a dualist system.

The duality of the system is reflected in the national consumer sales law of both countries. Article 1649*quater*, §5 of the Belgian Civil Code states that once the two-year period has expired, the warranty of latent defects of the common sales law will revive. The French legislator went even further and decided to make the dualist system available for consumers even when the two-year period has not yet expired. Thus, in France consumers are entitled to invoke at their own choice the 'non-conformity with the contract' and the remedies in respect of latent defects (Article L. 211-13 Code de la consommation).

The full harmonisation approach of the European legislator no longer leaves room for such dualist systems. If a French consumer would be allowed to use remedies against the seller based on different conceptual grounds which in practice present overlaps with 'non-conformity' of the goods, this would undermine the harmonising effect intended by the proposals.[171] Consequently, the full harmonisation endorsed by the new directives will prohibit not only the existence of alternative national schemes such as the liability for hidden defects in France but also the complementary regime for latent defects as is currently the case in Belgium.

4.2.2. National Fragmentation

To place the former analysis in a broader perspective it is illustrative to extend the comparison to Germany and the Netherlands. In both countries a monist

[171] S. Whittaker, 'Unfair Contract Terms and Consumer Guarantees', *ERCL* 2009, (223) 245.

system applies so that the implementation of the new proposals at first glance would not amount to major difficulties. Yet, in those countries the monist regime not only applies in *consumer* sales law, but also in the common sales law. In Germany, for instance, the implementation of the new proposals for directives will inevitably lead to a profound reform of the entire law of obligations ('*Schuldrechtsreform*') and of the conformity requirement that is now applicable to all contracts of sale. This is consequential on the implementation of the CSD, which apart from being applicable to consumer sales contracts, also extended to other contracts.

Likewise, the Dutch legislator endorsed the same approach and implemented the CSD into the Civil Code. Yet, in comparison with Germany, the amalgamation of the consumer sales law into the common sales law was less straightforward, leaving certain differences intact.

Nevertheless, the proposals for directives will confront those Member States with monist regimes, like Germany and the Netherlands, that went for so-called 'spontaneous harmonisation' between the consumer sales regime and the common sales law, with new challenges. Since the new proposals for directives would apply to consumer sales contracts only, these countries will have as such no incentive to amend their legislation for non-consumer sales contracts, with new fragmentation of sales law regimes as a result. Furthermore, if the implementation of the directives in those countries would be limited to B2C contracts it could lead to the adverse effect that the new provisions concerning consumer sales turn out to be less protective than the general contract law and that a consumer would be better off to be categorised as a non-consumer.[172] By elevating the current minimum standards to full harmonisation, general contract law then could turn out to be more favourable in some respects than the legislation transposing the proposals for directives into the national consumer sales legislation. That would mean that it could well be in the interest of the buyer to prove that he is not a consumer, or to prove that the seller was not acting in the exercise of his business or profession, as that would provide him with better protection than that which would apply if he were considered to be a consumer.[173] If, however, those Member States opt for an implementation of the new proposals through their consumer sales law and common sales law alike, then they will be forced to introduce rules that in comparison with existing legislation are less favourable for consumers, beside of course other rules that *are* in the consumer's favour.

---

172 R.R.R. Hardy and G.G. Hesen, 'Het voorstel voor een richtlijn betreffende consumentenrechten', *WPNR* 2009, (69) 71.

173 *Cf.* C. Twigg-Flesner and D. Metcalfe, 'The proposed Consumer Rights Directive. Less haste, more thought?', *ERCL* 2009, (368) 373; M. Loos, 'Consumer Sales Law in the Proposal for a Consumer Rights Directive', *ERPL* 2010, (15) 29.

5. CONCLUSION

The European legislature's preference for directives with full harmonisation comes as no surprise. As was pointed out above, it fits well into the existing Union's policy regarding consumer protection. The overall aim of the new proposals is to create a genuine digital single market based on a fully harmonised legal framework that eventually would increase the current level of consumer protection. Full harmonisation of the existing *consumer acquis* also serves the purposes of the internal market well.[174]

In general, the European Commission's policy of confidence building through total harmonisation of the existing *consumer acquis* must be welcomed. The shift towards full harmonisation of the acquis does not exclusively correspond to an inherent logic of markets becoming more integrated; it can also be justified by bad experiences with ineffective minimal harmonisation leaving too many divergences between national laws intact.[175]

However, full harmonisation in the field of contract law has always been highly controversial,[176] not so much because the consumer contract law acquis does not reveal areas where the law of the Member States differ considerably, but very much because Member States anxiously seek to preserve their contract law as it currently stands.

Whilst in those circumstances a fully harmonised framework of consumer sales law is, politically speaking, unattainable, the European legislature is forced to improve the fully harmonised minimum standards step by step, focusing on the most important rules for both the functioning of the internal market and the protection of consumers. This is exactly what the European Commission aims at with the current proposals for directives.

---

174 It would amount to maximum levels of protection beyond which consumer protection is considered to be excessive in the light of the internal market. Consequently it would make the law of host Member States predictable and fosters the establishment of the internal market.

175 The current minimum harmonisation has rather led to diversity among the Member States and is therefore considered as one of the obstacles which hampers the establishment of a genuine digital market.

176 Compare with N. Reich, 'Protection of Consumer's Economic Interests by EC Contract Law', *Sydney Law Review*, 2006, vol. 28, 60, who suggests, as a first step, to concentrate 'on a consolidation of existing consumer contract law which should be transferred into a "European Consumer Contract Law Regulation" (ECCLR)'. But also adds that this ECCLR as such could be based on Article 153(3)(b) EG as being a 'measure to support ... the policy pursued by Member States' (p. 61). See also S. Weatherill, 'Minimum Harmonisation as Oxymoron?' in H.-W. Micklitz (ed.), *Verbraucherrecht in Deutschland – Stand und Perspektiven*, Baden-Baden, Nomos, 2005, 35, who advocates diversity and the possibility of regulatory experimentation. Hence, 'EU rules would operate as minimum standards only – unless this was explicitly displaced by provision made by the legislature in the particular text concerned'.

Yet, the analysis of both proposals and their comparison with current Belgian legislation and the European legislative context result in findings which are not entirely in the favour of consumers across Europe.

5.1. ANALYSIS FROM A BELGIAN PERSPECTIVE

From a Belgian law perspective the analysis shows that the proposals deviate from the current Belgian legislation, sometimes in favour of the consumer and sometimes not. Among the changes that will be beneficial to consumers the following aspects may be ranged: the abolition of the obligation to notify the lack of conformity and consequently the prohibition on the seller stipulating such an obligation in the contract; the extension of the period during which the burden of proof is reversed from six months to two years, and the possibility for the consumer to terminate the contract unilaterally in the case of a distance sales contract, even if the lack of conformity is minor.

Also some novelties introduced in the proposals improve the level of protection for consumers. For instance the right to withhold performance and the right to damages for economic loss in the case of supply of digital content clearly improve the consumer's position, although, as will be pointed out below, the proposals merely regulate the principle of the remedy, leaving the framework for exercising those rights to the Member States themselves.

However, a major setback from a Belgian perspective will be that complementary regimes concerning latent defects will have to be abolished due to the full harmonisation endorsed in the proposals for directives.

5.2. ANALYSIS FROM A EUROPEAN PERSPECTIVE

The shift towards full harmonisation of minimum standards of protection will certainly contribute to increased legal certainty in cross-border shopping which is also in favour of consumers. Nevertheless the analysis demonstrates that the adoption of the proposals would entail the following shortcomings.

5.2.1. Fragmentation

First of all, the scope of application of the proposals is restricted to respectively electronic and other distance sales contracts and contracts for the supply of digital content. As a result the uniform rules regarding consumer sales would become fragmented again with the adoption of the new directives. Among face-to-face consumer sales contracts, contracts for the supply of digital content will be distinguished from other consumer sales contracts. The contracts for the supply of digital content themselves present in turn an overlap with the electronic and other distance sales contracts which will be subject to a different regime. This fragmentation evidently will render the legislation concerning consumer sales contracts more complex.

5.2.2. *Problems of Delineation*

Further, the criteria whereupon the overlap between both proposals is avoided will inevitably lead to delineation problems. Especially the way in which digital supply contracts are carved out of the general Consumer Sales Directive and removed from the scope of the new proposal for electronic and other distance sales contracts raises problems.[177]

5.2.3. *Problems Relating to the Lowering of Standards of Consumer Protection*

A comparison with the current level of consumer protection in the Belgian legal order leads to the result that consumers will no longer be capable of having recourse to the protective regime in the case of latent defects after the expiry of the guarantee period. On top of that the two-year period, which ever since the adoption of the CSD has been the subject of multiple critiques, will take the form of a long-stop period so that existing specific rules in domestic law concerning suspension or interruption of that period will become redundant.

Furthermore, besides maybe the rules incorporated in the CESL,[178] there is no convincing justification why the proposal for electronic and other distance sales contracts sets a two-year guarantee period during which the lack of conformity must become apparent whereas the proposal for digital content does not.

Finally, the upgrade of the minimum standards into fully harmonised rules will place Member States that already shifted towards a monist regime in an awkward position. They will have to decide whether the new directives should be implemented into the national consumer contracts law only or simultaneously into the general sales law. If the implementation of the directives would be confined to B2C contracts it could give rise to adverse effects, with consumers being better off under the general sales law than under the specific consumer sales law. Indeed, in the case where the transposition into the national legal order of the new proposals is confined to consumer sales contracts, the new provisions concerning consumer sales could turn out to be less protective than the general

177 See above and see also the chapter by R. Steennot and S. Geiregat in this volume.

178 See Article 105(2) of the Regulation on a Common European Sales Law, COM(2011) 635 final, which sets out a six months guarantee period unless this is incompatible with digital content and Article 105(4) of the Regulation on a Common European Sales Law, COM(2011) 635 final, that states that where the digital content must be subsequently updated by the trader, the trader must ensure that the digital content remains in conformity with the contract throughout the duration of the contract.

contract law so that consumers would be forced to strive for categorisation as a non-consumer. If the implementation of the new rules would take that form, it further would contribute to the creation of a new patchwork of sales contract laws in those Member States.

5.2.4. Conformity Criteria

It must be observed that the emphasis in contracts for the supply of digital content on subjective criteria of conformity may have an adverse impact on the level of consumer protection. It remains to be seen in that regard whether the consumer will find himself in a sufficiently strong bargaining position to influence the contract on this point.

5.2.5. Problems Relating to the Breadth of Harmonisation

One of the major drawbacks of the new proposals for directives is their rather limited scope of application. Only certain aspects of the specific types of consumer contracts will be fully harmonised, such as for instance the criteria for conformity with the contract mentioned in Section 5.2.4 above.

Although it was to be expected, given their sensitivity, that rules relating to the formation and the validity of the contract would remain within the ambit of domestic law, it must be observed that the proposals for directives do not even harmonise all or most relevant aspects of the areas they effectively deal with. For instance the prescription period, the right to damages and the right of redress are introduced in the proposals merely as a principle. Apart from the simple mentioning of the existence of these rights, the way in which the rights have to be exercised is completely left over to the Member States.

In this regard recital 14 of the proposal for a directive concerning electronic and other distance sales of goods may be recalled. It states that the directive must not affect contract laws of Member States in areas not regulated by it, and that

> Member States should also be free to provide more detailed conditions in relation to aspects regulated in this Directive to the extent those are not fully harmonised by this Directive: this concerns limitation periods for exercising the consumers' rights, commercial guarantees, and the right of redress of the seller.

In providing a closed list of areas in which Member States retain the freedom to provide more detailed rules, the wording of this proposal seems stricter than the wording of the corresponding recital 10 of the proposal for a directive concerning contracts for the supply of digital content, which spells out that national laws are not affected to the extent that the topics concerned are not regulated by this directive, such as national rules providing for obligations of the consumer towards the supplier of digital content or regulating the qualification, formation and validity of contracts or the legality of the content. It further states that

> Member States should also remain free to provide rules for the detailed conditions for the exercise of rights, *such as* the right to damages to the extent not covered by the Directive, or rules which provide for the consequences of termination of the contract which apply in addition to restitution rules regulated by this Directive (emphasis added).

Whereas the proposal on electronic and other distance sales seems to exclude the possibility of ruling in more detail how the new consumer rights guaranteed by the directive have to be exercised, the proposal on digital content, quite in contrast, seems to grant Member States much more leeway. In both cases the wording 'to the extent not covered/not fully harmonised by the directive' functions as a safeguard for uniformity but also leaves room for speculation about the precise extent of the harmonisation.

It follows that in certain areas consumers will be completely dependent upon the availability in their national legal system of protective rules. This will be, for instance, the case with the newly introduced right to withhold performance and rights to damages. Member States will remain free to regulate the modalities of those rights, even after the proposals would have been enacted. In that regard it is to be welcomed that some Member States will have to introduce a specific right to recover damages for economic loss in the case of contracts for the supply of digital content. But overall it may be concluded that the absence of more detailed rules in the proposals will lead to different levels of protection between Member States, which evidently undermines the uniformity aimed at in the proposals.

Even if it is acceptable to speculate to a certain extent on the unifying factor of the case law of the Court of Justice it will be nonetheless in this sensitive area of contract law a very time-consuming endeavour. Meanwhile it must be observed that consumers will not be secured the level playing-field which they were promised to enjoy in the new single digital market.

5.2.6. Securing Consumer Confidence in the Area of Consumer Sales?

Hence, in the light of the aforementioned shortcomings, the question may be raised whether the proposals under examination will be capable of achieving the proclaimed objectives of reducing the fragmentation of the rules between the Member States and securing consumer confidence in the area of consumer sales?

As is often the case in this type of evaluation, the overall answer must be nuanced. There are elements in the proposed directives that contribute to a more level playing-field and improve consumer protection, whereas other elements do not. The limited scope of the areas regulated by the directives as well as the way in which things were regulated, leaving many issues to the discretion of the Member States, points to the conclusion that the directives are, albeit an interesting one, only a first step towards a genuine level playing-field with a high level of consumer protection.

The analysis also shows that quite a number of issues remain unsolved. Therefore it seems legitimate to conclude that the contract law rules and correspondingly the level of consumer protection in the proposals for directives under examination must be worked out further into a proper and coherent system comparable to what was aimed at with the CESL. Hence, new complementary directives in the field under investigation are to be expected, but this will evidently take time. It is thereby not excluded that they may over time eventually result in an overall horizontal measure in the form of a Regulation or a Directive that consolidates the consumer sales acquis by eliminating existing contradictions and developing at EU level general concepts of consumer contract law. That way the fragmentation to which the adoption of the current proposals will certainly give rise could be overcome in the future.

Meanwhile the (procedural) autonomy of the Member States turns out to be an important obstacle for further harmonisation. As was mentioned above, speculation on the unifying impact of the case law of the European Court of Justice seems unsatisfactory. Even where the ECJ greatly contributed to a high level of consumer protection such as in the field of unfair contract terms, even based on a minimum harmonisation directive, it must be observed that this process turned out to be very time-consuming since it is necessarily based on a case-by-case approach and is not finished yet.

This is, however, not to say that further intrusion into the national legislation of Member States beyond the so-called existing 'consumer acquis', must not be strictly justified and any initiative with that aim closely scrutinised. Indeed, the case law with regard to free movement demonstrates that rather than a rule-based approach, an assessment is needed of the extent to which national rules really impact on the development of the internal market. Any attempt to further harmonise the divergent contract laws in the Member States must be balanced.[179] Yet, in the context of a well-established European-wide regime on unfair contract terms, the totally harmonised field of unfair commercial practices, the Consumer Rights Directive and the proposed developments in the field of consumer contract law, the European Union legislation now comes to a turning point where assessments for further unification of contract laws may lead to the removal of ostensibly more protective rules for consumers in some Member States.[180]

179 See G. Howells, 'The Rise of European Consumer Law – Whither National Consumer Law?', *Sydney Law Review*, 2006, vol. 28, 84.

180 Also S. Weatherill, 'Minimum Harmonisation as Oxymoron?' in H.-W. Micklitz (ed.), *Verbraucherrecht in Deutschland – Stand und Perspektiven*, Baden-Baden, Nomos, 2005, 35, who is in favour of regulatory diversity, admits that 'it might be necessary to identify improved methods for tracking diverse choices made by Member States'.

Such findings should not prevent the Community legislature from taking new initiatives that go beyond the full harmonisation that is proposed today in the field of contract law. Also the Member States themselves must be increasingly convinced of the benefits for consumers and traders of uniform legislation at European level. Thereto they should closely scrutinise whether existing rules ostensibly for the benefit of consumers effectively contribute to consumer protection. Turning back to the Belgian law context it is submitted that some of the national rules categorised as protective for consumers effectively pursue other objectives than the protection of consumers. To take the Belgian Code of Economic Law as an example, quite a number of its general, strict prohibitions boil down to disguised protection of local businesses with the specific purpose of lessening competition rather than protection of consumers.

With the markets becoming more open due to new technological evolutions and consumers increasingly prepared to shop across the borders, a certain openness (increased political willingness) of Member States towards further full harmonisation at European level would be welcomed even where certain inroads into national contract law are to be expected.

In that respect, the adoption of the CESL, with its comprehensive and balanced rules protecting traders' and consumers' interests, remains to be preferred, even if it would be characterised by the shortcoming of having an optional nature. Now that a comprehensive (optional?) contract law regime at EU level turns out to be politically impossible, we must do with proposals of directives with fully harmonised rules in some areas. This too could work in practice and create in the end the level playing-field for traders and consumers strived for, but rather than the current proposals for directives with their limited scope and partial arrangements of contract law aspects the Community legislature should have recourse to full harmonisation directives with well-chosen specific scopes that comprehensively regulate certain areas of consumer contract law. To that aim the CESL remains an important source of inspiration.

www.ingramcontent.com/pod-product-compliance
Ingram Content Group UK Ltd.
Pitfield, Milton Keynes, MK11 3LW, UK
UKHW051846100926
8556IPUK00005B/484